Charging Orders on Land

Law, Practice and Precedents

Second edition
Falcon Chambers

Charging Orders on Land

Law, Practice and Precedents

Second edition
Falcon Chambers

Editors
Cecily Crampin and Michael Ranson

Contributors
Edward Peters KC
Kavish Shah
Ashpen Rajah
Imogen Dodds
Fern Schofield
Thomas Rothwell
Mark Galtrey
Taylor Briggs

WS
&H

Wildy, Simmonds & Hill Publishing

ISBN: 9780854903436

British Library Cataloguing in Publication Data

A catalogue record for this book is available from the British Library

First edition 2013

This edition published in 2024 by

Wildy, Simmonds & Hill Publishing
Wildy & Sons Ltd
Lincoln's Inn Archway
Carey Street
London WC2A 2JD
www.wildy.com

Typeset by Heather Jones, North Petherton, Somerset.
Printed in Great Britain by CPI Group (UK) Ltd, Croydon CR0 4YY.

Foreword to the Second Edition

It is just over a decade since the first edition of this book was published. During that time much has changed in relation to the law and practice relating to charging orders. A new Civil Procedure Rules regime has been introduced, as well as limits on enforcement which would have been inconceivable in 2013, such as the breathing space and mental health crisis moratoria.

The case law has also not stood still with the law developing through authorities such as *Termhouse (Clarendon Court) Management Ltd v Al-Balhaa* [2021] EWCA Civ 1881 on the issue of direct enforcement in the county court of what is essentially a declaratory judgment by the First-tier Tribunal, and *McLinden v Lu* [2022] EWHC 2807 (Ch) on the importance of proving if there are beneficial interests other than the debtor's in debtor-owned property at the final charging order stage, and where the burden for doing so lies. The implications of *Lees v Kaye* [2022] EWHC 1151 (QB), an important case on the effect of the moratoria on property rights, is also considered in the context of charging orders.

In addition to a comprehensive updating of the law and practice, this second edition builds on the practical approach of the first edition by providing new precedent documents – including draft directions and various forms of final order – and new checklists and tables intended to assist readers through the practicalities of matters such as obtaining, varying and enforcing charging orders. This edition also includes an entirely new chapter on the corporate and personal insolvency issues frequently encountered by practitioners dealing with charging orders.

What remains the same is that this new edition has been written by an experienced team of Falcon Chambers barristers, all of whom are familiar not only with the law underpinning charging orders but also with the way judges approach charging orders on a day-to-day basis in court.

The law is stated as at 1 September 2023.

Cecily Crampin and Michael Ranson
Falcon Chambers, London
September 2023

Foreword to the First Edition

This book has been written by members of Falcon Chambers, all of whom specialise in litigation concerning land. All the contributors have knowledge and experience of such orders and the problems to which they may give rise. The book is not intended to cover the whole of the law on charging orders, whether under the Charging Orders Act 1979 or other statutes, but only the law which relates to charging orders on land.

The book is intended for use by all persons who may find themselves involved in the legal process of obtaining or challenging the making of a charging order on land. It seeks to address both the practical issues and the legal difficulties – some of them formidable – that can arise in relation to charging orders. The Charging Orders Act 1979 and the relevant provisions of the Civil Procedure Rules are included in the Appendix, as are a number of specimen precedents.

The law is stated as of 1 April 2013.

Charles Harpum
Falcon Chambers, London
5 May 2013

Contents

List of Abbreviations

AHA 1986	Agricultural Holdings Act 1986
AJA 1956	Administration of Justice Act 1956
AJA 1965	Administration of Justice Act 1965
CCA 1974	Consumer Credit Act 1974
CCA 1984	County Courts Act 1984
CCMCC	County Court Money Claims Centre
CCR	County Court Rules 1981–1998
CNBC	Civil National Business Centre
COA 1979	Charging Orders Act 1979
CPR	Civil Procedure Rules 1998 (SI 1998/3132)
CSA 1991	Child Support Act 1991
CT (A&E) Regs 1992	Council Tax (Administration and Enforcement) Regulations 1992 (SI 1992/613)
CVA	company voluntary arrangement
CVL	creditors' voluntary liquidation
Debt Respite Scheme Regs 2020	Debt Respite Scheme (Breathing Space Moratorium and Mental Health Crisis Moratorium) (England and Wales) Regulations 2020 (SI 2020/1311)
EEA	European Economic Area
European Convention on Human Rights	European Convention for the Protection of Human Rights and Fundamental Freedoms
FPR	Family Procedure Rules 2010 (SI 2010/2955)
FTT	First-tier Tribunal
HA 2004	Housing Act 2004
IA 1986	Insolvency Act 1986
IP	insolvency practitioner
IVA	individual voluntary arrangement
LASPO	Legal Aid, Sentencing and Punishment of Offenders Act 2012
LCA 1972	Land Charges Act 1972
LPA 1925	Law of Property Act 1925
LRA 1925	Land Registration Act 1925

LRA 2002	Land Registration Act 2002
LRR 2003	Land Registration Rules 2003 (SI 2003/1417)
LTA 1927	Landlord and Tenant Act 1927
MCA 2005	Mental Capacity Act 2005
MVL	members' voluntary liquidation
OFSI	Office of Financial Sanctions Implementation
PA 1890	Partnership Act 1890
RSC	Rules of the Supreme Court 1966–1998
SA 1974	Solicitors Act 1974
SLA 1925	Settled Land Act 1925
TA 1925	Trustee Act 1925
TCEA 2007	Tribunals, Courts and Enforcement Act 2007
TLATA 1996	Trusts of Land and Appointment of Trustees Act 1996

Civil and Family Procedure Rules – Comparison Tables

Civil Procedure Rules, Part 73	*Family Procedure Rules, Part 40 equivalent*
r 73.1	rr 40.1 and 40.2
r 73.2	r 40.3
r 73.3	r 40.4
r 73.4	n/a
r 73.5	n/a
r 73.6	r 40.5
r 73.7	r 40.6
r 73.10	n/a
r 73.10ZA	n/a
r 73.10A	r 40.8
r 73.10B	r 40.9
r 73.10C	n/a

Civil Procedure Rules, PD 73	*Family Procedure Rules, PD 40A equivalent*
para 1.1	para 1.2
para 1.2	para 1.3
para 1.3	para 1.4
para 1.4	n/a
para 2	para 2.1
para 3	para 3.1
para 3A	n/a

Civil Procedure Rules, PD 73	*Family Procedure Rules, PD 40A equivalent*
paras 4.1–4.5	para 4.1
para 4A.1	para 5.1
para 4A.2	para 5.2
para 4A.3	para 5.3

Table of Cases

References are to page numbers

Table of Statutes

References are to page numbers

Table of Statutory Instruments

References are to page numbers

Table of European Conventions

References are to page numbers

Table of Other Material

References are to page numbers

Chapter 1

Introduction

INTRODUCTION

1.1 The first part of this chapter provides an overview of charging orders against land.[1] This explains what charging orders are, their role in the enforcement of money judgments, and a summary of their advantages and disadvantages. In the second part, there is a brief history of charging orders – in particular, why and how the charging order has evolved into its modern form.[2]

1.2 As regards the remainder of this book:

(a) Chapter 2 explains the circumstances in which a charging order can be obtained, and against what property;
(b) Chapter 3 sets out the procedure for obtaining a charging order;
(c) Chapter 4 analyses issues of priority that can arise in relation to charging orders, and examines related conveyancing issues;
(d) Chapter 5 is concerned with the discharge of charging orders;
(e) Chapter 6 deals with the enforcement of charging orders, which is primarily by an order for sale;
(f) Chapter 7 considers certain specialist forms of charging order; and
(g) Chapter 8 provides an overview of the insolvency legislation and ways in which it might affect the obtaining and enforcement of charging orders.

---

1 See paras 1.3–1.35.

2 See paras 1.36–1.70.

OVERVIEW OF CHARGING ORDERS

Essence of a charging order

1.3 If one party to a civil claim (the judgment creditor) obtains a judgment against another party (the judgment debtor) for payment of a previously disputed or unpaid sum of money (whether debt or damages), the court will order the judgment debtor to pay the relevant sum to the judgment creditor within a specified period of time. That period is normally 14 or 21 days, unless the judgment debtor has a good reason for seeking a longer period. In many cases, the judgment debtor will have the funds to pay that sum (the judgment debt) and will pay it within the period specified by the order. If the judgment debtor lacks the funds to pay the judgment debt, or is unwilling to comply with the order, the judgment creditor must pursue one or more of the various methods of enforcing a money judgment, which are collectively known as 'execution'.

1.4 A charging order is a means of execution,[3] but an indirect one, in that it does not secure immediate payment of the judgment debt. Its nature has been summarised as follows:

> A charging order is an order made by the court charging some specified property of the judgment debtor with the ability to satisfy the judgment debt and is thus a mode of enforcement of money judgments and orders. It operates to give the judgment creditor security for the payment of the amount due under the judgment and produces the fruits of the judgment not at the time when the charge is imposed but at the time when the charge is enforced.[4]

1.5 There are three different types of charging order:

(a) charging orders against land;
(b) charging orders against securities (shares, etc); and
(c) charging orders against partnership property.

This book is concerned only with the first type, charging orders against land, which are the most common type of charging order.

1.6 A charging order over land is, as its name suggests, an order, made by the court, which creates a charge over specified land or a specified interest in land which belongs to the debtor.[5] The charge created by the charging order has effect

---

3 IA 1986, s 183(3) (and, previously, the now repealed Charging Orders Act 1979 (COA 1979), s 4, which was superseded by Insolvency Act 1985, s 179(5)).

4 *Report of the Committee on the Enforcement of Judgment Debts* (Cmnd 3909) (HMSO, 1969), para 855.

5 COA 1979, s 1.

and is enforceable in the same manner as a general equitable charge over the specified land.[6] The charging order provides security for the judgment debt and, normally, the judgment interest accruing on it.

1.7 A charging order over land can be made against any land or interest in land which belongs to the judgment debtor and is situated in England or Wales. If the debtor is the sole legal and beneficial owner of the land, the charging order can be made against the legal estate. If, however, the judgment debtor is one of two or more beneficial owners, a charging order in respect of a debt owed solely by that debtor can be made only against his beneficial interest.[7]

1.8 Any judgment creditor can apply for a charging order, but the court has a discretion as to whether or not to make the order. When deciding how to exercise its discretion, the court will have regard to all relevant circumstances, including not only the position of the judgment creditor, but also the interests of the judgment debtor and any third parties who might be adversely affected by the making of the order, such as other creditors of the judgment debtor, or others with an interest in the relevant land.[8]

1.9 Obtaining a charging order does not ensure swift payment of the judgment sum. Indeed, the judgment creditor will often seek a charging order precisely because he believes that the judgment debtor lacks sufficient liquid funds or saleable chattels to discharge the debt immediately. However, there are three main potential benefits for the judgment creditor who obtains a charging order:

(a) it provides the judgment creditor with some security for his judgment debt and the judgment interest accruing on it pending payment of the debt by the judgment debtor. A judgment creditor with a charging order will generally be in a better position than an unsecured creditor if the judgment debtor subsequently becomes insolvent;[9]
(b) a judgment creditor with the benefit of a charging order can apply to the court for an order for sale of the charged land or, where the charge is over the debtor's beneficial interest in the land, for an order for the sale of that beneficial interest or for the execution of the trust.[10] If the court orders a sale and the net proceeds are sufficient, then, following the payment of any prior

---

6 COA 1979, s 3(4).

7 COA 1979, s 2. See Chapter 2, para 2.12 *et seq*.

8 See Chapter 2, para 2.22 *et seq*.

9 There is of course, always the risk that the value of the charged land may be insufficient to discharge the judgment debt and interest, particularly if other creditors have prior security over the land.

10 In the latter case, under Trusts of Land and Appointment of Trustees Act 1996 (TLATA 1996), s 14: see Chapter 6, para 6.42 *et seq*.

secured creditors, they can be used to discharge the sums secured by the charging order; and

(c) the grant of the charging order over the debtor's land, which secures the judgment debt and interest, and carries with it the threat of an order for sale, may itself encourage the judgment debtor to discharge the judgment debt voluntarily if he is able to do so.

1.10 Many judgment debtors will have much of their wealth tied up in their family home. Obtaining a charging order against that home, or the debtor's beneficial interest in it, can therefore be an obvious and desirable means of enforcement for larger judgment debts. However, it can have very serious consequences for the debtor and his family.

Why seek a charging order rather than pursuing some other form of execution?

1.11 A charging order is only one means by which a judgment creditor can try to enforce payment of a judgment debt. Unlike some other forms of execution, it does not secure immediate payment of the debt. To understand the potential advantages and disadvantages of a charging order, and why a charging order will sometimes be the judgment creditor's preferred or only option, it is necessary to explain briefly the other methods of enforcement which are available to a judgment creditor, and the circumstances in which they will and will not be obtainable or useful.

Charging orders in context: various means by which a money judgment can be enforced

Execution against the debtor's goods

1.12 The most frequent form of execution, which is commonly called 'execution', is for the judgment creditor to direct a court-appointed official to seize goods and chattels belonging to the judgment debtor and sell them. The proceeds of sale are then applied in satisfaction of the judgment and to pay the costs of the execution. Any surplus is returned to the debtor. In the High Court such a direction is called a writ of control,[11] and the execution is carried out by

---

11 Formerly known as writs of *fieri facias* (commonly abbreviated to *fi fa*), meaning 'make or see it to be done', i.e. see to it, the writ being expressed in the form of a royal direction to a named court official (originally the Sheriff of the county in which the debtor resided). They were renamed with effect from 6 April 2014, by Tribunals, Courts and Enforcement Act 2007 (TCEA 2007), s 62(4)(a), which was brought into force by the Tribunals, Courts and Enforcement Act 2007 (Commencement No 11) Order 2014 (SI 2014/768).

the High Court enforcement officer.[12] In the county court and the family court such a direction is called a warrant of control,[13] and the execution is carried out by the bailiffs of the county court in question.[14] In many cases, this form of execution will be an effective means of securing payment of the judgment debt, particularly where the judgment debt is relatively small. If the debtor has sufficient chattels, it secures an immediate cash settlement of the judgment debt and costs. It may not be effective where the judgment debt is large, or where the debtor owns insufficient goods to satisfy the debt.

Attachment of earnings orders

1.13 The second most frequent form of execution is an attachment of earnings order, by which the court, normally the county court or family court, orders a judgment debtor's employer to make weekly or monthly deductions from the judgment debtor's earnings. Those deductions are paid by the employer to the court, which then pays them to the judgment creditor in, or towards, the satisfaction of the judgment debt.[15] Again, that can be a very effective form of execution. However:

(a) it cannot be used against an unemployed or self-employed debtor, or against a debtor whose earnings do not exceed the minimum subsistence level;
(b) it may be ineffective if the debtor subsequently changes jobs or becomes unemployed; and
(c) even a successful attachment order can take many months or years to discharge the debt.

1.14 There are also other, less frequently used, means of execution.

Third party debt orders

1.15 Where a third party debt order[16] is made, money owed to the judgment debtor by a third party, usually money in the debtor's bank account, must be paid by that third party to the judgment creditor rather than to the judgment debtor, in

---

12 See Civil Procedure Rules 1998 (SI 1998/3132, as amended) (CPR) Part 83.

13 Formerly known as warrants of execution, and renamed with effect from 6 April 2014, by TCEA 2007, s 62(4)(b).

14 See CPR Part 83.

15 See CPR Part 89.

16 Which replaced the old garnishee order.

reduction of the judgment debt.[17] Such an order is effective only if the judgment debtor has significant sums in his bank account or is otherwise owed some other debt.

Appointment of a receiver by way of equitable execution

1.16 This was originally an equitable remedy. However, following the reforms made on the recommendation of the Evershed Committee,[18] it can now be used against legal estates or interests in land.[19] It can be a useful remedy, in particular:

(a) where land belonging to the debtor is let and producing a rent, so that the receiver can collect the rents, and pay them to the judgment creditor; or
(b) in relation to assets, such as endowment policies, that cannot be the subject of third party debt orders until they have matured.

The appointment of such a receiver is usually of no practical value if the land owned by the judgment debtor (the debtor's home or workplace, for example) is not producing any income.

Insolvency

1.17 The judgment creditor can serve a bankruptcy or winding-up petition on the debtor, which may prompt the debtor to pay. However, if the debtor does not do so, and is, in fact, insolvent, an unsecured judgment creditor may receive little or no dividend from the debtor's estate. This is because the debts of secured and preferential creditors of the debtor will have priority.

Advantages and disadvantages of a charging order

1.18 The potential advantages and disadvantages of a charging order compared to those other forms of execution are as follows.

---

17 See CPR Part 72.

18 *Report of the Committee on Supreme Court Practice and Procedure* (Cmnd 8878) (HMSO, 1953) (*Supreme Court Practice and Procedure Report*). See para 1.51 *et seq*.

19 Originally under Administration of Justice Act 1956 (AJA 1956), s 36, and now under Senior Courts Act 1981, s 37 and County Courts Act 1984 (CCA 1984), s 107(1).

Judgment creditor's perspective

1.19 The three main advantages for a judgment creditor in obtaining a charging order are outlined above.[20] In addition to these, there are at least three other reasons why a judgment creditor might seek a charging order.

1.20 First, the chargee under a charging order enjoys priority over all other unsecured creditors. That is something which no other form of execution gives, pending actual payment of the debt. Even where goods are sold under a writ or warrant of control, the enforcement officer or bailiff must retain the proceeds of sale for a specified period of time, in case the bankruptcy or liquidation of the debtor occurs within that period. If it does, the proceeds of sale must be paid to the trustee in bankruptcy or liquidator. Furthermore, where a charging order has been made, if the value of the property charged rises over time, the value of the judgment creditor's security may in fact increase, so that a partially secured creditor may become fully secured.

1.21 Secondly, the usual procedure for obtaining a charging order is by means of an application for an interim charging order made without notice to the debtor, followed by an application for a final charging order made on notice.[21] This means that the charge can often be attached to the debtor's property before the debtor has an opportunity to defeat the application by further charging or disposing of it.

1.22 Thirdly, once a final charging order has been made, it can only be impeached in limited circumstances.[22] It can, in theory, be sold along with the judgment debt,[23] or bequeathed by the judgment creditor. Even if the judgment creditor does not seek an order for sale, he should be paid his share of the proceeds if the judgment debtor or a prior chargee subsequently sells the property.

1.23 There are potential drawbacks for a judgment creditor in obtaining a charging order.

1.24 First, a charging order can only be obtained if the debtor owns land or an interest in land which can be charged. Even if the debtor is the proprietor of land or owns an interest in land, that land or interest may not be good security for the judgment debt. For example:

---

20 See para 1.9.

21 See Chapter 2, para 2.22–2.25 and Chapter 3, para 3.3 *et seq*.

22 See Chapter 5.

23 In practice, only at a discount.

(a) the land may already be subject to existing charges or other incumbrances which secure debts that equal or exceed its value; or
(b) the judgment debtor may have or may claim to have no beneficial interest in the land or only a limited interest.

1.25 Secondly, if the debtor does own land or an interest in land, the court has a discretion whether or not to make a charging order. There may be good reasons why the court will or may decline to do so, for instance because of the particular personal circumstances of the debtor or because a charging order would cause undue prejudice to other creditors of the judgment debtor, as for example where:

(a) the debtor can satisfy the court he will be able to pay the judgment debt by other means within a short time;
(b) the debtor is insolvent or about to become so;
(c) the debtor's spouse is seeking a property transfer or adjustment order in matrimonial proceedings; or
(d) for some other reason, the judgment creditor should not obtain priority over another judgment or other creditor or creditors.[24]

1.26 Thirdly, the extent to which the judgment creditor's debt is secured will depend upon matters such as:

(a) the size of the debt relative to the net value of the charged land or interest in land;
(b) the amounts secured over the land by any prior charges and incumbrances; or
(c) where the judgment debtor is not the sole owner of the land, the size of the judgment debtor's beneficial interest in the land.

In many cases, the only land owned by the debtor will be his home, over which there will frequently already be an 'all monies' mortgage, and the debtor's spouse or partner may own a substantial beneficial interest in the property.

1.27 Fourthly, the security enjoyed by a judgment creditor with the benefit of a charging order may also worsen over time, as for example where:

(a) the value of the land falls;
(b) debts secured by a prior 'all monies' charge increase substantially, as where the debtor stops paying the monthly instalments due in respect of a first mortgage; or

---

[24] See Chapter 2, para 2.22 *et seq*.

(c) the judgment debt remains unpaid for many years and the accruing judgment interest comes to exceed the value of the land.

1.28 Fifthly, even if the value of the charged land is sufficient to provide adequate security for the judgment debt, the judgment creditor may still have to wait a substantial time before his debt is paid:

(a) a judgment creditor who has obtained a charging order and wishes to apply for an order for the sale of the charged property must issue a new claim; and
(b) the court has a discretion as to whether or not to order such a sale; and the court may decline to do so, as where:

    (i) the amount of the debt is small relative to the value of the land to be charged;
    (ii) the debtor satisfies the court that he will be able to pay the judgment debt by other means within a reasonable time;
    (iii) other secured creditors object to a sale; or
    (iv) the particular circumstances of the debtor or his co-owners or dependants dictate.[25]

Even ultimately successful proceedings for sale may be long and drawn out, and the sale itself may involve further time and difficulty.

1.29 Pending any proceedings for enforcement, a judgment creditor who has obtained a charging order against the legal estate in the debtor's land can protect the priority of his interest by appropriate registration of the charging order.[26] However, the position of a judgment creditor who has obtained a charging order against the beneficial interest of one co-owner of a property is much more vulnerable.[27] A conveyance or mortgage by the legal owners and trustees of the property will overreach both that beneficial interest and the charging order over it.[28] Unless the judgment creditor is informed before the disposition takes place, there is a danger that the proceeds of sale may be dissipated before he can take effective steps to obtain repayment. It is explained later that the standard form of protection by registration for a judgment creditor with a charging order over a beneficial interest in land is wholly inadequate in this regard.[29]

---

25 See Chapter 6, para 6.35 *et seq*.

26 See Chapter 4, paras 4.25–4.26 and 4.34–4.36 *et seq*.

27 A common case would be where a property is jointly owned by a husband and wife, and where the judgment creditor has obtained a charging order over the husband's half of the beneficial interest.

28 Law of Property Act 1925 (LPA 1925), ss 2(1)(ii) and 27(2).

29 See Chapter 4, paras 4.30–4.33 and 4.37–4.44.

1.30 The judgment creditor will always wish to consider whether, in the circumstances, he might better enforce his judgment by some other means. In particular, especially where the debt is relatively small, he may wish to do so by execution against the judgment debtor's goods, by a third party debt order or by an attachment of earnings order. In many cases, however, obtaining a charging order may still be the most effective option available.

Judgment debtor's perspective

1.31 For the judgment debtor, a charging order may be preferable to other forms of execution. Unlike execution against his goods, or an attachment of earnings order, it may not have any immediate impact on his way of life, because it may not lead to an immediate order for sale. It may give the debtor time to remedy or at least improve his financial position as, for example, by raising the money to discharge the judgment debt and charging order without the need for a sale of the charged property. Even if a sale of the charged property is the only means by which the judgment debt can be paid, the additional time may enable the judgment debtor to arrange a sale of the property at a higher price than could have been achieved on a forced sale at the behest of the judgment creditor.

1.32 There are, however, disadvantages. In particular:

(a) the existence of the unpaid judgment debt and the charging order are likely to damage the judgment debtor's credit rating and may, thereby, prevent the judgment debtor from raising further loans against the security of the charged land;
(b) interest on the judgment debt, which will also normally be secured by the charging order, will continue to accrue, and may in time come to exceed the judgment debt itself; and
(c) if the judgment debt is not paid voluntarily, the judgment creditor is in due course likely to seek an order for the sale of the charged land or interest in land.

Position of third parties

1.33 It is not only the judgment debtor who may be adversely affected by the making or enforcement of a charging order. It may affect third parties, as the following examples show:

(a) the debt of a judgment creditor who obtains a charging order will have priority over the debts of the judgment debtor's unsecured creditors, even if those debts pre-date the judgment debtor's;[30]

[30] For this reason, if the court knows that the judgment debtor's insolvency is imminent, it will normally refuse to grant a charging order: see Chapter 2, para 2.33 *et seq*.

(b) the debtor's spouse may be adversely affected, especially where a divorce is imminent, and that spouse wishes to seek a property transfer or adjustment order concerning the family home in matrimonial proceedings;[31]

(c) any family or dependants of the debtor will be affected if the charging order is made against his family home and a sale of that property is ordered; and

(d) where the debtor's beneficial interest is charged, the other co-owners of the property may be affected if the judgment creditor seeks to sell it in execution of the trust.

1.34 The potential effect of a charging order both on other creditors of the judgment debtor and on third parties is relevant to the exercise of the court's discretion when it decides whether to make a charging order or to enforce it by a sale. The court should balance the potential adverse impact on such persons against the potential advantages to the judgment creditor.[32] However, the court is not always in a position to do this because the judgment debtor may not appear, so that the court is not made aware of the concerns of other interested parties.

1.35 The need to balance the competing interests of judgment creditor, judgment debtor and relevant third parties is also evident in the history of the evolution of the modern charging order.

BRIEF HISTORY OF CHARGING ORDERS

Overview: balancing competing interests

1.36 The principal steps in the development of the modern charging order were the Judgments Act 1838,[33] the Administration of Justice Act 1956[34] and the Charging Orders Act 1979.[35]

1.37 That course of its development reflects how Parliament and the courts have, over time, sought to balance the competing and potentially irreconcilable interests of judgment creditors, judgment debtors and their dependants, third parties (especially other creditors and prospective purchasers or mortgagees of land), and the various and often conflicting interests of wider society.

---

31 See Chapter 2, para 2.46 *et seq*.

32 See Chapters 2 and 6.

33 See para 1.43 *et seq*.

34 See para 1.50 *et seq*.

35 See para 1.68 *et seq*.

1.38 A judgment creditor will wish to satisfy his judgment debt quickly and effectively from any assets which are owned by the debtor, including any interest in land. If the judgment creditor cannot force an immediate sale of the judgment debtor's land, he will at least wish to secure his judgment debt on the debtor's land, pending satisfaction of the judgment, with priority over subsequent creditors.

1.39 To give judgment creditors effective remedies encourages credit and commerce generally. That must be balanced against other factors, such as that:

(a) a judgment debtor's land may be worth considerably more than the judgment debt;
(b) the land may be of particular importance to the debtor, whether as a home, a workplace or an investment;
(c) there may be particular reasons why an immediate sale would not realise the potential value of the land.

A debtor may, therefore, want time to raise the money to satisfy the judgment rather than there being an immediate sale of the land. There may be a wider social interest in allowing the debtor to do this, particularly if the judgment creditor can be compensated for any delay by a grant over the debtor's land for the debt and the accruing interest.

1.40 Furthermore:

(a) if the first creditor to obtain a judgment against a debtor can achieve priority security for his debt against the debtor's land, regardless of when the original debt arose, that may unjustly disadvantage other creditors of the debtor; and
(b) if a judgment creditor can obtain security for his debt over the judgment debtor's land, any prospective mortgagee or purchaser of land should be able to ascertain by a simple means whether he has such security and whether it will bind that mortgagee or purchaser. Such facilitation of conveyancing transactions is in the public interest.

1.41 How those competing interests might be balanced has changed over the years. The law now favours judgment creditors far more than it did in 1800. However, the development of the law has not been a consistent or linear process, and it has been tempered by the development of various safeguards for debtors, other creditors and potential purchasers or mortgagees of a judgment debtor's land.

Judgment creditor's remedies against a debtor's land prior to 1838

1.42 Prior to the Judgments Act 1838, an ordinary judgment creditor was not entitled to a charge over any land belonging to the judgment debtor.[36] The creditor did, however, have some potential remedies against the debtor's land.[37] The choice of remedy was determined by the nature of the judgment debtor's estate or interest in the land. If the judgment debtor had a legal estate in real property, such as a fee simple, the judgment creditor could not force a sale of the land. However, if the debtor's interest was an interest in possession, the creditor could issue a writ of *elegit*,[38] which entitled the creditor to all the debtor's chattels and, until the judgment debt was paid, to possession and the rents and profits of half of the debtor's land.[39] If the judgment debtor was a lessee, the creditor was in a better position. He could issue a writ of *fi fa*,[40] requiring the sheriff of the relevant county to seize and sell the debtor's personalty, which for that purpose included not only chattels but also any leasehold interests ('chattels real'). If the judgment debtor had a mere equitable interest in real property, the judgment creditor's only remedy was to obtain the appointment of a receiver by way of equitable execution.[41]

---

36 The position of the Crown was different. It was able to satisfy a debt it was owed from any land which was *or had been* owned by the debtor, to the potential peril of purchasers of the land: see William Cornish, J Stuart Anderson, Ray Cocks, Michael Lobban, Patrick Polden and Keith Smith, *The Oxford History of the Laws of England, 1820–1914, Volume XII: Private Law* (Oxford University Press, 2010), Part One: Property (Stuart Anderson), pp 57 and 184–5 (*Oxford History of the Laws of England, Vol XII*).

37 For the evolution prior to 1838 of a creditor's remedies against the lands of a debtor, see E Jenks, *A Short History of English Law* (Methuen & Co Ltd, 5th edn, 1938), pp 254–5.

38 The writ of *elegit* was introduced by the Second Statute of Westminster 1285 (13 Edw I, c 18). As well as entitling the judgment creditor to become the tenant of half of the debtor's lands until the debt was satisfied, it gave the creditor a statutory right to protect his possession of the land by *novel disseisin*. Prior to the introduction of the writ of *elegit*, a judgment creditor was entitled to the profits of the land of the debtor in satisfaction of his judgment debt, but he was not entitled to possession of the land. Without possession it was, in practice, difficult to obtain the profits of the land. It was called a writ of '*elegit*', which means 'elect', because it gave the judgment creditor the right to choose to seek satisfaction of his debt by means of such a writ, rather than by a writ of *fi fa* (which was enforceable only against the debtor's chattels). See A W B Simpson, *A History of the Land Law* (Oxford University Press, 1st edn, 1961), p 134; T F T Plucknett, *A Concise History of the Common Law* (Butterworths, 5th edn, 1956), p 390.

39 The judgment creditor's right to possession was enforceable by the sheriff of the relevant county.

40 See para 1.12 and n 11.

41 *Oxford History of the Laws of England, Vol XII*, pp 184–6; *Charging Orders* (Cmnd 6412) (Law Com No 74) (HMSO, 1976), para 10 ((1976) Law Com No 74).

Judgments Act 1838 and the subsequent amendments to it: the creation and then effective abrogation of an automatic charge in favour of a judgment creditor

1.43 The Judgments Act 1838[42] was introduced to give judgment creditors additional remedies against debtors' real property, because, as the Act explained, 'the existing Law is defective in not providing adequate Means for enabling Judgment Creditors to obtain Satisfaction from the Property of their Debtors'.[43] The main provisions of the Act were as follows:

(a) it provided that a writ of *elegit* would entitle the creditor to possession and to the rents and profits of *all*, rather than half, of the debtor's lands;[44]
(b) it improved the writ of *fi fa*;[45] and
(c) it provided that a judgment would automatically create a charge over all lands[46] of the judgment debtor.[47] The creditor could not enforce the charge for one year and would not obtain any preference over other creditors if the debtor was made bankrupt within that year.[48] This gave the debtor an opportunity to discharge the debt and interest. Thereafter, the creditor could exercise the same remedies over the charged property as if the debtor 'had by Writing under his Hand agreed to charge the same with the Amount of such Judgment Debt and Interest thereon'. There was a dispute as to whether the charge created by those words gave the judgment creditor the remedies available to an equitable mortgagee, namely foreclosure or an order for sale, or only those of an equitable chargee, which were restricted to the appointment of a receiver or an order for sale. It was eventually settled that the creditor was entitled to foreclose.[49]

1.44 The Judgments Act 1838 sought to protect the interests of prospective purchasers or mortgagees of a judgment debtor's land by providing that no judgment would affect any lands or creditors of the judgment debtor, or any

---

42 1 & 2 Vict, c 110.

43 See the preamble to s 11. Conversely, it also largely abolished arrest on mesne process in civil claims (ss 1–7). It was intended by its promoter, the Attorney-General, John Campbell, as a prelude to the abolition of imprisonment for debt: *Oxford History of the Laws of England, Vol XII*, p 185.

44 Judgments Act 1838, s 11. It also extended the range of lands and tenures to which a writ of *elegit* could apply.

45 Judgments Act 1838, s 12. See para 1.12 and n 11.

46 Which was widely defined.

47 Judgments Act 1838, s 12.

48 Judgments Act 1838, s 13.

49 *Oxford History of the Laws of England, Vol XII*, p 61; *Messer v Boyle* (1856) 21 Beav 559; *Re Owen* [1894] 3 Ch 220.

subsequent mortgagee or purchaser of the debtor's lands, unless it was registered, under the name of the debtor, in a book kept by the Senior Master of the Court of Common Pleas at Westminster.[50] However, the Act also provided that 'nothing herein contained shall be deemed or taken to alter or affect any Doctrine of Courts of Equity whereby Protection is given to Purchasers for valuable Consideration without Notice'. That led to some uncertainty as to whether registration of a judgment meant that the charge automatically bound a purchaser and mortgagee of the debtor's land, even if the purchaser or mortgagee had not inspected the register and had no knowledge of the judgment.[51] Two subsequent amendments to the Judgments Act 1838, by the Judgments Act 1839[52] and the Judgments Act 1840,[53] made it clear that:

(a) registration was normally necessary if the charge created by the judgment was to be binding on a purchaser or a mortgagee; but
(b) registration would not in itself ensure that the charge was binding, since a purchaser or mortgagee for value but without notice of the judgment would not be bound.[54]

In practice, however, a purchaser or mortgagee might find it difficult to prove to the satisfaction of a court that he did not have notice of such a judgment and charge. As a result, most prospective mortgagees or purchasers of land still felt obliged to add a search of the register of judgments kept at the Court of Common Pleas to the existing list of necessary conveyancing searches and enquiries. In most cases, the search revealed that there were no registered judgments against the name of the relevant vendor or mortgagor, so this led to resentment by disponees because of the additional time and expense involved in carrying out such searches.[55]

1.45 That led to pressure for change by those who wished to reduce conveyancing costs and facilitate a free market in land, in particular north-country solicitors, who 'argued that the balance of public utility now lay in reducing the risks and costs of land transfers by curtailing the charge the Judgments Act 1838 had created'.[56] Two Acts of Parliament were enacted in response to such lobbying, namely:

---

50 Section 19. Registration of a judgment cost 5/-, inspection of the book 1/-.

51 See *Oxford History of the Laws of England, Vol XII*, p 186.

52 2 & 3 Vict, c 11.

53 2 & 3 Vict, c 82.

54 See *Oxford History of the Laws of England, Vol XII*, p 186. The Judgments Act 1839 also provided that registration would lapse after 5 years unless renewed.

55 See *Oxford History of the Laws of England, Vol XII*, p 187.

56 *Oxford History of the Laws of England, Vol XII*, p 188.

(a) the Law of Property Amendment Act 1860,[57] which provided that a judgment would only be binding on a purchaser or mortgagee if the judgment creditor, in addition to registering the judgment itself, also issued and registered a writ of execution, and then implemented the writ within 3 months of registration;[58]
(b) the Judgments Act 1864,[59] which provided that no future judgment would affect land until it had been actually executed by a writ of '*elegit* or other lawful authority'. However, it also provided judgment creditors with some compensation in the form of a summary power of sale.[60]

1.46 The unstated effect of the Judgments Act 1864 was as follows:

(a) it abolished the charge created by the Judgments Act 1838 but did not repeal it;
(b) it made the registration of judgments unnecessary; but
(c) it retained the registration of writs of execution 'to the puzzlement of judges'.[61]

The conveyancing process had been facilitated, but at the cost of reducing the rights and remedies of judgment creditors.

1.47 Subsequent judicial decisions once again increased the risk that a purchaser or mortgagee might find himself unexpectedly bound by the interest of a judgment creditor in the land, when it was held that:

(a) the interest of a judgment creditor who had taken possession under a writ of *elegit* would be binding on a purchaser or mortgagee even if it was not registered; and
(b) the 'appointment of a receiver was "other lawful authority" for the purposes of the Judgments Act 1864, [thereby] sanctioning in effect a new form of execution, one that would bind the land but which would often be undiscoverable by any reasonable inquiry'.[62]

---

57 23 & 24 Vict, c 38.

58 Law of Property Amendment Act 1860, ss 1–2.

59 27 & 28 Vict, c 112.

60 Under Judgments Act 1864, s 4.

61 *Oxford History of the Laws of England, Vol XII*, pp 188–9.

62 *Oxford History of the Laws of England, Vol XII*, p 189, commenting on the effect of *Re Pope* (1886) 17 QBD 743.

1900–1956: restoration of the automatic charge

1.48 Renewed lobbying from conveyancing solicitors about the unsatisfactory state of the law, not only in relation to judgment debts,[63] but also as to the registration of charges generally, led to a fundamental remodelling of the system for registering various charges against land. That was implemented by the Land Charges Registration and Searches Act 1888 and the Land Charges Act 1900. The latter Act closed the old registers of court judgments, and instead required creditors to register at HM Land Registry writs or orders for the *enforcement* of judgments, rather than the judgments themselves. Any such registered writs or orders would be identified by the new Land Registry 'official search' which could be carried out by a prospective purchaser or mortgagee.[64] The Judgments Act 1864 was also repealed, so that a judgment creditor could once again enjoy the benefit of the automatic statutory charge created by the Judgments Act 1838. That automatic charge would extend to all the judgment debtor's lands, provided that the creditor had duly registered his charge at HM Land Registry.[65]

1.49 The relevant provisions of the Judgments Act 1838 and the Land Charges Act 1900 were repealed in 1925, but were reproduced in consolidated form in section 195 of the Law of Property Act 1925. The legislative framework then remained unchanged until 1956.

Administration of Justice Act 1956: the emergence of the modern charging order

1.50 The legacy of the various legislative changes which had followed the Judgments Act 1838, and which were consolidated in 1925, 'was not altogether desirable', as the Law Commission later noted in its 1976 report, *Charging Orders*.[66] The 1838 Act had envisaged the statutory charge as something which was automatically created by the judgment itself, and which was entirely distinct from the execution process. However, under the scheme of registration which applied under the Land Charges Act 1900 and Law of Property Act 1925:

> the obtaining of a charge was no longer an alternative to issuing execution process, because no statutory charge could exist unless such process had already been issued. The execution process normally resorted to for the process of establishing the charge – the writ of *elegit* – was itself far from satisfactory; but one of the consequences of obliging the judgment creditor to issue such a writ in order to obtain a charge was that if he chose, despite the cumbersomeness of the procedure, to enforce the

---

63 As to which, see *Oxford History of the Laws of England, Vol XII*, pp 189–90.

64 Land Charges Act 1900, ss 1 and 2.

65 See *Oxford History of the Laws of England, Vol XII*, p 190; (1976) Law Com No 74, para 12.

66 (1976) Law Com No 74, paras 13–14.

judgment itself by proceeding with the writ, he avoided the twelve-month moratorium attached to the charge.[67]

1.51 In 1953, the Evershed Committee[68] recommended the abolition of the writ of *elegit*, and the extension of receivership as a means of execution, so that it could be exercised over both legal and equitable interests. Those recommendations were implemented by sections 34 and 36 of the Administration of Justice Act 1956.[69]

1.52 The Committee also advocated a new system of registration, under which it would be the judgment itself, rather than an order for its enforcement,[70] which would have to be registered. That recommendation was not implemented in 1956. Instead, a radical alteration in the charging scheme was made by section 35 of the Administration of Justice Act 1956.[71] Section 35 provided that the court could, for the purpose of enforcing a judgment or order for the payment of money, make an order imposing 'on any ... land or interest in land of the debtor as may be specified in the order a charge for securing the payment of any moneys due or to become due under the judgment or order',[72] either absolutely or subject to conditions,[73] and that such an order 'shall have the like effect and shall be enforceable in the same courts and in the same manner as an equitable charge created by the debtor by writing under his hand'.[74] Such a charging order therefore took effect as an equitable mortgage under hand (that is, as an equitable mortgage signed by the mortgagor but not made by deed).[75]

1.53 The new scheme inaugurated by section 35 of the Administration of Justice Act 1956 created, in essence, the modern form of 'charging order'. It was different from the system which it replaced in four fundamental respects:[76]

(a) unlike the scheme created by the Judgments Act 1838, a charge in favour of the judgment creditor was not created automatically by the making of the judgment. Nor did it automatically cover all of the debtor's lands. Instead, if the judgment creditor wanted a charge against land owned by the judgment debtor, the creditor had to apply for and obtain a specific order, the 'charging

67 (1976) Law Com No 74, para 13. For the 12-month moratorium, see para 1.43.

68 *Supreme Court Practice and Procedure Report.*

69 The writ of *elegit* had lasted for 671 years.

70 That is, under the proposed regime, an order appointing a receiver.

71 See (1976) Law Com No 74, paras 14–15.

72 Administration of Justice Act 1965 (AJA 1965), s 35(1).

73 AJA 1965, s 35(2).

74 AJA 1965, s 35(3).

75 (1976) Law Com No 74, para 99.

76 (1976) Law Com No 74, para 16.

order', which created a charge over the particular land specified in the order. The court had a discretion both as to whether or not to make such an order,[77] and as to whether to do so absolutely or subject to conditions;[78]

(b) the charge could take effect whether or not it was registered, although registration was necessary if the order was to be binding on subsequent mortgagees or purchasers;[79]

(c) what was registered was the charging order itself, rather than the original judgment or some other form of execution; and

(d) the charge could potentially be enforced at once if the court considered that appropriate in the exercise of its discretion. There was no automatic one-year moratorium for the debtor.

1.54 Section 35 of the Administration of Justice Act 1956 initially applied in both the High Court and the county court. However, the jurisdiction of the latter was subsequently derived from the identical terms of section 141 of the County Courts Act 1959.

1.55 The procedure for obtaining charging orders on land under the Administration of Justice Act 1956[80] was that, in the High Court, a charging order *nisi* was normally obtained on an *ex parte* application to the Master or District Registrar, and then either made absolute or discharged at a second hearing after notice was given to the judgment debtor.[81] In the county court, an application for a charging order was heard on notice to the debtor.[82] In either case, the application could be joined with an application for the appointment of a receiver.

1.56 Although the court's power to grant a charging order under the Administration of Justice Act 1956 was discretionary, in practice the courts tended to accede almost automatically to a judgment creditor's request for a charging order.[83]

---

77 Under AJA 1956, s 35(1).

78 Under AJA 1965, s 35(2).

79 AJA 1956, s 35(3). Registration was under the Land Registration Act 1925 (LRA 1925) as a caution (where title to the debtor's land was registered) or under the Land Charges Act 1925 and subsequently the Land Charges Act 1972 (LCA 1972) (where the title was unregistered).

80 See (1976) Law Com No 74, para 17.

81 Under the then RSC Ord 50, r 1.

82 Under the then CCR Ord 25, r 7 (County Court Rules 1936 (SR&O 1936/626), as amended).

83 (1976) Law Com No 74, para 43, although in *Rainbow v Moorgate Properties Ltd* [1975] 1 WLR 788, the Court of Appeal held that where the court was aware that the debtor was, or was likely to turn out to be, insolvent, it should hesitate to grant a charging order which would give one creditor an advantage over other unsecured creditors.

1976 Law Commission Report

1.57 In 1976 the Law Commission published a report which addressed three defects that had been identified in the law concerning charging orders on land obtainable under the Administration of Justice Act 1956, together with the Commission's recommendations as to how those defects should be cured and the law otherwise improved.[84]

Giving the grantee of a charging order automatic priority as a secured creditor

1.58 The first problem identified under the existing law arose from the decision of the Court of Appeal in *In re Overseas Aviation Engineering (GB) Ltd.*[85] In that case it was held that a charging order on land did not, by itself, give the judgment creditor's debt any priority over the debts of unsecured creditors in the event of the bankruptcy or winding-up of the judgment debtor.

1.59 Under the relevant insolvency legislation,[86] a judgment creditor only acquired priority over other creditors if the judgment creditor had taken some step which 'completed the execution' of the original judgment. Execution against land was deemed to be 'completed' only on the appointment of a receiver, or upon seizure under a writ of sequestration. Thus if a judgment creditor obtained a charging order, but wished to ensure that, in the event of a subsequent bankruptcy or winding-up, he had the status of a secure creditor, he had to make an application for the appointment of a receiver. This was so even when there was no prospect or intention that the receiver would ever do *anything* following his appointment.[87] Once that issue had been highlighted in *Overseas Aviation*, it presented no real difficulty to those who were aware of the problem. The application for the appointment of a receiver could be made simultaneously with the application for the charging order. However, it was usually an inappropriate and pointless requirement, which led to additional and pointless costs. It was also a potential trap to the unwary.

1.60 It was in principle appropriate that the charging order itself should give the judgment creditor priority. The grantee of an express charge obtained automatic priority as a secured creditor, and a charging order was intended to be analogous

---

84 (1976) Law Com No 74, which followed an earlier working paper, (1972) Law Com WP No 46.

85 *In re Overseas Aviation Engineering (GB) Ltd* [1963] Ch 24; see also *Barclays Bank Ltd v Moore* [1967] 1 WLR 1201 at 1205 and 1207; *Re a Debtor (No 39 of 1974), ex parte Okill* [1977] 1 WLR 1308.

86 At that time, Companies Act 1948, s 325 and Bankruptcy Act 1914, s 40.

87 There would no rents for the receiver to collect if, for example, the land subject to the charging order was occupied by the debtor as his home or workplace.

to such a charge. Although there was considerable force in the argument that it might sometimes be very unfair if the grantee of a charging order could obtain automatic priority over other unsecured creditors, a comprehensive review of the law of insolvency and priorities was not within the Law Commission's remit. Under the existing law, a well-advised grantee of a charging order could already obtain such priority by the appointment of a receiver.[88]

1.61 The Law Commission therefore recommended that legislation should be enacted to reverse the effect of the *Overseas Aviation* case, by providing that the making of a charging order was one of the events which amounted to the completion of execution.[89] It also recommended other changes that would give added protection both to the judgment debtor and to his other creditors. Those were as follows.

1.62 First, the Commission considered that the courts had hitherto tended to grant applications for charging orders without properly considering the potential adverse impact on debtors and other unsecured creditors. It recommended that any new legislation should make it clear that:

(a) the court had a wide discretion in deciding whether or not to make a charging order; and
(b) in exercising that discretion, the court should take into account evidence about:

    (i) the personal circumstances of the debtor; and
    (ii) other creditors, who might be unduly prejudiced if the charging order was granted.[90]

1.63 Secondly, the Commission considered that the High Court's jurisdiction to make charging orders should be limited to High Court judgment debts exceeding £1,000. The county court should have jurisdiction to make all other orders. If an application for a charging order was heard in the local county court, there was a much better chance that the judgment debtor would attend the hearing of the application. The court would then be informed both of the judgment debtor's circumstances and those of his other creditors. It could then have proper regard to them when deciding whether or not to make the charging order.[91]

---

88 See (1976) Law Com No 74, paras 22–39.

89 See (1976) Law Com No 74, paras 41–42.

90 See (1976) Law Com No 74, paras 43–44.

91 See (1976) Law Com No 74, paras 45–51.

Enabling any beneficial interest in land to be made the subject of charging orders

1.64 The second problem under the existing law identified by the Law Commission was that, because of the doctrine of conversion that then applied,[92] a beneficial interest in land held on trust for sale was not, for the purposes of section 35 of the Administration of Justice Act 1956, an 'interest in land', but an interest in the notional proceeds of sale of the land.[93] Such an interest could not therefore be made the subject of a charging order. This led to an anomaly: whereas interests under a bare trust or a settlement under the Settled Land Act 1925 could be the subject of a charging order, an interest under a trust for sale could not.[94]

1.65 The Commission recommended that the availability of charging orders should be extended to include a beneficial interest under a trust for sale of land. That would enable the judgment creditor in appropriate cases:

(a) to collect the debtor's share of any income from the property through the appointment of a receiver; and
(b) to apply to the court for an order for the sale of the charged beneficial interest.[95]

1.66 The Law Commission also recommended that where the judgment debtor was *both* a beneficiary under a trust *and* had the power to procure dealings with the legal estate for his own benefit, the judgment creditor should be entitled to charge the legal interest in the land. In such circumstances the legal estate should be treated as his own property for execution purposes. That applied where the judgment was against the trustees in their representative capacity as trustees, and where:

(a) there was only one beneficiary who was absolutely entitled under the trust,[96] and that beneficiary was the judgment debtor; or
(b) there were two or more beneficiaries who together were absolutely entitled under the trust, and where all the beneficiaries were debtors in respect of a single debt.[97]

---

92 It has since been abolished: see TLATA 1996, s 3.

93 See *Irani Finance Ltd v Singh* [1971] Ch 59.

94 See (1976) Law Com No 74, paras 54–95.

95 See (1976) Law Com No 74, paras 67–72. At that time, sale could be sought under LPA 1925, s 30. The relevant provision is now TLATA 1996, s 14.

96 'Absolutely entitled' meant, for that purpose, that the beneficiary held the whole of his beneficial interest under the trust unencumbered and for his own benefit, as where there was a bare trust. See further (1976) Law Com No 74, paras 65 and 73–77.

97 See (1976) Law Com No 74, paras 56–66.

Provision for the express discharge of charging orders

1.67 The third problem under the existing law was the uncertainty as to whether a judgment creditor could obtain a court order discharging his land from the charging order after satisfying the judgment. There was no express power to do so under section 35 of the Administration of Justice Act 1956, and while the rules of the High Court did permit such an order to be made, the position in the county court was uncertain. Accordingly, the Law Commission recommended that:

(a) both the High Court and the county court should be given power to make an order discharging the land subject to a charging order; and
(b) such an order should be sufficient to secure the removal of any entry at the Land Charges Department or HM Land Registry which might still subsist in respect of the charging order.[98]

Charging Orders Act 1979

1.68 The Law Commission's recommendations were embodied in a draft Bill annexed to its report. This was substantially enacted as the Charging Orders Act 1979. Much of the 1979 Act followed the wording of the Administration of Justice Act 1956. Accordingly, many decisions on the interpretation of the 1956 Act also apply to the 1979 Act. However, charging orders have become much more popular as a means of enforcing judgments since the 1979 Act than they were before. There are three main reasons for this:

(a) the improvements made by the 1979 Act, particularly the ability to charge beneficial interests in jointly owned properties;
(b) the greater prominence and publicity which the new Act gave to the charging order; and
(c) the subsequent increase in the percentage and value of individual home ownership.

1.69 The Charging Orders Act 1979 continues to form the basis of the current law of charging orders. There have been relatively few amendments to it over the four and half decades of its existence. The jurisdictional provisions concerning the High Court and county court, and now also the family court, have been revised from time to time.[99] Specific provisions have been added concerning charging orders in respect of judgment debts that are payable by instalments.[100] The

---

98 See (1976) Law Com No 74, paras 96–103.

99 See in particular the amendments made to COA 1979, ss 1 2 and 7, bringing them into their current form, made by the Administration of Justice Act 1982, the CCA 1984, the TCEA 2007, and the Crime and Courts Act 2013.

100 See COA 1979, s 1(6)–(8) and s 3(4A)–(4E), added by TCEA 2007, s 93.

provisions of section 4, concerning the completion of execution, were repealed and replaced by provisions now in the Insolvency Act 1986.[101] A power for the Lord Chancellor to set financial thresholds for charging orders has been added.[102] The provisions in the 1979 Act concerning the obtaining of charging orders over trust property have not themselves been amended,[103] but the way the 1979 Act applies to interests under trusts of land has been altered by the Trusts of Land and Appointment of Trustees Act 1996; and the references in the 1979 Act to the (now repealed) Land Registration Act 1925 have been superseded by references to the Land Registration Act 2002.[104]

1.70 The relevant procedure under the Charging Orders Act 1979 was originally governed by RSC Ord 50 and CCR Ord 31, but is now regulated by Part 73 of the Civil Procedure Rules. Part 73 came into force on 25 March 2002 and has been subject to various subsequent amendments.

---

101 IA 1986, s 183(3) (and, prior to that, Insolvency Act 1985, s 179(5)).

102 See COA 1979, s 3A, added by TCEA 2007, s 94.

103 COA 1979, s 2.

104 COA 1979, ss 3 and 7, as amended by the Land Registration Act 2002.

Chapter 2

Circumstances for Obtaining a Charging Order

INTRODUCTION

2.1 This chapter addresses the following issues:

(a) it explains who can apply for a charging order;
(b) it considers the property which may be charged by a charging order and, specifically, what interests in land may be the subject of such an order; ascertaining what land the debtor owns may not always be simple and searches and applications may need to be considered; and
(c) it examines how, on an application for a charging order, the court exercises its discretion in deciding whether such an order should be made; key issues to consider are whether the debtor is insolvent and whether they have any family or dependants who might be impacted.[1]

WHO CAN APPLY FOR A CHARGING ORDER?

Overview

- A court order, arbitral award, or order from certain tribunals requiring the payment of an ascertained sum can be enforced by a charging order.
- A charging order cannot be obtained to enforce a Tomlin order, an order which is strictly speaking purely declaratory, or a compensation order made in criminal proceedings.

---

1 The procedure for making an application for a charging order is explained in Chapter 3. Chapter 5 addresses the discharge or variation of a final charging order.

2.2 Under section 1(1) of the Charging Orders Act 1979, a creditor can obtain a charging order for the purpose of enforcing a judgment if:

(a) he has obtained a judgment or order of the High Court, the county court or the family court; and
(b) under that order, another person, called by the Act 'the debtor', is required to pay him a sum of money.

The charging order secures the payment of any money that is due or will become due under the judgment or order. An example of the latter would be instalment payments.[2] Money that may never become due does not fall within the statutory definition.[3]

2.3 Under that definition it is not possible to obtain a charging order in respect of:

(a) an unascertained sum;[4]
(b) an order to pay costs which have not been assessed;[5]
(c) a sum claimed in respect of which a defendant has been given leave to defend, conditional upon the payment into court of a specified sum, even if he is in breach of the condition and even if, following such failure, the claimant would be entitled to enter judgment in default.[6]

2.4 By contrast, a charging order can be obtained in respect of:

(a) a judgment given in foreign currency which has not been converted into sterling;[7]
(b) future interest, where the amount can be determined because it accrues at an ascertained rate.[8]

---

2 See COA 1979, s 1(7) which clarifies that the court is not prevented from making a charging order in respect of a sum even if there has been no default in the payment of instalments. See also *Monte Developments Ltd (In Administration) v Court Management Consultants Ltd* [2010] EWHC 3071 (Ch), [2011] 1 WLR 1579 at [33].

3 *Monte Developments Ltd (In Administration) v Court Management Consultants Ltd* [2010] EWHC 3071 (Ch), [2011] 1 WLR 1579 at [35].

4 *Widgery v Tepper (No 2)* (1877) 6 Ch D 364; *Ezekiel v Orakpo* [1997] 1 WLR 340.

5 *Monte Developments Ltd (In Administration) v Court Management Consultants Ltd* [2010] EWHC 3071 (Ch), [2011] 1 WLR 1579.

6 *Monte Developments Ltd (In Administration) v Court Management Consultants Ltd* [2010] EWHC 3071 (Ch), [2011] 1 WLR 1579.

7 *Carnegie v Giessen & Others* [2005] EWCA Civ 191, [2005] 1 WLR 2510.

8 *Ezekiel v Orakpo* [1997] 1 WLR 340.

2.5 The primary definition of orders or judgments which may be enforced under the Charging Orders Act 1979 is extended by the Act to include any judgment, order, decree or award (however called) of any court or arbitrator whether domestic or foreign which is or has become enforceable in whole or in part as if it were a judgment or order of the High Court, the county court or the family court.[9]

2.6 However, a charging order cannot be obtained in respect of a sum of money due in the schedule to a Tomlin order, unless and until the stay imposed by the Tomlin order is lifted for the purpose of enforcing the terms of the schedule and judgment is entered for the amount due.[10]

2.7 Further, in relation to domestic tribunals, a number of statutes provide for awards made by certain tribunals to be enforceable by execution or otherwise in a county court, as if they were an order of the county court. This means that a charging order may be made in respect of such an order. The types of awards in respect of which such an application may be made include the following:

(a) Employment Tribunal awards;[11]
(b) decisions of the First-tier Tribunal (FTT) or Upper Tribunal for the payment of sums (except in relation to certain judicial reviews);[12]
(b) awards for repayment to the Secretary of State for Work and Pensions;[13]
(c) fines and other penalties imposed by magistrates;[14] and
(d) awards of arbitrators.[15]

---

9 COA 1979, s 6(2).

The enforceability of judgments from European Economic Area (EEA) member states has become more complicated as a result of the United Kingdom's exit from the European Union and the ceasing of the application of Regulation (EU) No 1215/2012 [2012] OJ L 351/1, the Brussels Convention [1972] OJ L 299/32 and the Lugano Convention [2007] OJ L 339/3 in the United Kingdom. An exploration of when and how judgments of EEA countries can be made enforceable in England and Wales is outside the scope of this work and regard should be had to the Hague Convention on Choice of Court Agreements 2005, the Foreign Judgments (Reciprocal Enforcements) Act 1933, the Administration of Justice Act 1920, Civil Procedure Rules 1998 (Amendment) (EU Exit) Regulations 2019 (SI 2019/521), regs 26 and 27, and *Civil Procedure 2023* (Sweet & Maxwell, 2023), Part 74.

10 *T Class Security Ltd v Latchworth Ltd* [2021] EWHC 3579 (Ch).

11 Employment Tribunals Act 1996, s 15.

12 TCEA 2007, s 27.

13 Social Security and Housing Benefits Act 1982, s 41.

14 Magistrates' Courts Act 1980, s 87.

15 Arbitration Act 1996, s 66.

2.8 As regards the enforcement of such awards, except arbitration awards,[16] where an enactment provides that a decision of a court, tribunal, body or person other than the High Court or the county court[17] may be enforced as if it were a court order, an application must be made:

(a) to the court for the district where the person against whom the order is sought resides or carries on business, unless the court otherwise orders;[18] and
(b) in the prescribed form.[19]

In the case of an arbitration award, an application for permission to enforce the award is made without notice in an arbitration claim form.[20]

2.9 Care must be taken to ensure that the award by a tribunal actually requires the payment of sums. If the reality is that the decision of the tribunal is purely declaratory, then a charging order cannot be made in respect of it.[21] For example, where the FTT (Property Chamber) determines an application under section 27A of the Landlord and Tenant Act 1985, as to whether a service charge is payable, such a determination is strictly speaking simply a declaration rather than an order that the sums must be paid within a certain timeframe. Following such a determination, a claim would need to be begun in the courts for payment of the sums, in which the decision of the FTT (between the same parties) would be binding (although different/additional defences may be available). That court order might then be enforced by charging order.

2.10 A person who is the ultimate beneficiary of a compensation order made in criminal proceedings cannot apply for a charging order, because he is not a creditor within the meaning of section 1 of the Charging Orders Act 1979.[22]

2.11 There are other situations where it is not possible to obtain a charging order because it is precluded by statute. For example, as a result of section 25(4) of the Crown Proceedings Act 1947, no charging order may be obtained against the Crown. Similarly, no charging order can be made where the debtor has an

---

16 See CPR r 70.5(2)(b).

17 For enforcement of orders of the family court, please refer to FPR Part 40, which sets out that an application must be made to the family court or High Court, as appropriate. Please also refer to Chapter 3, para 3.25.

18 See CPR r 70.5(3) and (4)(b).

19 CPR r 70.5(5).

20 CPR r 62.18(1)(a).

21 *Termhouse (Clarendon Court) Management Ltd v Al-Balhaa* [2021] EWCA Civ 1881.

22 *Osbourne v Kendrick* [2001] EWCA Civ 690.

interest in property which is 'property of a state's central bank or other monetary authority' within the meaning of section 14(4) of the State Immunity Act 1978.[23]

PROPERTY WHICH MAY BE CHARGED

Overview

- Generally, land that is beneficially owned by the judgment debtor may be charged.
- Where a judgment debt is incurred by trustees, land held by the trustees for that trust may be charged.
- A charging order will sever a beneficial joint tenancy.
- If the judgment creditor does not know what land the judgment debtor owns, it may be necessary to apply to the court for HM Land Registry to carry out an index search, to look at mortgage charges in a Companies House search, or to search the Register of Overseas Entities.

2.12 Although charging orders may be made over a number of different types of property, this book is concerned only with charging orders over land, which are the commonest type of order.[24] The Charging Orders Act 1979 does not define 'land' and, in determining what is land for the purposes of the Act, it is therefore necessary to apply the provisions of the Interpretation Act 1978, by which land 'includes buildings and other structures, land covered with water, and any estate, interest, easement, servitude or right in or over land'.[25]

2.13 The interests in land which, under section 2 of the Charging Orders Act 1979, may be the subject of a charging order are:

(a) land that is legally and beneficially owned by the judgment debtor;[26]
(b) an interest in land held by the debtor beneficially under a trust; and
(c) any interest in land that is held by a trustee in circumstances where:

---

23 *AIG Capital Partners Inc v Republic of Kazakhstan* [2005] EWHC 2239 (Comm), [2006] 1 WLR 1420. State Immunity Act 1978, s 14(4) provides that, 'Property of a State's central bank or other monetary authority shall not be regarded for the purposes of subsection (4) of section 13 above as in use or intended for use for commercial purposes; and where any such bank or authority is a separate entity subsections (1) to (3) of that section shall apply to it as if references to a State were references to the bank or authority'. Such property is immune from the jurisdiction of the courts of England and Wales and therefore its enforcement process.

24 See Chapter 1, para 1.5.

25 Interpretation Act 1978, s 5 and Sch 1.

26 COA 1979, s 2(1)(a)(i) and (2)(a).

(i) the charge is made in respect of a judgment or order made against a person as trustee of the trust;[27]
(ii) there is a bare trust for the judgment debtor;[28] or
(iii) the land is held in trust for two or more debtors, who are liable for the same debt and who have between them, the whole beneficial interest in the land.[29]

2.14 Prior to the coming into force of the Charging Orders Act 1979, the court could only make a charging order on 'any land or interest in land'.[30] Those words had been held not to include the interest of a beneficiary under a trust for sale, which, under the doctrine of conversion then applicable,[31] was treated as being an interest in the proceeds of sale and not in the land itself.[32] At that time, beneficially co-owned land was necessarily held on a trust for sale. That shortcoming was remedied by the 1979 Act, which provided that a charging order might be made over land which the debtor owned jointly with another person, such as his or her spouse.[33]

2.15 As regards the three categories of interest in land, set out at para 2.13, that may be the subject of a charging order:

(a) category (a) is self-explanatory, although there may be cases in which, for other reasons, a charging order cannot be imposed on such property;[34]
(b) category (b) applies to any beneficial interest under a trust of land which belongs to the judgment debtor, whether that interest is a joint beneficial interest or held in common. Where the beneficial interest is a joint tenancy, the effect of a charging order is to sever the owners' joint beneficial interest, so that they are thereafter beneficial tenants in common in equal shares;[35]
(c) category (c), which is concerned with 'any interest held by a person as trustee of trust',[36] is more difficult and its component parts require further explanation.

2.16 Looking more closely at category (b), a beneficial interest under a trust of land can arise in a variety of circumstances. Co-ownership can for example be

---

27 COA 1979, s 2(1)(b)(i) and (2)(a).

28 COA 1979, s 2(1)(b)(ii) and (2)(a).

29 COA 1979, s 2(1)(b)(iii) and (2)(a).

30 AJA 1956, s 35.

31 The doctrine of conversion has since been abolished: see TLATA 1996, s 3.

32 *Irani Finance Ltd v Singh* [1971] Ch 59; see Chapter 1, para 1.64.

33 *National Westminster Bank Ltd v Stockman* [1981] 1 WLR 67.

34 See paras 2.9–2.11.

35 *C Putnam & Sons v Taylor* [2009] EWHC 317 (Ch), [2009] BPIR 769.

36 COA 1979, s 2(1)(b)(i).

expressly declared by the co-owners, it can arise from a resulting trust (e.g. if part of the purchase price is provided by another) or it can arise from a common intention constructive trust. That latter option is common in domestic situations and is often raised in response to charging order applications. In respect of the legal estate, co-ownership can only be in a joint tenancy.[37] A joint tenancy provides that as against the rest of the world, the joint tenants are in the position of a single owner:[38] they are all entitled to possession of the land, under the same interest, under the same title, and from the same time.[39] If one joint tenant dies, their interest passes to the other joint tenants by the right of survivorship. A beneficial interest can exist as a joint tenancy or a tenancy in common. In a tenancy in common, there is no right of survivorship and each co-owner owns an (undivided) share of the land; there is still unity of possession. Generally, a joint tenancy for the beneficial interest is presumed and co-owners may have drawn up their wills (or not drawn up wills at all) on the presumed basis of survivorship applying to their interest in land. As stated above, a charging order will sever such a joint tenancy into a tenancy in common in equal shares. Those drafting wills may wish to bear this in mind.

2.17 Category (c)(i)[40] was enacted to cover the case where the trustees, acting as such, have incurred the debt which is the subject of the judgment on behalf of the trust.[41] The charging order in such a case is over the trustees' estate in the land.[42] This is entirely logical, because the trustees are entitled to be reimbursed out of trust funds for expenses which they incur,[43] as where they employ solicitors or other agents to act for the trust. A charging order in this category has been made in respect of a costs order made against X in litigation, where X was acting throughout as nominee for Y. The order was made over a beneficial interest in land which X held on a bare trust for Y.[44] The order was also made where the liability had been incurred without the consent or knowledge of the beneficiary.[45] The authors consider that a further example that should come within this category is where trustees hold leasehold property and an order is made against them in respect of rent, service charges, or administration charges for that property; it should follow that a charging order can be made against that leasehold property

---

37 LPA 1925, s 36(2).

38 *Hammersmith & Fulham LBC v Monk* [1992] 1 AC 478 at 492.

39 *AG Securities v Vaughan* [1990] 1 AC 417 at 472 and 474.

40 COA 1979, s 2(1)(b)(i).

41 See (1976) Law Com No 74, para 63; *Beckenham MC Ltd v Centralex Ltd* [2004] EWHC 1287 (Ch), [2004] 2 BCLC 764 at [30]–[31].

42 This will normally be a legal estate, but in some cases it may be merely an equitable interest: see *Nelson v Greening & Sykes (Builders) Ltd* [2007] EWCA Civ 1358, [2008] 1 EGLR 59.

43 See Trustee Act 2000, s 31(1) (replacing earlier legislation).

44 *Nelson v Greening & Sykes (Builders) Ltd* [2007] EWCA Civ 1358, [2008] 1 EGLR 59.

45 *Kamran (Humera) v Davenport* [2017] EWHC 1844 (QB).

as it would be in respect of an order made against the legal owners as trustees of the trust in land.

2.18 Category (c)(ii)[46] is straightforward. Where the judgment debtor is absolutely entitled to the land held in trust, a charging order may be made over the interest held by the bare trustee. The reason for this is obvious. A beneficiary under a bare trust can at any time require the trustee to transfer the title to the asset to himself or at his direction.

2.19 Category (c)(iii)[47] is very similar. It is concerned with the situation where land (or an interest in land) is held in trust for two or more beneficiaries and where all of those beneficiaries are liable to the creditor for the same debt. A charging order may be made over the interest held by the trustees.[48] The underlying reason is the same as with category (c)(ii). The beneficial owners – the joint judgment debtors – can require the trustees to convey the land (or interest) at their direction under the rule in *Saunders v Vautier*.[49]

2.20 A judgment creditor may not always know what property is owned by a judgment debtor.[50] The public cannot search HM Land Registry's index of proprietors' names. A person (or their trustee in bankruptcy or their personal representative) can apply to HM Land Registry for such a search,[51] but this right does not extend to a judgment creditor. However, a judgment creditor can apply to the court, under section 34(2) of the Senior Courts Act 1981 and its inherent jurisdiction, for HM Land Registry to carry out such a search.[52] The results of such a search will show what property is legally owned by the judgment debtor (but will not show information relating to beneficial interests).

2.21 For a company, a Companies House search can bring up data relating to mortgage charges, which is likely to assist in ascertaining the identity of at least some properties owned by the judgment debtor company. Overseas entities that own property in England and Wales that they bought on or after 1 January 1999, or that now want to buy, sell, or transfer land in the United Kingdom, are also

---

46 COA 1979, s 2(1)(b)(ii).

47 COA 1979, s 2(1)(b)(iii).

48 See e.g. *Clark v Chief Land Registrar* [1994] Ch 370, where A and B held land on trust for themselves and a charging order was imposed on the land in respect of a debt which both A and B owed to the judgment creditor.

49 *Saunders v Vautier* (1841) 4 Beav 115. *Cf* (1976) Law Com No 74, para 62.

50 A judgment creditor may wish to engage an enquiry agent to locate properties owned by a judgment debtor.

51 Land Registration Rules 2003 (SI 2003/1417), r 11(3).

52 *Parkinson v Hawthorne* [2008] EWHC 3499 (Ch), [2009] 1 WLR 1665. See also *Barfoot Farms Ltd v Revuckas* [2021] EWHC 2423 (QB).

now required to disclose to Companies House who has certain beneficial interests.[53] Most information given to Companies House about such beneficial owners will be publicly available on the Register of Overseas Entities.[54] Whilst the meaning of 'beneficial owner' for the purposes of the Register of Overseas Entities is not the same as the meaning of beneficial ownership under the Charging Orders Act 1979, information on the Register of Overseas Entities may be useful in establishing lines of enquiry.

EXERCISE OF THE COURT'S DISCRETION

Overview

- A court will first make an interim charging order before making a final charging order.
- At both stages, the court has a discretion. The court will consider all the circumstances of the case.
- Where bankruptcy/insolvency of the judgment debtor has commenced, the court will usually decline to make a charging order so that the assets can instead fall part of the statutory scheme to protect all the creditors.
- Family circumstances of the debtor can complicate the discretion but often the court will make the charging order on the basis that those circumstances are better explored at the sale stage.
- Recent legislation (e.g. on commercial rent arrears during the pandemic and for debt breathing spaces and mental health crises) has introduced moratoriums which might restrict the ability to obtain a charging order.

Role of discretion

2.22 A charging order, as a form of enforcement of a debt, is not available as of right, but only in exercise of the court's discretion. The discretion is statutory,[55] and must be exercised judicially.[56] In deciding whether to make a charging order the court has to consider all the circumstances, and, in particular, any evidence before it as to: (a) the personal circumstances of the debtor; and (b) whether any other creditor of the debtor would be likely to be unduly prejudiced by the making of the order.[57] It has been said that the effect of that provision 'is to confer upon

---

53 Land Registration Act 2002, Sch 4A.

54 Economic Crime (Transparency and Enforcement) Act 2022, s 21.

55 COA 1979, s 1(1).

56 *First National Securities Ltd v Hegerty* [1985] QB 850.

57 COA 1979, s 1(5).

the judge a general discretion neither governed nor limited by any statutory language'.[58]

2.23 Part 73 of the Civil Procedure Rules, following the practice that had applied under section 35 of the Administration of Justice Act 1956, provides for a two-stage process in determining whether a charging order should be made.[59] The first stage is the consideration by the court of the question whether to grant an interim charging order ('the interim charging order'). The second stage is a consideration by the court of whether to make the interim charging order final. The court has a discretion, both at the stage of making an interim charging order and when making a final order.[60] The same principles must apply to the exercise of discretion at each stage, namely those set out at para 2.22.[61] However, for the procedural reasons explained below, the court may be less well informed when considering whether to make an interim charging order in the first place than it will be when deciding whether to make an interim charging order final.

2.24 The application for a charging order will be dealt with initially without a hearing.[62] At that stage, the court may make an interim charging order imposing a charge over the debtor's interest in the assets to which the application relates. Before the court makes an interim charging order, it will need to be satisfied from the application that a sum of money is payable to the applicant under a judgment, that the judgment debtor is in default,[63] and that the judgment debtor either owns a legal estate in the land or has a beneficial interest under a trust of land. Those are seldom substantial hurdles for the applicant.[64]

2.25 At the subsequent determination of whether the interim order should be made final, the court may, by order:

(a) make a final charging order confirming that the charge imposed by the interim charging order shall continue, with or without modification;
(b) discharge the interim charging order and dismiss the application;
(c) decide any issue in dispute between the parties, or between the parties and any other person objecting to the making of a final charging order;
(d) direct the trial of any issue, and give directions accordingly;[65] or
(e) make such other order as the court considers appropriate.

---

58 *Kremen v Agrest* [2013] EWCA Civ 41, [2013] 2 FLR 187 at [28], per Thorpe LJ.

59 See further Chapter 3, para 3.46.

60 See *Clarke v Coutts & Co (A Firm)* [2002] EWCA Civ 943, [2002] BPIR 916 at [35].

61 See COA 1979, s 1(5).

62 CPR rr 73.4(2) and 73.6(2).

63 Except where COA 1979, s 1(7) and (8) applies: see para 2.50.

64 See Chapter 3, para 3.39.

65 CPR rr 73.10(7) and 73.10A(3)). See Chapter 3, para 3.95.

Principles applicable to the exercise of discretion

2.26 As already explained, the Charging Orders Act 1979 sets out the matters that a court must consider in exercising its discretion.[66] There has been some judicial guidance as to the exercise of the discretion and, in particular, in the judgment of Lord Brandon of Oakbrook in *Roberts Petroleum Ltd v Bernard Kenny Ltd*[67] in the Court of Appeal, to the extent that it was not affected by the subsequent decision of the House of Lords.[68] Those remarks were made in the context of whether an interim charging order should be made final.

2.27 The five principles stated by Lord Brandon that were unaffected are as follows:

(a) The question whether an interim charging order should be made final is one for the discretion of the court.
(b) The burden of showing cause why an interim charging order shall not be made final is on the judgment debtor.
(c) For the purpose of the exercise of the court's discretion there is no material difference between third party debt orders and charging orders.[69]
(d) In exercising its discretion, the court must take into account all the relevant circumstances whether they arose before or after the interim charging order.
(e) The court should exercise its discretion equitably having regard to the interests of all parties involved, including other unsecured creditors, as well as those of the judgment creditor and the judgment debtor.[70]

The second of those five principles, which was based upon the wording of the then applicable court rules,[71] may not represent the present law, because the court rules are differently worded.[72] The point has been left open by the Court of Appeal.[73] Nonetheless, the High Court has determined that where the party applying for an interim charging order to be made final is seeking to displace the presumption that the beneficial title follows the legal title, the burden on that issue is on the said party.[74] In another case, the High Court held that the burden is on

---

66 COA 1979, s 1(5); see para 2.22.

67 *Roberts Petroleum Ltd v Bernard Kenny Ltd* [1982] 1 WLR 301 at 307, CA.

68 *Roberts Petroleum Ltd v Bernard Kenny Ltd (In Liquidation)* [1983] 2 AC 192, HL. Of Lord Brandon's seven propositions, the first five were unaffected by the decision of the House of Lords.

69 A third party debt order used to be known as a garnishee order. For such orders, see CPR Part 72.

70 *Cf* COA 1979, s 1(5)(b).

71 RSC Ord 50, r 1.

72 See CPR rr 73.10 and 73.10A.

73 See *National Guild of Removers and Storers Ltd v Jones and Coid* [2012] EWCA Civ 216, [2012] 1 WLR 2501 at [13]–[16]. See Chapter 3, para 3.61.

74 *National Crime Agency v Persico* [2021] EWHC 3476 (QB) at [30].

the party applying for the final charging order to establish that the debtor owns the property which can be discharged by referring to the registered title; the burden then shifts to any party seeking to say that they in fact own the beneficial interest in that property to establish that fact.[75]

2.28 The court can only consider the evidence before it when exercising the discretion and must make its decision on the basis of that evidence.[76] Accordingly, where the applicant for a charging order did not know that another creditor had presented a bankruptcy petition in respect of the judgment debtor,[77] it could not be said that either the interim charging order or the final charging order should not have been made, because 'hindsight cannot be relied on in this context'.[78]

2.29 Although the Charging Orders Act 1979 specifically requires the court to have regard both to the personal circumstances of the judgment debtor[79] and to whether any other creditor of that debtor would be likely to be unduly prejudiced by the making of the order,[80] its overriding obligation is to consider all the circumstances of the case.[81] Those circumstances will necessarily include the effect on third parties[82] and also the position of the creditor who is applying for the charging order.

2.30 As regards the position of the judgment creditor, it has been held that:

(a) The purpose of making a final charging order was not to punish the debtor but to provide security for the judgment debt.[83]
(b) It was not a proper exercise of discretion to suspend the accrual of interest when adjourning an application for a final charging order.[84]

---

75 *Ashraf v Phonepayplus Ltd* [2016] EWHC 1026 (Ch) at [47].

76 COA 1979, s 1(5) and *C & W Berry Ltd v Armstrong-Moakes* [2007] EWHC 2101 (QB) at [8].

77 As to the effect of such a petition on the exercise of discretion, see para 2.38.

78 *C & W Berry Ltd v Armstrong-Moakes* [2007] EWHC 2101 (QB) at [8], per David Clarke J. The decision is briefly reported at [2008] 1 P & CR DG1. The charging order was set aside under an application under COA 1979, s 3(5), on other grounds. For applications under s 3(5), see Chapter 5.

79 COA 1979, s 1(5)(a).

80 COA 1979, s 1(5)(b).

81 COA 1979, s 1(5).

82 See *Howell v Montey* (1990) 61 P & CR 18, considered at Chapter 4, para 4.29.

83 *National Guild of Removers and Storers Ltd v Jones and Coid* [2012] EWCA Civ 216, [2012] 1 WLR 2501 at [21].

84 *National Guild of Removers and Storers Ltd v Jones and Coid* [2012] EWCA Civ 216, [2012] 1 WLR 2501 at [17]–[19]. No reason had been given for such a suspension. The Court of Appeal left open whether it could ever be proper to do so.

(c) It was not a proper exercise of discretion to refuse the creditor a final charging order and, instead, to order the debtor to make small periodical payments in respect of the debt.[85]

2.31 Conversely, there may be conduct by the judgment creditor that may adversely affect his chances of obtaining a final charging order. For example, if the creditor had an opportunity to take other security for his debt when it was incurred but failed to take it, that is relevant to the exercise of discretion, and may lead to the refusal of such an order. Thus in one case,[86] charity trustees had a statutory power, with the Charity Commissioners' consent, to borrow on the security of the charity property.[87] However, the lender chose not to take that security. The court declined to make a final charging order in the lender's favour because (among other reasons):

(a) the lender knew he could have taken security but chose not to take it and he would otherwise 'thereby obtain by the back door what he knowingly did not insist on obtaining by the front door';
(b) in borrowing unsecured, the trustees were acting in breach of trust 'the consequences of which ought not lightly to be visited upon the assets still available for the fulfilment of the trust's charitable purposes';
(c) the charging order if granted would not be in a form that complied with the statutory requirements for a mortgage by charity trustees.

Personal circumstances of the debtor

2.32 The personal circumstances which will weigh the most heavily with the court are:

(a) the judgment debtor's financial circumstances and, in particular (but not exclusively), where the judgment debtor is bankrupt or in liquidation;[88]
(b) the situation of the judgment debtor's family and dependants.[89]

---

85 *National Guild of Removers and Storers Ltd v Jones and Coid* [2012] EWCA Civ 216, [2012] 1 WLR 2501 at [23].

86 *White v Williams* [2011] EWHC 494 (Ch), [2011] PTSR 1151.

87 Pursuant to Charities Act 1993, s 38. That provision is now Charities Act 2011, s 124.

88 This is because of COA 1979, s 1(5)(b).

89 See COA 1979, s 1(5)(a).

Financial circumstances

Insolvency

2.33 The effect of the insolvency of a judgment debtor in relation to an application for a charging order is as follows.[90]

2.34 First, in a case where:

(a) the judgment debtor is an individual who has been adjudged bankrupt; and
(b) the judgment creditor has, before the commencement of bankruptcy, issued execution against the judgment creditor's land;

that creditor is not entitled, as against the official receiver or trustee of the bankrupt's estate, to retain the benefit of the execution unless the execution was completed before the commencement of the bankruptcy.[91]

2.35 For these purposes:

(a) bankruptcy commences on the day upon which a bankruptcy order is made and continues until the individual is discharged under the relevant statutory provisions;[92]
(b) execution against land is completed by the making of a charging order under section 1 of the Charging Orders Act 1979;[93] and
(c) in this context, the making of a charging order means the making of a final charging order.[94]

2.36 This restriction is subject to a dispensing power conferred on the court in favour of the creditor who has issued the execution, whereby it may permit such execution.[95] However, it is a jurisdiction to be exercised with great caution and only in exceptional cases.[96] The general approach of the court will be influenced by the principles that are set out at paras 2.38–2.41.

---

90 See also, Chapter 8.

91 Insolvency Act 1986 (IA 1986), s 346(1). See Chapter 8, para 8.129.

92 See IA 1986, Part IX, Chapter I.

93 IA 1986, s 346(5)(b).

94 *Roberts Petroleum Ltd v Bernard Kenny Ltd (In Liquidation)* [1983] 2 AC 192 at 212, HL.

95 IA 1986, s 346(6).

96 See *Tagore Investments SA v Official Receiver* [2008] EWHC 3495 (Ch), [2009] BPIR 392, especially at [43]–[48], where Mann J summarised the factors relevant to the exercise of this discretion.

2.37 There are equivalent provisions to those set out at paras 2.34–2.36 in a case where a judgment creditor has issued execution against the land of a company that is subsequently wound up.[97]

2.38 Secondly, where the judgment debtor is an individual, and:

(a) an interim charging order has been made against him, but not a final charging order; and
(b) that individual's bankruptcy has then commenced;

the court has a discretion whether or not to make a final order.[98] However, in practice, it will generally decline to make such an order, so that the property will fall within the statutory scheme that became applicable on bankruptcy in order to protect all of the debtor's creditors. These principles are derived by analogy from the leading case on corporate insolvency, *Roberts Petroleum Ltd v Bernard Kenny Ltd*,[99] which is explained below. Even if no bankruptcy order has been made, but a bankruptcy petition has been presented, a court is likely, in its discretion, to refuse to make a final charging order. Once again, this is because of the potentially adverse impact that such an order might have on the judgment debtor's other creditors.[100]

2.39 The same principles apply where an interim charging order has been made against a judgment debtor which is a company, but where, before a final charging order is made, a winding-up order is made or a winding-up resolution is passed in relation to the judgment debtor. In those circumstances, although the court has a discretion in the matter, it will, in exercising it, normally decline to make a final order. This principle was settled by the House of Lords in *Roberts Petroleum Ltd v Bernard Kenny Ltd*.[101]

2.40 In that case, the judgment creditor applied for an interim charging order over two of the judgment debtor's filling stations, knowing that the debtor was insolvent and with a view to obtaining an advantage over its other unsecured creditors. After obtaining the interim order, the debtor company resolved to put

---

97 See IA 1986, s 183.

98 *Cf Re a Debtor (Nos 31/32/33 of 1993), Calor Gas Ltd v Piercy* [1994] BCC 69 at 79 *et seq*.

99 *Roberts Petroleum Ltd v Bernard Kenny Ltd (In Liquidation)* [1983] 2 AC 192, HL, especially at 208–209.

100 See e.g. *Sandhu v Sidhu* [2011] EWHC 3675 (Ch). See also, Chapter 4, para 4.73.

101 *Roberts Petroleum Ltd v Bernard Kenny Ltd (In Liquidation)* [1983] 2 AC 192, HL. The case concerned a charging order imposed under AJA 1956, s 35(1), the wording of which is not materially different from COA 1979, s 1(1).

itself into voluntary liquidation to deprive the creditor of that advantage. The issue was whether the court should, in its discretion, make the charging order final.

2.41 The main elements in the judgments[102] were as follows:

(a) As a matter of principle, if 'the statutory scheme for dealing with the assets of the company has been irrevocably imposed on the company, by resolution or winding up order, before the court has irrevocably determined to give the creditor the benefit of a charging order ... the statutory scheme should prevail'.[103]
(b) Although an interim charging order imposed an immediate charge, that charge was defeasible. There was not, therefore, any irrevocable determination that the judgment creditor should have the benefit of a charging order.
(c) The imposition on the assets of an insolvent company of the statutory scheme for the distribution of those assets among the unsecured creditors was a sufficient cause for not converting the interim order into a final order.[104] Lord Brightman made clear the policy: 'I do not see why a creditor should gain an advantage merely because he has a revocable order for security at the time when the statutory scheme comes into existence'.[105]

Accordingly, the House of Lords held, reversing the Court of Appeal, that the interim charging order should not be made final.[106]

2.42 Thirdly, where the judgment debtor is an individual and he has obtained from the court an interim order under the Insolvency Act 1986 because he intends to enter into a voluntary arrangement with his creditors, the court's consent is required to any application for an interim or final charging order.[107] The court

---

102 Lord Brightman gave the only reasoned judgment with which the other judges concurred.

103 *Roberts Petroleum Ltd v Bernard Kenny Ltd (In Liquidation)* [1983] 2 AC 192 at 208, HL, per Lord Brightman.

104 The words 'sufficient cause' appeared in the court rules then applicable: see RSC Ord 50, r 1. There is no equivalent provision in the present equivalent rule, CPR r 72(8). However, this does not affect the principle laid down in *Roberts* and its application to cases under the COA 1979 and CPR Part 72. See *Clarke v Coutts & Co (A Firm)* [2002] EWCA Civ 943, [2002] BPIR 916 at [39]–[41].

105 *Roberts Petroleum Ltd v Bernard Kenny Ltd (In Liquidation)* [1983] 2 AC 192 at 209, HL.

106 See also *Monte Developments Ltd (In Administration) v Court Management Consultants Ltd* [2010] EWHC 3071 (Ch), [2011] 1 WLR 1579 at [43], where Floyd J explained that notice of the intention to appoint administrators, where that intended administration was appropriately invoked, was 'plainly a powerful factor to be taken into consideration. Were it not so, a creditor with notice of the administration would be able to gain an advantage over the other creditors, who will all be subject to the statutory scheme'.

107 IA 1986, s 252.

may, in its discretion, decide to allow such an application,[108] although it would have a particular concern to ensure that other creditors of the judgment debtor will not be unduly prejudiced by such an order.[109] If a court, in ignorance of such an interim order, makes a charging order, although that order is not a nullity, it must be set aside unless the court's consent is retrospectively sought.[110]

2.43 Similar provisions apply in relation to a company, where the directors propose a voluntary arrangement under Part A1 of the Insolvency Act 1986 and obtain a moratorium. During the period of such a moratorium, the court's consent is required to any application for an interim or final charging order.[111] The position set out at para 2.42 would apply equally to any such application.

2.44 Fourthly, the question whether, where a final charging order has been made prior to the insolvency of the judgment debtor, that charging order can be set aside on an application by the debtor's trustee in bankruptcy or liquidator[112] is considered in both Chapters 4,[113] 5[114] and 8.

Size of the debt

2.45 There is some authority to the effect 'it would not be a proper exercise of discretion to make a charging order on an asset of considerable or substantial value in respect of a relatively small debt payable by the debtor'.[115] To impose a charging order in such circumstances could be disproportionate and unfair to other creditors.[116] However, in a subsequent authority on the enforcement of a charging order, it has been suggested that 'it is potentially dangerous for a court to identify any hard and fast rules that seek to link the size of the debt with the ability to obtain a charging order or an order for sale'. Not only were there difficulties in determining what constituted a small debt for these purposes, but it 'offends against common sense' to say that 'the greater the value of the asset (and therefore the greater the default on the part of the debtor in failing to realise any

---

108 See *Re a Debtor (Nos 31/32/33 of 1993), Calor Gas Ltd v Piercy* [1994] BCC 69.

109 COA 1979, s 1(5)(b).

110 See *Clarke v Coutts & Co (A Firm)* [2002] EWCA Civ 943, [2002] BPIR 916 (where such retrospective permission had not been sought).

111 See IA 1986, s A21.

112 The application would be under COA 1979, s 3(5).

113 See Chapter 4, para 4.69 *et seq*.

114 See Chapter 5, para 5.20.

115 *Re Goldspan Ltd* [2003] BPIR 93, [2001] All ER (D) 412 (Oct), per Leslie Kosmin QC, applying *Robinson v Bailey* [1942] Ch 268 (judgment for annual payments of £50: charging order over stock worth £3,333 refused). See further Chapter 6, para 6.38.

116 *Re Goldspan Ltd* [2003] BPIR 93, [2001] All ER (D) 412 (Oct).

part of that asset to pay the debt), the greater the chance the debtor would have of avoiding a charging order or an order for sale'.[117]

Personal circumstances: the family home

2.46 Acute conflicts can arise where a judgment creditor seeks a charging order against the family home of the judgment debtor. These cases usually arise where the spouses or cohabitants are co-owners of the family home. The courts have accepted, on the one hand, that 'a judgment creditor is in general entitled to enforce a money judgment which he has lawfully obtained against a judgment debtor by all or any of the means of execution prescribed by the relevant rules of court'.[118] However, that must be balanced against the claims of the judgment debtor's spouse (or, in many cases, former or divorcing spouse) and any children who live in the property to be charged.

2.47 The approach to this balancing exercise was recently summarised by the Court of Appeal as follows:

> when striking a balance between the interests of the judgment creditor and those of the wife, the interests of the judgment creditor should be respected, save to the extent that it is necessary to override them in order to make appropriate provision for the wife and any minor children. In some cases that can be achieved by an order postponing the sale of the property (usually known as a *Mesher* order – see *Mesher v Mesher and Hall* [1980] 1 All ER 126), or in a more extreme case by withholding a charging order altogether and transferring the husband's interest to the wife free of any encumbrance.[119]

2.48 In *Harman v Glencross*,[120] the Court of Appeal gave some guidance as to how these cases should be dealt with, where the spouses were, or were likely to be, divorcing:

---

117 *Packman Lucas Ltd v Mentmore Towers Ltd* [2010] EWHC 1037 (TCC) at [25]–[26], per Coulson J. In that case judgment debts owed by two debtors, which together totalled about £250,000, were secured by charging orders over two multi-million-pound properties, each owned by one of the debtors. On an application for sale the court ordered that one property be sold for a minimum of £16 million. Had the only issue been the relative size of the debt when compared to value, the court would not have been persuaded that an order for sale of the other property (itself worth at least £15 million) was inappropriate (at [31]). However, because there was also the possibility of an imminent sale of the second property, the court gave the second debtor a final opportunity either to pay the outstanding sums or to realise its own sale.

118 *Roberts Petroleum Ltd v Bernard Kenny Ltd* [1982] 1 WLR 301 at 307, per Lord Brandon. See also *First National Securities Ltd v Hegerty* [1985] QB 850 at 866–7.

119 *Kremen v Agrest* [2013] EWCA Civ 41, [2013] 2 FLR 187 at [13], per Moore-Bick LJ.

120 *Harman v Glencross* [1986] Fam 81 at 99–100, per Balcombe LJ.

(a) Where a judgment creditor had obtained an interim charging order on the husband's share in the matrimonial home and his application to have that order made absolute was heard before the wife had started divorce proceedings, the case could only be heard by the court to which the application for a charging order was made. There was no competing claim from the wife. In those circumstances, there were no good reasons for the court to refuse to make the charging order absolute.

(b) Where the interim charging order had been made after the wife's petition, then on the application for a charging order absolute the court should consider whether the circumstances are such that it is proper to make the charging order absolute, even before the wife's application for ancillary relief has been heard by the family court. The value of the family home might be such that even if the charging order was made absolute, and the charge was then realised by a sale of the house, the proceeds of sale would be clearly sufficient to provide adequate alternative accommodation for the wife and children.

(c) Unless it appeared to the court hearing the application for the charging order absolute that the circumstances were so clear that it was proper to make an immediate order, the usual practice should be to transfer the application to the family court to be heard with the wife's application for ancillary relief so that one court could be in a position to consider all the circumstances of the case. If the equity in the house was not sufficient to enable the charging order to be made absolute and realised at once, the court should make only such order as was necessary to protect the wife's right to occupy the matrimonial home with any children. The court would normally postpone the sale by means of a *Mesher* order for such period as was necessary to protect the right of occupation.[121] If the judgment creditor would accept such a *Mesher* order, 'it would require exceptional circumstances before the court should make an order for the outright transfer of the husband's share in the house to the wife'.[122] The court should also consider whether there was any point in refusing to make the charging order absolute if the wife's rights of occupation could in any event be defeated by the judgment creditor making the husband bankrupt.[123]

(d) Once the charging order absolute has been made, it would normally require some special circumstances for the court to set the charging order aside under section 3(5) of the Charging Orders Act 1979, so as to deprive the judgment creditor of his vested right.[124]

---

121 As happened in *Austin-Fell v Austin-Fell* [1990] Fam 172.

122 *Harman v Glencross* [1986] Fam 81 at 100, per Balcombe LJ.

123 See IA 1986, ss 335A and 336.

124 See Chapter 5, para 5.3.

2.49 In the end, however, each case depends on its own facts and 'there can never be automatic predominance for any claim; each case depends upon striking a fair balance between the normal expectations of the judgment creditor and the hardship to the wife and children if a charging order is made'.[125] It might have been expected that the courts would take into account the European Convention for the Protection of Human Rights and Fundamental Freedoms,[126] in exercising their discretion in such cases. However, it has not been specifically mentioned, although the balancing exercise in which the courts engage is entirely compatible with the requirements of the Convention. This matter is considered more fully below.[127]

Instalments

2.50 As from 1 October 2012,[128] where, under a judgment or order of the High Court, the county court or the family court a debtor is required to pay a sum of money by instalments, the fact that there has been no default in payment of the instalments does not prevent a charging order from being made in respect of that sum.[129] However, where there has been no default by the debtor, that is a factor that the court must take into account when considering the circumstances of the case under section 1(5) of the Charging Orders Act 1979.[130]

2.51 These provisions mirror the position that had previously applied in the High Court, and reverse the previous county court position, in which it had been held that section 86(1) of the County Courts Act 1984[131] prevented the making of an interim charging order until after default.[132] Even in the county court, where the interim charging order preceded the making of any instalment order in respect

---

125 *Kremen v Agrest* [2013] EWCA Civ 41, [2013] 2 FLR 187 at [13], per Moore-Bick LJ. In that case, the husband had transferred his interest in the family home to C to try to defeat the wife's claim on divorce. The sale was set aside and the husband was required to indemnify C for his costs. C then applied for a charging order over the matrimonial home. Having regard to all the circumstances, the Court of Appeal upheld the trial judge's refusal to make a final charging order.

126 European Convention on Human Rights.

127 See para 2.53.

128 See Tribunals, Courts and Enforcement Act 2007 (Commencement No 8) Order 2012 (SI 2012/1312), art 3.

129 COA 1979, s 1(6) and (7), added by TCEA 2007, s 93(1) and (2).

130 COA 1979, s 1(8). For COA 1979, s 1(5), see para 2.22.

131 Which provides that, 'Where the court has made an order for payment of any sum of money by instalments, execution on the order shall not be issued until after default in payment of some instalment according to the order'.

132 See *Mercantile Credit Co Ltd v Huxtable* (1987) *The Times*, 1 April 1987.

of the underlying judgment, it had been held that that charging order might be confirmed by a final order even if there was no default.[133]

2.52 The old rules continue to apply to judgments and orders made before 1 October 2012.[134]

European Convention on Human Rights

2.53 The final issue in relation to discretion is whether the European Convention on Human Rights is ever engaged when a court exercises its discretion whether or not to make a charging order under section 1(5) of the Charging Orders Act 1979. It is well settled[135] that two provisions of the Convention may be engaged when a court has to consider whether, where land is already subject to a final charging order, an *order for sale* should be made.[136]

2.54 The two provisions of the European Convention on Human Rights are Article 1 of the First Protocol (the enjoyment of possessions), which applies to the rights of the judgment creditor, and Article 8 of the Convention (right to respect to family and private life), which will apply in relation to the interests of, for example, the judgment debtor's spouse or partner, particularly where that person has a beneficial interest in the property in question.[137]

2.55 In the context of an application for a sale of land subject to a charging order, the courts acknowledge that:

> It is of course in accordance with the law that a charging order has been made and, to the extent that it is now enforced, that will be in accordance with the law also. It will also be in the public interest to enforce charging orders generally because of the economic importance of ensuring that there is an efficient machinery for the enforcement of debt obligations, even though, unlike in the case of a legal mortgagee, this is not a debt obligation which was voluntarily provided as a secured obligation.[138]

---

133 *Ropaigealach v Allied Irish Bank plc* [2001] EWCA Civ 1790, [2002] 1 EGLR 83.

134 TCEA 2007, s 93(6) and Tribunals, Courts and Enforcement Act 2007 (Commencement No 8) Order 2012, art 3.

135 See *Close Invoice Finance Ltd v Pile* [2008] EWHC 1580 (Ch), [2009] 1 FLR 873; *C Putnam & Sons v Taylor* [2009] EWHC 317 (Ch), [2009] BPIR 769; *National Westminster Bank plc v Rushmer* [2010] EWHC 554 (Ch), [2010] 2 FLR 362.

136 The court exercises a discretion in such cases under CPR Part 73, which is considered in Chapter 6.

137 As will be the case where the charging order is over the judgment debtor's beneficial interest.

138 *Close Invoice Finance Ltd v Pile* [2008] EWHC 1580 (Ch), [2009] 1 FLR 873 at [12], per HHJ Purle QC. See also *National Westminster Bank plc v Rushmer* [2010] EWHC 554 (Ch), [2010] 2 FLR 362 at [48].

The courts have also accepted that:

> in applying the court's discretion, it must be applied in a way which gives due respect to the right of all those living in the property, not just the debtors, to have respect for their family life and their home. Against that must be weighed the rights of the chargee under the equitable charge, that is to say the Claimant, not to have to wait indefinitely for payment or to have no means of enforcing its security.[139]

2.56 The European Convention on Human Rights could in some cases, as in the situations considered at paras 2.32–2.49, apply to the exercise of discretion under section 1(5) of the Charging Orders Act 1979. This is because a charging order may lead to a sale of the family home, which is why, in some divorce cases, the court may refuse to make a final charging order unless the judgment creditor is prepared to accept a *Mesher* order deferring the date of any possible sale.[140] It is suggested that the balancing exercise that the courts undertake in these situations complies with the requirements of the Convention, as the first passage quoted in para 2.55 suggests.

COMMERCIAL RENT (CORONAVIRUS) ACT 2022

2.57 During the COVID-19 pandemic, the UK government instituted various measures to protect business tenants, such as a temporary ban on forfeiting business leases for non-payment of rent.[141] On 24 March 2022, this assistance developed in the form of the Commercial Rent (Coronavirus) Act 2022. Paragraph 3 of Schedule 2 to the 2022 Act provides that for any claim which is made between (and including) 10 November 2021 and 23 March 2022, by a landlord against a tenant, relating to a protected rent debt as defined under the Act, no enforcement of any judgment debt relating to such protected rent debt or interest can be enforced by the landlord before the end of the moratorium period. This moratorium period ended on 24 September 2022, or the day on which an arbitration under the Act concludes. Therefore, during this period, a charging order was unavailable to a landlord to enforce a protected rent debt or interest on it and remains unavailable in cases where an arbitration still proceeds.

---

139 *Close Invoice Finance Ltd v Pile* [2008] EWHC 1580 (Ch), [2009] 1 FLR 873 at [13], per HHJ Purle QC. See also *National Westminster Bank plc v Rushmer* [2010] EWHC 554 (Ch), [2010] 2 FLR 362 at [48].

140 See para 2.48.

141 See e.g. Coronavirus Act 2020, s 82.

BREATHING SPACE MORATORIUM AND MENTAL HEALTH CRISIS MORATORIUM

2.58 If a debtor is covered by a breathing space moratorium or a mental health crisis moratorium,[142] then a creditor is, for the period of such moratorium, not permitted to take any steps to enforce a judgment issued by a court or tribunal before or during the moratorium, in respect of a moratorium debt.[143] These moratoriums are only available to individuals who live or usually reside in England or Wales.

2.59 The period of a breathing space moratorium will normally last 60 days[144] whereas the period of a mental health crisis moratorium is more fact dependent.[145] If such a moratorium applies then, during such period, a creditor will be unable to apply for a charging order against a debtor in respect of a moratorium debt. Whilst a creditor should have been contacted by the Secretary of State in relation to the commencement of a moratorium,[146] a creditor ought always to investigate the register held by the government to check whether a moratorium applies to a debtor.

2.60 If a creditor needs to apply for a charging order sooner than the ordinary end of a moratorium, they will need to consider requesting a review of the moratorium. It can request such a review if the moratorium unfairly prejudices the interest of the creditor or there has been some material irregularity in relation to:

(a) the debtor not meeting the relevant eligibility criteria when the application for the moratorium was made;[147]
(b) the moratorium debt is not a qualifying debt;[148] or
(c) the debtor has sufficient funds to discharge or liquidate their debt as it falls due.

---

142 See Chapter 8 for a discussion of the debt respite provisions.

143 Debt Respite Scheme (Breathing Space Moratorium and Mental Health Crisis Moratorium) (England and Wales) Regulations 2020 (SI 2020/1311) (Debt Respite Scheme Regs 2020), reg 7(7)(b).

144 Debt Respite Scheme Regs 2020, reg 26.

145 Debt Respite Scheme Regs 2020, reg 32.

146 Debt Respite Scheme Regs 2020, regs 25 and 31.

147 For which, refer to Debt Respite Scheme Regs 2020, regs 24 and 30.

148 For which, refer to Debt Respite Scheme Regs 2020, regs 24 and 30.

Such a request must be made within the period of 20 days beginning with the day on which the moratorium took effect. If the request to the debt advice provider does not result in the cancellation of some or all of the moratorium debts, then the creditor may make an application to the county court on the same grounds within the period of 50 days beginning with the day on which the moratorium started in respect of the relevant debt.[149]

[149] Debt Respite Scheme Regs 2020, reg 19.

Chapter 3

Procedure for Obtaining a Charging Order

PROCEDURAL FRAMEWORK

3.1 This chapter is concerned with the procedure for obtaining charging orders. The three principal stages of any application that are considered are:

(a) the application to the court;
(b) the making of an interim charging order by the court;
(c) the making of a final charging order by the court.

3.2 The procedural framework in this regard is provided by section 1 of the Charging Orders Act 1979 and either Part 73 and Practice Direction 73 of the Civil Procedure Rules (where the application is made to the county court or to the High Court exercising its civil jurisdiction), or Part 40 and Practice Direction 40A of the Family Procedure Rules (where the application is made to the family court or to the High Court (Family Division)).

3.3 In summary, as already explained,[1] a charging order is obtained in a two-stage process, which is initiated by an application to the court made by the judgment creditor. The first stage generally leads to the making of an interim charging order which is made without notice to the debtor or other interested parties. At the second stage, interested parties are given an opportunity to object and the interim order is then either made final or discharged. A more detailed summary of the procedural steps is set out in Tables 3.1 and 3.2 at the end of this chapter.

3.4 Despite the well-established procedure for obtaining a charging order considered in this chapter, in some instances it may be possible for the judgment creditor to bypass the standard two-stage process by inviting the trial judge who

---

[1] See Chapter 2, para 2.23.

gives judgment in its favour to make a final charging order there and then. There are several family cases in which a judge has done so, on the basis that the broad wording of section 3(1) of the Charging Orders Act 1979 empowered the judge to grant an immediate absolute order without notice.[2] It is considered that such an application is only likely to be granted in limited circumstances, such as where it is obvious that the debtor will not pay and it has been established in the underlying litigation that the debtor owns land which may be charged and which he is likely to dispose of unless a charge (and/or freezing order) is in place.

APPLICATION TO THE COURT

Overview

- Only a judgment creditor can apply.
- The application must be in the relevant prescribed form and contain certain specified information.
- It must be made to either the High Court, the county court or the family court, depending on the type of order being enforced.
- All applications made to the county court must be made to the Civil National Business Centre (CNBC). The procedure in the CNBC is different to that in the High Court or the family court.
- The application is made without notice and so the judgment creditor owes a duty to make full and frank disclosure of all material facts, including those adverse to its application.
- The judgment creditor should consider whether to protect the application as a pending land action.

Application: by whom?

3.5 An application for a charging order may only be made by a judgment creditor.[3] A charging order, if made, is imposed 'for the purpose of enforcing [a] judgment or order',[4] and not otherwise. Only the person who obtained the judgment which is the subject of the proposed charging order (or the personal representatives of such person or other assignees of the judgment debt[5]) can make the application. Other general creditors of the debtor who are strangers to the proceedings in which the subject judgment was obtained cannot apply therein for

---

2 *Bhura v Bhura* [2012] EWHC 3633 (Fam), [2013] 2 FLR 44; *Veluppillai v Veluppillai* [2015] EWHC 3095 (Fam), [2016] 2 FLR 681; *Green v Adams* [2017] EWFC 24, [2017] 2 FLR 1413. See also *AA v AB*, 19 March 2021, unreported, at [74], Family Court.

3 See Chapter 2, paras 2.2–2.11.

4 COA 1979, s 1(1).

5 CPR r 70.1(2)(a).

a charging order. If they are entitled to apply in their own right, i.e. if they have the benefit of other judgments in their favour against the debtor, they must apply separately on their own account relying on their own judgments.

Not the only available option for a judgment creditor

3.6 A judgment creditor is not generally required to elect between different available remedies by way of enforcement. Except where an enactment, rule or practice direction provides otherwise, the creditor may use more than one method of enforcement either concurrently or consecutively.[6] Thus a judgment creditor may apply for a charging order while applying separately for, say, a third party debt order.

Which court?

3.7 An application for a charging order over land must be made to the 'appropriate court',[7] as defined by section 1(2) of the Charging Orders Act 1979. This is determined as follows:

(a) Where the order to be enforced is an order of the family court, the application must be made to the family court;[8]
(b) Where the order to be enforced is a maintenance order[9] of the High Court or an order for costs made in family proceedings[10] in the High Court, the High Court and the family court will have concurrent jurisdiction;[11]

---

6 CPR r 70.2(2)(b); Family Procedure Rules 2010 (SI 2010/2955) (FPR) r 33.2. However, note that a judgment creditor needs the leave of the court to issue execution against property of a judgment debtor whilst an attachment of earnings order is in force: Attachment of Earnings Act 1971, s 8(2)(b).

7 COA 1979, s 1(1).

8 COA 1979, s 1(2)(ba).

9 'Maintenance order' has the same meaning as in the Attachment of Earnings Act 1971: COA 1979, s 1(2).

10 'Family proceedings' means proceedings in the Family Division of the High Court which are business assigned, by or under Senior Courts Act 1981, s 61 (and Sch 1), to that Division of the High Court and no other: COA 1979, s 1(9).

11 COA 1979, s 1(2)(a). This is subject to FPR r 5.4, which provides that where both the family court and the High Court have jurisdiction to deal with a matter, the proceedings must be started in the family court unless either: proceedings between the same parties are already being heard in the High Court; any rule, other enactment or Practice Direction provides otherwise; or the court otherwise directs. See *VS v RE (Family Court: Allocation of Cases)* [2018] EWFC 30, [2018] 1 WLR 3757.

(c) Where the order to be enforced is an order of the High Court, other than an order falling within (b), for a sum that exceeds the county court limit,[12] the High Court and the county court will have concurrent jurisdiction;[13]
(d) In all other cases (i.e. where the order to be enforced is an order of the county court or an order of the High Court not satisfying either (b) or (c)), the county court will have exclusive jurisdiction.[14]

3.8 The provisions of the Charging Orders Act 1979 in relation to judgments or orders of the High Court apply equally in relation to judgments or orders of the Court of Appeal Civil Division.[15] In other words, for the purposes of execution or enforcement by means of a charging order, judgments and orders of the Court of Appeal are treated as if made by the High Court and the appropriate forum for the charging order application is determined accordingly.

3.9 Since 2016, all applications to the county court for charging orders over land have been required to be made to a central processing centre.[16] This was originally the County Court Money Claims Centre (CCMCC) but, as of August 2023, is now the CNBC.[17] The handling of applications for charging orders in the CNBC differs in a number of significant respects from the procedure in other courts. In particular, in the CNBC:

(a) the interim charging order can generally be made by a court officer, rather than a judge;[18]
(b) the time limits in relation to the service of the interim charging order documents by the judgment creditor, and the filing and service of an objection by the judgment debtor, are different;[19]
(c) unless an objection to the making of a final order is filed, or a judge determines that a hearing is appropriate, the consideration of a final charging order will be on paper;[20] and

---

12 The 'county court limit' means the limit for the time being specified in an Order in Council under CCA 1984, s 145 as the limit for the purposes of COA 1979, s 1: COA 1979, s 1(2). That limit is currently £5,000: County Court Jurisdiction Order 2014 (SI 2014/503), art 3.

13 COA 1979, s 1(2)(c).

14 COA 1979, s 1(2)(d).

15 Senior Courts Act 1981, s 15(4).

16 CPR r 73.3(2). This change was introduced with effect from 6 April 2016 by the Civil Procedure (Amendment) Rules 2016 (SI 2016/234).

17 In October 2022, the handling of charging orders was shifted from the CCMCC to the County Court Business Centre in Northampton, before both centres were combined into the CNBC in August 2023. Paper applications should be addressed to: Civil National Business Centre, St Katharine's House, 21–27 St Katharine's Street, Northampton NN1 2LH.

18 See paras 3.35–3.38.

19 See paras 3.54–3.55 and 3.58–3.59.

20 See paras 3.76–3.77.

(d) where the consideration of a final order takes place without a hearing, it may be carried out by a legal adviser rather than a judge, although the legal adviser's options for dealing with the application are more limited.[21]

3.10 The reformed county court procedure is intended to centralise and streamline the process, particularly where the application is straightforward and unopposed. In those cases, the application may be dealt with from start to finish without a hearing and may not even require the involvement of a judge.

Multiple judgment debts

3.11 Subject to the preceding rules as to the appropriate court to which an application for a charging order must be issued, a judgment creditor may apply for a single charging order in respect of more than one judgment or order against the same debtor.[22] Indeed, a judgment creditor who has the benefit of multiple judgments against the same debtor ought normally to make a combined application.

3.12 Where an application is made to enforce more than one judgment or order by way of charging order, if the High Court would be the (or an) appropriate court in relation to one or more of the judgments or orders concerned, then it is the (or an) appropriate court in relation to the composite application.[23] In that type of case, the High Court is empowered to deal with the whole of the application, notwithstanding that it might otherwise have lacked jurisdiction to entertain an application for a charging order in respect of some of the judgments or orders in question.

Multiple judgment debtors

3.13 Historically, a separate application notice and court fee was required for each judgment debtor against whom a charging order was sought. However, prior to the shift of cases to the CNBC, the CCMCC appeared to have adopted a practice of permitting multiple judgment debtors to be dealt with in a single application (and with a single fee payable) where: (a) there was a joint judgment against the debtors; and (b) the property sought to be charged was the same for each debtor.

3.14 Before adopting this approach, it would be sensible to check with the relevant court whether it will accept such an application. Since the prescribed forms do not provide space for identifying multiple judgment debtors, the relevant

---

[21] See paras 3.78–3.88.

[22] CPR r 73.3(4); FPR r 40.4(3).

[23] COA 1979, s 1(4).

details should be provided in an annexed schedule. A single interim charging order should then be made, naming all the judgment debtors.

Multiple assets

3.15 A judgment creditor may apply in a single application notice for charging orders over more than one asset.[24] However, if the court makes interim charging orders over more than one asset, it will draw up a separate order in relation to each.[25] It seems that a separate fee is payable in respect of each charging order applied for.

Application for non-standard restriction

3.16 Before making the application, it is worth giving some thought to how the priority of the eventual charging order will be protected.[26] In particular, where the charging order sought is over a beneficial interest in registered land (e.g. because the judgment debtor is one of two registered proprietors) then it will not be possible to place a notice on the register, and a restriction will need to be entered instead. In those circumstances, the standard restriction is that in Form K of Schedule 4 to the Land Registration Rules 2003.[27] As explained in Chapter 4,[28] the Form K restriction provides very little protection to the judgment creditor and for that reason creditors sometimes seek an order from the court under section 46(1) of the Land Registration Act 2002 for the entry of a non-standard restriction.

3.17 As set out in a guidance note from District Judge Ivan Ranson, then Liaison Judge for the CCMCC, in March 2021, an application for a non-standard restriction is a separate application, albeit ancillary to the charging order application. It ought not, therefore, to be made by 'request' in a covering letter, or in Land Registry Form RX1 (which is a form of application prescribed for use by HM Land Registry, not the courts). Instead, the application ought to be included in the charging order application form[29] or made as a separate application under Part 23 of the Civil Procedure Rules.[30] The application can also be made at

---

24 CPR PD 73, para 1.3; FPR PD 40A, para 1.4.

25 CPR PD 73, para 1.3; FPR PD 40A, para 1.4.

26 See Chapter 4, paras 4.34–4.44 and 4.52–4.61.

27 SI 2003/1417 (LRR 2003).

28 Chapter 4, paras 4.39–4.43.

29 The N87 precedent order in Appendix Precedent B6 contains a suggested text ordering entry of a non-standard restriction. As for the application, the form does not provide space for such an additional application for a non-standard restriction so it may be necessary to make a separate application. Suggested wording is included in Appendix Precedent B6A.

30 *Civil Procedure 2023* (Sweet & Maxwell, 2023), Vol 1, para 73.4.3.1.

a hearing for the consideration of whether the interim order should be made final. However, where the application is made to the CNBC there may not be such a hearing.

3.18 In any case, the application will need to set out the wording of the proposed non-standard restriction and give reasons why it is 'necessary or desirable', bearing in mind the default entitlement to a Form K restriction on the grant of a charging order. The non-standard form of restriction that is usually sought is that notice should be given to the judgment creditor 14 days prior to the disposition. Although there is a two-stage process for charging orders (interim and final), the application for a non-standard restriction will not be considered until the court is making a final charging order, at which point the court has power to 'make such other order as the court considers appropriate'.[31]

Duty of full and frank disclosure

3.19 As with all applications made without notice, the judgment creditor is bound to make full and frank disclosure of all material facts, including those adverse to its application.[32] This duty reflects the fact that the judgment debtor, and any other interested persons, do not have an opportunity to be heard or to make representations before an interim order is made.[33] The duty will also apply where an application is made without notice at the end of a trial, in the circumstances described at para 3.4.

3.20 The judgment creditor must therefore identify any matters of fact and law that might be relevant to the exercise of the court's discretion.[34] This extends to any matters that the judgment creditor would have discovered had proper enquiries been made.[35] At a minimum, that ought to include any insolvency orders that could have been found through an appropriate search of the Insolvency Service's Individual Insolvency Register (for individuals) or Companies House (for companies) and the identities of any other persons who could have been identified from the registered title as having a potential interest in the land.[36]

---

31 CPR r 73.10(7)(e); *cf* rr 73.4 and 73.6.

32 *Fitzgerald v Williams* [1996] QB 657 at 667.

33 Although they will be able to object to the making of a final charging order, see para 3.57 *et seq*.

34 *Alliance Bank v Zhunus* [2015] EWHC 714 (Comm) at [65].

35 *Brink's-Mat Ltd Elcombe & Others* [1988] 3 All ER 188 at 1357A–B; *Dar Al Arkan Real Estate Development Company & Another v Majid Al-Sayed Bader Hashim Al Refai & Others* [2012] EWHC 3539 (Comm) at [97].

36 For example where the legal title is held together with a co-owner, or by a third party on trust for the judgment debtor, or where there is a home rights notice on the title.

3.21 In the context of charging orders, it is particularly important that the judgment creditor provide details of all other known creditors. This is because the court will investigate the possibility of insolvency[37] and, further, the competing interests of the various creditors must be considered and weighed by the court when deciding whether or not to make a charging order.[38] Strictly speaking, in order to give the court the most complete picture of the circumstances of the case, details of *all* creditors, including those who are secured creditors (and who thus will not be 'unduly prejudiced by the making of the order'[39] and will be unlikely to make any representations in response to the application), are required.

3.22 Additionally, it may be necessary to bring other matters to the court's attention, such as where the judgment debtor has applied for permission to appeal the judgment sought to be enforced.[40]

3.23 The judgment creditor's duty of disclosure continues after the application notice has been filed,[41] until service of the interim charging order (if made).[42] Therefore, if the judgment creditor becomes aware of new material facts in the intervening period, this information should be brought to the court's attention, preferably by filing a short witness statement.

3.24 Where a judgment creditor has breached the duty of full and frank disclosure, the court may set aside the interim charging order on that basis alone, particularly where the non-disclosure is substantial or deliberate.[43] In other cases, the court may instead take the breach into account as part of 'all the circumstances'[44] when considering whether to make a final charging order.[45]

---

37 For the relevance of insolvency to the exercise of discretion whether or not to make a charging order, see Chapter 2, para 2.33 *et seq*.

38 COA 1979, s 1(5)(b).

39 COA 1979, s 1(5)(b).

40 As in *Ittihadieh v Metcalfe*, 9 February 2017, unreported.

41 *Commercial Bank of the Near East v A, B, C and D* [1989] 2 Lloyd's Rep 319; *O'Regan v Iambic Productions Ltd* (1989) 139 NLJ 1378.

42 *JSC BTA Bank v Ablyazov* [2018] EWHC 259 (Comm).

43 *Re OJSC Ank Yugraneft* [2008] EWHC 2614 (Ch), [2009] 1 BCLC 298. The court may set aside the interim order even where it would still have been made if the undisclosed information had been provided: *R v Kensington Income Tax Commissioners, ex parte de Polignac* [1917] 1 KB 486 at 514. The court will take into account the policy interest in depriving the wrongdoer of an advantage improperly obtained and deterring others from breaching the duty.

44 COA 1979, s 1(5).

45 In *Ittihadieh v Metcalfe*, 9 February 2017, unreported, a final charging order was made despite the judgment creditor's breach of duty.

Application notice

3.25 The correct form of application notice will depend upon the court to which the application is made:

(a) If the application is made to the county court or to the High Court exercising its civil jurisdiction, the application notice must be in Practice Form N379[46] and contain the information required by Practice Direction 73 of the Civil Procedure Rules.[47]
(b) If the application is made to the family court or to the High Court (Family Division), the application notice must be in Form FE6[48] and contain the information required by Practice Direction 40A of the Family Procedure Rules.[49]

3.26 In either case, the application notice must contain:[50]

(a) the name and address of the judgment debtor;
(b) details of the judgment or order sought to be enforced;
(c) the amount of money remaining due under the judgment or order;
(d) if the judgment debt is payable by instalments:

    (i) whether the order was made on or after 1 October 2012;[51] and
    (ii) the amount of any instalments which have fallen due and remain unpaid;

(e) if the judgment creditor knows of the existence of any other creditors of the judgment debtor, their names and (if known) their addresses;
(f) identification of the asset or assets which it is intended to charge including, where applicable, the title number under which any land upon which it is sought to impose a charge is registered;

---

46 CPR PD 73, para 1.1.

47 CPR r 73.3(5)(a).

48 In fact, FPR PD 40A, para 1.2 states that the relevant form is Practice Form N379. However, the form listed in FPR PD 5A is Form FE6 and this is understood to be the form now used in practice in family proceedings: see *The Family Court Practice 2023* (Jordan Publishing, 2023) at 3.1677[1].

49 FPR r 40.4(4)(a).

50 CPR PD 73, para 1.2; FPR PD 40A, para 1.3.

51 Technically, this information is only expressly required by CPR PD 73 and not FPR PD 40A, but it is still necessary in order to complete Form FE6. The relevance of 1 October 2012 is that the law changed with effect from that date to permit enforcement of an instalment order by charging order even in the absence of a default in payment. The old rules continue to apply to the enforcement of judgments or orders made, or applied for, before that date. See Chapter 2, paras 2.50–2.52.

(g) details of the judgment debtor's interest in the asset; and
(h) the names and addresses of the persons on whom an interim charging order must be served (under rule 73.7 of the Civil Procedure Rules or rule 40.6 of the Family Procedure Rules, as applicable).[52]

3.27 Precedents for a completed Form N379 and Form FE6 are included in Appendix Precedent B1 and Precedent B2, respectively.

3.28 The two forms are very similar and largely self-explanatory. However, the following commentary is offered by way of guidance:

(a) A copy of the judgment or order sought to be made the subject of a charging order should be attached to the application notice.
(b) If the application is intended to relate to multiple judgment debtors[53] the details for each debtor should be set out in an attached schedule and a note should be added to section 2 of the form referring to the schedule.
(c) In section 3, in relation to the amount owing under the judgment debt (including further interest that has accrued since judgment), the forms only leave space for a figure to be inserted. In some cases it may not be obvious how this figure has been arrived at and so the judgment creditor may need to provide further explanation by, for example, giving details of payments made by the debtor and/or setting out the interest calculation. This information could be provided in the 'Further Information' section or as an attached schedule.
(d) Where the underlying order provides for payment by instalments, the forms themselves could be read as only requiring the judgment creditor to specify the amount of any instalments which have fallen due and remain unpaid if the order was made before 1 October 2012. However, Practice Direction 73 of the Civil Procedure Rules requires this information to be included in any event. Further, the court must take into account whether there has been a default when exercising its discretion.[54] Details of any missed instalments should therefore be provided in all cases, regardless of the date on which the underlying order was made.
(e) Where the judgment debt is expressed in a foreign currency, the application notice ought to include words to the effect of:

---

[52] For discussion of the persons on whom an interim charging order must be served, see paras 3.50–3.52.

[53] See paras 3.13–3.14.

[54] COA 1979, s 1(8).

> The rate current in London for the purchase of *[unit of foreign currency in which the judgment is expressed]* at the close of business on *[nearest preceding date to the date of signing the statement of truth]* was *[give details]* to the £ sterling. At this rate the sum of *[amount in the foreign currency]* currently owed (including interest payable on the judgment debt) amounts to £*[number] [and the instalments due and unpaid amount to £[number]]*. I have obtained this information from *[source]* and believe it to be true.[55]

(f) Where the application is being made in respect of a liability order made by the magistrates' court under the Council Tax (Administration and Enforcement) Regulations 1992,[56] section 3B should be completed rather than section 3A and evidence of the debt will need to be attached.

(g) Clear identification of the land sought to be charged is essential. A full and accurate postal address (or other appropriate description) should be given. Where the title to the land is registered, the title number(s) must be stated and an official copy of the register(s) of title must be attached to the application form. In some cases, for example involving unregistered open land that cannot easily be identified by description, or where it is intended to charge only part of the land within a registered title, it will be sensible to annex a plan.

(h) So far as demonstrating the judgment debtor's interest (legal and/or beneficial) in the asset sought to be charged (and the extent of that interest) is concerned, this is relatively straightforward in the case of registered land[57] since the official copy of the register[58] will evidence the debtor's title and, further, there is a *prima facie* presumption that beneficial ownership mirrors the legal title.[59] If, however, the title to the land is unregistered or the land is registered in, say, the sole name of the debtor's spouse, matters may be more complicated and the judgment creditor will need to state the grounds for believing that the debtor is interested in the land in question. This may be based on knowledge of ownership acquired from the debtor in the proceedings which resulted in the judgment or order, whether through sight

---

55 Wording adapted from that suggested by the *King's Bench Guide* (Courts and Tribunals Judiciary, March 2023), paras 22.17 and 22.27.

56 SI 1992/613 (CT (A&E) Regs 1992). See paras 7.2–7.8.

57 If it is not known whether a corporate judgment debtor owns land in England and Wales (or what such land is), it is open to the judgment creditor to apply to HM Land Registry for a search to be made of the index of proprietors' names: LRR 2003, r 11. But no such application may be made in respect of the name of an individual, unless the applicant can demonstrate that it is interested generally in the property of that person, and it is unlikely that being a judgment creditor is sufficient in this context.

58 Which is admissible as evidence of the matters mentioned therein, to the same extent as the register itself: Land Registration Act 2002 (LRA 2002), s 67(1).

59 See e.g. *Stack v Dowden* [2007] UKHL 17, [2007] 2 AC 432; *Jones v Kernott* [2011] UKSC 53, [2012] 1 AC 776.

of the title deeds or otherwise, or from some other source (e.g. an enquiry agent).[60] Appropriate details must be given.

(i) The judgment creditor must identify all known creditors of the judgment debtor, bearing in mind his own duty of full and frank disclosure.[61]

(j) The persons on whom an interim charging order will be served who have to be identified within the forms include any persons who have or may have an interest in the property, including any co-owners, trustees and persons with rights of occupation.[62] Given that the court has a discretion as to on whom the order is served,[63] the judgment creditor would be well advised in relevant cases (e.g. where the land in question is held by trustees) to suggest, supported by any necessary evidence and reasons, who ought or ought not to be served, and to explain any difficulties that may be foreseen in relation to service, in order that the court can make any appropriate directions.

(k) The forms provide an opportunity for the judgment creditor to put before the court any further information which it is desired the court should take into account. This opportunity should be seized. Indeed, the burden at the stage of the written application must be upon the judgment creditor to demonstrate why it requires the protection of a charging order.[64] An astute applicant will wish to present as strong a case up front as possible, bearing in mind that this will be all the 'evidence before'[65] the court when it comes to decide whether to make the interim charging order. It may therefore be appropriate for the application to set out details of some or all of the following:

  (i) the judgment creditor's own financial position;
  (ii) any deliberate refusal to pay by the judgment debtor;
  (iii) the failure of any other methods of enforcement previously attempted by the creditor;

---

60 The judgment creditor may be able to obtain information on land owned by the judgment debtor at a hearing held pursuant to CPR r 71 (orders to obtain information from judgment debtors), FPR r 33.3(3) or r 33.23. If the provisions of TCEA 2007, ss 95–105 regarding information requests and orders ever come into force, a judgment creditor could also seek to invoke those powers in order to elicit information regarding the debtor's assets. However, at the time of writing, those provisions have yet to be brought into force and it was announced in a Written Ministerial Statement on 17 March 2009 that there was no intention to do so.

61 See paras 3.19–3.24.

62 See Form N379, panel 7 and Form FE6, panel 7.

63 See paras 3.50–3.52.

64 *National Guild of Removers and Storers Ltd v Jones and Coid* [2012] EWCA Civ 216, [2012] 1 WLR 2501 at [15], per Pitchford LJ.

65 COA 1979, s 1(5). See also para 3.63.

(iv) details of a recent valuation of the property, if available (attaching a copy of the valuation report to the application notice);
(v) whether there are any known insolvency proceedings against the debtor.

(l) The 'Further Information' section of Forms N379 and FE6 should also be used to set out any other material facts relevant to the application, including those adverse to the judgment creditor.[66]
(m) In an appropriate case, the judgment creditor may wish to include an application for a non-standard restriction in the application form.[67]
(n) Form N379 (but not Form FE6) expressly requires that where the judgment creditor is a firm, company or other corporation, the person completing the form must confirm that they have made proper enquiry of all relevant persons within the organisation who might have knowledge of the facts. It is thus evident that they need not have actual knowledge of the information; hearsay (second-hand) knowledge will suffice. However, the requirement should at least focus the mind on the need for comprehensive and diligent research to be undertaken before the application is signed off.
(o) Form FE6 (but not Form N379) contains the old form of statement of truth and has not been updated to include the wording now required by paragraph 2.1 of Practice Direction 17A of the Family Procedure Rules.[68] Specifically, the missing wording is:

> *[I understand] / [the creditor understands]*[69] that proceedings for contempt of court may be brought against anyone who makes or causes to be made, a false statement in a document verified by a statement of truth without an honest belief in its truth.

As a matter of best practice, this wording should be added when completing the form, as shown in Appendix Precedent B2.
(p) Remember to complete the 'Notice to judgment creditor' checklist at the end of the form, which confirms that certain requirements have been complied with.

3.29 The application notice must be verified by a statement of truth,[70] which must be signed by the judgment creditor, his litigation friend or the legal representative of the creditor or litigation friend (as the case may be).[71]

---

66 See discussion of the duty of full and frank disclosure at paras 3.19–3.24.

67 See paras 3.16–3.18 and Chapter 4, paras 4.34–4.44 and 4.52–4.61.

68 Which is very similar to the wording now required by CPR PD 22, para 2.1.

69 Delete as appropriate.

70 CPR r 73.3(5)(b); FPR r 40.4(4)(b).

71 CPR r 22.1(6)(a); FPR r 22.1(6)(a).

Consequently, provided the correct form of statement of truth is used, the contents of the notice constitute evidence before the court which may be relied on at any hearing other than a trial.[72] In the circumstances there is no need for separate evidence (in the form of a witness statement) to be filed in any but the most complicated of cases.

3.30 The application must be accompanied by the appropriate fee.[73] A separate fee is payable in respect of each charging order applied for. So, if more than one parcel of land is intended to be charged, then more than one fee must be paid.

Service of the application notice

3.31 An application for a charging order may be, and generally is, made without notice.[74] Hence there is no need to serve the application on anyone, whether the debtor or any third party. It must simply be sent to the appropriate court.

Protection of the application

3.32 In an appropriate case, the judgment creditor may wish to consider protecting the application for a charging order as a pending land action.[75] However, in practice this added tier of complexity and costs is usually unnecessary, especially when the typical short timeframe between the making of an application and the following interim charging order is borne in mind.[76]

---

72 CPR r 32.6(2)(b); FPR r 22.7(2)(b). If a trial were later directed, the maker of the statement would (if the evidence were disputed) have to attend to give oral evidence and be cross-examined, failing which the statement would stand as hearsay evidence only (and probably be given little, if any, weight by the court). The possibility of the need for the statement maker to attend court should be borne in mind when deciding who should sign the statement of truth. It will usually be preferable (if possible) for the judgment creditor (with first-hand knowledge of the relevant facts), rather than its solicitor, to do so.

73 At the time of writing, the fee is £119 in the county court or the High Court (except for the Family Division): Civil Proceedings Fees Order 2008 (SI 2008/1053). The fee in the family court and the High Court (Family Division) is £38: Family Proceedings Fees Order 2008 (SI 2008/1054).

74 CPR r 73.3(1); FPR r 40.4(1).

75 See Chapter 4, paras 4.48–4.56.

76 For the up-to-date processing times in the CNBC, see www.gov.uk/government/publications/hmcts-civil-business-centres-performance-information.

INTERIM CHARGING ORDER

Overview

- The application will initially be considered on paper and without a hearing. Unless the application is defective, the court will ordinarily make an interim charging order.
- In the High Court or the family court, the interim charging order will be made by a judge. In the CNBC, it will generally be made by a court officer and either party can request that the decision be reconsidered by a District Judge.
- An interim charging order imposes an immediate charge over the judgment debtor's interest in the land to which the application relates. It is intended to hold the position until the court has further considered the application and determined whether to make a final charging order or to discharge the interim charging order.
- Once an interim charging order has been made, the judgment creditor is required to serve copies of the order, the application notice, and any documents filed in support on the judgment debtor and various other persons.
- The judgment creditor should take steps to protect the priority of his interim charging order. Where the charged land is registered, this will involve entering an appropriate notice or restriction against the registered title.
- In the event of the judgment debtor's subsequent insolvency, an interim charging order provides substantially less security than a final charging order.

No hearing at this stage

3.33 All applications for a charging order are initially dealt with on paper and without a hearing.[77] In this respect the process is distinctly advantageous to the judgment creditor since, because the interim order is made without notice to the debtor, the charge attaches to the land before the debtor can dispose of it in order to defeat the application. This does not, of course, prevent the debtor from disposing of the property because he apprehends that an application for a charging order might be about to be made or be working its way through the court system.

---

[77] CPR rr 73.4(2) and 73.6(2); FPR r 40.5(1).

Decision-maker

3.34 Applications made to the High Court or the family court are initially handled by a judge.[78]

3.35 However, where an application for a charging order over land is made to the CNBC,[79] it may be initially dealt with by a court officer instead, unless:[80]

(a) the application is made under section 2(1)(b)(i) of the Charging Orders Act 1979;[81]
(b) the application is for a charging order on the interest of a partner in the partnership property under section 23 of the Partnership Act 1890;[82]
(c) the order sought to be enforced is an instalment order made before 1 October 2012;[83] or
(d) the court officer otherwise considers that the application should be dealt with by a judge.

3.36 Therefore, in the CNBC, the decision over whether to grant an interim charging order is generally made by a court officer.[84] In practice, the court officer will have a checklist of prescribed criteria and, if these are met, will generally make the interim charging order. If the criteria are not met, the court officer will instead refer the matter to a judge.

Reconsideration of court officer's decision

3.37 Where the decision has been made by a court officer, any party can request that it be reconsidered by a District Judge.[85] To do so, that party must file a written request within 14 days of being served with notice of the decision.[86] There is no need for an application to be made under Part 23 of the Civil Procedure Rules or for an application fee to be paid. Although the Civil Procedure Rules do not

---

78 CPR r 73.6(2); FPR r 40.5(1). This includes a deputy or Master: CPR r 2.3(1)(c).

79 All applications for charging orders over land made to the county court must be made to the CNBC: CPR r 73.3(2).

80 CPR r 73.4(3) and (4).

81 See Chapter 2, para 2.17.

82 See Chapter 7, paras 7.55–7.61.

83 See Chapter 2, paras 2.50–2.52.

84 CPR r 73.4(5). It should be noted that wherever a step is to be taken by a court officer: (a) the court officer may consult a judge before taking that step; and (b) the step may be taken by a judge instead of the court officer: CPR r 3.2.

85 CPR r 73.5(1). A similar procedure is available under CPR r 73.10ZA where a decision on a final charging order has been made by a legal adviser. See paras 3.86–3.88.

86 CPR r 73.5(2).

expressly state this,[87] the request ought to explain the party's reasons for seeking a reconsideration.

3.38 Whilst there is a degree of similarity, it is important to distinguish between an objection to the making of a final order[88] and a request for reconsideration of the interim order. The former will cause the application to be listed for a hearing and is likely to be more appropriate where the objector seeks to rely on 'all the circumstances'. Reconsideration, on the other hand, takes place without a hearing[89] and is intended to cover situations where the application is technically defective or has proceeded on a mistaken basis, for example where it is alleged by the debtor that the judgment debt has been satisfied.

Discretion in relation to interim order

3.39 Assuming that the application is not so manifestly deficient or ill-founded as to justify its dismissal, an interim charging order (formerly known as a charging order *nisi*) is likely to be made.[90] Although strictly speaking the process entails the exercise of a discretion,[91] in practice – and because the court will have no 'evidence before it'[92] except that which the judgment creditor has presented – the making of an interim charging order is usually a formality. Provided therefore that the court is satisfied that the basic threshold requirements[93] for obtaining a charging order are met, the chances are that an interim charging order will be granted.[94] The published statistics reflect a high success rate for applications for charging orders.[95]

3.40 The onus is on the judgment creditor to prove on the balance of probabilities that the debtor has an interest in the land sought to be charged. Although increasingly straightforward in registered land situations, this may

---

87 There is no equivalent in CPR r 73.5 of CPR r 73.10ZA(3).

88 See para 3.57 *et seq*.

89 CPR r 73.5(3).

90 CPR r 73.6(3); FPR r 40.5(2).

91 Note the word 'may' in COA 1979, s 1(1); CPR r 73.4(5) and (6) and r 73.6(3); and FPR r 40.5(2).

92 COA 1979, s 1(5) and see also para 3.63.

93 As to which, see Chapter 2, para 2.24.

94 Realistically, the available options for the court at this stage are the diametric opposites of: (a) granting the interim order; or (b) dismissing the application (in the unlikely event that the application is materially deficient in some significant respect). It is improbable that the court will have the reason or material to adopt some middle course of action.

95 Of the 21,329 applications for charging orders made in the county court in 2021, 18,859 (88%) resulted in charging orders being made: *Civil Justice Statistics Quarterly: January to March 2022 Tables*, see www.gov.uk/government/statistics/civil-justice-statistics-quarterly-january-to-march-2022.

present difficulties where the judgment debtor has only a beneficial interest or in the now comparatively rare cases where the title to the land is unregistered.[96] However, even if there is some doubt as to whether the judgment debtor has an interest in the land sought to be charged, the court may nonetheless be prepared to grant an interim charging order, limited to 'such interest, if any, as the judgment debtor may have' in the asset. An order in those terms will give the judgment creditor security over any interest which the judgment debtor does in fact have. Yet if it later transpires that the judgment debtor does not have any interest in the land, no effective interim charge will have been imposed (since there will have been nothing to which the charge could have attached) and so it is unlikely that any real harm (that cannot be compensated by a costs order) will have been done. Nevertheless, before a final charging order is made, it will need to be established that the judgment debtor does indeed have a beneficial interest in the land,[97] although that interest need not necessarily be quantified.[98]

Effect of the interim order

3.41 An interim order imposes a charge over the judgment debtor's interest in the asset to which the application relates.[99] If the application identifies multiple assets, the court will draw up a separate order in relation to each asset that is intended to be charged.[100] An interim charging order is immediate in its effect but transitory in nature.[101] It serves to maintain a balance pending the determination of whether the charge should be made permanent by making a final charging order. It should be noted, however, that there are important differences between the security provided by an interim charging order and a final charging order in the event of the debtor's insolvency. Where a judgment debtor is wound-up or made bankrupt, the judgment creditor can generally rely on any final charging orders that had been made prior to the commencement of the relevant insolvency process, but will lose the benefit of any interim charging orders that had not yet been made final.[102]

3.42 The interim order will therefore also make provision for the further consideration of the application by either:

---

96 See para 3.28(h).

97 *McLinden v Lu* [2021] EWHC 3171 (Ch), [2022] BPIR 433.

98 *Walton v Allman* [2015] EWHC 3325 (Ch), [2016] 1 WLR 2053. It will be necessary for the interest to be quantified before an order for sale is made.

99 CPR rr 73.4(5) and (6)(a) and r 73.6(3)(a); FPR r 40.5(2)(a).

100 CPR PD 73, para 1.3; FPR PD 40A, para 1.4.

101 For the defeasible nature of an interim charging order, see Chapter 2, para 2.41.

102 See Chapter 8, paras 8.116–8.120 and 8.127–8.131.

(a) fixing a date for a hearing at which the court will consider whether to make a final charging order;
(b) stating that the application will be dealt with without a hearing unless an objection to a final order is filed and served within 28 days of service of the interim order; or
(c) transferring the proceedings from the CNBC to the judgment debtor's home court so that a hearing can be listed.

3.43 In respect of (a), a hearing date will be fixed in all cases where the application has been made to a court other than the CNBC.[103] In view of the requirement that the interim order must be served at least 21 days before the date fixed for the hearing to determine whether to make a final charging order,[104] in practice the hearing date must be set for at least one month in the future (to allow time for service).

3.44 Where the application was instead made to the CNBC and has been dealt with by a court officer,[105] or by a judge who has determined that a hearing is not appropriate,[106] option (b) will apply and a hearing will only take place if the application is contested.[107]

3.45 The court will transfer the proceedings to the judgment debtor's home court under (c) where a judge of the CNBC has determined that it is appropriate for a hearing to take place.[108] A transfer is required before a hearing can be fixed because the CNBC is not itself a hearing centre. In these circumstances,[109] the judgment debtor's home court is defined as:[110]

(a) in the case of an application under the Council Tax (Administration and Enforcement) Regulations 1992, the county court hearing centre for the district in which the relevant dwelling[111] is situated; or
(b) in other cases, the county court hearing centre for the district in which the judgment debtor resides or carries on business.

---

[103] CPR r 73.6(3)(b); FPR r 40.5(2)(b).

[104] See para 3.55.

[105] CPR r 73.4(5).

[106] CPR r 73.4(6)(b).

[107] See para 3.76 *et seq*.

[108] CPR r 73.4(6)(b).

[109] A separate definition of the judgment debtor's home court applies where the application for a charging order is proceeding in the High Court: CPR r 73.1(2)(c)(ii). See para 3.93.

[110] CPR r 73.1(2)(c)(i).

[111] As defined in CT (A&E) Regs 1992, reg 50(3)(b).

3.46 Interim charging orders are not expressly provided for by name in the Charging Orders Act 1979. However, historically it has always been the practice of the courts to adopt a two-stage approach.[112] Moreover, authority for this procedure is derived from section 3(1) of the Charging Orders Act 1979, which states that, 'A charging order may be made either absolutely or subject to conditions as to notifying the debtor or as to the time when the charge is to become enforceable, or as to other matters'. A standard interim charging order so provides. Further, as appears from the above, the Civil Procedure Rules and the Family Procedure Rules now expressly embrace the concept of interim charging orders.[113]

Form of the interim order

3.47 An interim charging order will generally be in Form N86. A precedent for a completed Form N86 is included in Appendix Precedent B3.

3.48 It is worth noting that the current version of Form N86 has not been updated to reflect the possibility that, where an interim charging order has been made in the CNBC, the further consideration of the application may now be by a legal adviser.[114] Therefore, the standard wording where a hearing is not envisaged provides that in the absence of an objection the application will be considered by a District Judge without a hearing. Preferably, the words 'or Legal Adviser' should be inserted after each of the two references to 'District Judge'.

3.49 Interim charging orders made in the family court generally use Standard Order 4.13 as a template rather than Form N86. A copy of Standard Order 4.13 is included in Appendix Precedent B7.[115]

Service of the interim order, etc

3.50 Once an interim charging order against land has been made, copies of the order, the application notice and any documents filed in support of it must be served by the judgment creditor[116] on the following persons:[117]

---

112 See Chapter 1, para 1.55 and Chapter 2, para 2.23.

113 CPR r 73.1(2)(e); FPR r 40.2.

114 As of 30 March 2020. See paras 3.78–3.88.

115 Standard Order 4.13 can also be accessed at www.judiciary.uk/guidance-and-resources/update-standard-orders-issued-by-mr-justice-mostyn/.

116 CPR r 73.7(1) and (5); FPR r 40.6(1).

117 CPR r 73.7(7); FPR r 40.6(3).

(a) the judgment debtor;[118]
(b) any co-owner(s);
(c) the judgment debtor's spouse or civil partner (if known);
(d) such other creditors as are identified in the application notice or as the court directs; and
(e) if the order relates to an interest under a trust, on such of the trustees as the court directs.

3.51 Service on spouses, civil partners and co-owners is therefore always necessary. However, there is no specific requirement for service on other persons with rights of occupation, or on a former spouse or civil partner whose application for financial relief has been registered as a pending action against the property. This is in tension with the prescribed application notices, which require all persons who have or may have an interest in the property to be identified under the section 'Other persons to be served'. In practice, the court will usually direct that such persons should be served, together with anyone else who is in possession of the land.[119] This is so that the court is properly able to consider 'all the circumstances of the case'[120] when deciding whether to make a final charging order.

3.52 In relation to point (d), service must be effected on all creditors (except for the judgment creditor) identified in the application notice, which should include all those of whom the judgment creditor is aware.[121] Given that the application for an interim charging order is ordinarily made without notice, it will be unusual for the court to itself be aware of any additional creditors. Where it is, the court will usually direct that they should also be served, although this may be unnecessary for existing secured creditors since their rights will rank above, and be unaffected by, the charge imposed by the charging order.

3.53 As of 1 October 2022, any persons required to be served with the interim charging order who are outside the jurisdiction may be served without the permission of the court.[122]

---

118 If the judgment debtor is a partnership, service must be effected on a member of the partnership within the jurisdiction, a person authorised by a partner, or some other person having the control or management of the partnership business: CPR PD 73, para 4A.2; FPR PD 40A, para 5.2.

119 In line with those who must be identified by the judgment creditor when proceeding to enforce a charging order by sale under CPR r 73.10: see CPR PD 73, para 4.3(6) and (7).

120 As required by COA 1979, s 1(5) and see Chapter 2, para 2.22.

121 CPR PD 73, para 1.2(5); FPR PD 40A, para 1.3(5).

122 CPR r 73.7(8). This is a deviation from the general rules under CPR rr 6.36 and 6.38.

3.54 If the interim charging order has been made at the CNBC and the application has not been transferred to the judgment debtor's home court,[123] the judgment creditor must effect service within 21 days of the date of the interim charging order.[124] The judgment creditor must then file a certificate of service in relation to each person served, together with a statement of the amount due under the judgment or order including any costs and interest,[125] within 28 days of the date of the interim charging order.[126] An application for an extension of time for either of those deadlines must be made to the CNBC and will be dealt with without a hearing.[127]

3.55 In all other cases, the time limits are calculated by reference to the date of the upcoming hearing. The judgment creditor must effect service not less than 21 days before the hearing for the determination of whether to make a final charging order.[128] The judgment creditor must also either file a certificate of service in relation to each person served, not less than 2 days before the hearing, or produce a certificate of service at the hearing.[129]

Protecting the priority of the interim order

3.56 As soon as an interim charging order is made, the judgment creditor should take steps to protect his priority, so far as possible. Where the land is registered, this will involve entering an appropriate notice or restriction against the registered title.[130] The creditor need not, and should not, wait until the charging order is made final before doing so. Unless this basic and essential protective step is taken, the creditor risks losing the benefit of the interim charging order, the priority of which might be defeated in the event of a disposition of the land by the debtor.[131]

---

123 Under CPR r 73.4(6).

124 CPR r 73.7(1).

125 There is no prescribed form for the statement of amount due, but it ought to at least contain the same information as required by Section 3 of Form N379 (with the figures updated) and should preferably include a signed statement of truth.

126 CPR r 73.7(2).

127 CPR r 73.7(3).

128 CPR r 73.7(5); FPR r 40.6(1).

129 CPR r 73.7(6); FPR r 40.6(2).

130 For details of the registration process, see Chapter 4, para 4.34 *et seq*.

131 The importance of swift registration is highlighted by *Howell v Montey* (1990) 61 P & CR 18, in which an interim charging order was made but not registered before the debtors contracted to sell the land in question. For further details of this case, see n 197.

FINAL CHARGING ORDER

Overview

- Anyone opposed to the making of a final charging order should file and serve a written objection, within the applicable time limit, setting out the grounds on which a final charging order should be refused or subjected to conditions.
- The procedure for determining whether to make a final charging order is different in the CNBC. In the CNBC, but not other courts, that decision may take place without a hearing and may be carried out by a legal adviser rather than a judge.
- A final charging order confirms the interim order and the two orders both relate to a single charge. The interim order creates a conditional charge that becomes unconditional on the making of a final charging order.
- The final charging order takes effect from the date of the interim order. Provided the priority of the interim order has been protected, any intervening dispositions or proceedings will not affect the charge.
- The costs recoverable by the judgment creditor are limited to fixed costs.

Objection to the making of a final charging order

3.57 If any person objects to the court making a final charging order, that person must file and serve on the judgment creditor written evidence stating the grounds of its objections. The objector will typically be the judgment debtor but could also be an interested third party (such as a creditor, co-owner or spouse) who, having been served with the interim order, wishes to contest its finalisation.

Time limits for making an objection

3.58 Where the interim charging order was made at the CNBC and has not been transferred to the judgment debtor's home court under rule 73.4(6) of the Civil Procedure Rules for a hearing,[132] the written evidence of objection must be filed and served not later than 28 days after the objector was served with the application notice and interim order.[133]

3.59 In all other cases, the written evidence must be filed and served not less than 7 days before the hearing.[134] Therefore, a person wishing to oppose the

---

132 It will be recalled that this is a power available where a judge is dealing with a charging order application in the CNBC and considers that a hearing would be appropriate for the consideration of a final order. See para 3.45.

133 CPR r 73.10(2).

134 CPR r 73.10A(2); FPR r 40.8(1).

making of the final order ought not simply to attend the hearing for further consideration without first having complied with this requirement.

3.60 Although the rules regarding the timely filing of written evidence are couched in mandatory terms, a breach does not mean that the debtor is non-suited. The court will decide whether to grant relief against the consequences of the failure[135] and, in this regard, may make an order of its own initiative.[136] Especially in cases where a court other than the CNBC is dealing with self-represented litigants, some flexibility may be shown and the court may be prepared to entertain oral representations despite the absence of written evidence, subject to any application by the creditor to adjourn the proceedings (if made).[137] The consequences of delay are likely to be more serious in the CNBC since, in the absence of any objection or application for an extension of time within the permitted period, the court may proceed to make a final order without a hearing.[138]

Evidence in opposition and advice to judgment debtors

3.61 It has traditionally been considered that the burden of showing why an interim charging order should not be made final rests with the judgment debtor.[139] However, the decision to that effect was the consequence of the rules in force prior to the Charging Orders Act 1979,[140] which are not replicated in the 1979 Act or the current procedural rules. Accordingly, it is now open to question whether such a specific burden (which is nowhere explicit in the current legislation or rules) rests upon the judgment debtor.[141] There is an argument that there is no such legal burden on the debtor at the final hearing and that it may simply be the case that at the final hearing the judge must consider all relevant matters[142] and exercise the statutory discretion accordingly.

---

135 Pursuant to CPR r 3.10; FPR r 4.7.

136 CPR r 3.3; FPR r 4.3.

137 *National Guild of Removers and Storers Ltd v Jones and Coid* [2012] EWCA Civ 216, [2012] 1 WLR 2501 at [17], per Pitchford LJ (*obiter*).

138 See para 3.76 *et seq*.

139 *Roberts Petroleum Ltd v Kenny* [1982] 1 WLR 301, CA (unaffected by [1983] 2 AC 192, HL) in which Lord Brandon of Oakbrook said, 'The burden of showing cause why a charging order nisi should not be made absolute is on the judgment debtor'.

140 RSC Ord 50, r 1(6), which read, '[the court] shall, unless it appears (whether on the representation of the judgment debtor or otherwise) that there is sufficient cause to the contrary, make the order absolute with or without modifications'.

141 *National Guild of Removers and Storers Ltd v Jones and Coid* [2012] EWCA Civ 216, [2012] 1 WLR 2501 at [11]–[16], per Pitchford LJ, where the point was raised but left undecided. Some relevant authority was not cited to the Court of Appeal: see further Chapter 4, paras 4.72 and 4.73.

142 As to which, see COA 1979, s 1(5).

3.62 In any event, in practical terms it remains incumbent on the debtor to provide a firm evidential foundation for any opposition to the confirmation of the interim order. The evidence ought to go directly to the reason why, in the particular case, it is claimed that the interim order should be discharged and not made final (or, if made final, should be made conditional[143]). In practice, it will most likely need to address one or other of the recognised grounds on which the court may incline to dismiss the creditor's application.[144]

3.63 The court is only required to, and in practice obviously can only, act on 'any evidence before it'.[145] Hindsight cannot be relied on in this context.[146] A decision to make a charging order final cannot be impugned as such (although it may still be open to the debtor or other interested party to apply for discharge or variation of the charging order[147]) if the judge takes into account all the often limited material before the court at the relevant time.[148] This demonstrates why it is important for the debtor to take advantage of the opportunity afforded by the court procedure to adduce any evidence that may assist its case.

3.64 The evidence in opposition should ideally take the form of a witness statement, verified by a statement of truth. In practice, however, courts will often accept a letter from the judgment debtor, especially if (as is recommended) the debtor attends the hearing, makes representations and is able to verify and, if necessary, explain and amplify the contents of any correspondence.

3.65 The evidence in support of the debtor's case needs to be both credible and cogent, and as detailed as possible in the circumstances. This is so whether, for instance, further time is sought, an instalment plan is proposed,[149] or there is a fundamental challenge to the basis of the charging order, such as that the debt has been repaid.

3.66 The evidence should outline why it is claimed that the charging order should not be made or, if made, should only be made on terms. A debtor should consider the various elements of the creditor's case and challenge any contentions which are considered to be incorrect. By way of example, assertions of the debtor's title to and ownership of the land should be challenged if these are disputed.

---

143 See para 3.104 in relation to the conditions subject to which a final order may be granted.

144 As to which, see para 3.105.

145 COA 1979, s 1(5).

146 *C & W Berry Ltd v Armstrong-Moakes* [2007] EWHC 2101 (QB) at [8].

147 Under COA 1979, s 3(5). As to discharge generally, see Chapter 5.

148 *C & W Berry Ltd v Armstrong-Moakes* [2007] EWHC 2101 (QB) at [8].

149 See para 3.104.

3.67 A debtor who resists the making of a final order altogether on financial grounds or who, failing that, seeks either time for payment of the debt (e.g. by instalments) or conditions on the enforcement of the charging order,[150] should provide details of income and outgoings, together with information in relation to any and all other debts and assets, so that the court is fully informed of its overall financial circumstances. This material may also assist the court in determining whether the debtor's insolvency is likely. Ultimately, the most important consideration in the majority of cases is likely to be the offer the debtor can put forward in relation to the indebtedness.

3.68 If it is the case that the value of the debtor's share in the subject land is negative (after taking account of any existing mortgages), the debtor might consider adducing some valuation evidence. This would enable an argument that a charging order should not be made because it would not give the judgment creditor any security in practical terms. That argument alone, however, is unlikely to carry the day given that the market might well subsequently improve so that the charge does provide meaningful security. The judgment debtor can make a stronger version of this argument where he is also in the process of selling the property, since the making of a charging order that would not be discharged on purchase, would (provided its priority is protected) be likely to prevent the sale.

3.69 It may be useful for the debtor to give details of any arrangements with other creditors, as where extra time to pay has been given, or where interest has been frozen. For instance, if the debtor has payment plans in place with those other creditors and believes that the ability to honour those arrangements will be jeopardised if a charging order is made, this should be covered in the evidence. Further, it may be that the history underlying the judgment debt will be relevant (when it comes to balancing the rights of multiple creditors), as where the debt which is the subject of the charging order stems from an unsecured loan which is at a high rate of interest precisely because it was unsecured.

3.70 The debtor may wish to seek the imposition of conditions on the enforcement of any charging order so as to defer any possible sale of the land. In those circumstances, the considerations that the debtor might want to put before the court could include:

(a) confirmation (if it be the case) that the land is the debtor's home;
(b) details of any children or dependent adults living there; and
(c) an explanation of any disabilities or relevant medical issues which the debtor or the residents have.

[150] As to which, see para 3.104.

3.71 Clearly, the debtor's track record, his attempts to reach a repayment agreement with the creditor, and his proposals (if realistic) in relation to repaying the debt, may also influence the court's decision.

3.72 A debtor should be realistic about the prospects of successfully challenging the application to make the interim charging order final. In this context it is also important that a debtor properly understands the nature and effect of a charging order and, in particular, that he understands the difference in terms of consequences between:

(a) the *imposition* of a charging order, which itself merely secures the debt; and
(b) the subsequent *enforcement* of a charging order by a sale of the land charged.[151]

3.73 Many debtors are thought to waste time and money in the mistaken belief that a final order will mean that the land will be sold immediately.

3.74 Advice may be obtained from bodies such as Citizens Advice,[152] Law Centres or National Debtline.[153]

3.75 A sample witness statement in opposition is included in Appendix Precedent B4.

Further consideration of interim order made by the Civil National Business Centre

Hearing not always required

3.76 Where the interim charging order was made in the CNBC, the consideration of whether to make a final charging order does not always require a hearing.

3.77 A hearing will not be required where:

(a) either:

    (i) the interim order was made by a court officer; or
    (ii) the interim order was made by a judge who did not consider it appropriate to transfer the application to the judgment debtor's home court for a hearing;[154] and

---

151 See Chapter 1, paras 1.4 and 1.9. For enforcement, see Chapter 6.

152 See e.g. www.citizensadvice.org.uk/debt-and-money/action-your-creditor-can-take/charging-orders/.

153 See e.g. www.nationaldebtline.org/fact-sheet-library/charging-orders-ew/.

154 CPR r 73.10(1).

(b) no objection to the making of a final order has been filed and the time limits for doing so have expired.[155]

Determination by judge or legal adviser without a hearing

3.78 If a hearing is not required, the application will remain in the CNBC and be dealt with on paper[156] by either a judge or a legal adviser.[157]

3.79 Where the application is considered by a judge, the judge's powers are the same as at a hearing.[158]

3.80 However, a legal adviser's options for dealing with the application are more limited. A legal adviser may only:[159]

(a) make a final charging order, if it provides that the charge imposed by the interim charging order is to continue without modification (except for the amount secured);
(b) discharge the interim charging order and dismiss the application, if the applicant has requested it;
(c) refer the matter to a judge; or
(d) in certain circumstances, make an unless order.

3.81 The circumstances in which a legal adviser can make an unless order are where the judgment creditor has not complied with the provisions for the service of the interim charging order and has either failed to apply for an extension of time within the relevant period or has failed to meet the extended deadline.[160] Where that applies, the legal adviser must either:

(a) order that unless, by a date specified in the order, the judgment creditor files a certificate in relation to each person served (together with a statement of the amount due under the judgment or order including any costs and interest), the application for a charging order is to be dismissed and the interim charging order discharged; or
(b) refer the matter to a judge to consider whether to dismiss the application and discharge the interim charging order.

---

155 CPR r 73.10(6).

156 CPR r 73.10(6D) and (7).

157 CPR r 73.10(6) and 73.1(2)(ea). The standard form interim charging order, Form N86, has not yet been updated to reflect the possibility that the decision may be made by a legal adviser: see paras 3.78–3.88.

158 CPR r 73.10(7). See para 3.95 and Chapter 2, para 2.25.

159 CPR r 73.10(6A).

160 CPR r 73.10(6B).

3.82 A legal adviser therefore has no power to:

(a) modify the charge imposed by the interim charging order except as to the amount secured;
(b) discharge the interim order and dismiss the application, unless the applicant has requested it;
(c) decide issues in dispute between the parties, or between any of the parties and any other person who objects to the court making a final charging order;
(d) direct a trial of such issues; or
(e) make such other order as is considered appropriate.

3.83 For any of these to happen, the legal adviser would first need to refer the matter to a judge, who could then consider taking the relevant step.

3.84 In any event, in most cases the judge or legal adviser will simply confirm that the interim order continues unconditionally. This is hardly surprising, because:

(a) if the application is being considered on paper then, by definition, it must be uncontested;
(b) a judge or court officer will already have satisfied himself that the application was in order when making the interim order;[161]
(c) there will be nothing before the court to contradict the applicant's evidence.

3.85 In the absence of unusual circumstances, there is therefore no reason why the court should refuse the application.

Reconsideration of legal adviser's decision

3.86 An interested person can request that a legal adviser's decision be reconsidered by a District Judge.[162] To do so, the interested person must file a written request within 14 days of being served with notice of the decision, or becoming aware of the decision.[163] There is no need for an application to be made under Part 23 of the Civil Procedure Rules or for an application fee to be paid.

---

161 See para 3.39.

162 CPR r 73.10ZA(1). This supplements the general provision that a party (rather than 'any interested person') can request that any decision of a legal adviser in the CNBC be reconsidered by a District Judge: CPR PD 2E, paras 3.2–3.5.

163 CPR r 73.10ZA(2). A similar procedure is available under CPR r 73.5 where an interim charging order has been made by a court officer. See paras 3.37–3.38.

3.87 The interested person may include in the request a summary of the issue and an explanation of why the reconsideration is sought.[164] Although technically optional, this is clearly advisable, and the interested person should take the opportunity to explain why the judge ought to make a different order.

3.88 Reconsideration may take place without a hearing[165] and the District Judge may exercise any of the powers ordinarily available to a judge when considering an application.[166] In other words, the District Judge is not limited to the powers that were available to the legal adviser.

Transfer to judgment debtor's home court for a hearing

3.89 Where an interim charging order has been made in the CNBC, a hearing is only required where, either:

(a) the interim charging order was made by a judge, who considered it appropriate to transfer the application to the judgment debtor's home court for a hearing;[167] or
(b) an objection to the making of a final charging order has been filed.[168]

3.90 In either case, the application will be transferred to the judgment debtor's home court[169] and listed for a hearing. In the first scenario, the transfer is ordered as part of the interim charging order.[170] In the second, the court transfers the application once all persons served with the interim order have filed an objection or once the time period for the service of an objection by the last person served with the interim order has expired, whichever is the earlier.[171]

3.91 The court will serve notice of the hearing on the judgment creditor and all persons served with the interim charging order.[172] The procedure and powers of the court at the hearing are considered at para 3.95 *et seq.*

---

164 CPR r 73.10ZA(3).

165 CPR r 73.10ZA(4).

166 CPR r 73.10ZA(5).

167 CPR r 73.4(6)(b).

168 CPR r 73.10(3); CPR PD 73, para 3. The objection should also have been served on the judgment creditor: CPR r 73.10(2)(b).

169 The CNBC is not itself a hearing centre.

170 CPR r 73.4(6)(b).

171 CPR r 73.10(4).

172 CPR rr 73.4(7) and 73.10(5)

Further consideration of interim order made by the High Court or the family court

Hearing always required

3.92 As already explained,[173] where the interim charging order is made by a court other than the CNBC, it will fix a hearing date for the further consideration of the application. The procedure and powers of the court at the hearing are considered at para 3.95 *et seq*.

Transfer to another court

3.93 Where the application is being dealt with by the High Court (other than the Family Division), and an objection to the making of a final order is filed, the court may transfer the application to the judgment debtor's home court.[174] In these circumstances, that court will be the district registry for the district in which the judgment debtor resides or carries on business or, where there is no such district registry, the Royal Courts of Justice.[175] However, unlike the equivalent situation in the CNBC,[176] the transfer is not mandatory.[177] Therefore, if the judgment debtor would like the proceedings to be transferred, it would be sensible for this to be stated in the written evidence of objection, together with an explanation of why a transfer is appropriate. Note that it is only the application that is transferred, not the claim itself, and any subsequent applications within the claim should still be made to the court in which the claim is based.[178]

3.94 There is no specific provision for the transfer of the application where an objection is filed with the family court or the High Court (Family Division). The general framework under rules 29.17 and 29.18 of the Family Procedure Rules therefore applies.

---

[173] See para 3.43.

[174] CPR PD 73, para 3.

[175] CPR r 73.1(2)(c)(ii). A different definition applies where the application for a charging order is proceeding in the county court: CPR r 73.1(2)(c)(i). See para 3.45.

[176] CPR r 73.10(3). See paras 3.89–3.90.

[177] CPR PD 73, para 3.

[178] *Chancery Guide 2022* (Courts and Tribunals Judiciary, July 2022; updated October 2022 and June 2023), para 31.30.

Hearing for further consideration

Procedure and powers of the court at the hearing

3.95 As already explained,[179] at the hearing, the judge may:[180]

(a) make a final charging order confirming that the charge imposed by the interim charging order is to continue, with or without modification;
(b) discharge the interim charging order and dismiss the application;
(c) decide any issues in dispute between the parties, or between any of the parties and any other person who objects to the court making a final charging order;
(d) direct a trial of any such issues, and if necessary give directions; or
(e) make such other order as the court considers appropriate.

3.96 Further, in the exercise of its general case management powers,[181] the court may adjourn the hearing to a later date in appropriate circumstances, for example if it is desirable that an objector should have additional time in which to put together his case, or if the debtor requests a short deferment to enable him to discharge the debt in full and the court is satisfied that this is appropriate in the particular circumstances.[182]

3.97 Any adjournment should be to a fixed date, rather than an adjournment generally. This is because an interim charging order ought not to be left in place against a debtor's land indefinitely. It is designed only as a temporary measure. By its very nature and terms, the court is supposed to proceed to determine whether to confirm or discharge it. This determination should not be left in limbo indefinitely.

3.98 If an adjournment is appropriate, the court can, and typically will, extend the interim charging order until the rescheduled final hearing[183] since otherwise the interim order will lapse, its registration be liable to be cancelled, and the judgment creditor will be denied any security in the meantime. In such a scenario the debtor might be able to divest himself of the asset before the resumed hearing, thus rendering the creditor's application nugatory. There is no prescribed form for such an order.

---

[179] See Chapter 2, para 2.25.

[180] CPR rr 73.10(7) and 73.10A(3); FPR r 40.8(2).

[181] As to which, see CPR r 3.1(2)(b) and FPR r 4.1(3)(c).

[182] *National Guild of Removers and Storers Ltd v Jones and Coid* [2012] EWCA Civ 216, [2012] 1 WLR 2501 at [17], per Pitchford LJ.

[183] *National Guild of Removers and Storers Ltd v Jones and Coid* [2012] EWCA Civ 216, [2012] 1 WLR 2501 at [4], [6(2)] and [17], per Pitchford LJ.

3.99 Also, in appropriate cases, such as where the court becomes aware of the existence of other relevant litigation (such as divorce proceedings or proceedings directly concerned with and/or impacting on the judgment debtor's financial status and solvency), the court may decide to adjourn the hearing for further consideration and transfer the application to the other court in order that all matters can be investigated and dealt with together.[184]

3.100 What the court will do and what the outcome might be will necessarily depend on a combination of considerations including:

(a) whether any objection is made;
(b) the nature of the objection;
(c) the type and extent of any issues arising from the objection; and
(d) the quality and completeness of the evidence and material before the court at the hearing.

3.101 The court's approach and its decision at the hearing will reflect the principles which it must apply when deciding whether to make a charging order[185] and the grounds on which a charging order may be resisted. These are explained in Chapter 2.[186]

Uncontested hearing

3.102 If neither the judgment debtor nor any other notified person decides to contest the making of a final charging order, the overwhelming likelihood is that the court will simply confirm the interim order unconditionally. In this situation the hearing is in practice little more than a formality.[187]

Contested hearing

Confirmation of the interim order

3.103 If, despite any objection, the court is satisfied that the debtor has title to the asset charged, is solvent but unable to satisfy the judgment within a reasonable time, and that, in all the circumstances, it is desirable that the applicant creditor has security for the unpaid debt, it will generally confirm the interim order unconditionally.

---

184 See Chapter 2, para 2.46 *et seq*.

185 See COA 1979, s 1(5).

186 See Chapter 2, para 2.22 *et seq*.

187 See paras 3.84–3.85.

3.104 The court may confirm the interim order subject to conditions.[188] It might provide, for example, that the charge should not be enforced provided that the debtor pays the debt by specified instalments.[189] That course would have close parallels with the fact that it is statutorily provided that a charging order may not be enforced (e.g. by sale) if it was made in respect of a sum payable in instalments under a court judgment or order and there has not been default in payment of an instalment.[190] Similarly, the court may grant the final order subject to a moratorium on further enforcement action (such as an application for an order for sale) by the creditor, either indefinitely or until a specified date.[191]

Discharge of the interim order

3.105 At the hearing, in the exercise of the court's discretion, a charging order may be refused and the judgment creditor's application dismissed for a number of reasons which reflect the principles to be applied when the court is considering whether to make a charging order.[192] The following is a non-exhaustive list of possible instances:

(a) The underlying judgment has been successfully appealed or set aside.
(b) The judgment debt has been paid.
(c) Possibly, the judgment debt is small in comparison with the value of the land against which the charge is sought.[193]
(d) The charging order is to secure future liabilities of the judgment debtor, and the amount thereof is low compared with the value of the land sought to be charged.[194]

---

188 COA 1979, s 3(1).

189 The fact that a judgment is payable in instalments does not in principle preclude a charging order being made to secure the entire judgment debt, even if there has been no default in payment of the instalments: see COA 1979, s 1(6)–(8); Chapter 2, para 2.50–2.52.

190 COA 1979, s 3(4A)–(4E), inserted by TCEA 2007, s 93.

191 *Austin-Fell* v *Austin-Fell* [1990] Fam 172, in which a postponed enforcement order was made, this representing the fairest balance between the competing claims of the divorced wife and a judgment creditor of the debtor. Enforcement was suspended until the youngest of the minor children of the debtor attained majority. See Chapter 2, paras 2.47–2.48.

192 See Chapter 2, para 2.22 *et seq.*

193 See Chapter 2, para 2.45. There is currently no minimum level set by statute or the court rules for a judgment creditor to obtain a charging order. What is more, the making of a charging order itself merely gives security, leaving any question of enforcement (as by sale) to a future occasion. Therefore, it is hard to see how or why a charging order should be refused on such basis, certainly where the debt exceeds the bankruptcy level (£5,000). However, see further Chapter 3, para 3.106.

194 *Robinson v Bailey* [1942] Ch 268 (in which the defendant had been ordered to pay £50 per year until certain documents were executed). See also COA 1979, s 1(6)–(8); Chapter 2, para 2.45.

(e) The debtor is proved to be insolvent, or a bankruptcy or winding-up petition has been presented against the debtor.[195]
(f) There is about to be an arrangement whereby the debtor's assets will be distributed between the various creditors pro rata.[196]
(g) The evidence shows that there are so many other creditors and/or that the debtor's indebtedness is so great, that a charging order is not appropriate.
(h) It is established that the debtor has no interest in the land in question.[197]
(i) The interim charging order is shown to have been obtained by the judgment creditor without making full and frank disclosure of material facts.

3.106 In relation to point (c), it is possible that the law may change. The Lord Chancellor may by regulations provide that a charge may not be imposed by a charging order for securing the payment of money of an amount below that determined in accordance with the regulations.[198] At the time of writing, no regulations have been made under this power.[199]

3.107 If the interim order is discharged, the charge necessarily falls away and any notice or restriction entered against the land should be cancelled. To ensure that this occurs, the court will frequently direct that any relevant registration entry be cancelled and that a copy of the discharging order be sent to the Land Charges

---

195 See Chapter 2, paras 2.38–2.41. See Chapter 8, para 8.108 *et seq*.

196 See Chapter 2, paras 2.42–2.43.

197 In determining whether the judgment debtor has a beneficial interest in land subject to an interim charging order, the initial burden lies with the judgment creditor but, if that is discharged, it thereafter rests with whichever side would lose on the basis of the weight of the overall evidence: *Nightingale Mayfair Ltd v Mehta* [2000] WTLR 901, [1999] All ER (D) 1501. In *Howell v Montey* (1990) 61 P & CR 18 an interim charging order was made but not registered before the debtors contracted to sell the land in question. On completion of the sale, because of a failure to register title within the priority period afforded by an official certificate of search at HM Land Registry, the purchasers' registration took place subject to the charging order, and the charging order was subsequently made final. In a dispute between the purchaser and the judgment creditor as to their relative priority it was held that the fact the charging order had been made final at a time when the debtors no longer had any beneficial interest in the land and thus against the property of a bona fide purchaser justified the discharge of the charging order. See further Chapter 4, para 4.24.

198 COA 1979, s 3A(1), inserted by TCEA 2007, s 94.

199 If and when a threshold is imposed, it is anticipated that it might be around £1,000, which is also: (a) the level of outstanding liability required before a local authority can seek a charging order in respect of unpaid council tax: see CT (A&E) Regs 1992, reg 50(1)(c); and (b) the minimum threshold for the level of Consumer Credit Act 1974 (CCA 1974) debts in relation to applications for orders for sale: see the Charging Orders (Orders for Sale: Financial Thresholds) Regulations 2013 (SI 2013/491), which came into force on 6 April, 2013: see Chapter 6, para 6.5.

Department (in the case of unregistered land) or HM Land Registry (in the case of registered land).[200]

3.108 A precedent for an appropriate form of discharge order is included in Appendix Precedent B5.

Deciding issues in dispute and the direction of a trial

3.109 If an issue arises within the charging order proceedings, for example, as to the title to the land to be charged, or as to whether the debtor has already satisfied the judgment in full, the court will determine it in the manner it considers appropriate, giving the parties a fair opportunity to contest the issue.

3.110 The court may well, and often will, adopt a summary procedure and decide matters at the hearing, at least where it is able to resolve the dispute with relative ease. However, in more complicated cases, or where it requires further evidence from either or both parties, the court may direct that the issue be tried and give directions for the trial, for example, disclosure of documentation and the exchange of witness statements. Oral (as opposed to written) evidence is likely to be required if the court directs a trial.

3.111 If an issue is not decided immediately, the practice is to adjourn the application to make the charging order final until after the trial of the issue, with the interim charging order continued in the meantime.[201]

Such other order as the court considers appropriate

3.112 As already discussed,[202] and explained further in Chapter 4,[203] a judgment creditor applying for a charging order over a beneficial interest in registered land might ask the court to order the registrar to enter a non-standard restriction against the registered title,[204] in order to protect its charge. That second application will

---

200 Where an application for discharge of a charging order is made under COA 1979, s 3(5), the court is expressly empowered to make such a direction: s 3(6). It is considered that a corresponding power exists when an interim order is further considered and a final order refused.

201 *Rosseel NV v Oriental Commercial and Shipping (UK) Ltd* 8 October 1991, briefly reported at [1991] EGCS 94, CA.

202 See para 3.16–3.18.

203 See Chapter 4, para 4.39–4.43.

204 The court has power to require the registrar to enter a restriction in the register if it appears to the court to be necessary or desirable for the purpose of protecting a right of claim: LRA 2002, s 46(1).

typically be dealt with alongside the decision to grant a final charging order, under the court's general power to 'make such other order as the court considers appropriate'.

Final order

3.113 A final charging order should generally be in Form N87.[205] A precedent for a completed Form N87 is included in Appendix Precedent B6. Final charging orders made in the family court generally use Standard Order 4.14 as a template rather than Form N87. A copy of Standard Order 4.14 is included in Appendix Precedent B8.[206]

3.114 Both Form N87 and Standard Order 4.14 expressly state that the charge is security not only for the outstanding balance of the judgment debt (including interest to date), but also the costs of the charging order application and any further interest accruing after the date of the order. The position is the same even if the order does not state this expressly.[207]

3.115 Any order made upon further consideration of the application, either on the papers or at a hearing, must be served on all the persons on whom the interim charging order was required to be served.[208] The order will be served by the court,[209] except where the order is made at a hearing in the family court or the High Court (Family Division), in which case service will be by the judgment creditor.[210] The most significant orders that the court may make are the final charging order, if the interim order is confirmed, or the discharge of the interim order, if it is not.

3.116 Since a final order merely confirms the interim order,[211] it is not strictly necessary to take steps to protect its priority, provided that the interim order has been properly protected. However, it is generally prudent to enter a separate notice/restriction for the final order, so that it is clear from the register that a final order was in fact made.[212]

---

205 CPR PD 4, Annex A.

206 Standard Order 4.14 can also be accessed at www.judiciary.uk/guidance-and-resources/update-standard-orders-issued-by-mr-justice-mostyn/.

207 *Ezekiel v Orakpo* [1997] 1 WLR 340.

208 CPR rr 73.10(9) and 73.10A(5); FPR r 40.8(4). Note that CPR r 73.10(6C) provides that an unless order made under CPR r 73.10(6B) must be served by the court on all the parties but does not expressly exclude the application of the general provision in CPR r 73.10(9).

209 CPR rr 73.10(9) and 73.10A(5).

210 FPR r 40.8(4).

211 CPR r 73.1(2)(ca); FPR r 40.8(2)(a).

212 For details of the registration process, see Chapter 4, para 4.34 *et seq.*

3.117 Because the final order is confirmatory of the interim order, the charge relates back to, and takes effect from, the date of the interim order.[213] Therefore, subject to appropriate registration, any intervening dispositions or proceedings (other than insolvency) cannot affect it.[214]

Costs

3.118 Fixed costs apply in relation to the obtaining of a charging order.[215] Consequently, unless the court orders otherwise,[216] the solicitors' costs allowed against the judgment debtor on the making of a final charging order are (currently) fixed at £110.[217] Any appropriate court fee is recoverable in addition.[218] The court may also allow reasonable disbursements in respect of search fees and the registration of the order.[219] The judgment creditor should have details and proof of any disbursements incurred available at the hearing.

INSOLVENCY RESTRICTIONS

3.119 A judgment debtor's insolvency can have a significant impact on the ability of a judgment creditor to apply for a charging order, to have an interim order made final, or to enforce a charging order by sale. Any judgment creditor who has reason to believe that the debtor may be insolvent, or about to become so, should immediately and carefully consider the ramifications of the relevant statutory provisions before proceeding any further. For a summary of the various insolvency regimes and their significance in the context of charging orders, see Chapter 8.

---

213 *Ropaigealach v Allied Irish Bank plc* [2001] EWCA Civ 1790, [2002] 1 EGLR 83.

214 *Haly v Barry* (1868) LR 3 Ch App 452; and see *Brereton v Edwards* (1888) 21 QBD 226 (affirmed, at 488).

215 CPR r 45.1(2)(g); FPR r 28.2.

216 CPR r 45.1(1); *Blacknest Gate Ltd v Seymour Realty Ltd* [2020] EWHC 3878 (TCC). By way of example, if the debtor or other interested party opposes the making of the final order and such opposition means that: (a) the hearing for further consideration is adjourned to a later date with a longer time-estimate; or (b) a trial is directed – but ultimately the opposition fails and is shown to have been misconceived, the court may in its discretion be prepared to disapply the fixed costs regime and to award more costs to the judgment creditor.

217 CPR r 45.8.

218 CPR r 45.1(4). For the applicable court fees, see n 73.

219 CPR r 45.8. For registration, see para 3.56 and Chapter 4.

BASIC PROCEDURE TABLES

3.120 There follow two tables outlining the basic procedure for obtaining a charging order by application to the county court (Table 3.1) or by application to the High Court or the family court (Table 3.2). Each table outlines the steps required, the rules and timeframes and, where appropriate, the relevant forms. The tables should be read in conjunction with the more detailed commentary set out above.

Table 3.1: Procedure in the Civil National Business Centre

<table>
<tr><th>Step</th><th>Form</th><th>Rule</th><th>Timeframe</th></tr>
<tr><td>Without notice application to the CNBC</td><td>N379</td><td>CPR r 73.3
CPR PD 73, paras 1.1–1.3</td><td></td></tr>
<tr><td>Interim charging order (made by a judge or court officer without a hearing)</td><td>N86</td><td>CPR r 73.4</td><td></td></tr>
<tr><td colspan="4">If made by a judge, the interim charging order may transfer the proceedings to the judgment debtor's home court (CPR r 73.4(6)(b)), in which case the procedure set out in Table 3.2 will apply from this point on.</td></tr>
<tr><td>Application to HM Land Registry to enter a notice or restriction on the registered title</td><td></td><td></td><td></td></tr>
<tr><td>Service of interim charging order</td><td></td><td>CPR r 73.7(1), (3) and (7)</td><td>Within 21 days of the date of the interim charging order (unless an extension of time is granted)</td></tr>
<tr><td>Filing of certificate of service and
statement of amount due under the judgment</td><td>N215
None prescribed</td><td>CPR r 73.7(2) and (3)
CPR r 6.29</td><td>Within 28 days of the date of the interim charging order (unless an extension of time is granted)</td></tr>
</table>

Step	*Form*	*Rule*	*Timeframe*
If interim order made by court officer, any written request for reconsideration (which will take place without a hearing)	None prescribed	CPR r 73.5	Within 14 days of the party being served with notice of the decision
Filing and service of written evidence stating the grounds of objection	None prescribed	CPR r 73.10(2)	Not later than 28 days after service on that person of the application notice and interim charging order
If an objection is received, the court will transfer the proceedings to the judgment debtor's home court for further consideration at a hearing		CPR r 73.10(3)–(5) CPR PD 73, para 3	Once all persons served have filed an objection or once 28 days has expired since the final person was served
If no objection is received, the application will be considered by a judge or legal adviser without a hearing		CPR r 73.10(6)	
Ultimately, either a final charging order will be made or the interim charging order will be discharged		CPR r 73.10(6A)–(7) CPR rr 45.1(2)(g) and 45.8	
Service of final charging order by the court		CPR r 73.10(9)	
If the final decision is made by a legal adviser, any written request for reconsideration (which may take place without a hearing)		CPR r 73.10ZA	Within 14 days of being served with notice of the decision, or becoming aware of the decision

Table 3.2: Procedure other than in the Civil National Business Centre

Step	*Form*	*Rule*	*Timeframe*
Without notice application	N379 (in civil proceedings)	CPR r 73.3 CPR PD 73, paras 1.1–1.3	
	FE6 (in family proceedings)	FPR r 40.4 FPR PD 40A, paras 1.1–1.4 FPR PD 5A	
Interim charging order (made without a hearing)	N86	CPR r 73.6	
		FPR r 40.5	
Service of interim charging order		CPR r 73.7(5) and (7)	At least 21 days before the hearing for further consideration
		FPR r 40.6(1) and (3)	
Application to HM Land Registry to enter a notice or restriction on the registered title			
Filing and service of written evidence stating the grounds of objection	None prescribed	CPR r 73.10A(2)	At least 7 days before the hearing for further consideration
		FPR r 40.8(2)	
Filing of certificate of service	N215	CPR r 73.7(6) CPR r 6.29	At least 2 days before the hearing for further consideration (or the certificate must be produced at the hearing)
		FPR r 40.6(2) FPR r 6.37	
Hearing for further consideration, ultimately leading to a final charging order or discharge of the interim charging order		CPR r 73.10A(3) and (5) CPR rr 45.1(2)(g) and 45.8	
		FPR r 40.9(2) and (4) FPR r 28.2 CPR r 45.8	

Step	*Form*	*Rule*	*Timeframe*
Service of final charging order by the court or (in family proceedings) the judgment creditor		CPR r 73.10A(5) FPR r 40.8(4)	

Chapter 4

Priorities and Problems

BASIC RULE OF PRIORITY

Priority and the protection of priority

4.1 This chapter is concerned with the priority of charging orders, the means by which that priority can be protected, and some of the consequential issues that arise.

Overview

- A charging order takes effect as an equitable charge.
- The interim and the final charging order are the same equitable charge and hence the priority of the final order is the same as that of the interim order.
- A charging order's priority as against other equitable interests will be determined by reference to the date of creation.
- If the charging order is over a registered estate, its priority will depend on the priority rules in the Land Registration Act 2002. On a registered disposition for value, the charging order will likely lose priority unless protected by a notice on the title.
- A charging order over a beneficial interest can be made the subject of a restriction on the title. The standard Form K restriction is of little assistance.

4.2 A few general points need to be made at the outset.

4.3 First, the charge which is imposed by a charging order has the same effect as an equitable charge created by a debtor under hand (i.e. in signed writing).[1] The principles for determining the priority of such a charge follow from its character as an equitable charge.

4.4 However, the means by which that priority is protected differs from ordinary equitable charges. Section 3(2) of the Charging Orders Act 1979 provides that charging orders are required to be protected under the provisions of the Land Registration Act 2002 (where land is registered) and the Land Charges Act 1972 (where it is not) in the same way that those Acts apply in relation to other orders or writs issued or made for the purpose of enforcing judgments.[2] It follows that charging orders are protected as forms of execution, not equitable charges.

4.5 An important consequence of section 3(2) and its references only to the 2002 and 1972 Acts is that (because no other statute has relevance to the protection of charging orders) a charging order over the assets of a company is not registrable as a charge under Part 25 of the Companies Act 2006.[3]

4.6 Lastly, as set out below, questions of priority often (although not always) turn on the date on which an interest is created. In the case of a charging order, the date of creation is the date on which the interim charging order was made (not the date on which the order was made final or added to any relevant register).[4]

TYPES OF INTEREST OVER WHICH A CHARGING ORDER CAN BE MADE

4.7 Two key questions need to be asked first when considering issues of priority.

(a) First, is the relevant land registered or unregistered?
(b) Secondly, what is the nature of the interest over which the order has been made?

---

1 COA 1979, s 3(4); Chapter 1, para 1.6.

2 COA 1979, s 3(2). The position was the same under the AJA 1956: see AJA 1956, s 35(3).

3 See *In Re Overseas Aviation Engineering (GB) Ltd* [1963] Ch 24, a decision of the Court of Appeal on Companies Act 1948, s 95, and AJA 1956, s 35. The equivalent provision of the Companies Act 2006 is s 859H.

4 *Ropaigealach v Allied Irish Bank plc* [2001] EWCA Civ 1790, [2002] 1 EGLR 83 at 84, applying *Haly v Barry* (1868) LR 3 Ch App 452.

4.8 As set out in Chapter 2,[5] this book is concerned with charging orders over the following types of property:

(a) land that is legally and beneficially owned by the judgment debtor;[6]
(b) a beneficial interest in land that is held in trust; and
(c) land that is held in trust in circumstances where:

  (i) the charge is made in respect of a judgment or order made against a person as trustee of the trust;[7]
  (ii) there is a bare trust for the judgment debtor; or
  (iii) the land is held in trust for two or more debtors, who are liable for the same debt and who have, between them, the whole beneficial interest in the land.[8]

As we have already seen, a charging order obtained in situation (b) takes effect over the beneficial interest only. It is therefore protected in a different way from a charging order that has been obtained in situations (a) and (c), which will take effect over the legal title.

4.9 Where land is held on trust for two or more persons as beneficial joint tenants, and a creditor obtains a charging order over the interest of one of the joint tenants, the effect of that order will be to sever the joint tenancy in relation to the share of that joint tenant.[9] Because the charging order takes effect as an equitable charge created in writing under the hand of the debtor,[10] it necessarily operates as a partial alienation of the joint tenant's beneficial interest and thereby severs the joint tenancy.[11] This can be very important if one of the co-owners dies. Under the doctrine of survivorship, where one joint tenant dies, the property is

---

5 See Chapter 2, paras 2.12–2.13.

6 The meaning of 'land' in the COA 1979, see Chapter 2, para 2.13.

7 This situation could only arise if the judgment was binding on all the trustees (if, as is usual with land, there were more than one).

8 *Cf* COA 1979, s 2(1) and (2)(a).

9 See *Walker v Lundborg* [2008] UKPC 17 at [8], per Lord Walker of Gestingthorpe (concerning Bahamian Supreme Court Act 1996, s 63, which is in similar terms to the COA 1979); *C Putnam & Sons v Taylor* [2009] EWHC 317 (Ch), [2009] BPIR 769 at [20], per HHJ Purle.

10 COA 1979, s 3(4).

11 In the leading case of *Williams v Hensman* (1861) 1 J & H 546 at 547, Page Wood V-C set out the three methods by which a joint tenancy might be severed at common law. The first of these was that, 'an act of any one of the persons interested operating upon his own share may create a severance as to that share'. It had long been settled that a *mortgage* by a joint tenant operated as a severance (see *York v Stone* (1709) 1 Salk 158, per Lord Cowper LC), although at that time a mortgage required an outright conveyance of the mortgagor's interest.

automatically vested in the survivors. However, where there are tenants in common, their interests devolve under the ordinary principles relating to wills and intestacy.

Registered land

Priority rules

4.10 Where land is registered, the priority of competing interests affecting that land is governed by the Land Registration Act 2002 – most importantly, sections 28–30.

Section 28 – the basic rule

4.11 Section 28 of the Land Registration Act 2002 sets out the 'basic rule' that save as provided by sections 29 and 30, the priority of an interest affecting a registered estate (or registered charge) is not affected by a disposition of that estate (or charge). In other words, the starting point is that the interest which was first in time prevails.[12]

4.12 Strictly, section 28 does not apply to any disposition of a beneficial interest under a trust over registered land. Instead, where there are competing equitable interests affecting a beneficial interest (rather than the registered estate or charge itself) the common law rules which govern unregistered land apply. However, in such a case the rule is again that the competing interests rank in the order in which they are created (as stated by the maxim 'where the equities are equal, the first in time prevails').[13] For the purposes of this rule, it is irrelevant that the party who acquired the later interest had no notice of the earlier interest, even if he gave value.[14]

---

12 See *Hughmans Solicitors v Central Stream Services Ltd (In Liquidation)* [2012] EWHC 1222 (Ch), [2012] BPIR 1013 at [19]. By contrast, the priority of registered charges depends upon the order in which they appear in the register: see LRA 2002, s 48.

13 Although the general rule is subject to an exception in cases of competing assignments of beneficial interests – an exception known as the rule in *Dearle v Hall* – that exception does not apply in relation to the priority of charging orders over beneficial interests: *United Bank of Kuwait plc v Sahib* [1997] Ch 107 at 119, per Chadwick J. The reasons for the rule in *Dearle v Hall* (1828) 3 Russ 1 did not apply where a judgment creditor was attempting to obtain such security as he could for credit already given to the judgment debtor. The point did not arise on the subsequent appeal to the Court of Appeal.

14 The principle was summarised by Millett J in *Macmillan Inc v Bishopsgate Investment Trust plc (No 3)* [1995] 1 WLR 978 at 999–1000.

Sections 29 and 30 – the special rule

4.13 The Land Registration Act 2002 contains an important exception to the basic rule considered above. This is laid down by section 29 (where there are competing interests which affect a registered estate) and the lesser used section 30 (where the competing interests instead affect a registered charge).

4.14 These provisions provide that where there is a registrable disposition of the registered estate (or charge) for valuable consideration, completion of that disposition by registration will postpone to the interest under that disposition any interest affecting the estate (or charge) immediately before the disposition whose priority was not protected at the time of registration. In other words, registrable dispositions will, once registered, trump any pre-existing interest the priority of which has not been protected as at the time of registration.

4.15 What constitutes a registrable disposition and how that disposition must be registered are set out in the Land Registration Act 2002.[15] In essence, a registrable disposition is one which creates or transfers a legal estate or interest. Transfers, the granting of longer leases, and the granting of charges by deed by way of legal mortgage are common examples. The burden of proving that there has been a registrable disposition for valuable consideration lies on the party asserting it.[16]

4.16 We now consider the application of these rules to charging orders specifically.

Priority of charging orders in relation to subsisting interests

4.17 The making of a charging order is not a registrable disposition for the purposes of the Land Registration Act 2002.[17] Furthermore, a judgment creditor

---

15 See LRA 2002, ss 27 and 132(1) and Sch 2.

16 See *Halifax plc v Curry Popeck* [2008] EWHC 1692 (Ch) at [46]; *Hughmans Solicitors v Central Stream Services Ltd (In Liquidation)* [2012] EWHC 1222 (Ch), [2012] BPIR 1013 at [21].

17 Registrable dispositions are those listed in LRA 2002, s 27(2): see s 132(1). Charging orders are not listed in s 27(2). Although in *Hughmans Solicitors v Central Stream Services Ltd (In Liquidation)* [2012] EWHC 1222 (Ch), [2012] BPIR 1013 at [21], Briggs J was prevailed upon by counsel to treat the making of a charging order as a registrable disposition for the purposes of the priority provisions of LRA 2002, s 29, that is plainly wrong and *per incuriam*. The point was, in the circumstances, merely *obiter*. *Cf Palace Gate Worldwide Ltd v Palacegate Agencies Ltd and Oddbins Ltd*, REC/2009/0007 at [135], per Simon Brilliant sitting as Deputy Adjudicator to HM Land Registry: see https://landregistrationdivision.decisions.tribunals.gov.uk/public/summary.aspx?id=238.

who obtains a charging order receives no valuable consideration when the charging order is made and as such is regarded as a volunteer.[18]

4.18 It follows from this that a judgment creditor can never take advantage of the special provisions of the Land Registration Act 2002 that confer priority on a registrable disposition for valuable consideration where a prior interest was unprotected at the date of registration of that disposition (i.e. the special rule in sections 29 and 30).

4.19 Accordingly, the judgment creditor will always take subject to interests in the land charged that pre-date the imposition of the charging order in his favour, whether equitable or legal, because the basic first in time of creation rule of priority[19] must apply.[20]

Priority of competing charging orders

4.20 Because a charging order has the same effect as an equitable charge created under hand,[21] once an interim charging order has been made,[22] that charging order must have priority over any subsequent charging order that may be made over the same registered estate or charge. This follows from the basic first in time rule of priority for equitable interests. The same must also be true where a charging order is made over a beneficial interest in registered land that is held in trust or under a settlement.

---

18 *United Bank of Kuwait plc v Sahib* [1997] Ch 107 at 118–19, per Chadwick J; *Hughmans Solicitors v Central Stream Services Ltd (In Liquidation)* [2012] EWHC 1222 (Ch), [2012] BPIR 1013 at [23]–[25], per Briggs J. The view of Briggs J on this issue was not challenged on appeal: [2012] EWCA Civ 1720.

19 See LRA 2002, s 28

20 *Hughmans Solicitors v Central Stream Services Ltd (In Liquidation)* [2012] EWHC 1222 (Ch), [2012] BPIR 1013 at [24]–[25]. The fact that an existing interest is binding on the chargee does not mean that it should have a paramountcy when it comes to enforcement of the charge: *Pritchard Englefield (A Firm) v Steinberg* [2004] EWHC 1908 (Ch), [2004] All ER (D) 580 (Jul) at [59]. In that case, the chargee's charging order was subject to the prior right of the mother of the judgment debtor to remain in occupation for life pursuant to a constructive trust that was binding on the judgment debtor. However, that fact did not frustrate the chargee's legitimate desire to realise its charge. An order for sale was made with vacant possession, subject to postponement for 2 months to enable a purchaser to be found who was prepared to acquire the property subject to the mother's right to occupy.

It should be borne in mind that where a purchaser has made a part-payment under a contract to acquire an estate in land, that purchaser will acquire a purchaser's lien in the nature of an equitable charge. See *Williams & Another v Alter Domus Trustees (UK) Ltd & Another* [2023] EWHC 1820 (Ch).

21 COA 1979, s 3(4).

22 It is the date of the interim order that is relevant: see para 4.6.

4.21 Where there are competing interim charging orders and the question arises as to whether, as a matter of discretion, those orders should be made final (where statutory insolvency provisions are not engaged), the courts will often apply the principle of 'first past the post'.[23] The charging orders will therefore rank in priority in the order in which they are made. However, there may be other cases where it is appropriate to refuse to make an interim charging order in favour of a judgment creditor who obtained his interim charging order first, and instead to make an order giving effect to some different priority (using the powers under rule 73.10(7) or rule 73.10A(3) of the Civil Procedure Rules as applicable).[24]

Priority of charging orders in relation to subsequent interests

4.22 Where the subsequent interest is not one which satisfies the requirements of the 'special rule' in section 29 or section 30 (it is not a registrable disposition of the registered estate or charge for valuable consideration, which is completed by registration), a pre-existing charging order will take priority.[25]

4.23 However, where the subsequent interest does satisfy those requirements, it is necessary to consider whether the priority of the charging order was protected at the time of registration. If not, it will be postponed and the later interest will take priority under the special rule.[26]

PROTECTION OF PRIORITY UNDER THE LAND REGISTRATION ACT 2002 – A SUMMARY

4.24 The following paragraphs set out the various methods of protection under the Land Registration Act 2002 generally, before considering protection of charging orders in particular.

---

23 See e.g. *Midtown Acquisitions LP v Essar Global Fund Ltd* [2018] EWHC 789 (Comm), in which two creditors with interim charging orders applied to make them final, with the second in time seeking equal priority. Knowles J accepted that the court had power to order such but declined to do so.

24 See *British Arab Commercial Bank plc v Algosaibi and Bros Co* [2011] EWHC 2444 (Comm), [2011] 2 CLC 736 at [53], per Flaux J. *Cf Nathan v Orchard* [2004] EWHC 344 (QB) (not cited in *Algosaibi*), where the charging orders were not over land, but over a fund in court. At [21], Pitchers J held that, 'first in time' was one circumstance in deciding whether an interim charging order should be made final, when a subsequent interim charging order had been made, but it did not automatically overpower all other factors. See also *Midtown Acquisitions LP v Essar Global Fund Ltd* [2018] EWHC 789 (Comm), in which Knowles J noted that whilst there might be debate over whether 'first past the post' would only be disapplied in 'exceptional' cases, or whether that was to 'put things too high', such debate did not require resolution in the case before him.

25 LRA 2002, s 28

26 LRA 2002, s 29 or s 30.

Notices

4.25 The principal means of protecting an incumbrance under the Land Registration Act 2002 is by the entry of a notice on the register.[27] Under that Act, a notice is 'an entry in the register in respect of the burden of an interest affecting a registered estate or charge'.[28] The entry of a notice does not necessarily mean that the interest is valid. However, if it is, the notice will protect its priority.[29] Certain interests cannot be protected by the entry of a notice. In particular, no notice may be entered in respect of an interest under a trust of land.[30]

4.26 A notice may either be a unilateral notice or an agreed notice.[31] The registrar may only approve an application for an agreed notice if the registered proprietor (or a person entitled to be registered as proprietor) either makes or consents to the application, or if the registrar is satisfied as to the validity of the applicant's claim.[32] In any other case, except where rules otherwise require,[33] the notice will be registered as a unilateral notice, and the registrar will then be bound to give notice of the entry to the proprietor of the registered estate or charge to which it relates.[34] The registered proprietor may apply for the cancellation of the notice if he considers that it should not have been entered.[35]

Overriding interests

4.27 Many interests in registered land that are capable of being protected by a notice can, in the alternative, be protected as an overriding interest if the person having the benefit of the interest is in actual occupation of the land affected by it.[36]

---

27 The same was true under the LRA 1925: see LRA 1925, s 49(1)(g).

28 LRA 2002, s 32(1) and s 29(2)(a)(i).

29 LRA 2002, s 32(3).

30 LRA 2002, s 33(a).

31 LRA 2002, s 34(2). Application for an agreed notice is made using Form AN1: LRR 2003, r 81. Application for a unilateral notice is by Form UN1: LRR 2003, r 83.

32 LRA 2002, s 34(3).

33 See LRA 2002, s 34(2). It is provided by LRR 2003, r 80, that certain interests can be protected by an agreed notice. None of those interests is relevant for present purposes. However, see para 4.35.

34 LRA 2002, s 35(1). The notice is entered prior to such notification.

35 LRA 2002, s 36.

36 See LRA 2002, ss 29(2)(a)(ii) and 30(2)(a)(ii) and Sch 3, para 2.

Indirect ways to protect priority – priority searches

4.28 In addition to the rules of priority set out above, there is a system of priority searches that enable an intending purchaser to protect a forthcoming purchase of land.[37] In this context, the date upon which an interim charging order is protected by the entry of a notice may be relevant to the exercise of the court's discretion in determining whether that charging order should be made final.[38]

4.29 In one case,[39] A obtained an interim charging order over B's house, the title to which was registered. Shortly afterwards, B contracted to sell the house to C. C made a priority search of the register in respect of the house a few weeks before completion. It expired after completion of the sale but before the transfer from B to C had been registered. After completion, but before the expiry of C's priority search, A applied to register his interim charging order. C could not have known of the charging order when he completed his purchase of the house and C was not given notice of the subsequent hearing at which A's charging order was made absolute. In those circumstances, the Court of Appeal upheld the decision of the county court judge to set aside the charging order. The interim charging order should never have been made absolute because the balance of the equities decisively favoured C as against A.[40]

Restrictions

4.30 As indicated above, interests under trusts cannot be protected by the entry of a notice.[41] The correct mechanism where there are beneficial interests is to ensure that, on any disposition of the land affected by them, the interests are overreached and attach instead to the proceeds of sale. The trustees must then account for the proceeds to the beneficiaries.[42] For overreaching to occur, the

---

37 See LRA 2002, s 72; LRR 2003, r 147 *et seq*.

38 For the exercise of discretion in deciding whether to make an interim charging order final, see Chapter 2, para 2.26 *et seq*.

39 *Howell v Montey* (1990) 61 P & CR 18.

40 *Howell v Montey* (1990) 61 P & CR 18 at 22, where Fox LJ said, 'it does not seem to me to be just to impose upon land of which the purchasers were the absolute beneficial owners, a charge in respect of a debt which they did not incur, for which they had no contractual liability at all, and which charge did not appear on the title to the property when they bought it and of which they had no knowledge at all when they bought the land'.

41 See para 4.25.

42 See LPA 1925, s 105; and para 4.63.

proceeds of the disposition must be paid to the trustees, of whom there must be at least two, unless the trustee is a trust corporation.[43]

4.31 To ensure that overreaching does occur, the Land Registration Act 2002 utilises a form of entry known as a restriction.[44] A restriction is an entry in the register regulating the circumstances in which a disposition of a registered estate or charge may be the subject of an entry in the register.[45] A restriction is usually made on application.[46] When a restriction has been entered in the register, it prevents any entry in the register in respect of a disposition to which it applies except in accordance with the terms of that restriction.[47] The registrar is expressly empowered to enter a restriction for the purpose of securing that an interest that can be overreached on a disposition of a registered estate or charge is overreached.[48]

4.32 An application for a restriction may be made by or with the consent of the registered proprietor (or person entitled to be registered as proprietor) or by a person having a sufficient interest in making the entry.[49] Normally, the application is for a standard form of restriction.[50] These standard forms are set out in Schedule 4 to the Land Registration Rules 2003.

4.33 As explained below, the only means of protecting a charging order over a beneficial interest in land that is held in trust or in a settlement is by means of the entry of a restriction.[51]

---

43 See LPA 1925, ss 2(1) and 27(2); Settled Land Act 1925 (SLA 1925), ss 18(1) and 94. See also *Banwaitt v Dewji* [2015] EWHC 3441 (Ch), where the transfer (by Form TR1, for valuable consideration) by two co-owners A and B, to B alone, was held not to have overreached a charging order over A's share. Notwithstanding the use of a single transfer, the parties' true intention was to transfer A's beneficial share to B, with a subsequent gratuitous transfer of the legal title, such that no overarching had taken place.

44 A Form A restriction which prevents registration of a disposition unless the proceeds of the disposition are paid to two trustees or a trust corporation.

45 LRA 2002, s 40(1).

46 LRA 2002, s 43. Application is normally made using Form RX1: see LRR 2003, r 92.

47 LRA 2002, s 41(1). The registrar is empowered to disapply or modify the restriction: see LRA 2002, s 41(2).

48 LRA 2002, s 42(1)(b).

49 LRA 2002, s 43(1). Note that the Registrar must enter the trust Form A restriction if he thinks there is a trust.

50 *Cf* LRA 2002, s 43(2)(d); and see LRR 2003, r 91.

51 See para 4.38.

Charging orders and applications for charging orders

Protecting charging orders over registered land or registered charge (legal title)

4.34 A charging order over registered land or a registered charge can be protected by a notice. This is due to a combination of section 87(1)(b) of the Land Registration Act 2002, which provides that references in that Act to an interest affecting an estate or charge (which by section 32(1) are protectable by notice) include writs or orders affecting land issued or made by any court for the purposes of enforcing a judgment, and section 3(2) of the Charging Orders Act 1979, which brings charging orders within the scope of section 87(1)(b) of the Land Registration Act 2002.

4.35 A charging order may be protected by means of either a unilateral notice or an agreed notice.[52] Because the application will be supported by the court order, the registrar should be satisfied as to the validity of the applicant's claim, and so register an agreed notice.[53] The advantage of such a registration is that the notice cannot be cancelled unless and until the registrar is satisfied that the interest has come to an end,[54] which would only be the case where the charging order has been discharged. Even if the charging order is registered as a unilateral notice,[55] the registered proprietor would in practice be unsuccessful in any application to cancel the unilateral notice while the charging order subsisted, unless the judgment creditor failed to object to that application. There would in those circumstances be no grounds for its removal. The chief risk for a judgment creditor who uses a unilateral rather than agreed notice might, therefore, lie in the consequences of their failure to object to removal of the notice but this alone is not a reason to seek an agreed rather than unilateral notice.

4.36 It is not possible for a charging order to be protected as an overriding interest (i.e. by virtual of actual occupation).[56]

Protecting charging orders over beneficial interests

4.37 Neither an interest under a trust or settlement of land nor a charging order over such interest can be protected by a notice.[57]

---

52 See HM Land Registry, *Practice Guide 76: charging orders* (15 August 2022), para 3.2.

53 See LRA 2002, s 34(3); see also para 4.26.

54 LRR 2003, r 87.

55 Pursuant to LRA 2002, s 36.

56 LRA 2002, s 87(3).

57 LRA 2002, s 33(a).

4.38 Instead, the Land Registration Act 2002 makes specific provision for the entry of a restriction where a charging order is made over such a beneficial interest. The registrar is empowered to enter a restriction if it is necessary or desirable for the purpose of protecting a right or claim in relation to a registered estate or charge.[58] The Act provides that a person who is entitled to the benefit of a charging order relating to an interest under a trust is to be treated as having a right or claim in relation to the trust property.[59]

4.39 The purpose of a restriction where land is held in trust is to ensure that overreaching takes place. The judgment creditor wishes to ensure that his monetary claim against the debtor can be met out of the proceeds of any disposition of the land subject to the trust to which the trusts will attach after the disposition. It might have been expected that an appropriate form of restriction would be devised to meet this need. However, this has not happened.

4.40 There is a standard form of restriction that has been prescribed for the situation where there is a charging order over a beneficial interest under a trust or settlement of land,[60] namely the restriction in Form K of Schedule 4 to the Land Registration Rules 2003.[61] This restriction prohibits the registration of the registered estate or charge subject to the trust without a certificate, signed by the applicant for registration or their conveyancer, that written notice of the disposition was given to the judgment creditor who has the benefit of the interim or final charging order.

4.41 As a means of protecting the judgment creditor, the Form K restriction is ineffective, because it does not require written notice to the judgment creditor to be given prior to the making of the disposition. This means that he may find that, by the time he has been notified of the disposition, the proceeds of the sale of the property have been dissipated and are not available to satisfy his debt. Because the trusts will have been overreached, the judgment creditor will no longer have

---

58 LRA 2002, s 42(1)(c).

59 LRA 2002, s 42(4).

60 See LRR 2003, r 93(k); Sch 4, Form K.

61 'Charging order affecting beneficial interest – certificate required'. Form K is as follows:

> No disposition of the
>
> *[choose whichever bulleted clause is appropriate]*
>
> – registered estate, other than a disposition by the proprietor of any registered charge registered before the entry of this restriction,
>
> – registered charge dated *[date]* referred to above, other than a disposition by the proprietor of any registered sub-charge of that charge registered before the entry of this restriction,
>
> is to be registered without a certificate signed by the applicant for registration or their conveyancer that written notice of the disposition was given to *[name of person with the benefit of the charging order]* at *[address for service]*, being the person with the benefit of *[an interim or a final]* charging order on the beneficial interest of *[name of judgment debtor]* made by the *[name of court]* on *[date]* (Court reference *[insert reference]*).

any form of security, even if the proceeds of the disposition have been applied in the purchase of another property.

4.42 The undemanding nature of the Form K restriction has been heavily criticised.[62] One consequence of the Form K restriction's shortcomings is that, at the hearing when the court decides whether an interim charging order should be made final, the judgment creditor often also seeks an order from the court for the entry of a non-standard restriction to protect the charging order.[63] The non-standard form of restriction that is normally sought is that notice should be given to the judgment creditor a sufficient period prior to the disposition – usually a period of 14 days – to enable him to take steps to protect his interest.[64] However, the Law Commission has recommended that this practice should stop, and that the legislation make clear that the form of restriction must be Form K.[65]

4.43 If a judgment creditor with only a charge over a beneficial share does find himself in the position where a sale has been effected in compliance with Form K, then it may well be that (regardless of whether overreaching has occurred) the creditor acquires a security interest in the sale proceeds, entitling him to restrain their dissipation.[66] If the proceeds have already been dissipated, it is less clear that the judgment creditor can pursue third parties who were previously holding them, in particular, the judgment debtor's solicitors who may have paid out those proceeds to the judgment debtor. It is far from clear that such a person as the solicitor would without more themselves be under any trust-like duty to pay the

---

62 See e.g. *Civil Procedure 2023* (Sweet & Maxwell, 2023), Vol 1, at para 73.4.3.1, although the Law Commission's view is that it gives an adequate level of protection, and that additional control should not be given to creditors. See Law Commission, *Updating the Land Registration Act 2002*, Law Com No 380 (2018), at para 10.94.

63 The court has power to require the registrar to enter a restriction in the register if it appears to the court to be necessary or desirable for the purpose of protecting a right or claim: LRA 2002, s 46(1).

64 *Civil Procedure 2023* (Sweet & Maxwell, 2023), Vol 1 at para 73.4.3.1.

65 See Law Commission, *Updating the Land Registration Act 2002*, Law Com No 380 (2018), at para 10.97.

66 *Buhr v Barclays Bank Plc* [2001] EWCA Civ 1223, although see *Menelaou v Bank of Cyprus* [2012] EWHC 1991 (Ch) at [15], per David Donaldson QC, sitting as a Deputy High Court Judge, in which it was suggested that the decision in *Buhr* may not apply where the mortgagee has consented to the sale. The Court of Appeal and Supreme Court in *Menelaou* declined to consider the true ratio of *Buhr*. *Buhr* might also be distinguished on the basis that a charging order takes effect as a mere charge, rather than an equitable mortgage (as was considered in *Buhr*). This ought not to matter, however. See *Amari Lifestyle ltd v Warnes* [2017] EWHC 1891 (Ch) at [32], where it was said that, 'the essential characteristic of an equitable charge is that the owner of the property assumes an obligation to deal with that specific property for the benefit of the creditor, so that the creditor has a security interest in the property, and can require that, when sold, the proceeds of sale are to be appropriated to the payment of the debt [owed] to the creditor' (per Stephen Jourdan QC, sitting as a Deputy High Court Judge). The person with a charging order ought to have a sufficient proprietary interest in the proceeds of sale to restrain their dissipation.

proceeds over to the judgment creditor, for example under the constructive trust suggested in *Buhr & Others v Barclays Bank Plc*.[67] The agent of a constructive trustee does not become himself a constructive trustee when he simply holds the proceeds to the trustee's order and when he does what the trustee directs, even if he knows of another call on the money. He may however be liable if, knowing of the trust, and without the trustee's instructions, he acts inconsistently with the trust. Alternatively, the solicitor may be liable for dishonest assistance if he induces or assists in the breach of trust which occurs when the trustee deals with the proceeds without paying the judgment creditor with the benefit of a charging order, if the solicitor does so dishonestly, for example perhaps were he positively to advise the trustee not to pay.

4.44 Quite apart from the inadequacies of the Form K restriction, the protection given by a charging order over a beneficial interest in land is inherently weak. This weakness is particularly apparent where the disposition takes the form of a legal charge over the property which is subject to the trust. Although often any such charge may secure a further advance by the legal chargee, out of which the judgment creditor could be satisfied, it could alternatively secure some pre-existing indebtedness without there being any payment to the registered proprietors of the land. If the legal charge is executed by all the legal owners of the land held in trust, of whom there must be at least two (unless the legal title is vested in a trust corporation),[68] that charge will overreach all beneficial interests, even if no capital monies arise at the time when the charge is made. In this situation, the judgment creditor does not even have the possibility that his debt will be satisfied out of an advance by the legal chargee.

Should issues as to trust ownership be determined at the charging order or enforcement stage?

4.45 One issue which can arise is whether a court should determine disputes as to trust ownership of property at the charging order stage or the enforcement stage. Of course, any such issues can only be resolved if the person asserting the beneficial interest and their claim are known.[69] Assuming that is so, then

---

67 In *Buhr & Others v Barclays Bank Plc* [2001] EWCA Civ 1223, this was conceded (see [44]) by the chargor's solicitors if the court found (as it did) that the chargeholder had a proprietary interest in the proceeds of sale. It is hard to see how, without more, the solicitor as his principal's agent could be fixed with being a constructive trustee for someone with a charging order over a beneficial interest.

68 See LPA 1925, ss 2(1)(ii) and 27(2).

69 The register of title can often indicate the existence of third party beneficial interests. In particular, if there is a sole registered proprietor, the presence of a Form A, B, C, Q or II restriction; or joint proprietors, a Form B, C or K restriction. See HM Land Registry, *Practice Guide 76: charging orders* (15 August 2022), paras 3.1.1.1 and 3.1.2.1.

(notwithstanding the usual practice of some judges to the contrary) it is suggested that such issues are best determined at the earlier, charging order stage.[70]

4.46 The contrary approach carries risks for both the judgment creditor (who may otherwise proceed to enforcement only to find himself without security, or security worth considerably less than he had believed) and the person asserting the beneficial interest (who may find himself facing an allegation of abuse of process for failing to conclusively establish his interest when he could have done so earlier).[71] Moreover, although judges sometimes take the view that a charging order wrongly noted on the legal title does no harm, it may in practice affect the owner's ability to remortgage or make other dispositions.

Protecting applications for charging orders over land or registered charge (legal title)

4.47 Section 87(1)(a) of the Land Registration Act 2002 extends that Act's definition of an 'interest affecting an estate or charge' (which, as seen above, can be protected by notice) to include a pending land action within the meaning of the Land Charges Act 1972.

4.48 A pending land action is an action or proceeding in court in which the claimant claims some proprietary right in the land.[72] Its purpose is to put on notice any purchaser 'that there is a dispute that might affect the title to the land' of which he would not otherwise have any means of knowing.[73]

4.49 On this basis, an application for a charging order over either a legal estate in land or a legal mortgage or charge is registrable as a pending land action, because it is a claim to a proprietary right in the land, mortgage or charge. As it falls within these words, an application for a charging order over a registered estate or charge is an 'interest' for the purposes of the Land Registration Act 2002 and so can be protected by the entry of a notice.[74]

4.50 Although it will seldom be necessary to protect an application for a charging order in this way, it would be prudent to do so where the judgment

---

70 See *McLinden v Lu* [2022] EWHC 2807 (Ch) at [14] and [31], per Deputy Master Bowles; *Rosseel N.V. v Oriental Commercial and Shipping (UK) Ltd* [1991] 10 WLUK 97.

71 See *McLinden v Lu* [2022] EWHC 2807 (Ch), where it was ultimately decided that there had been no abuse of process.

72 *Calgary and Edmonton Land Co Ltd v Dobinson* [1974] Ch 102 at 107, per Megarry J.

73 *Godfrey v Torpey* [2006] EWHC 1423 (Ch), [2007] BPIR 1063 at [6], per Peter Smith J.

74 See HM Land Registry, *Practice Guide 19: notices, restrictions and the protection of third-party interests in the register* (20 February 2023), Appendix A, para 6.1.

creditor has grounds to think that some other disposition of the land in question is about to be made.

Protecting applications for charging orders over beneficial interests

4.51 Conversely, an application for a charging order over a form of beneficial interest under a trust of land or settlement (such as a life interest) is not a pending land action.[75] A beneficial interest is not within the scope of the definition of 'land' (or therefore 'pending land action') under the Land Charges Act 1972.[76] As such, the priority of this type of application cannot be protected.

Unregistered land

4.52 Where land is unregistered the priority rules can be summarised as follows:

(a) the basic rule is that estates and interests rank in order of creation (i.e. the first in time prevails;
(b) however, a bona fide purchaser of a legal estate for value will take priority over prior equitable interests, provided he did not have notice thereof.

4.53 However, these rules were considerably modified by the Land Charges Act 1972, which requires registration of many rights over unregistered land (as opposed to the land itself).

4.54 The benefit of registration under the Land Charges Act 1972 is that (by section 198 of the Law of Property Act 1925) registration is generally[77] deemed to constitute actual notice of the instrument or matter which has been registered. There are, however, potentially serious consequences if a right is not registered when the 1972 Act requires it to be, which are prescribed by the Act.

---

75 See HM Land Registry, *Practice Guide 19: notices, restrictions and the protection of third-party interests in the register* (20 February 2023), Appendix A, para 6.1.

76 The definition of 'land' in the LCA 1972 excludes an undivided share in land; LCA 1972, s 17(1); *Perry v Phoenix Assurance plc* [1988] 1 WLR 940. Moreover, under the 1972 Act, registration of the land charge has to be against the name of the estate owner or other person whose estate or interest is intended to be affected. However, the legal owner's estate or interest will not be affected by the application, which is concerned only with obtaining security over a beneficial interest under a trust of land or settlement. Any such beneficial interest can be overreached on any sale of the land which complies with the statutory requirements as to payment of the purchase price. For those requirements, see LPA 1925, ss 2(1) and 27(2); SLA 1925, ss 18(1) and 94. See also *Perry v Phoenix Assurance plc* [1988] 1 WLR 940 at 945.

77 The exceptions are set out in LPA 1925, ss 94(1)(c) and 96(2).

4.55 The registrability of each type of interest within the scope of this book is as follows:

(a) *Charging orders over legal estate or charge*: a charging order made against a legal estate or charge is one of the rights which the 1972 Act requires to be registered. It falls within the scope of section 6 of the 1972 Act in the register of writs and orders affecting land. Registration is made in the name of the estate owner or other person whose land is affected by the charging order.[78] By section 6(4), if the charging order is not so registered, it is void as against a purchaser of the land, whether that purchaser acquires a legal or equitable interest.[79]
(b) *Applications for charging orders over legal estate or charge*: where a person has applied for a charging order over an estate in or a legal charge over unregistered land, that application is a pending land action.[80] It can therefore be protected by registration as a land charge in the register of pending actions.[81] Registration is again in the name of the estate owner or other person whose estate or interest is intended to be affected.[82] Such a pending land action will not bind 'a purchaser without express notice of it' unless it is registered in this way,[83] and for these purposes, 'purchaser' means 'any person (including a mortgagee or lessee) who, for valuable consideration, takes any interest in land or in a charge on land'.[84] It will be noted that a 'purchaser' for these purposes does not have to acquire a legal estate or interest, but merely an interest. An application for a charging order could therefore be defeated if, before the charging order was made, the land to which the application relates was sold, or it could lose its priority, if the land was mortgaged. However, for reasons already given, it is unlikely that the application will in practice be so registered.[85]

---

78 LCA 1972, s 6(2). Application to register the charging order is made on Form K4 under Land Charges Rules 1974 (SI 1974/1286), r 5.

79 LCA 1972, s 6(4). For the meaning of 'purchaser', see LCA 1972, s 17(1).

80 See para 4.48.

81 LCA 1972, s 5(1)(a).

82 LCA 1972, s 5(4). Application to register the pending land action is made on Form K3 under Land Charges Rules 1974, r 5.

83 LCA 1972, s 5(7). An error in the name registered does not invalidate the registration if the name given may fairly be called a version of the correct name; but a purchaser who searches in the correct name is protected even if it fails to reveal an entry: *Oak Co-Operative Building Society v Blackburn* [1968] Ch 730.

84 LCA 1972, s 17(1).

85 See para 4.50.

(c) *Charging orders over interests under a trust of land*: a charging order over an interest under a trust of land cannot be registered as a land charge in the register of writs and orders affecting land because the Land Charges Act 1972 expressly prohibits it.[86] Nor would it appear to be possible to register a charging order over an interest under a Settled Land Act 1925 settlement, because the charge has to be registered in the name of the estate owner or other person whose land is affected by the charging order.[87] However, the land itself is not affected at all by the charging order, but only the beneficial interest in it.

(d) *Applications for charging orders over interest under trust of land*: for much the same reasons as at para 4.51 (which considers protection of such applications in relation to registered land), it does not appear possible to register such an application.

4.56 Almost any disposition of the legal estate will now trigger the requirement of compulsory first registration of title under the Land Registration Act 2002.[88] A person with a beneficial interest under a trust or settlement of unregistered land has standing under that Act to apply for a caution against the first registration of the land in which he has an interest.[89] Once a caution against first registration has been registered in the cautions register kept by HM Land Registry,[90] if there is any application to register the legal estate which is the subject of the caution, the registrar must give the cautioner notice of the application and of his right to object to it.[91] The registrar cannot determine the application for first registration before the end of 15 business days,[92] unless the cautioner has exercised his right to object to the application or given the registrar notice that he does not intend to do so.[93] The registration of a caution against first registration has no effect on the validity or priority of any interest of the cautioner in the legal estate to which the caution relates.[94] It is simply a procedure by which a person can be alerted to a disposition that triggers first registration, thereby enabling that person to take steps to protect his interest in an appropriate way.

---

86 LCA 1972, s 6(1A).

87 LCA 1972, s 6(2)

88 See LRA 2002, s 4(1) (as amended).

89 LRA 2002, s 15(1)(b) and (2). Application for such a caution is by means of HM Land Registry Form CT1: see LRR 2003, r 42.

90 See LRA 2002, s 19(1); LRR 2003, rr 39–41.

91 LRA 2002, s 16(1).

92 See LRR 2003, r 53.

93 LRA 2002, s 16(2).

94 LRA 2002, s 16(3).

Priority of charging orders in relation to subsequent disposition

4.57 In the light of the principles set out above, the effect of any subsequent disposition of land which is subject to a charging order that has not been registered in the register of writs and orders affecting land under the Land Charges Act 1972,[95] may be summarised as follows.

4.58 First, where the charging order was made against a legal estate or charge and could therefore have been registered as a land charge under the Land Charges Act 1972, but was not, it will be void as against a purchaser of the land, whether that purchaser acquires a legal or equitable interest in the land.

4.59 Secondly, where the charging order was made against a beneficial interest, so that it could not be registered as a land charge under the Land Charges Act 1972, the position is as follows:

(a) The charging order will have priority over any subsequent disposition of the beneficial interest charged, because the charging order would be first in time, and the usual equitable rule as to priorities would apply.
(b) Any disposition of the legal estate that the trustees or life tenant had power to make would overreach the beneficial interests under the trust so that the charging order would apply instead to the proceeds of sale of that disposition, provided the statutory requirements for overreaching were met.[96]

4.60 The difficulty which faces any judgment creditor in relation to point (b) is that he is unlikely to be aware that any disposition has taken place. However, there is one form of protection that is available to the judgment creditor in this situation that will normally ensure that he is alerted to an overreaching disposition having taken place.

Priority of charging orders in relation to subsisting interests

4.61 As already explained, a judgment creditor who obtains a charging order is not a purchaser, but is treated as a volunteer. It must follow that the judgment creditor will always be bound by any prior interest in the land or beneficial interest over which he obtains his charging order, including any prior charging order. This will be so even if that interest was registrable under the Land Charges Act 1972 but had not been so registered. Under the provisions of that Act, an interest or matter that is capable of registration as a land charge will be void against a

---

95 That is LCA 1972, s 6(1)(a).

96 See LPA 1925, ss 2(1)(i) and (ii) and 27(2); SLA 1925, s 94.

purchaser for non-registration.[97] A judgment creditor who has obtained a charging order cannot be a purchaser for these purposes because he does not take a charge on land for valuable consideration as the Act requires:[98] 'the debtor receives no consideration from the judgment creditor at the time that the charge is created'.[99]

CHARGING ORDERS, MORTGAGES AND SALES

4.62 Two specific issues arise where land is subject to a mortgage and a charging order, namely:

(a) What is the situation where a mortgagee exercises its power of sale?
(b) What is the situation where the judgment creditor obtains an order for sale?

The same principles govern both situations.

Where the mortgagee exercises its power of sale

4.63 Where a mortgagee exercises its power of sale, it holds the proceeds of sale upon a statutory trust, imposed by section 105 of the Law of Property Act 1925, to apply them in the order set out in the section.[100] That order is as follows:

(a) First, in discharge of any prior incumbrances or by a payment into court of a sum to meet any prior incumbrances.
(b) Secondly, in payment of all costs, charges, and expenses that were properly incurred by the mortgagee as incident to the sale or any attempted sale, or otherwise.
(c) Thirdly, in discharge of the mortgage money, interest, and costs, and other money, if any, due under the mortgage.
(d) Fourthly, if there is any residue, that should be paid to the person entitled to the mortgaged property, or authorised to give receipts for the proceeds of the sale of that property.

---

97 Precisely what type of purchaser will defeat the unregistered interest or matter is not uniform under the LCA 1972, but varies from land charge to land charge. In some cases, the purchaser must be a purchaser of a legal estate. In other cases, it is enough that he is a purchaser of *some* interest. In some cases, it suffices that the purchase is for valuable consideration, whereas in others, the purchase must have been for money or money's worth.

98 See the definition of 'purchaser' in LCA 1972, s 17(1).

99 *United Bank of Kuwait plc v Sahib* [1997] Ch 107 at 119, per Chadwick J.

100 See also Chapter 6, para 6.122.

4.64 It follows from this that, if the charging order has priority over the mortgage under which the property is sold, which will only be the case where the charging order pre-dated the mortgage and had been appropriately protected in the relevant register (or in the case of registered land, if the mortgage is merely equitable and later in time), the mortgagee must first apply the proceeds of sale in discharge of the debt secured by the charging order.

4.65 Where the title to the land is unregistered, the charging order will only be protected if it is registered as a land charge in the register of writs and orders affecting land.[101] Such registration is important for another reason. It constitutes notice of the charging order to all persons and for all purposes connected with the land affected.[102] Accordingly, even if the charging order does not have priority over the mortgage under which the property is sold, its registration serves as notice to any prior mortgagee of the charge. A mortgagee who holds any residue of the proceeds of sale after payment of the first three matters listed at para 4.63 must, therefore, check the registers kept under the Land Charges Act 1972 to see if there are any charging orders. This is because the judgment creditor will have priority over the mortgagor (at least where the charging order is final) and will therefore be entitled to be paid out of the surplus in preference to the mortgagor.[103] Even if the registration of a charging order did not provide notice to the selling mortgagee, that mortgagee is a trustee of the surplus by reason of section 105 of the Law of Property Act 1925, and as such, it is his duty 'to ascertain the parties entitled to the trust fund, the shares of the fund to which they are respectively entitled and to distribute the fund accordingly'.[104]

4.66 Where the title to the land is registered, a charging order over the land will only be protected so to have priority over the subsequent mortgage if it is the subject of a notice in the register. It is specifically provided by section 54 of the Land Registration Act 2002 that, for the purposes of section 105 of the Law of Property Act 1925, the mortgagee is taken to have notice of anything in the register immediately before the disposition on sale.

---

101 LCA 1972, s 6(1).

102 LPA 1925, s 198(1).

103 For the position where the charging order that has been registered is merely an interim and not a final order, see para 4.73.

104 *Re Thompson's Mortgage Trusts* [1920] 1 Ch 508 at 514, per Eve J. The provisions of s 105 do not require the mortgagee having to determine the priority entitlement of subsequent incumbrancers. The whole of the surplus remaining in the mortgagee's hands is paid to the next incumbrancer.

Where the judgment creditor obtains an order for sale

4.67 The Law of Property Act 1925 defines 'mortgage' widely so as to include 'any charge or lien on any property for securing money or money's worth'.[105] Accordingly, where a judgment creditor, whose debt is secured by a charging order, obtains an order for the sale of the property affected, the trust imposed on a selling mortgagee by section 105 of that Act applies equally to him. The rules set out at paras 4.63–4.66, in relation to the case where a mortgagee sells, apply equally to a judgment creditor who sells the charged property.

OTHER PRIORITY PROBLEMS

4.68 The remainder of this chapter addresses four other issues of priority that may arise in relation to charging orders.

Priority of charging orders when the judgment debtor becomes insolvent

4.69 Where the judgment debtor is adjudicated bankrupt[106] or enters into liquidation,[107] the following statutory restrictions apply:[108]

---

105 LPA 1925, s 205(1)(xvi).

106 The bankruptcy commences on the day on which the bankruptcy order is made not the presentation of the petition for bankruptcy: IA 1986, s 278; *Nationwide Building Society v Wright* [2009] EWCA Civ 811, [2010] Ch 318.

107 In a case where a company is wound up by the court (except where there has been an earlier resolution for voluntary winding-up, when the winding-up is deemed to have commenced at the time of the passing of the resolution) the winding-up is deemed to commence at the time of the presentation of the petition for winding-up: IA 1986, s 129(2).

108 In addition to the matters set out in the text, the following should be noted: (a) where a petition for bankruptcy is issued the court may stay any action, execution or other legal process against the property of the judgment debtor: IA 1986, s 285; (b) after the presentation of a winding-up petition and before a winding-up order has been made, the company and any creditor may apply to restrain any proceedings: IA 1986, s 126(1); (c) a resolution for voluntary winding-up does not operate as a stay of proceedings, or invalidate executions or prevent claims or other proceedings being brought or continued against the company. The court has, however, jurisdiction to stay any claim or execution against the company upon such terms as it thinks fit: *Westbury v Twigg & Co Ltd* [1892] 1 QB 77; (d) where a company is wound up by the court any execution put in force against the estate or effects of the company after the commencement of the winding-up is void: IA 1986, s 128(1).

See also Chapter 2, paras 2.33–2.44 and, for a more detailed discussion as to the restrictions upon commencing and pursuing an application for a charging order upon the insolvency of the judgment debtor, Chapter 3, para 3.119.

(a) Where the judgment debtor is adjudicated bankrupt, the creditor is not entitled, as against the official receiver or trustee in bankruptcy, to retain the benefit of any execution against land of the judgment debtor unless he has completed the execution before the commencement of the bankruptcy.[109] The court may permit the judgment creditor to retain the benefit of the execution.[110]

(b) Where the judgment debtor is a company which is subsequently wound up, the creditor is not, as against the liquidator, entitled to retain the benefit of any execution against land of the company unless he has completed the execution before the commencement of the winding-up.[111] The court may permit the judgment creditor to retain the benefit of the execution.[112]

4.70 For the purpose of these statutory provisions, the execution process is not complete unless the charging order is made final.[113] However, these provisions only come into play *after* a charging order has been made final,[114] and restrict the right of the creditor only as against the official receiver, trustee in bankruptcy or liquidator. Where the charging order is made final before a bankruptcy order is made, the judgment creditor is not to be deprived, by the exercise of the general power to discharge a charging order,[115] of the benefit of his security by reason of the bankruptcy alone.[116]

4.71 If a creditor has obtained an interim charging order,[117] but before it can be made final, a bankruptcy order is made against the judgment debtor or, if the debtor is a company, the company is put into liquidation, should the court in its discretion[118] make the charging order final, or should it discharge it? If the charging order is discharged, the judgment creditor will be an unsecured creditor in the bankruptcy or liquidation, thereby losing the priority that the interim order

---

109 IA 1986, s 346(1). By s 346(5)(b), it is provided that, 'an execution against land is completed by ... the making of a charging order' under COA 1979, s 1.

110 IA 1986, s 346(6).

111 IA 1986, s 183. By s 183(3)(c) it is provided that, 'an execution against land is completed by ... the making of a charging order' under COA 1979, s 1.

112 IA 1986, s 183(2)(c).

113 *Roberts Petroleum Ltd v Bernard Kenny Ltd (In Liquidation)* [1983] 2 AC 192 at 212 and 213B, HL, per Lord Brightman (based on the now-repealed Companies Act 1948, s 325, which was similar to IA 1986, s 183). See also *Clarke v Coutts & Co (A Firm)* [2002] EWCA Civ 943, [2002] BPIR 916 at [39], per Peter Gibson LJ (in the context of the provisions of IA 1986, s 252, relating to an interim order for an IVA).

114 *Roberts Petroleum Ltd v Bernard Kenny Ltd (In Liquidation)* [1983] 2 AC 192 at 212G–H, HL.

115 Under COA 1979, s 3(5).

116 *Nationwide Building Society v Wright* [2009] EWCA Civ 811, [2010] Ch 318.

117 An interim charging order is made without a hearing: see CPR r 73.4(1).

118 See COA 1979, s 1(5), Chapter 2, paras 2.38–2.44.

had (provisionally and defeasibly) given him.[119] On bankruptcy or liquidation, a statutory scheme comes into existence for dealing with the assets of the insolvent person or company.[120] If an interim charging order could be made final after that event, the asset subject to the order would fall outside that statutory scheme.

4.72 In relation to a charging order that had been obtained under the legislation prior to the Charging Orders Act 1979, it had been held by the House of Lords that, in those circumstances, a court, in exercising its discretion, should normally decline to make the charging order final. In the absence of any other factors, the imposition of the statutory scheme on insolvency was a sufficient reason for refusing to make the interim charging order final.[121] Admittedly, the wording of the relevant legislation was notably different from the present provisions.[122]

4.73 The Charging Orders Act 1979 does provide specifically that, in deciding whether to make a charging order the court must consider all the circumstances of the case, including, in particular, whether any other creditor of the debtor would be likely to be unduly prejudiced by the making of the order.[123] It has not been finally decided whether there is any legal or evidential burden upon the judgment debtor to show cause why an interim charging order should not be made final.[124]

---

119 *Cf Roberts Petroleum Ltd v Bernard Kenny Ltd (In Liquidation)* [1983] 2 AC 192 at 205, HL, per Lord Brightman. See also *Clarke v Coutts & Co (A Firm)* [2002] EWCA Civ 943, [2002] BPIR 916 at [39], per Peter Gibson LJ.

120 Where one of two or more joint tenants is adjudicated bankrupt, the joint tenancy is severed when his property is vested in his trustee in bankruptcy: *Bedson v Bedson* [1965] 2 QB 666 at 690; *Re Rushton* [1972] Ch 197 at 283; *Re Gorman* [1990] 1 WLR 616 at 620. Where there are joint proprietors, it is only the bankrupt's beneficial interest that vests in the trustee in bankruptcy: IA 1986, s 283(1)(a).

121 *Roberts Petroleum Ltd v Bernard Kenny Ltd (In Liquidation)* [1983] 2 AC 192, HL (a case involving the voluntary winding-up of the judgment debtor).

122 See *National Guild of Removers and Storers Ltd v Jones* [2012] EWCA Civ 216, [2012] 1 WLR 2501 at [13]–[14]. RSC Ord 50, r 1(6) provided that a court, in considering whether to make the charging order final, should, 'unless it appears ... that there is sufficient cause to the contrary, make the order absolute with or without modifications'. The application of the respective statutory schemes on insolvency was held in *Roberts Petroleum Ltd v Bernard Kenny Ltd (In Liquidation)* [1983] 2 AC 192, HL to be 'sufficient cause to the contrary'.

123 COA 1979, s 1(5)(b). It is not enough that other creditors will be prejudiced, because a charging order will invariably have that effect. The prejudice must be 'undue': see *British Arab Commercial Bank plc v Algosaibi and Bros Co* [2011] EWHC 2444 (Comm), [2011] 2 CLC 736.

124 See *National Guild of Removers and Storers Ltd v Jones* [2012] EWCA Civ 216, [2012] 1 WLR 2501 at [16], per Pitchford LJ. However, the Court of Appeal's attention was not drawn to earlier authority, including a previous decision of the Court of Appeal, *Rosseel NV v Oriental Commercial and Shipping (UK) Ltd*, 8 October 1991, briefly reported at [1991] EGCS 94, and followed in *Midland Bank plc v Wyatt* [1997] 1 BCLC 242, in which it was held that, 'the burden of showing cause why a charging order nisi should not be made absolute lies on the judgment debtor or a third party and not, in any event, on the judgment creditor': *Habib Bank Ltd v Ahmed* [2003] EWHC 1697 (QB), [2004] BPIR 35 at [28], per Simon J.

However, although the wording of the legislation has changed, the former approach is still followed in practice,[125] and the courts are likely to regard supervening or impending[126] insolvency after the making of an interim charging order as a ground for refusing to making the order final in most cases, just as they did under the statutory regime that applied prior to the 1979 Act.[127]

4.74 The fact that the judgment debtor has become insolvent is not in itself a bar to the court exercising its statutory discretion as to whether to make the charging order final.[128] Furthermore, where the relevant statutory regime does not apply, as where the insolvent judgment debtor is domiciled outside the United Kingdom, the considerations set out above do not apply, and the court will generally make the charging order final unless to do so would cause undue prejudice to other creditors.[129]

---

125 See e.g. *Re a Debtor (Nos 31/32/33 of 1993), Calor Gas Ltd v Piercy* [1994] BCC 69 at 80, where HHJ Paul Baker QC, after referring to *Roberts Petroleum Ltd v Bernard Kenny Ltd (In Liquidation)* [1983] 2 AC 192, HL, said, 'I take that still to be the law, despite the changes in statute law since that time'. See also *JGD Construction Ltd v Mills* [2013] EWHC 572 (Ch), which concerned the discretion to make a third party debt order final.

126 It is clear that the principle expressed in *Roberts Petroleum Ltd v Bernard Kenny Ltd (In Liquidation)* [1983] 2 AC 192, HL does apply where the insolvency of the judgment debtor is pending, for example, where, after the interim order, a bankruptcy petition is served: see at 209H–201E, where Lord Brightman referred with approval to a number of decisions where a final order was refused, the judgment debtor having become prospectively subject to a statutory scheme applicable to insolvency. However, in *JGD Construction Ltd v Mills* [2013] EWHC 572 (Ch), HHJ McCahill QC, sitting as a Judge of the High Court considered (at [39]) there to be a 'spectrum of insolvency' (with the issuing of a statutory demand at one end, and a compulsory winding-up order of considerable duration at the other), with the weight of the argument for or against ordering a final charging order varying accordingly. See also *Industrial Diseases Compensation Ltd v Marrons* [2001] BPIR 600 (garnishee application, but the principles are the same); *Nationwide Building Society v Wright* [2009] EWCA Civ 811, [2010] Ch 318 at [25] and [26]. Where insolvency is pending, the appropriate course is for the judge to adjourn the application for the order to be made absolute until after the hearing of the bankruptcy petition: *Nationwide Building Society* at [26]. The court may refuse to make an interim order final in view of the judgment debtor's impending bankruptcy even though no petition for bankruptcy has yet been served: *Sandhu v Sidhu* [2011] EWHC 3675 (Ch). See also Chapter 2, para 2.38.

127 See e.g. *National Westminster Bank plc v Caldeira* [1999] CLY 3225 (Hull County Court).

128 See *Re a Debtor (Nos 31/32/33 of 1993), Calor Gas Ltd v Piercy* [1994] BCC 69. The case was an exceptional one because all the other creditors of the judgment debtor were only creditors for small sums, so that on administration and sale by the trustee in bankruptcy, they would only receive a very small sum. Accordingly, the judge was able to conclude that they would not be 'unduly prejudiced' within the meaning of COA 1979, s 1(5) if the order were made absolute in favour of the judgment creditor.

129 *British Arab Commercial Bank plc v Algosaibi and Bros Co* [2011] EWHC 2444 (Comm), [2011] 2 CLC 736.

Where a company debtor enters a moratorium under Part A1 of the Insolvency Act 1986

4.75 As set out in more detail in Chapter 8, Part A1 of the Insolvency Act 1986, introduced by the Corporate Insolvency and Governance Act 2020, has created a new moratorium procedure for companies to obtain a moratorium giving it protection from certain creditors during the moratorium, subject to the oversight of a monitor.

4.76 The company is placed under restrictions as to the disposal of its property. By section A29(5), property subject to a security interest may only be disposed of in accordance with the terms of the security, or section A31(1).

4.77 Section A31 is an important provision because it sets out that the company may, with the permission of the court, dispose of property which is subject to a security interest as if it were not subject to the security interest (although permission will only be granted if the sale will support the rescue of the company as a going concern).

4.78 Where permission is given in relation to property subject to a fixed charge, section A31(3) provides that the company must apply: (a) the net proceeds of disposal; and (b) any money required to be added to the net proceeds so as to produce the amount determined by the court as the net amount which would be realised on a sale of the property in the open market by a willing vendor, to discharging the sums secured. Failing to comply with section A31(3) is an offence by the company and also by any officer of the company who authorised or permitted the failure without reasonable excuse.

4.79 Where the permission relates to multiple security interests, section A31(4) provides that the money has to be applied in the order of priority of the security interests.

Inherent jurisdiction to remove register entries

4.80 In a similar vein (although not limited to corporate borrowers), the court has an inherent jurisdiction to vacate any entry on the register which is unaffected the enactment of the Land Registration Act 2002 and applies to both restrictions[130] and notices.[131]

---

130 *Quay House Admirals Way Land Ltd v Rockwell Properties Ltd* [2022] EWHC 545 (Ch) (although permission to appeal has been granted).

131 *Nugent v Nugent* [2013] EWHC 4095 (Ch), [2015] Ch 121, which concerned a unilateral notice.

4.81 Where there is no good arguable claim or the entry is without substance, then the court should order the vacation of the entry. However, where there is a good arguable claim to the entry, the test to be applied is the test which governs the granting of an interim injunction (i.e. whether there is a serious issue to be tried, whether an award of damages would be an adequate remedy and consideration of where the balance of convenience lies). The court is likely to require an undertaking in damages from the party seeking to have the entry vacated.

4.82 In an appropriate case, this could facilitate the sale of a property free from a charging order over it or the beneficial interest.

Where an interim charging order is never made final

4.83 Another troublesome situation arises where an interim charging order is never made final because it cannot be. This might happen, for example, where a mortgagee of a property, which was subject to an interim charging order over which the legal charge had priority, exercised its power of sale before the judgment creditor could obtain a final order. As already explained,[132] the selling mortgagee is a trustee and is obliged to pay any surplus following the discharge of its mortgage to the person entitled to the mortgaged property.[133] If there is another secured creditor whose security ranks behind the mortgage, that person would therefore be entitled to the mortgaged property. If that person's security is defeasible, as will be the case with an interim charging order, the mortgagee cannot be sure that the creditor is in fact the person entitled to the mortgaged property.[134]

4.84 In the circumstances set out at para 4.83, the mortgagee will be well advised to pay the surplus into court pursuant to section 63 of the Trustee Act

---

132 See para 4.63.

133 See LPA 1925, s 105.

134 There appears to be no authority on this point.

1925.[135] That will be a good discharge for the mortgagee.[136] The mortgagee should give notice of what it has done both to the judgment creditor, who has the benefit of the charging order, and to the mortgagor/judgment debtor. The correct recipient of the surplus can then be determined on an application to the court by either the judgment creditor or the judgment debtor to have the money paid out. In that way, the judgment debtor could challenge the correctness of the interim charging order by seeking its discharge.[137]

Priority agreements

4.85 Secured lenders may agree between themselves to vary the priority of their securities, and such agreements are common. In the absence of some express provision in the mortgage deed, such a variation does not require the mortgagor's consent.[138] In general, because such agreements are no more than contracts between the two lenders, they cannot affect third parties. However, where the land subject to the charges is registered, as will usually be the case, any variation of priority may be shown in the register, and the charges will be ranked in order of priority.[139]

4.86 Provided that the charging order is duly protected by a notice in the register when the interim order is made, such priority agreements cannot affect the priority of a charging order. An example may be given to illustrate this in the usual situation where the title to the land is registered, and where:

(a) 'L' is the landowner;
(b) 'A' is the first legal chargee in time to create a charge over L's land, and the charge secures a debt of £100,000;

---

135 Trustee Act 1925 (TA 1925), s 63(1) specifically authorises trustees 'having in their hands or under their control money or securities belonging to a trust ... to pay the same into court'. A payment into court may also be advisable where, after a sale by the mortgagee, there is a dispute between subsequent incumbrancers about who is entitled to the balance of any proceeds after the mortgagee has satisfied his debt. This is a real rather than theoretical problem. The mortgagee as trustee may be liable for breach of trust if the fund, namely, the balance of the proceeds, is incorrectly distributed. A trustee must satisfy himself beyond doubt, before he parts with the possession of the property, who are the parties legally and equitably entitled to it. A trustee is entitled to call upon those who claim to be beneficiaries to prove their title: *Hurst v Hurst* (1874) 9 Ch App 762. A 'trustee' within TA 1925, s 63, includes a chargee holding surplus proceeds: *Charles v Jones* (1887) 35 Ch D 544. See further Chapter 6, paras 6.123 and 6.131.

136 TA 1925, s 63(2).

137 See COA 1979, s 3(5).

138 *Cheah Theam Swee v Equiticorp Finance Group Ltd* [1992] 1 AC 472.

139 LRA 2002, s 48; LRR 2003, r 102. The same was previously true under LRA 1925: see s 29.

(c) 'B' is the second legal chargee in time to create a charge over L's land, and the charge secures a debt of £150,000; and
(d) 'C' is a judgment creditor who obtains a charging order over L's land in respect of a debt of £50,000.

4.87 In the first example, the sequence of events is as follows:

(a) 1 February: A's charge is created and registered as a legal charge on L's title.
(b) 1 March: C obtains a charging order over L's land and protects it by a notice against L's title.[140]
(c) 1 April: B's charge is created and registered as a legal charge on L's title.
(d) 1 May: A and B enter into an agreement under which B's charge is to have priority over A's charge. That agreement is duly registered, and the register is amended so that B's legal charge appears in the register prior to A's charge.
(e) 1 July: B exercises its power of sale and sells L's land for £225,000, which is £75,000 less than the amount for which it stood as security.

4.88 Although B's legal charge ranks in priority to A's legal charge in consequence of the agreement between A and B, that cannot give B an advantage over C's charging order, because C was not privy and has not consented to the variation agreement between A and B.

4.89 Accordingly, after the payment of the costs, charges and expenses that were an incident to B's sale, B would have to make payments out of the proceeds as follows:

(a) as to £100,000 towards the discharge of B's legal charge;
(b) as to the next £50,000 to C in respect of his judgment debt secured by the charging order;
(c) as to the next £50,000 in discharge of B's legal charge;
(d) as to whatever was left, to A, in partial discharge of A's legal charge.

4.90 The position would obviously be different if:

(a) both the legal charges predated C's charging order; or
(b) at the time of the creation of B's charge, C's charging order had not been protected, so that the priority of C's charging order was postponed to B's charge.[141]

---

140 See para 4.34.

141 See LRA 2002, s 29; see para 4.23.

In either of those circumstances, the charges of A and B would have priority over C's charging order.

Priority by subrogation

4.91 Under the principles of equitable subrogation, where X's money is used to pay off the claim of Y, who is a secured creditor of Z's, X is regarded in equity as if he had an assignment to him of Y's rights as a secured creditor.[142] There will only be such a right of subrogation, however, where X was intended to obtain a particular security over Z's property, but for some reason failed to do so, whether in whole or in part.[143] Subrogation does not operate as an assignment of the prior security, but gives the subrogated lender the same rights as if there had been such a transfer.[144] Equitable subrogation rests upon the principles of unjust enrichment.[145] Typically, the unjust enrichment will not be of the landowner whose property is charged, but some other secured creditor with a charge over that land.[146]

4.92 An example[147] arises out of the following sequence of events:

(a) Z's land was subject to a legal charge in favour of Y.
(b) Z agreed a remortgage with X, in consequence of which X discharged Y's charge and obtained an executed charge over the property from Z.
(c) X failed to register the charge, but Y's charge remained on the register.
(d) Z then granted W a further charge over the property, which W registered.
(e) X realised what had happened and protected its charge as an equitable charge by way of a notice.[148]
(f) X claims to be subrogated to Y's charge, so as to have priority over both W's charge and V's charging order.

4.93 Notwithstanding X's negligence in failing to register its legal charge, X will be subrogated to Y's rights under Y's charge. If that were not so, W would be unjustly enriched by obtaining the priority of a first charge, which W never

---

142 See *Cheltenham & Gloucester plc v Appleyard* [2004] EWCA Civ 291 at [25] and [32]–[44].

143 *Cheltenham & Gloucester plc v Appleyard* [2004] EWCA Civ 291 at [37]–[38].

144 *Banque Financière de la Cité v Parc (Battersea) Ltd* [1999] 1 AC 221 at 236.

145 *Banque Financière de la Cité v Parc (Battersea) Ltd* [1999] 1 AC 221.

146 *Anfield (UK) Ltd v Bank of Scotland* [2010] EWHC 2374 (Ch), [2011] 1 WLR 2414.

147 The facts are a simplified version of what occurred in *Anfield (UK) Ltd v Bank of Scotland* [2010] EWHC 2374 (Ch), [2011] 1 WLR 2414.

148 This will have been because W's charge will have forbidden the creation of any subsequent legal charge without W's consent. Such provisions are common form.

thought it was obtaining, and X would only have an equitable charge over the property even though it had advanced the funds that discharged Y's charge.[149]

4.94 As the example above shows, subrogation may affect priorities. In that example, W had a legal charge, but W's charge could have been an equitable charge created by a charging order over which X sought priority.[150] Equally, there could be subrogation to a charging order itself, as where X advanced money to pay off Z's judgment debt to W, which was secured by a charging order.

Marshalling

4.95 Marshalling is an equitable principle which applies where there are two creditors (A and B) of a single debtor, in circumstances where the first creditor A has multiple securities for his debt, but the second creditor B has only one (which is common with those of A). In such a case, if A looks to the common security to recoup his debt, it is possible for B to be subrogated to A's rights in the other security/securities. This is an equitable remedy which must be granted by the court and will be refused where it would be to the injury of a third chargeholder.[151]

4.96 There does not seem to be any reason why marshalling would not in principle be available to someone with the benefit of a charging order.[152] Contrary to the security considered in *National Crime Agency v Szepietowski*[153] (which was security over the balance of the proceeds of sale of a property once other charges had been paid off, which the Supreme Court determined did not entitle the chargeholder to marshall), a charging order does secure an underlying debt – the judgment debt.

---

149 See *Anfield (UK) Ltd v Bank of Scotland* [2010] EWHC 2374 (Ch), [2011] 1 WLR 2414.

150 In *Anfield (UK) Ltd v Bank of Scotland* [2010] EWHC 2374 (Ch), [2011] 1 WLR 2414, there was in fact a charging order, which was made after W's charge and before X entered a notice to protect its charge.

151 *Aldrich v Cooper* (1803) 8 Ves 382.

152 This appears to have been assumed in *Pourghazi v Kamyab* [2019] EWHC 1300 (Ch).

153 *National Crime Agency v Szepietowski* [2013] UKSC 65, [2010] 2 WLR 1097.

Chapter 5

Discharge or Variation of a Charging Order

INTRODUCTION

5.1 There are two points in time when charging orders are typically challenged: after an interim order has been made but before it has become final, and after a final order has been made. Challenges brought at the first of those stages are dealt with in Chapter 2 and this chapter deals with the court's power to discharge or vary a charging order (in practice, usually a final charging order).

Overview

- The court has a discretion to set aside or vary a charging order.
- Once a charging order is made final, the debtor must show some 'special circumstances' for it to be set aside or varied.
- If the judgment debt has been paid the charging order should be discharged. Likewise, if the underlying order under which the judgment debt arises is set aside, the charging order should be set aside.
- Circumstances of a type which may suffice for set aside of a charging order are the debtor's non-attendance at court for the final charging with good reason, material non-disclosure by the judgment creditor at the charging order hearing or insolvency, but each case will turn on its facts.
- Circumstances of a type which may suffice for variation of a charging order include where the judgment debtor needs to raise money from the property to finance legal representation for litigation against the judgment creditor, or where the property is not worth sufficient to repay the judgment debt but the judgment debtor seeks to sell it to repay it in part.

5.2 The power to discharge or vary a charging order is expressly conferred by section 3(5) of the Charging Orders Act 1979 which grants the court the power to discharge or vary a charging order which it made.[1]

5.3 Once a charging order has been made absolute, the judgment creditor is generally entitled to assume that he has security for the debt. Accordingly, some 'special circumstances' must be shown by a person applying for the order to be discharged or set aside.[2] The first part of this chapter is concerned with identifying the categories of 'special circumstances' which can justify the discharge or variation of a charging order.

5.4 It should be noted that, as at other stages of the charging order process, the decision whether to discharge or vary a charging order is a matter for the court's discretion, and there are no fixed rules as to when the power will be exercised. It depends on the facts and circumstances of the particular case. However, some guidance is given, where possible, in the following paragraphs to indicate how a court is likely to deal with a particular application on the grounds identified. The court may, on the application under section 3(5) of the Charging Orders Act 1979, make any order such as it could make on an application for a charging order.[3]

5.5 At the end of this chapter there is a procedural guide for making an application for discharge or variation of a charging order (Table 5.1).[4] It also deals with the procedure where a reference is made to the FTT as the result of an application to HM Land Registry in relation to registration matters relating to a charging order.

5.6 The cases have given little consideration to the object of the power to discharge a charging order. In particular, there is no authoritative comment as to the relationship between this power and any entitlement to apply to set aside, or to appeal from the making of, a charging order. The Law Commission report which led to the Charging Orders Act 1979[5] suggested that the primary intention behind section 3(5) was to provide a mechanism for terminating charging orders when the underlying debt had been discharged,[6] or some

---

1 It provides that, 'The court by which a charging order was made may at any time, on the application of the debtor or of any person interested in any property to which the order relates, make an order discharging or varying the charging order'. As to who may be a 'person interested' within this subsection, see para 5.44.

2 *Harman v Glencross* [1986] Fam 81.

3 *Harman v Glencross* [1986] Fam 81 at 101, per Fox LJ.

4 See para 5.77.

5 (1976) Law Com No 74, para 96 *et seq*.

6 This argument was considered and rejected in *Harman v Glencross* [1986] Fam 81 at 91, per Balcombe LJ. See para 5.8.

other matter had occurred since the order was made which would justify a reconsideration of the order.

5.7 In addition, it has been held that the fact that a court has made an order which it would not have made had other evidence been before it which was available at the time is not of itself a ground for the discharge of the order.[7] That also suggests that the only grounds for an application to discharge are those arising from events which occurred after the date of the final order. If that is the full extent of the power, there is no overlap with any other entitlement which a person aggrieved by a charging order may have to set aside or appeal the order. On this basis, if the ground of complaint relates to a matter which could have been or was drawn to the court's attention, the applicant's only prospect of redress would depend upon the availability of an appeal or of a right to set aside the original order.

5.8 However, there is authority that the discharge provision will not be interpreted as narrowly as the above analysis might suggest. It is thought that this broader view is likely to be followed. In *Harman v Glencross*,[8] the Court of Appeal rejected, as a matter of construction, the argument that the main purpose of the power conferred by section 3(5) of the Charging Orders Act 1979 was merely to resolve a doubt whether a charging order on land could be discharged once the judgment debt had been paid. Whatever may have been the reason behind the subsection, its wording was quite general and there was no justification for limiting it as suggested. Accordingly, if it appears that there is a good reason to discharge the charging order, the court has power under section 3(5) to do so.

GROUNDS WHICH ARE OPEN TO PARTICULAR APPLICANTS

5.9 Notwithstanding the wider interpretation that has been given to section 3(5) of the Charging Orders Act 1979, it is suggested that as a matter of policy, and in the interests of consistency of practice in relation to challenges to court orders in other areas of the law, certain applicants should be precluded from relying on certain grounds when seeking the discharge of a charging order under that subsection. It is suggested that the following principles provide a working rule for determining whether a particular ground is open to an applicant.

---

7 *C & W Berry Ltd v Armstrong-Moakes* [2007] EWHC 2101 (QB). As David Clarke J explained at [8], the crucial words in COA 1979, s 1(5) are 'any evidence before it', which demonstrate that hindsight cannot be relied upon in this context.

8 *Harman v Glencross* [1986] Fam 81 at 90–91, per Balcombe LJ.

5.10 First, a ground that was in fact advanced unsuccessfully at the time the charging order was made cannot be relied on in an application to discharge the order. An appeal from the original decision should be the only remedy in such a case.

5.11 Secondly, on an application to discharge a charging order, a party who attended the final hearing, whether or not self-represented, should not be able either to adduce evidence that was available, or to advance arguments that were open to him, at the time when the charging order was made. Again, the appropriate course is to appeal.[9]

5.12 A party who did not attend the final hearing at which the charging order was made, and who seeks to have the order discharged on grounds that were available to him at the time, should seek to have the application relisted pursuant to rule 23.11 of the Civil Procedure Rules, rather than making an application under section 3(5) of the Charging Orders Act 1979.[10] That rule provides that:

(a) if an applicant does not attend the hearing of an application, the court may proceed in his absence; but
(b) if the court makes an order at such a hearing, it may relist the application either on its own initiative, or on application.

5.13 In so doing, the court should proceed under the overarching guidance given in rule 1.2 of the Civil Procedure Rules, to consider the same factors as would apply under rule 39.3, in a case where a party failed to attend a trial.[11] Those factors are as follows:

(a) there must have been a good reason for the non-attendance;
(b) the non-attending party must demonstrate an arguable case on the merits that he has a valid reason to object to the making of the charging order; and
(c) the non-attending party must have applied to set aside the order promptly.[12]

---

9 See by analogy *Lloyds Investment (Scandinavian) Ltd v Ager-Hanssen* [2003] EWHC 1740 (Ch) at [15], and also the comments in *Heifer International Ltd v Christiansen* [2013] EWHC 721 (TCC) at [13]. However, the safest course may well be both to seek to appeal and also to apply for discharge under s 3(5) in such situations.

10 CPR r 23.11 is applicable because in charging order proceedings the case generally proceeds by a series of applications, even if these result in final orders. CPR r 39.3, which is concerned with a failure to attend a trial, does not therefore apply: see *Taylor v Diamond* [2012] EWHC 2900 (Ch) at [66], per Norris J.

11 A helpful summary of the principles to be derived from the authorities under this rule can be found in *Anne Alexander Hotels v Anne Blake-Coulter* [2016] EWHC 1457 (QB) at [27] per Soole J.

12 See CPR r 39.3(5).

5.14 Those factors will not be given the force of mandatory requirements which restrict the exercise of the court's broad discretion.[13] However, if the applicant cannot satisfy all the factors (which are to be considered collectively, rather than sequentially),[14] he may be restricted to an appeal, if that is available.[15]

5.15 It follows that a person, whether the debtor, the debtor's spouse or a third party such as a secured creditor,[16] who was not served with the interim order and notice of the hearing should not assume that he will be entitled to the discharge of the charging order for that reason alone. The significance of non-service is that it provides a good reason for non-attendance. However, the applicant must still show both that he acted promptly, and that he has a valid ground for objecting to the charging order. He will, of course, be entitled to put forward any grounds which could have been advanced at the time of the original hearing, so that he may seek to impugn the order on the merits.[17]

5.16 Notwithstanding all the matters set out above, events occurring after the date of the final order are still likely to form the basis of the application to discharge in the majority of cases. These are therefore considered first.

GROUNDS FOR DISCHARGE

Post-order events

5.17 The easiest way to persuade the court to discharge the charging order is to show that the debt itself has either been paid in full or discharged in some other way. The debt will only be discharged in full if all interest and costs forming part of the sums secured are paid. Even if the charging order makes no mention of interest, the judgment creditor will be entitled to interest, and it will form part of the sums secured by the charging order.[18] If the debt secured by the charging order

---

13 *Taylor v Diamond* [2012] EWHC 2900 (Ch) at [67], per Norris J; see also, e.g. *Fineland Investments Ltd v Pritchard* [2011] EWHC 3901 (Ch) at [40], per Norris J.

14 *Anne Alexander Hotels v Anne Blake-Coulter* [2016] EWHC 1457 (QB) at [28], per Soole J.

15 See *Bank of Scotland v Pereira* [2011] EWCA Civ 241, [2011] 1 WLR 2391 at [24]. Further, the appellate court may take a great deal of persuading to depart from a conclusion reached by the judge hearing an unsuccessful set-aside application. To do so in the absence of good reason would be invidious (at [27]). Similarly, a party will not normally be allowed to raise the same arguments on appeal as made in a set-aside application which had failed on the basis that there was no reasonable prospect of success.

16 Such persons have standing to apply to discharge or vary the charging order: see paras 5.44–5.46.

17 *Harman v Glencross* [1986] Fam 81; *Howell v Montey* (1990) 61 P & CR 18.

18 *Ezekiel v Orakpo* [1997] 1 WLR 340; *Mehta v Nolan*, 11 June 2009, unreported, QBD.

is discharged in full, whether by the debtor or someone else,[19] there is no ground upon which the court can refuse an application to discharge the charging order. This is so, even if the creditor has secured other judgments against the debtor which have not been discharged.[20] Therefore, those acting for the debtor should expressly appropriate any payments that are made to the debt secured by the charging order, if that is what is intended, and if there is any possibility that other debts might be owed to the creditor.

5.18 Other matters which can occur after the final order is made which may justify the discharge of the charging order include, by way of example, the following situations:

(a) where the underlying judgment is set aside; and
(b) where a document is rectified which has the effect, retrospectively, of removing any beneficial interest in the property from the debtor.

5.19 In those situations, there is no basis upon which the court can refuse an application to discharge the charging order.

5.20 If the debtor becomes bankrupt or goes into liquidation after the final charging order is made, does that constitute a ground upon which the final charging order can be discharged? Where the final order is made before the commencement of the winding-up or bankruptcy respectively, the creditor is entitled to retain the benefit of the charging order.[21] However, even in those circumstances, the court has a discretion under section 3(5) of the Charging Orders Act 1979 to discharge the charging order, but some additional feature will be needed before it will do so.[22] In particular, the judgment debtor may have to

---

19 *Al-Khayat v Al-Khayat* [2008] CLY 286, ChD (Master Moncaster).

20 *Al-Khayat v Al-Khayat* [2008] CLY 286, ChD (Master Moncaster).

21 See IA 1986, s 183 (winding up) and s 346 (bankruptcy). The purpose of both sections is to make it clear that if execution has not been completed by that time, the creditor is *not* entitled to the benefit of it. For the relevant time of commencement, see IA 1986, s 86 (commencement of voluntary winding up), s 129 (commencement of winding-up by the court) and s 278 (commencement and continuance of bankruptcy). See also Chapter 8, which gives a general overview of insolvency, in particular paras 8.15 and 8.98.

22 *Nationwide Building Society v Wright* [2009] EWCA Civ 811, [2010] Ch 318, esp at [18]; *C & W Berry Ltd v Armstrong-Moakes* [2007] EWHC 2101 (QB). In *Banque Nationale de Paris plc v Montman* [2000] 1 BCLC 576 the judge considered that, in circumstances where (as was the case before her) the final order had been made before the commencement of the company's insolvency, IA 1986, s 183 would probably provide a complete answer to any application under s 3(5). The judge's view was said to be 'correct' by Sir John Chadwick in *Nationwide Building Society v Wright* [2009] EWCA Civ 811, [2010] Ch 318 at [24].

show more compelling grounds for discharging the charging order than would have to be shown to secure the discharge of an interim charging order at the final hearing.[23]

5.21 In a case where a final charging order pre-dates the commencement of winding-up or bankruptcy, it is suggested that the following matters are likely to be relevant in any application for the discharge of the order:

(a) If at the time the charging order was made final, no steps had been taken to start the process of commencing the winding up of the company or the bankruptcy of an individual, the court is unlikely to exercise its discretion to set the charging order aside.[24]
(b) If at the time the charging order was made final, such steps had been taken and the judgment creditor was then aware of it, that would be a ground for exercising the discretion to set the order aside.[25]
(c) If the judgment creditor was not aware that such steps had been taken, the court is unlikely to set aside the charging order, in the absence of something more.[26]

5.22 By way of example, in one case, the final charging order was set aside because of the following additional factors:

(a) the judgment creditor had proved in the bankruptcy for the debt and had not referred to his charging order over the course of many years of dealings with the trustee in bankruptcy; and
(b) the debtor's wife had purchased the debtor's interest in the property from the trustee in bankruptcy without realising the charging order was in place.[27]

---

23 *Jelle Zwemstra Ltd v Walton and Stuart* [1997] CLY 3002 (Scarborough County Court).

24 See *Jelle Zwemstra Ltd v Walton and Stuart* [1997] CLY 3002 where the charging order was not discharged because the chargee had properly pursued his debt through the courts and obtained a charging order a year before the bankruptcy, whereas the other creditors had not. See also *Banque Nationale de Paris plc v Montman* [2000] 1 BCLC 576.

25 See para 5.26. In *National Westminster Bank plc v Caldeira* [1999] CLY 3225 (Hull County Court), a final order, which had been made 2 days before the making of a bankruptcy order, was discharged. It is not clear from the short report whether the creditor was aware of the impending bankruptcy. The decision can only be correct if the creditor was aware of the debtor's insolvency. A notice of intention to appoint administrators is not to be treated as a conclusive reason for refusing to make a charging order final. However, an intended administration is a powerful factor to be taken into consideration. A creditor with notice of the administration should not be able to gain an advantage over the other creditors, who will all be subject to the statutory scheme: *Monte Developments Ltd (In Administration) v Court Management Consultants Ltd* [2010] EWHC 3071 (Ch), [2011] 1 WLR 1579.

26 *Nationwide Building Society v Wright* [2009] EWCA Civ 811, [2010] Ch 318.

27 *C & W Berry Ltd v Armstrong-Moakes* [2007] EWHC 2101 (QB).

5.23 Even where the debtor has not been adjudicated bankrupt or gone into liquidation, the judgment creditor's conduct after the final charging order is made may provide grounds for its discharge. If the judgment creditor acts in such a way as to induce the other party reasonably to believe that the charging order will not be relied upon,[28] and the other party acts to his detriment in reliance on that inducement, the judgment creditor will be estopped from relying on his charging order. In those circumstances, the charging order should be discharged.

Delay in enforcement

5.24 The mere passage of time does not justify an order for the discharge of a charging order. Even if 12 years or more have passed since the final order was made and the judgment creditor has taken no steps to enforce the charging order, the creditor is entitled to retain the charging order in order to recoup the sums due to it as and when the property is sold.[29]

Lack of jurisdiction to make charging order

5.25 If the court had no jurisdiction to make the charging order, it should be discharged. This situation can arise, for example, where there was no underlying money judgment in favour of the person who obtained the charging order,[30] or where the debtor had no interest in the property that was charged by the order.[31]

---

28 An assurance that the charging order will not be enforced is not enough to create an estoppel.

29 See *Yorkshire Bank Finance v Mulhall* [2008] EWCA Civ 1156; and Chapter 6, para 6.151.

30 As e.g. in *Monte Developments Ltd (In Administration) v Court Managements Consultants Ltd* [2010] EWHC 3071 (Ch), [2011] 1 WLR 1579 and in *T Class Security Ltd v Latchworth Ltd* [2021] EWHC 3579 (Ch).

31 This might happen where, for example, the transfer to the debtor of the property charged was a forgery, or the debtor had validly disposed of any beneficial interest in the property by entering a specifically performable contract to sell, or otherwise creating a trust, prior to the date of the charging order. The relevant date in this context is the date when the interim order is made, although if the position has changed by the time of the final order, that is a matter which the court should take into account in exercising its discretion: *Howell v Montey* (1990) 61 P & CR 18. See also Chapter 2, para 2.22.

Creditor's failure to disclose all material information to the court

5.26 The creditor is obliged to put certain information before the court.[32] If it later transpires that the creditor failed to comply with that duty, or actively misled the court in a material way, the court is likely to discharge the charging order.[33]

Debtor's lack of beneficial interest in the charged property

5.27 As long as the court is satisfied that the debtor has some beneficial interest in the property, it may make a charging order over that beneficial interest, without it being necessary to quantify the extent of the beneficial interest; the proper time for quantification is on sale of the charged property.[34] It is therefore possible that having made a charging order, being satisfied that the debtor had some beneficial interest in the property at that time, a court would decline to discharge it because the debtor asserted he no longer had a beneficial interest in the charged property (perhaps by operation of a common intention constructive trust) without there already being a determination to that effect (such as a judgment in other proceedings). Absent some reason to determine the matter, it may be more appropriate to wait until such time as the property is sold.

Other matters going to the court's discretion

5.28 A charging order will not usually be set aside because the court that imposed the charging order should have taken additional material into account (that being material beyond that which the creditor was under a duty to provide to the court; failure to provide that information is likely to result in discharge[35]). This is because the person seeking to set aside the charging order could have presented such evidence or advanced such arguments at the time. However, there are occasions where this is not so, particularly where the applicant is not the debtor and did not have notice of the hearing. In such circumstances, the court must consider whether the charging order would have been made if, at the time of making the final order, the court had been aware of all the information now before it.[36] It should be borne in mind that it is at the stage of making a charging

---

32 See Chapter 3, paras 3.19–3.24.

33 *C & W Berry Ltd v Armstrong-Moakes* [2007] EWHC 2101 (QB).

34 *Walton v Allman* [2015] EWHC 3325 (Ch), [2016] 1 WLR 2053.

35 See para 5.26.

36 See *Howell v Montey* (1990) 61 P & CR 18.

order final that the court should decide whether the debtor has a beneficial interest in the property.[37]

5.29 One particular example is that of a spouse who has issued a petition for divorce and is seeking a property adjustment order. If the court is aware of those proceedings before it makes the final order, the practice is to adjourn the final hearing to the family court so that all matters can be considered together.[38] However, if this does not occur, the spouse's application to discharge should be considered by the family court.

GROUNDS FOR VARIATION

5.30 Although there is a power to vary a charging order in addition to the power to discharge it, this power is rarely used. Cases in which it would be appropriate to do so include the following:

(a) where, by mistake, a charging order had been made over a whole property instead of just the debtor's beneficial interest in that property; or
(b) where the wrong sum was stated to be secured in the charging order.

5.31 The court's power to vary a charging order may be invoked by a judgment creditor who seeks to resist an application to discharge the charging order. The court may vary the charging order instead of discharging it altogether. The effect is to leave the original charging order in place but with modified terms. This outcome may be important because of its effect upon priorities.[39]

5.32 It is also clear that events which occurred since the making of a final charging order may justify the variation of that order. In one case, a charging order was varied so as to permit the debtor to use either part of the proceeds of sale of the property charged or sums raised by way of charge over the security, to obtain legal representation for further litigation against the judgment creditor. This appears to have been on the basis that otherwise the charging order would stifle the debtor's defence.[40] One might also query whether a court might vary a charging order so as to enable a sale in circumstances where the value of the property is insufficient to discharge the debt. The court could vary the charging order so as to secure a lower sum which can be realised, enabling discharge of the

---

37 See Chapter 3, para 3.40 and Chapter 4, para 4.45.

38 See Chapter 2, para 2.48.

39 See Chapter 4.

40 *Perotti v Watson*, 19 May 2000, unreported, CA. The transcript does not indicate whether the court considered whether this ground was open to the applicant, or whether he could and should have raised this at the time the final charging order was made.

order on sale. Further or alternatively, the court could elect to discharge the order, and require any notice protecting it to be cancelled (so as to enable the sale), either by exercising its power under section 3(6) of the Charging Orders Act 1979, or by the exercise of its inherent jurisdiction.[41] An applicant for such an order might consider offering an undertaking to pay the sale proceeds into court or to the judgment creditor, following application of sale proceeds to any prior charges.

PROCEDURE IN THE COURTS

Overview

- An application for discharge or variation of a charging order can be made by the judgment debtor or anyone else with an interest in the charged property.
- The judgment debtor or applicant should first approach the judgment creditor to agree discharge or variation.
- Any application should be made promptly once the applicant is aware of grounds for the application.
- The application should be made by Form N244 to the court which made the charging order.
- Any application should be supported by evidence.

Approach the judgment creditor

5.33 In some cases where a debtor seeks to have the charging order discharged, an application to the court may not be necessary. If the debt has been paid, a discharge can in practice be obtained by obtaining from the judgment creditor:

(a) a receipt for payment, confirming that payment in full has been made; and
(b) a completed application for discharge of the relevant entries at HM Land Registry.[42]

5.34 A court order is only required if both of those cannot be obtained.

5.35 If a receipt can be obtained, but the judgment creditor will not complete the necessary forms for discharging HM Land Registry entries, an application can

41 *Quay House Admirals Way Land Ltd v Rockwell Properties Ltd* [2022] EWHC 545 (Ch). It should be noted that permission to appeal was granted: [2022] EWHC 742 (Ch).

42 In the case of a unilateral notice, a Form UN2 will be required. In the case of a restriction, Form RX4 should be used.

probably be made to HM Land Registry by the debtor[43] without the need for a court order,[44] although it may be safer to apply to the court in such a case.

5.36 If the judgment creditor agrees to a variation of the charging order, the application notice should be in the form referred to at para 5.33, and the creditor's consent should be produced in the evidence.

5.37 In any case, before any application is made, the debtor should in practice approach the judgment creditor to ascertain his attitude to the application. An attempt by the applicant to resolve the matter with the judgment creditor prior to issuing proceedings will be relevant to the costs of the application, which may in consequence fall on the judgment creditor. Accordingly, any pre-application communications with the other party should be included in the evidence.

Time for making application

5.38 Although there is no statutory time limit for making an application to discharge or vary a charging order, the application should be made promptly after the potential applicant becomes aware of the ground upon which discharge or variation may be sought. Delay in making the application is a factor that could influence the exercise of the court's discretion.

5.39 It is difficult to see how an application for the discharge of a charging order could be successfully pursued *after* the security had been sold. Not only will third party rights have intervened, but the charge imposed by the charging order will in fact have been discharged on the sale. However, there is no reason in principle why an application should not be made up to the point of sale.

Which court or tribunal?

5.40 Having regard to section 3(5) of the Charging Orders Act 1979,[45] the application for the discharge or variation of a charging order should be made to the court which made the charging order. If the order was made by the CNBC[46] without a hearing, then the application must be made in the first instance to the CNBC, which will then transfer it to the debtor's home court for hearing.[47] It is unclear whether, in circumstances where a charging order was made in the county court but the proceedings are subsequently transferred to the High Court,

---

43 On Form UN4 in the case of a notice, and on Form RX3 in the case of a restriction.

44 See para 5.34.

45 See para 5.2.

46 Or, prior to August 2023, by the CCMCC or the CCBC.

47 CPR r 73.10B.

section 5 of the County Courts Act 1984 is sufficient to enable the High Court judge to discharge the charging order, or whether the matter must be transferred to the county court for that purpose.[48]

5.41 Other courts should neither discharge the charging order nor order the removal of entries in the register relating to it, even if seized of a claim to determine, for example, whether the debtor had any beneficial interest at the date the charging order was made. A separate application to the court which made the charging order is required. The findings made in the other proceedings will necessarily bind the judgment creditor on that application provided he was a party to them.[49]

5.42 Similarly, a person cannot apply to HM Land Registry to remove the entries on the register of title relating to the charging order unless he has the judgment creditor's consent.[50] An order discharging the charging order, from the court that made it, should first be obtained.

5.43 If, notwithstanding what is said at para 5.42, an application *is* made to HM Land Registry, and an objection is made to it which HM Land Registry does not consider groundless, the matter must be referred to the FTT[51] for determination.[52] The applicable procedure is dealt with in more detail at para 5.63 *et seq*.

Applications to the court: who can apply?

5.44 An application to the court under section 3(5) of the Charging Orders Act 1979 can be made by the debtor, or 'any person interested in any property to which the order relates'. The quoted words have been interpreted to include:

(a) anyone with an interest in the property (including other chargeholders[53]), whether or not that interest is subject to the charging order according to its terms;

---

48 See *T Class Security Ltd v Latchworth Ltd* [2021] EWHC 3579 (Ch).

49 *Palace Gate Worldwide Ltd v Palacegate Agencies Ltd and Oddbins Ltd*, REC/2009/0007 at [125] *et seq* (especially at [133]), per Simon Brilliant, sitting as Deputy Adjudicator to HM Land Registry, see https://landregistrationdivision.decisions.tribunals.gov.uk//Public/summary.aspx?id=238.

50 See para 5.33.

51 This function was formerly performed by the Adjudicator to HM Land Registry. The functions of the Adjudicator were transferred from 1 July 2013 to the FTT by the Transfer of Tribunal Functions Order 2013 (SI 2013/1036).

52 See LRA 2002, s 73.

53 As in *T Class Security Ltd v Latchworth Ltd* [2021] EWHC 3579 (Ch) (holder of subsequent charging order was entitled to apply for discharge of previous charging order).

(b) anyone with a right to occupy the property, even if the property charged is only a share of the beneficial interest; and
(c) a person who has made an application for a property adjustment order in respect of the property.[54]

5.45 Furthermore, in principle, the debtor's trustee in bankruptcy (if he is insolvent) or his personal representatives (if he is deceased) can apply, as each stands in the debtor's shoes.

5.46 Unsecured creditors of the debtor have no standing to apply.[55] This follows from the wording of section 3(5) of the Charging Orders Act 1979, which requires an applicant to be a person 'interested in any property to which the order relates'.[56] However, this does lead to an unsatisfactory mismatch between the persons who are entitled to be heard at the final hearing, at which 'any person' may object, and those who are entitled thereafter to apply to discharge the final order. This may discourage judgment creditors from serving other creditors prior to the charging order being made final. An aggrieved creditor who was not served may perhaps be able to seek to have the application relisted under rule 23.11 of the Civil Procedure Rules.[57] Failing that, he might either:

(a) attempt to persuade the debtor to make an application for the discharge of the charging order because of the failure by the judgment creditor to serve a creditor; or
(b) seek to bankrupt the debtor and persuade his trustee in bankruptcy to apply for the discharge of the order.

Application notice

5.47 The application notice should be in Form N244. A specimen is in Appendix Precedent B9.[58]

5.48 The judgment creditor should always be a respondent to the application, even if he consents to it. If there were other parties named in the charging order, they should either be joined as parties to the application or at least listed as persons on whom the application should be served.

---

54 See *Harman v Glencross* [1986] Fam 81 in which the wife of the debtor was considered to be interested in the property when, in separate matrimonial proceedings, she claimed a property adjustment order by which she would be entitled to the husband's interest.

55 *Banque Nationale de Paris v Montman* [2000] 1 BCLC 576.

56 *Banque Nationale de Paris v Montman* [2000] 1 BCLC 576 at 581.

57 See para 5.12.

58 See CPR r 4(1) and PD 4, para 1.1.

5.49 The court will list the application for a hearing when the application notice is issued. As with any application, the hearing may be set for a date many weeks after the date upon which the application is issued. The shorter the time estimate given for the hearing in the application notice, the quicker it is likely to come on. An opposed application is likely to be heard later than an unopposed one. It is therefore prudent to contact the judgment creditor prior to making the application to ascertain his position.[59] An unopposed application is likely to be suitable for a 30-minute hearing. In the case of an opposed hearing, the estimated length of hearing will depend on the nature of the dispute and amount of evidence for the court to consider.

Evidence in support

5.50 The applicant should ensure that he has set out fully his ground for seeking the discharge or variation of the charging order, and demonstrated (if necessary) that he is not precluded from relying on it. Commonly, the applicant must therefore outline what event has occurred since the date of the final order or explain why he did not advance his arguments at the time the final order was made. This will ordinarily be by way of a witness statement made by the applicant or his solicitor.[60] Although the form of the witness statement will necessarily be determined by the ground relied upon, an illustrative example of a witness statement is provided in Appendix Precedent B10.

Fee

5.51 The applicant must pay a fee on the issue of the application. At the time of writing, the fee is £275.[61]

Service

5.52 The application notice and evidence in support should be served as soon as possible. The rules require service at least 3 clear days before the hearing as a

---

59 See para 5.37. If the applicant does not know whether the application will be opposed, a short hearing of, say, 20 minutes should be requested. If the application is unopposed that is likely to suffice. If it is opposed, the hearing can be used for case management directions.

60 The general rule is that evidence at hearings other than a trial is to be by witness statement unless the court, a practice direction or any other enactment requires otherwise: CPR r 32.6(1). The applicant may rely on matters set out in the application notice if this is verified by a statement of truth: CPR r 22.1(3); CPR r 32.6(2).

61 Civil Proceedings Fees Order 2008 (SI 2008/1053), Sch 1, para 2.4(a). This is the general application fee. If the application is made by the debtor, and is for a variation rather than discharge, there is an argument that a lower fee of £14 should be payable under Sch 1, para 2.7 (which applies where the application is to vary a judgment or suspend enforcement).

minimum.[62] However, it is sensible to give the respondent (and any other persons to be served) as long as practicable to prepare for the hearing to avoid any risk that the hearing may have to be adjourned.

5.53 The applicant (or his solicitor) should serve the application notice,[63] and should be ready to prove service. A certificate of service (in Form N215) identifying how and when the application was served, will generally suffice.

Evidence in response

5.54 The court may give directions for the filing of evidence in response.[64] Such directions should be complied with, if given. In any event, if a person served with the application wishes to oppose it, he should prepare and serve his evidence as soon as possible. If time is short, he may either try to agree directions with the applicant or seek an adjournment from the court. A judgment creditor may wish to adduce evidence of any hardship which he would suffer if the charging order were discharged.[65] He may also wish to challenge any factual assertions made in the applicant's evidence which are not accepted, for example, as to his knowledge of the previous hearing.

Hearing

5.55 At the hearing, the judge[66] will first consider whether any additional parties should be joined or the application served on them.[67] Service is likely to be required on all those who were served with or appeared when the final order was made. If this has not happened, proceedings are likely be adjourned so that such persons can be served and have an opportunity to file any evidence in opposition.

5.56 If the applicant is a spouse who has also commenced divorce proceedings and is seeking the discharge of the charging order on the ground that he or she has sought a property adjustment order, the court will normally adjourn the

---

62 CPR r 23.7. The court has power to allow a shorter period: see CPR r 23.7(4). An application for discharge of a charging order will seldom be sufficiently urgent to justify it. CPR r 6.26 specifies the time at which documents are deemed to be served by various methods.

63 By one of the methods set out in CPR r 6.20.

64 CPR PD 23, para 9.2.

65 *Harman v Glencross* [1986] Fam 81.

66 The case is normally heard before a District Judge in the county court and a Master in the High Court. However, if the final order was made by a more senior judge, the application to discharge or vary should be made to a judge of that level.

67 Pursuant to CPR r 73.10B(4).

application to the family court. In this way it can be considered together with the ancillary relief application.

5.57 In other cases, once the court is ready to hear the application, it will consider the merits of the grounds, and either dismiss the application, or discharge or vary the charging order. In most cases, the hearing will proceed by way of submissions on the written evidence by the applicant's representative, submissions on behalf of any respondents who wish to address the court, and a reply on behalf of the applicant.[68] The court will generally make its decision immediately, reserving judgment only in the most complex cases.

Order

5.58 A draft order should in practice be annexed to the application notice. A precedent is given in Appendix Precedent B11.

5.59 In the county court, the court office usually produces the order itself and sends it to the parties. In the High Court, the applicant is likely to be asked to prepare a minute of order after the hearing, if represented by counsel. The court will then nominate one party (typically the applicant) as the serving party, and send that party one sealed copy of the order. The nominated party will then be responsible for serving the order on the other parties.

5.60 The order should be served on all parties on whom the final charging order was required to be served,[69] and also on any other parties who were involved in the application for discharge.

Registration issues following discharge

5.61 When discharging an order under section 3(5) of the Charging Orders Act 1979, the court can and in practice will direct that any protecting entry under the Land Charges Act 1972 or the Land Registration Act 2002 be cancelled.[70] On production of the order, the registrar will remove the relevant notice or restriction. The application to HM Land Registry should be on HM Land Registry Form UN4 (in the case of a unilateral notice) or Form RX3 (in the case of a restriction). Only the registered proprietor of the estate to which the notice relates, or a person who

---

68 Oral evidence is very rare. It might be permitted in relation to whether a person had been aware of the final hearing, if that matter is relevant to the ground of application.

69 CPR r 73.10B(5).

70 COA 1979, s 3(6).

is entitled to be so registered, can apply for the cancellation of a unilateral notice.[71] A Form DS1 is not required.

Costs

5.62 The costs of the application are in the discretion of the court. Costs will normally follow the event but conduct will also be relevant.[72] Thus, if the applicant had notice of the original hearing and chose not to attend, the court may award the judgment creditor his costs even if he loses, unless he has acted unreasonably in opposing the application.

THE PROCEDURE ON A REFERENCE TO THE FIRST-TIER TRIBUNAL

When and how a reference is made to the First-tier Tribunal

5.63 This procedure applies if an application is made to HM Land Registry in relation to a charging order (e.g. for the entry or removal of a restriction to protect it) and an objection is made to the application which HM Land Registry does not consider groundless. The matter must be referred to the FTT[73] for determination.

5.64 The way in which matters are referred to the FTT by the registrar is governed by the Land Registration (Referral to the Adjudicator to HM Land Registry) Rules 2003.[74] The Rules have not been renamed notwithstanding the replacement of the functions of the Adjudicator by the FTT.

5.65 Once the matter has been transferred to the FTT (Property Chamber), procedure is governed by the Tribunal Procedure (First-tier Tribunal) (Property Chamber) Rules 2013. The Civil Procedure Rules do not apply in the FTT.

---

71 LRA 2002, s 36.

72 See generally CPR r 44.3.

73 This function was formerly performed by the Adjudicator to HM Land Registry. The functions of the Adjudicator were transferred from 1 July 2013 to the FTT by the Transfer of Tribunal Functions Order 2013 (SI 2013/1036).

74 SI 2003/2114.

What happens when a reference to the First-tier Tribunal is made?

5.66 In all cases where a matter is referred to the FTT by the registrar under section 73(7) of the Land Registration Act 2002, the registrar will first prepare a case summary, which is sent to the parties for their comment.[75] The case summary (amended, if appropriate, in light of the parties' comments) will then be sent to the FTT together with copies of the documents listed in it. The parties will be informed that the matter has been referred to the Tribunal.[76]

5.67 The FTT will consider the case summary, and will provide the parties with a notice stating when the FTT received the matter, the names and addresses of the parties, and directing which of them will be the applicant and which will be the respondent.[77]

Decisions the First-tier Tribunal may make

5.68 Once a reference has been made to the FTT, the FTT may then follow one of three courses of action:

(a) It may strike out the application on the ground that, by reason of section 3(5) of the Charging Orders Act 1979, an application to the court that made the charging order is required before any application can be made to HM Land Registry. The FTT can do so without a hearing.[78]
(b) It may instead direct the applicant to commence court proceedings.[79] Pending the final court order, the FTT proceedings will be automatically stayed.[80] If an order of the FTT is then required to implement the court's order, the FTT can then do so, without a hearing.[81]
(c) It may decide to accept the case and determine the dispute between the parties.

5.69 The FTT has a discretion to decide which of those three courses of action to take. However, the general practice that has been adopted seems to be as follows.

---

75 Land Registration (Referral to the Adjudicator to HM Land Registry) Rules 2003 (SI 2003/2114), r 3.

76 Land Registration (Referral to the Adjudicator to HM Land Registry) Rules 2003, r 5.

77 Tribunal Procedure (First-tier Tribunal) (Property Chamber) Rules 2013 (SI 2013/1169), r 28.

78 Tribunal Procedure (First-tier Tribunal) (Property Chamber) Rules 2013, r 31(4).

79 See LRA 2002, s 110.

80 Tribunal Procedure (First-tier Tribunal) (Property Chamber) Rules 2013, r 29(2).

81 Tribunal Procedure (First-tier Tribunal) (Property Chamber) Rules 2013, rr 39(4) and 31(4).

5.70 First, the FTT will never go behind a judgment or an order of the court. If the basis of the application is that the underlying judgment was wrong and there was no debt, the application will be dismissed.

5.71 Secondly, the FTT may well be prepared to determine a dispute as to whether the debt has been paid off in full since the date when the charging order was made, because this does not involve going behind a court order. It is understandable that a debtor who considers that he had paid the debt off in full should apply to HM Land Registry for the removal of the entry relating to the charging order, without considering that it is necessary to go back to court. In principle, the debtor ought to be able to do so, at least in cases where he has no reason to suspect that there will be a dispute as to whether he has in fact discharged the debt.[82]

5.72 Thirdly, the FTT will sometimes determine whether the debtor had any beneficial interest in the property when the charging order was made. It is unsatisfactory that the practice in the FTT is far from consistent.

5.73 For examples of cases where the FTT has determined whether or not a party had a beneficial interest, see the following:

(a) In *Yorkshire Bank plc v Elliott & Elliott*,[83] the Deputy Adjudicator[84] rejected the contention that the making of a final charging order was conclusive as to whether the debtor had any beneficial interest in the property on the making of the order, and went on to determine that she did not.
(b) In *F & H Didsbury Ltd v Plant*,[85] the Deputy Adjudicator was also prepared to decide whether the debtor had a beneficial interest. This was because there was evidence before him that, when considering whether to make the final charging order, the District Judge had indicated that he would not decide that matter and would leave it to be determined by HM Land Registry.
(c) In *Arrow Global Guernsey Limited v Avornyo*,[86] the FTT determined that a written agreement predating the charging order had operated to transfer the debtor's beneficial interest, and therefore ordered that the restriction protecting the charging order should be cancelled.

5.74 For examples of cases where the FTT declined to determine whether or not a party had a beneficial interest, see the following:

---

82 If the debtor approaches the creditor as suggested at para 5.37, this issue should not arise.

83 REF/2005/0256.

84 As then fulfilling the functions now performed by the FTT: see para 5.64.

85 REF/2012/0614.

86 REF/2016/0521.

(a) In *Commercial First Business Ltd v Choudhry*,[87] the Deputy Adjudicator[88] held that it was not open to an applicant to suggest that the debtor had no beneficial interest in the charged asset; the appropriate route was either to pursue a court application for variation or discharge of the charging order, or for the matter to be considered in the context of an order for sale.
(b) In *Arrow Global Guernsey Limited v Jacomb & McEnnerney-Stevens*,[89] the District Judge, when making the charging order, had expressed that while his view was that a particular deed had not divested the debtor of her beneficial interest in the property, the FTT might reach a different conclusion. The FTT (while it would have come to the same conclusion as the judge had it been able to) did not consider that it was open to it to go behind the court's order.
(c) In *Aldemore Bank plc v Stephanson & Grimes*,[90] the FTT refused to go behind the charging order to investigate the parties' beneficial interests, and said that any challenge to the charging order ought to be by way of court proceedings.

5.75 There is therefore an unwelcome element of chance involved in whether or not the FTT will determine the beneficial ownership of property. In the experience of the authors, the safest approach for advisers is likely to be to tell clients that whilst the FTT on occasion does so, it is unlikely to accept a case which involves having to determine the nature of a beneficial ownership, even where the court has indicated that the FTT might in the future do so.

5.76 The FTT has jurisdiction to make costs awards in land registration matters.[91] In deciding what if any order to make, the FTT will have regard to all the circumstances of the case, including the extent to which a party has been successful and the parties' conduct.[92]

BASIC PROCEDURE TABLE

5.77 There follows a table outlining the basic procedure for obtaining the discharge or variation of a charging order by way of an application to the court (Table 5.1). The table outlines the steps required, the relevant forms, rules and

---

87 REF/2011/0713.

88 As then fulfilling the functions now performed by the FTT: see para 5.64.

89 REF/2016/0536.

90 REF/2018/0139.

91 Tribunal Procedure (First-tier Tribunal) (Property Chamber) Rules 2013, r 13(1)(c).

92 The full list of factors to be taken into account can be found in Practice Directions – Property Chamber, First-Tier Tribunal Land Registration, para 9, see www.judiciary.uk/wp-content/uploads/JCO/Documents/Practice+Directions/ftt-land-registration-pc-300713.pdf.

timeframes. The table should be read in conjunction with the more detailed commentary set out above.

Table 5.1: Procedure for obtaining the discharge or variation of a charging order

Step	*Form*	*Rule*	*Timeframe*
Application for discharge issued in court which made the final order	N244 plus a witness statement	CPR r 73.10B	Promptly after grounds come to applicant's attention
Fee of £275 payable		Civil Proceedings Fees Order 2008, Sch 1, para 2.4(a)	On issue
Application (together with supporting evidence) served on judgment debtor and any other parties		CPR r 23.7	As soon as possible and no later than 3 clear days before the hearing
If necessary, directions hearing			As per court listing
If necessary, court orders any other persons to be joined or served		CPR r 73.10B(4)	
Evidence in answer			As directed
Evidence in reply			As directed
Substantive hearing of the application			As per court listing
Order served on parties and, if granted, on anyone else on whom original order was served		CPR r 73.10B(5)	
Debtor (or other interested party) applies to HM Land Registry for cancellation of the notice/restriction	UN4 (for a notice) or RX3 (for a restriction)		

Chapter 6

Enforcement

INTRODUCTION

6.1 Since a charging order against land gives a judgment creditor security for his judgment debt, in order to obtain satisfaction of the debt, the judgment creditor may simply choose to wait for a sale of the land by the debtor or another interested party[1] and receive his share of the proceeds then. However, if there is no prospect of such a sale, or if the judgment creditor wants swifter payment, he may take steps to enforce the charging order himself, either by seeking an order for sale (together with an order for possession if required), or by the appointment of a receiver. This chapter is concerned with the means of such enforcement, its basis and the applicable procedure.

Overview

- A charging order can be enforced by obtaining a court order for the appointment of a receiver, or an order for sale. Obtaining an order for sale is the more common and practical route.
- A new claim for such an order will need to be issued in the court which granted the charging order, or if necessary for jurisdictional reasons, the High Court.
- Where the charging order is over a legal interest in land, a claim for an order for sale is brought on the basis of the court's equitable jurisdiction to assist in the enforcement of an equitable charge.
- Where the charging order is over a beneficial interest in land, the claim will be made under section 14 of the Trusts of Land and Appointment of Trustees Act 1996.

---

1 For example, another secured creditor or, in cases where the charging order has been made against property of which the debtor is a joint beneficial owner, the trustees.

- In each case the court will have a discretion whether to make such an order, and as to the terms of the order. Where the property charged is a family home, the welfare of any children may be relevant, but the court will also want to see the judgment debt repaid.

6.2 This chapter deals with the following matters:

(a) The court's jurisdiction to enforce charging orders, through orders for sale and possession, or the appointment of a receiver. It also considers the appropriate court in which to bring an enforcement claim.
(b) Various aspects of the most common means of enforcement, namely, orders for sale, and in particular:

  (i) the process of establishing a judgment debtor's title in the property to be sold;
  (ii) the source and exercise of the court's discretion to order sale;
  (iii) the procedure on an application for an order for sale, including the relevant provisions of the Civil Procedure Rules;
  (iv) the necessary evidence to be adduced;
  (v) the forms of order that can be made; the mechanics by which the sale is conducted; and the application of the proceeds of sale; and
  (vi) enforcement, if necessary, against the proceeds of sale.

(c) Enforcement by the appointment of a receiver and the circumstances in which that might be advantageous, and the process and consequences of such an appointment.
(d) The extent to which limitation periods affect the enforcement of charging orders.

6.3 As explained in previous chapters, a charging order may be made against land of which the debtor is the sole legal and beneficial owner, or against a debtor's interest in land held on trust of which he is a co-beneficial owner. At almost every stage of the enforcement process, the debtor's status as either a sole legal and beneficial owner or as a co-beneficial owner is determinative. It is relevant to:

(a) the jurisdiction under which enforcement may be granted;
(b) the type of application that should be made;
(c) the evidence that must be adduced; and
(d) the order which may ultimately be made.

The question of whether the charging order has been made against property of which the debtor is a sole legal and beneficial owner, or a co-beneficial owner, should thus be established at the outset[2] and is relevant throughout the enforcement process.

COURT'S JURISDICTION AND THE APPROPRIATE COURT

Court's jurisdiction

Alternative means of enforcement: orders for sale and possession, and orders for the appointment of a receiver

6.4 The usual method of enforcement of a charging order is by way of a court order for the sale of the land which is subject to the charging order, or in which the debtor has his charged beneficial interest. A creditor who obtains an order for sale may, subject to the interests of any prior incumbrancers, apply the sale proceeds to satisfy the sums secured by the charging order – the judgment debt, interest and his costs.[3] A possession order will not in itself satisfy the judgment debt, but is often made together with an order for sale, in order that the property may be conveyed to the purchaser with vacant possession, which will usually result in a higher sale price being achieved.[4]

6.5 Originally, the court's jurisdiction to enforce a charging order by an order for sale was not subject to any legislative restriction by reference to the value of the sum that the judgment creditor sought to recover. However, since 6 April 2013, there has been a minimum financial threshold in relation to charging orders which secure a debt arising from a regulated consumer credit agreement.[5] These cannot be enforced by an order for sale to recover a sum below £1,000.[6]

6.6 An alternative means of enforcement is the appointment by the court of a receiver over the debtor's land or interest in land, but a creditor will usually only seek the appointment of a receiver in certain limited situations.[7]

---

2 As to establishing the nature of the debtor's title, see paras 6.28–6.34.

3 For a full discussion of the application of the proceeds of sale, see paras 6.121–6.131.

4 Although a sale with vacant possession will not always be preferable, for example if the charged land consists of commercial premises let to third parties at market rents.

5 As defined by CCA 1974, s 189.

6 See the Charging Orders (Orders for Sale: Financial Thresholds) Regulations 2013 (SI 2013/491). The Regulations were made by the Lord Chancellor under COA 1979, s 3A.

7 See paras 6.138–6.149.

Basis of jurisdiction for enforcement by order for sale: where there is a charging order against the legal estate

6.7 Where a charging order is obtained over property of which the debtor is the sole legal and beneficial owner, the court's jurisdiction to order sale arises from a statutory engagement of its inherent equitable jurisdiction, and is further confirmed by the Civil Procedure Rules.

6.8 Section 3(4) of the Charging Orders Act 1979 provides that, 'subject to the provisions of this Act, a charging order shall have the like effect and shall be enforceable in the same courts and in the same manner as an equitable charge created by the debtor by writing under his hand'. In proceedings for the enforcement of a charging order, that entitles the court to exercise its inherent jurisdiction to grant any of the equitable remedies which it can grant to the creditor under an equitable charge, the most commonly exercised of which remedies is an order for sale.[8]

6.9 The court's jurisdiction to make an order for sale to enforce a charging order is confirmed by rule 73.10C(1) of the Civil Procedure Rules, which provides that 'subject to the provisions of any enactment, the court may, upon a claim by a person who has obtained a charging order over an interest in property, order the sale of the property to enforce the charging order'.

Basis of jurisdiction for enforcement by order for sale: where there is a charging order against the debtor's beneficial interest

6.10 Where a charging order is obtained over the debtor's beneficial interest in property of which he is a co-beneficial owner under a trust of land,[9] the charge does not attach to the legal estate or the entire beneficial interest in the property sought

---

8 The jurisdiction to order sale is one of a range of equitable remedies at the court's disposal on application by the creditor under an equitable charge: the court's equitable jurisdiction extends also to appointing a receiver. However, an equitable chargee has no right to foreclosure nor, *per se* or without a court order, to possession: *Garfitt v Allen* (1887) 37 Ch D 48 at 50, per North J; and *Yorkshire Bank Finance Ltd v Mulhall* [2008] EWCA Civ 1156. On the court's jurisdiction to grant remedies to the creditor under an equitable charge, see generally *Tennant v Trenchard* (1869) LR 4 Ch App 537 and specifically, e.g. *Carreras Rothmans Ltd v Freeman Mathews Treasure Ltd (In Liquidation)* [1985] Ch 207 at 227, per Peter Gibson J.

9 It has only been possible to obtain a charging order over a debtor's beneficial interest in co-owned property since the enactment of COA 1979, s 2(1)(a)(ii). Under the previous law, it had been held in *Irani Finance Ltd v Singh* [1971] Ch 59 that the predecessor provision, AJA 1956, s 35(3), which specified that a charging order could be granted over an 'interest in land', did not permit the grant of a charging order over a beneficial interest in the proceeds of sale under a trust for sale. See Chapter 1, para 1.64.

to be sold, but only to the debtor's beneficial interest in the property.[10] In this situation, the court's inherent jurisdiction to order sale of any property subject to an equitable charge, as engaged by section 3(4) of the Charging Orders Act 1979,[11] could be invoked to sell only the debtor's beneficial interest in the property, rather than the legal estate in the property as a whole: such a course would seldom be practicable or raise much value.[12]

6.11 However, section 14 of the Trusts of Land and Appointment of Trustees Act 1996 gives the court jurisdiction to make orders in relation to property held on trust, including orders for execution of the trust by way of sale of the legal estate, upon an application by 'any person who is a trustee of land or has an interest in property subject to a trust of land'.[13] A creditor with a charging order over a debtor's beneficial interest in property held on trust is a person with 'an interest in property subject to a trust of land' for the purposes of section 14, and so may apply for an order under that section.[14]

Orders for possession in conjunction with orders for sale

6.12 Where the court makes an order for sale, it may also make an order for possession to enable the property to be conveyed with vacant possession,[15] which will usually result in a higher sale price.[16] The court's jurisdiction to make orders

---

10 This situation will arise, for example, where the debtor, and his or her spouse or cohabitant, are joint beneficial owners of the family home. Note that this would also apply if the debtor were the beneficial owner under a bare trust of land where the legal title was held by his nominee.

11 See paras 6.7–6.9 for this source of jurisdiction.

12 See *Midland Bank v Pike and Pike* [1988] 2 All ER 434 at 435J, per Edward Nugee QC; *National Westminster Bank v King* [2008] EWHC 280 (Ch), [2008] Ch 385 at [11].

13 TLATA 1996, s 14(1).

14 This was established conclusively in *Midland Bank v Pike and Pike* [1988] 2 All ER 434, a case decided under LPA 1925, s 30, the predecessor provision to TLATA 1996, s 14. In that case, the deputy judge held that the charge holder over a husband's beneficial interest in the co-owned marital home was 'a person interested' in the trust for sale on which the property was held by and for the husband and his wife. The deputy judge cited several authorities in which this principle had been taken for granted: *Thames Guaranty Ltd v Campbell* [1985] QB 210 at 238–9, per Slade LJ; *First National Securities Ltd v Hegerty* [1985] QB 850; *Harman v Glencross* [1986] Fam 81.

15 See *Garfitt v Allen* (1887) 37 Ch D 48; *Yorkshire Bank Finance Ltd v Mulhall* [2008] EWCA Civ 1156. The two sample orders for sale at CPR PD 73, Appendix A (applicable in cases where the debtor is sole legal and beneficial owner and co-beneficial owner, respectively) each contain provision for the defendant(s) to deliver possession of the property to the claimant at para 5.

16 Although a sale with vacant possession will not always be preferable, for example if the charged land consists of commercial premises let to third parties at market rents.

allowing a judgment creditor to take steps to terminate any tenancies of the property is considered further below.[17]

Basis of jurisdiction for enforcement by the appointment of a receiver

6.13 The court's jurisdiction to appoint a receiver to enforce a charging order arises from its inherent jurisdiction to enforce equitable charges, engaged by section 3(4) of the Charging Orders Act 1979, which provides that a charging order has like effect and is enforceable in the same way as an equitable charge.[18]

6.14 The court's jurisdiction to appoint receivers, including to enforce a charging order, now has a statutory footing, in the High Court pursuant to section 37 of the Senior Courts Act 1981[19] and in the county court pursuant to section 38 of the County Courts Act 1984.[20]

6.15 It should be noted that, in addition to the jurisdiction to appoint a receiver for the purpose of enforcing a charging order, a receiver may be appointed by way of equitable execution without a charging order first being obtained or over land of the debtor which is not subject to the charging order.[21] The appointment of a receiver is itself a distinct and stand-alone method of enforcement.[22] Section 107 of the County Courts Act 1984 provides expressly that the county court may

---

17 See paras 6.95–6.96 and 6.107.

18 The court has an equitable jurisdiction to appoint a receiver over property subject to an equitable charge: *Tennant v Trenchard* (1869) LR 4 Ch App 537; *Carreras Rothmans Ltd v Freeman Mathews Treasure Ltd (In Liquidation)* [1985] Ch 207 at 227, per Peter Gibson J.

19 Section 37(1) provides that, 'the High Court may by order (whether interlocutory or final) grant an injunction or appoint a receiver in all cases in which it appears to the court just and convenient to do so'. Section 37(2) provides that such an order may be made unconditionally or on such terms and conditions as the court considers just.

20 Section 38 provides that the county court may make any order which could be made by the High Court if the proceedings were in the High Court; thus the High Court's jurisdiction under Senior Courts Act 1981, s 37(1) is conferred also on the county court.

21 The appointment of receivers by way of equitable execution itself has now become less common because of the availability of charging orders, as discussed at para 6.138 *et seq*. Receivers are now most commonly appointed either to collect rents from a property or to prevent a beneficial co-owner taking his share of the sale proceeds upon sale of the trust property to the exclusion of his judgment creditor.

22 See further Chapter 1, para 1.16; and para 6.138 *et seq*.

appoint a receiver by way of equitable execution, whether or not a charging order has been imposed on the land.[23]

Appropriate court

High Court

6.16 The High Court has unlimited jurisdiction to enforce charging orders, regardless of the quantum or source of the debt which they secure, except in cases where the debt arises from a regulated consumer credit agreement under the Consumer Credit Act 1974. In those cases, the county court has exclusive jurisdiction[24] and proceedings brought in the High Court to enforce a charging order arising from a regulated consumer credit agreement must be transferred to the county court.[25] As already noted, there is a minimum financial threshold of £1,000 before a sale can be ordered to enforce a charging order arising from a regulated consumer credit agreement.[26]

6.17 Where proceedings to enforce a charging order by way of order for sale are brought in the High Court, paragraph 4.2 of Practice Direction 73 of the Civil Procedure Rules provides that the claim 'must be started in Chancery Chambers at the Royal Courts of Justice, or a Chancery district registry'. However, in *Packman Lucas Ltd v Mentmore Towers Ltd*,[27] Coulson J pointed out that the old rule 73.10[28] did not itself contain such a requirement and held that an order for sale could be made in the Technology and Construction Court, part of the (then)

---

23 CCA 1984, s 107(1) provides that, 'The power of the county court to appoint a receiver by way of equitable execution shall operate in relation to all legal estates and interests in land'. CCA 1984, s 107(2) further provides that, 'The said power may be exercised in relation to an estate or interest in land whether or not a charge has been imposed on that land under section 1 of the Charging Orders Act 1979 for the purpose of enforcing the judgment, decree, order or award in question, and the said power shall be in addition to and not in derogation of any power of any court to appoint a receiver in proceedings for enforcing such a charge'.

24 CCA 1974, s 141(1) provides that, 'in England and Wales the county court shall have jurisdiction to hear and determine (a) any action brought by the creditor or owner to enforce a regulated agreement or any security relating to it; (b) any action to enforce any linked transaction against the debtor or hirer or his relative, and such an action shall not be brought in any other court'. A 'regulated agreement' is defined at CCA 1974, s 189(1). See also High Court and County Courts Jurisdiction Order 1991 (SI 1991/724), art 8(1A).

25 CCA 1974, s 141(2) provides that, 'where an action or application is brought in the High Court which, by virtue of this Act, ought to have been brought in the county court it shall not be treated as improperly brought, but shall be transferred to the county court'.

26 See para 6.5.

27 *Packman Lucas Ltd v Mentmore Towers Ltd* [2010] EWHC 1037 (TCC) at [9] and [10].

28 The relevant rule relating to the enforcement orders, albeit in similar terms, is now CPR r 73.10C.

Queen's Bench Division.[29] Thus, while an order for sale should generally be sought in the Chancery Division, it appears that such a claim may be brought elsewhere in appropriate circumstances.[30]

6.18 Where proceedings for the enforcement of a charging order are brought in the High Court, the High Court may transfer the proceedings to the county court under section 40(2) of the County Courts Act 1984,[31] even if the county court would not otherwise have jurisdiction.[32] Where enforcement proceedings are transferred, the appropriate county court will be either the court which originally made the charging order or, if this was the CNBC,[33] the debtor's home court.[34]

County court

6.19 Enforcing a charging order by way of an order for sale of property of which the debtor is the sole legal and beneficial owner is an exercise of the county court's equitable jurisdiction,[35] and so is subject to the fetters on that jurisdiction imposed by section 23 of the County Courts Act 1984.[36] Section 23(c) limits the county court's equitable jurisdiction to enforce a charge to cases where the amount owing at the commencement of the proceedings[37] does not

---

29 On this point, Coulson J followed his own earlier decision in *Harlow and Milner Ltd v Teasdale* [2006] EWHC 1708 (TCC). No jurisdiction or forum point was taken by the parties in *Packman Lucas Ltd v Mentmore Towers Ltd* [2010] EWHC 1037 (TCC) at any stage in the proceedings, as all parties were keen that the TCC should deal with the applications for orders for sale. Coulson J considered that, 'whilst it will usually be appropriate to seek such orders in the Chancery Division, there will be occasions when it is both proportionate and sensible for orders of sale to be made by other divisions of the High Court'.

30 Note that the decision in *Packman Lucas* was cited with approval in the subsequent case of *Harker v Reynolds* [2015] EWHC 3127 (Ch).

31 CCA 1984, s 40(2) provides that, 'the High Court may order the transfer of any proceedings before it to a county court'. The factors which the High Court will consider before making such a transfer are listed in CPR r 30.3.

32 Where proceedings are transferred by the High Court to the county court in this way, the transfer itself effectively confers jurisdiction on the county court: *National Westminster Bank plc v King* [2008] EWCA Civ 280 (Ch), [2008] Ch 385, per David Richards J.

33 Or, prior to August 2023, by the CCMCC or the CCBC.

34 See CPR r 73.10C(2) and (3).

35 See paras 6.7–6.9.

36 This is confirmed in CPR PD 73, para 4.1A.

37 This limit applies to the debt as owing at the date of issue: *Shields, Whitley and District Amalgamated Model Building Society v Richards* [1901] 84 LT 587. Accordingly, the county court will have jurisdiction, for example, in cases where the debt initially exceeded £350,000, but has fallen below £350,000 by the date of issue.

exceed the county court limit of £350,000.[38] This was significantly increased from £30,000 in 2014.[39]

6.20 The above amendment has, however, given rise to a potential difficulty. This is because, in cases where a claim to enforce a charging order is made against a sole legal and beneficial owner of a property, it will invariably be necessary to seek an order vesting a term of years in the creditor under section 90(1) of the Law of Property Act 1925 to enable the debtor's entire interest to be sold.[40]

6.21 The county court limit under section 90(3) of the Law of Property Act 1925 has not been increased and remains at £30,000. This would suggest that, in cases where an order under section 90(1) is a necessary step to ensure successful enforcement of the charging order, it remains the position that proceedings should only be commenced in the county court if the sum owing under the charging order at the date of the commencement of the proceedings does not exceed £30,000.

6.22 That said, given that the clear intention behind the increase in the county court limit was to broaden the number of claims in the lower courts, it seems unlikely that the county court would now decline jurisdiction where the amount owing is less than £350,000. Indeed, in the authors' experience, the point is not generally taken. On a strict view, however, the point remains undetermined and may, for example, yet be raised by a defendant seeking to buy time.[41]

6.23 Section 24 of the County Court Act 1984 does allow the parties to agree, by signed memorandum, that the county court shall have jurisdiction in cases where the county court limit under sections 23 of the County Courts Act 1984

---

38 CCA 1984, s 23 provides that, 'a county court shall have all the jurisdiction of the High Court to hear and determine–... (c) proceedings for foreclosure or redemption of any mortgage or for enforcing any charge or lien, where the amount owing in respect of the mortgage, charge or lien does not exceed the county court limit'. This limit on the county court's jurisdiction is restated at CPR PD 73, para 4.1: 'a county court has jurisdiction to determine a claim under rule 73.10C for the enforcement of a charging order if the amount owing under the charge does not exceed the county court limit'.

39 County Court Jurisdiction Order 2014 (SI 2014/503).

40 The mechanics of LPA 1925, s 90 are discussed in greater detail below, see paras 6.91–6.96.

41 It might, for example, be said that CPR PD 73, paras 4 and 4.1A cannot unilaterally have the effect of re-writing the jurisdictional requirements set out in primary legislation: see, on that point, *National Westminster Bank v King* [2008] EWHC 280 (Ch), [2008] Ch 385 at [11]–[12], per David Richards J.

and/or s 90 of the Law of Property Act 1925 is exceeded.[42] In a case where there is any doubt, such an agreement may be sensible where the sum owing at the start of the proceedings is more than £30,000 but less than £350,000 or if the sum owing exceeds £350,000. Alternatively, proceedings could be issued in the High Court and an application then made to transfer the proceedings to the county court. The latter strategy, however, is unlikely to be a creditor's first port of call.[43]

6.24 Where an order for sale is sought to enforce a charging order under section 14 of the Trusts of Land and Appointment of Trustees Act 1996 over a property of which the debtor is a beneficial owner only or a co-beneficial owner under a trust of land, the county court would *prima facie* appear to have an unlimited jurisdiction, regardless of the amount in issue, by virtue of article 2(1)(p) of the High Court and County Courts Jurisdiction Order 1991.[44] However, it was stated, *obiter*, in *National Westminster Bank v King*,[45] that the limit imposed on the county court's jurisdiction under section 23 of the County Courts Act 1984 prevails over the general jurisdiction conferred in the 1991 Order. This is because section 23 is primary legislation and the 1991 Order is secondary legislation. If that is correct, the county court's jurisdiction in applications to enforce a charging order by way of order for sale under the 1996 Act is limited to cases where the judgment debt does not exceed £350,000.[46]

6.25 Strictly speaking, until there is appellate authority on this point, a cautious creditor may wish to issue proceedings in the High Court where the judgment exceeds £350,000. An application could then be made for the claim to be transferred to the county court, if appropriate. Alternatively, the parties could simply agree, by signed memorandum, for the claim to be brought in the county court under section 24 of the 1984 Act. The authors are, however, aware of

---

42 CCA 1984, s 24(1), provides that, 'If, as respects any proceedings to which this section applies, the parties agree, by a memorandum signed by them or by their respective legal representatives or agents, that a county court specified in the memorandum shall have jurisdiction in the proceedings, that court shall, notwithstanding anything in any enactment, have jurisdiction to hear and determine the proceedings accordingly'. The proceedings to which that section applies include CCA 1984, s 23 and LPA 1925, s 90 : see CCA 1984, s 24(2)(c) and (g).

43 If such an application were granted, this would in itself confer jurisdiction on the county court, even if the county court otherwise did not have jurisdiction: see para 6.18.

44 SI 1991/724. Article 2(1) provides that, 'a county court shall have jurisdiction under– ... (p) sections 13 and 14 of the Trusts of Land and Appointment of Trustees Act 1996, ... whatever the amount involved in the proceedings and whatever the value of any asset or fund connected with the proceedings'.

45 *National Westminster Bank v King* [2008] EWHC 280 (Ch), [2008] Ch 385 at [11]–[12], per David Richards J

46 With respect, the judge's *obiter* view may be open to doubt. CCA 1984, s 23 applies to equity proceedings, and it is not clear that the limit in that section applies to claims brought under TLATA 1996, s 14, which confers a statutory, rather than an equitable, jurisdiction on the county court.

the county court widely accepting jurisdiction for claims under the 1996 Act, whatever their value, so the point may in fact arise rarely in practice.

6.26 The county court does have unlimited jurisdiction where the judgment debt which the charging order secures arises out of a regulated consumer credit agreement under the Consumer Credit Act 1974.[47] However, as already noted, since 6 April 2013, there has been a minimum financial threshold for enforcement by way of order for sale of charging orders arising from regulated consumer credit agreements.[48]

6.27 The county court's limited jurisdiction to enforce charging orders by way of order for sale is in notable contrast to its unlimited jurisdiction to impose charging orders.[49] However, there is a rationale behind the distinction. As the White Book notes to rule 73.10C of the Civil Procedure Rules explain,[50] 'it is one thing to make an order giving security to the judgment creditor and quite another to order a sale of a judgment debtor's property ... To order sale is a draconian step to satisfy a simple debt'.[51]

ORDERS FOR SALE

Establishing the debtor's title

6.28 Before making an order for sale, the court must be satisfied as to the nature of the debtor's title to the charged property. Evidence as to the nature of the debtor's title will already have been adduced at the stages of applying for and obtaining an interim and final charging order.[52] However, evidence which sufficed at those stages may not be sufficient at the stage of enforcement. At those earlier stages, if there had been doubt as to the nature of the debtor's title, a charge may nonetheless have been granted, as it could only ever have attached to such interest as the debtor did in fact have in the property.[53] If it transpired that he had none, then no charge would in fact have been imposed.[54] However, at the stage of enforcing the charging order, the court must be satisfied that the debtor in fact has

---

47 CCA 1974, s 141 and High Court and County Courts Jurisdiction Order 1991, art 8(1).

48 See para 6.5.

49 See Chapter 3, paras 3.7–3.8.

50 *Civil Procedure 2023* (Sweet & Maxwell, 2023).

51 David Richards J referred to the notes to the old CPR r 73.10 (now CPR r 73.10C) in explaining the county court's limited jurisdiction to enforce charging orders in *National Westminster Bank plc v King* [2008] EWHC 280 (Ch), [2008] Ch 385 at [8].

52 As to which, see Chapter 3, para 3.28(h).

53 *Walton v Allman* [2015] EWHC 3325 (Ch).

54 See further Chapter 3, para 3.40.

an interest in the property to be sold, and as to the nature of that interest. A summary of the particular steps to be taken, from initial investigations to the conclusive establishment of the nature of the debtor's title, is given below.

6.29 The method of proving title will differ according to whether the property is registered (which it is likely to be in most cases) or unregistered. If the creditor does not already know whether the property is registered or unregistered, this can be easily discovered by making an official search of the Index Map maintained by HM Land Registry,[55] either on paper or online. The certificate of result issued by HM Land Registry will show whether the property is registered, subject to a pending application for first registration, or subject to a caution against first registration.

Identifying the legal owner (registered land and unregistered land)

6.30 Where the property is registered, then proving title will be relatively straightforward in most cases. The creditor should obtain an official copy of the registered title from HM Land Registry, which will give details not only of the registered proprietor of the property, but also of any prior charges and incumbrances which have priority over the creditor's charging order. An official copy is admissible as evidence of the matters mentioned therein, to the same extent as the register itself, without the need for a witness to be called.[56] If the official copy shows the debtor as the sole registered proprietor, then his title to the legal estate will be established. So too will his beneficial ownership, as there is a presumption that beneficial ownership mirrors the legal title.[57] If, however, the property is registered in the joint names of the debtor and others, or if the property is registered in another's name and not the debtor's, then the debtor will, at best, be a beneficial co-owner of the property.[58] The creditor will then need to prove the debtor's beneficial interest[59] and seek enforcement of the charging order by an application under section 14 of the Trusts of Land and Appointment of Trustees Act 1996.

---

55 LRR 2003, rr 10 and 145.

56 LRA 2002, s 67(1).

57 See e.g. *Stack v Dowden* [2007] UKHL 17, [2007] 2 AC 432; *Jones v Kernott* [2011] UKSC 53, [2012] 1 AC 776.

58 When considering the registered title, practitioners should look out for a Form A restriction, which will indicate a beneficial tenancy in common: see HM Land Registry, Practice Guide 19*: notices, restrictions and the protection of third-party interests in the register* (20 February 2023) and *Practice Guide 24: private trusts of land* (3 July 2023). If there is an express trust containing terms requiring consents, etc there may also be further restrictions on the title.

59 See para 6.33 *et seq*.

6.31 Where the property is unregistered, proving the debtor's title in the legal estate may be more difficult. Ultimately, it will be necessary to have recourse to the title deeds to show in whom the legal estate is vested.[60] Those title deeds may be held by the legal owner or by a mortgagee of the property or may have been lost. The judgment creditor may already be aware of the debtor's title, through sight of the title deeds in the proceedings which led to the judgment or charging order. Otherwise, a number of options are open to the creditor.

6.32 The creditor may use Part 71 of the Civil Procedure Rules (Orders to Obtain Information from Judgment Debtors). By rule 71.2, the creditor may obtain an order for the debtor to attend court and be questioned on oath as to any matter about which information is needed to enforce a judgment or order. If this reveals that the title deeds are held by the debtor, then the creditor may obtain an injunction requiring the debtor to lodge the title deeds at court together with an affidavit as to the completeness of the deeds. An enquiry under Part 71 may reveal that the title deeds are held by a mortgagee. If that is so, enquiries should be made of the mortgagee as to the names on the title deeds. If it transpires that the title deeds have been lost, unless the debtor is able to give evidence that he has acquired title by adverse possession, the creditor may face an evidential difficulty.

Identifying the beneficial owner and the extent of their interest

6.33 A creditor who has obtained a charging order over a debtor's beneficial interest will usually have adduced evidence of the debtor's beneficial interest at the stage of obtaining the interim and final orders: only with such evidence can the charging order have been made expressly over the debtor's beneficial interest.[61] At the stage of enforcement, however, the creditor will, if he has not already done so, be required to provide evidence of the extent of the debtor's beneficial interest.[62]

6.34 The form which the evidence of the nature and extent of the debtor's beneficial interest takes will depend on the circumstances. It may be that the equitable interests of the debtor and his co-owner(s) were defined expressly by a

---

60 For the deduction of title to unregistered land, see e.g. S Bridge, E Cooke and M Dixon, *Megarry & Wade, The Law of Real Property* (Sweet & Maxwell, 9th edn, 2019), paras 5-027–5-032.

61 See further Chapter 3, para 3.28(h).

62 This will be needed to ensure that the correct order is made with respect to the application of the proceeds of sale. See paras 6.126–6.131.

trust instrument,[63] in which case the trust instrument itself will be decisive, except in cases where there has been a subsequent variation in the equitable interests by agreement or by court order.[64] If the debtor and his beneficial co-owners had held the equitable interests in the property as joint tenants, then the making of the charging order will have severed the joint tenancy and created a tenancy in common: under the equitable maxim of 'equality is equity', the debtor and his beneficial co-owners will then be taken to hold the equitable interest in the property in equal shares, unless the debtor or a co-beneficiary can adduce evidence to support an alternative apportionment.[65] In cases where the debtor's equitable interest has arisen impliedly, for example by way of a resulting or constructive trust, the extent of the beneficial co-owners' equitable interests in the property will have been determined by the court in the claim which established the resulting or constructive trust and so will be defined in the court's judgment and any subsequent order.

Exercise of the court's discretion

6.35 The court's discretion, already engaged in deciding whether to make an interim and then a final charging order,[66] is engaged for a third time upon the creditor's application to enforce the charging order by way of an order for sale. An order for sale of property of which the debtor is the sole legal and beneficial owner is, as already explained,[67] an equitable remedy and is, therefore, like all equitable remedies, discretionary. An order for sale of charged property of which the debtor is a co-beneficial owner is made under section 14 of the Trusts of Land and Appointment of Trustees Act 1996,[68] which itself confers a discretion on the court in deciding whether or not to make an order.[69]

6.36 The courts have often emphasised that there is a considerable difference between merely deciding to grant a creditor security by way of a charging order, and then deciding to enforce the charging order by way of granting an order for sale. The latter is seen as an extreme remedy for which clear justification will be

---

63 For example, a transfer by which the legal title in the property was conveyed to the debtor and his spouse or cohabitant to hold on trust for themselves as joint tenants or as tenants in common in defined shares.

64 For example, an order under the Matrimonial Causes Act 1973.

65 *Cf Goodman v Gallant* [1986] Fam 106 at 119.

66 As to which, see Chapter 2.

67 See paras 6.7–6.9.

68 See para 6.11.

69 Section 14(2) provides that, 'on an application for an order under this section the court *may* make any such order ... as the court thinks fit' (emphasis added).

required.[70] The commentary at note 73.10C.1 in the White Book is often cited by judges when articulating these principles.[71] Thus, while the matters pertinent to the court's discretion when granting a charging order remain relevant when the court is considering whether or not to make an order for sale, the court must expand its view to consider all the circumstances when deciding whether to make an order for sale – and the emphasis placed on those matters which were considered when the charging order was granted may change.[72]

Factors relevant to the exercise of the court's discretion in all cases

6.37 Where the property is the debtor's and/or his family's home, the welfare of those in occupation of the property[73] will be relevant to the exercise of the

---

70 In *National Guild of Removers and Storers Ltd v Jones and Coid* [2012] EWCA Civ 216, [2012] 1 WLR 2501 at [9], Pitchford LJ identified the 'important distinction between providing security for the judgment debt and the order for sale of the property on which the judgment debt is secured' and described the order for sale as the 'ultimate sanction' for which 'powerful reasons will be required'. In *Royal Oak Property Co Ltd v Iktilat* [2008] EWHC 1703 (Ch) at [9], Floyd J said that, 'the sanction [of an order for sale] is an extreme one which should be resorted to only in extreme cases, particularly where the property to be sold is the debtor's home. Nevertheless where it is clear that the debt will not be paid unless an order for sale is made, the order may be justified'.

71 The following note to the old CPR r 73.10.1, which remains in unaltered form in the notes to the new CPR r 73.10C.1 in *Civil Procedure 2023* (Sweet & Maxwell, 2023), was referred to in *Forrester Ketley & Co v Brent and Pallette* [2009] EWHC 3441 (Ch) at [52], per Vos J, 'It is one thing to make a charging order giving security to the judgment creditor and quite another thing to order a sale of the judgment debtor's property. Just as the court has a discretion whether or not to make the charging order so it has discretion whether or not to order the sale. It would be an extreme sanction and all circumstances would have to be considered. Where the property is the debtor's home, the Court will have to consider the provisions of Art 8 European Convention of Human Rights. To order sale is a draconian step to satisfy a simple debt and is likely to be ordered for example, in a case of the judgment debtor's contumelious neglect or refusal to pay or in a case where in reality without a sale the judgment debt will not be paid (see, *e.g.*, *Barclays Bank v Hendricks* [1996] 1 FLR 258 where the court ordered a sale even though the proceeds would amount to only about 20 per cent of the debt). Even where a sale is ordered, the Court could suspend the order on terms as to payment by instalments, or postpone the sale until a specified future date (see, *e.g.*, *Austin-Fell v Austin-Fell* [1990] Fam 172). Of course, different considerations would apply if it were not the debtor's home and they held the property as a second home or as an investment. In all cases relevant factors will include the size of the judgment debt and the value of the property.'

72 For instance, now that the creditor is secured, the debtor's potential insolvency would be of less concern at the stage of ordering a sale than it was at the stage of granting a charging order in the first place, at which time the creditor was promoted from being an unsecured to a secured creditor.

73 As explained at para 6.77, CPR PD 73, para 4.3(6) and (7) requires the claimant for an order for sale under CPR r 73.10C to identify in his written evidence details of any person in possession of the property, to the best of the claimant's knowledge, and details of any spouse on whose behalf a Class F land charge or a notice under Family Law Act 1996, s 31(10) has been registered. Where the order for sale is sought under TLATA 1996, the identity of those in occupation of the property is likely to emerge from the evidence relating to the trust of land on which the property is held.

court's discretion,[74] both where the order for sale is sought under section 14 of the Trusts of Land and Appointment of Trustees Act 1996, against a property of which the debtor is a joint beneficial owner, and also, it now appears,[75] where the order is sought against a property of which the debtor is the sole legal and beneficial owner. In both types of case, it is clear that regard must be had to the occupiers' rights under Article 8 of the European Convention on Human Rights and that the court's discretion must be exercised compatibly with Convention rights.[76]

6.38 The ratio of the debt to the value of the charged asset may be considered by the court when it is asked to make an order for sale, as it is when the court is asked to make an interim or final charging order.[77] However, that factor is likely to be given far greater weight in the context of an application for an order for sale. It is one thing for the court to grant security for a relatively small debt, but the

---

74 Welfare considerations have included, in *Forrester Ketley & Co v Brent and Pallette* [2009] EWHC 3441 (Ch), the fact that the property had been the home of the debtor and his wife for a period of 8 years, the health of the occupants and the stress caused by ordering possession.

75 See *Close Invoice Finance Ltd v Pile* [2009] EWHC 1580 (Ch), [2009] 1 FLR 873, in which earlier authority to the contrary in *Pickering v Wells* [2002] 2 P & CR DG 23 was not followed. In *Pickering*, David Oliver QC, sitting as a Deputy Judge of the Chancery Division, held that, in determining whether or not to make an order for sale against property of which the debtor was the sole legal and beneficial owner, the court was limited to considering the competing proprietary interests of other occupiers of the property, but not their welfare: this was contrasted by the deputy judge with the position on an application for an order for sale under TLATA 1996, s 14, where s 15 requires the court to have regard to the welfare of any minor occupying the property. The deputy judge held that the then RSC Ord 88, r 5(A)(2)(f) – now CPR PD 73, para 4.3(6) and (7) – was intended to give the court notice of occupiers' competing proprietary interests, but not to bring those persons' welfare into consideration. The deputy judge held that this was entirely consistent with the policy of law that a creditor is entitled to be paid and to be paid in due time; and that this was not inconsistent with European Convention on Human Rights, Art 8. In *Close*, however, HHJ Purle QC, sitting as a Judge of the Chancery Division, did not follow *Pickering*: he held that it would be 'somewhat capricious' if the welfare of other occupiers fell to be considered where the debtor was a joint beneficial owner (and hence the claim for an order for sale was made under TLATA 1996), but not where the debtor was a sole legal and beneficial owner. It is suggested that the decision in *Close* is clearly to be preferred.

76 See e.g. *Forrester Ketley & Co v Brent and Pallette* [2009] EWHC 3441 (Ch); *Close Invoice Finance Ltd v Pile* [2009] EWHC 1580 (Ch), [2009] 1 FLR 873; *C Putnam & Sons v Taylor* [2009] EWHC 317 (Ch), [2009] BPIR 769. In cases brought under TLATA 1996, consideration of the factors listed in s 15 will often satisfy in itself the need to balance the creditor's rights under First Protocol, Art 1 and the debtor's rights under Art 8. There may be circumstances where it is necessary for the court to go beyond this and explicitly consider whether an order for sale is a proportionate interference with the Art 8 rights of those affected, but that will not always be necessary: see *National Westminster Bank plc v Rushmer* [2010] EWHC 554 (Ch), [2010] 2 FLR 362 at [50], per Arnold J. See also Chapter 2, para 2.53 *et seq*.

77 The court may exercise its discretion against making an interim or final charging order where the debt is very small relative to the value of the asset to be charged: see *Robinson v Bailey* [1942] Ch 268 at 271; *Re Goldspan Ltd* [2003] BPIR 93, [2001] All ER (D) 412 (Oct); but see Chapter 2, para 2.45.

court is far more likely to be reluctant to allow an order for sale where it perceives that it is 'being used as a sledge-hammer to crack a nut', that is, where the debt is very small relative to the value of the asset.[78] However, there are no hard-and-fast rules in this regard and the fact that a debt is small compared to the value of the property will not necessarily prevent an order for sale being made – and may sometimes, in fact, tip the balance towards an order, where it demonstrates the debtor's unwillingness to pay despite having the means to do so.[79] Where there is sufficient equity in the property to enable the debtor and his or her spouse to be able to afford another home, albeit a smaller one, after discharge of the charging order and prior incumbrances, this may weigh in favour of an order for sale being made.[80]

6.39 The attitude of other secured creditors, if known, will be relevant to the exercise of the court's discretion. The claimant who seeks an order for sale under rule 73.10C of the Civil Procedure Rules must state in his evidence[81] who the prior incumbrancers are, how much they are owed and (if known) their order of priority.[82] When gathering this information, it may be possible for the judgment creditor to canvass these other secured creditors' attitude to a sale. If there is a majority view in favour of a sale, that may assist in persuading the court to order a sale.

6.40 The right of the judgment creditor to enforce his security, the attitude of the judgment debtor towards paying the debt, and the prospects of payment without an order for sale, are all factors to be considered and weighed against the

---

78 This was the view expressed in G C P Walker and M E Buckley, *Charging Orders Against Land: Law, Procedure & Precedents* (Barry Rose Law Publishers, 2nd edn, 2004), p 249 (Walker and Buckley).

79 In such cases, a suspended or postponed order may be made to prompt the debtor into payment. See also *Packman Lucas Ltd v Mentmore Towers Ltd* [2010] EWHC 1037 (TCC). In that case, it was argued that an order for sale should not be made as the debt was only £35,000 and the property was worth £15 million. Pointing out that the argument would not be available if the house were a modest one worth £250,000 and that the greater the value of the asset, the greater is the default, Coulson J rejected the argument as offending against common sense and at [31] added, 'if the only point had been the relative size of the debt when compared to the value of the property, I would not have been persuaded that an order for sale was inappropriate'.

80 See e.g. *C Putnam & Sons v Taylor* [2009] EWHC 317 (Ch), [2009] BPIR 769 at [6].

81 *Cf* the position when applying for a charging order in the first place. At that stage, there is no requirement for a judgment creditor to specify the quantum of the debts owed to other creditors; the judgment creditor must simply state if he knows of the existence of any other creditors and, if known, their names and addresses: CPR PD 73, para 1.2(5).

82 CPR PD 73, para 4.3(4).

interests and rights of the judgment debtor and other occupiers of the property.[83] Where a debtor has, as a matter of choice, kept a judgment creditor out of his money under a policy that payment will only be made as a last resort, the court is likely to be better disposed towards making an order for sale.[84]

6.41 In a case where a creditor has obtained judgment against multiple debtors who are jointly and severally liable, and has obtained charging orders over each of their properties, the court will have to decide whether an order for sale should be made in respect of each (or any) of the properties and, if so, in what order. In *Re Shri Guru Ravidass Sabha Southall*,[85] the High Court decided that all three of the debtors' properties should be sold together. It was said that the court's role was not to give marks for good or bad conduct but rather to control the enforcement process. On the facts of that case, it would have been unfair and unjust to order only one property to be sold, leaving one of the debtors to fund a contribution claim against the others.

Factors relevant to the exercise of the court's discretion where the charging order is against the debtor's beneficial interest

6.42 Where the debtor has a beneficial interest in the charged property but is not the owner or sole owner of the legal title, and the application for an order for sale is accordingly made under section 14 of the Trusts of Land and Appointment of Trustees Act 1996,[86] then section 15 provides that the court must[87] have regard to the following (non-exhaustive) list of factors when considering whether to make the order:

---

83 In *Close Invoice Finance Ltd v Pile* [2008] EWHC 1580 (Ch), [2009] 1 FLR 873, the judge had regard to the rights of the creditor not to have to wait indefinitely for payment and not to be left without means of enforcing his security. In *Forrester Ketley v Brent and Pallette* [2009] EWHC 3441 (Ch), Vos J took into account the debtor's previous refusal to comply with court orders; the evidence that the debtor had made no efforts to raise monies to discharge the debt; and the absence of any substantial reason why the property should not be used for that payment. See also the note to CPR r 73.10C.1 in *Civil Procedure 2023* (Sweet & Maxwell, 2023), suggesting that an order for sale will be appropriate 'in a case of the judgment debtor's contumelious neglect or refusal to pay or in a case where in reality without a sale the judgment debt will not be paid'.

84 *The Secretary of State for Communities and Local Government v Bartlet* [2017] 1 WLUK 433.

85 [2017] EWHC 1255 (Ch).

86 This will apply whether the debtor owns the entire beneficial interest (and the legal title is thus held by a nominee) or whether the debtor co-owns the beneficial interest with other persons.

87 TLATA 1996, s 15(1) provides that, 'the matters to which the court *is to have regard* in determining an application for an order under s 14 include ...' (emphasis added).

(a) the intentions of the person or persons (if any) who created the trust;[88]
(b) the purposes for which the property subject to the trust is held;[89]
(c) the welfare of any minor who occupies or might reasonably be expected to occupy any land subject to the trust as his home;[90]
(d) the interests of any secured creditor of any beneficiary;[91] and
(e) the circumstances and wishes of any beneficiaries of full age and entitled to an interest in possession in property subject to the trust or (in case of dispute) of the majority (according to the value of their combined interests).[92]

6.43 In *Mortgage Corporation v Shaire*,[93] Neuberger J contrasted the position under sections 14 and 15 of the Trusts of Land and Appointment of Trustees Act 1996 with that which had prevailed under its predecessor provision, section 30 of the Law of Property Act 1925.[94] He held that the list of factors set out in section 15 had tipped the balance more in favour of families and against banks and other chargees when the court was deciding whether to order the sale of property held on trust under section 14 than had been the case under section 30. Nevertheless, it remains a powerful consideration that a creditor will be kept out of his money. The fact that greater weight is to be placed on the interests of families does not necessarily mean that their interests will outweigh those of creditors.[95] Moreover, a judgment creditor with the benefit of a charging order may well be more impecunious than a typical institutional lender, and may suffer real financial hardship if he is unable to secure payment of his judgment debt by enforcement of the charging order.

Suspension of the order

6.44 The court may give effect to its discretion by making a postponed or suspended order for possession and/or sale, rather than choosing between an

---

88 TLATA 1996, s 15(1)(a).

89 TLATA 1996, s 15(1)(b).

90 TLATA 1996, s 15(1)(c).

91 TLATA 1996, s 15(1)(d).

92 TLATA 1996, s 15(2) and (3).

93 *Mortgage Corporation v Shaire* [2001] EWHC 452 (Ch), [2001] Ch 743.

94 LPA 1925, s 30 conferred power on the court to order sale in cases where trustees for sale refused to exercise their powers. The TLATA 1996 abolished trusts for sale, replacing them with trusts of land, repealed s 30, and replaced it with s 14.

95 See e.g. *Bank of Ireland Home Mortgage Ltd v Bell* [2001] 2 All ER (Comm) 920, esp at [30]; *Fred Perry (Holdings) Ltd v Genis* [2015] 2 P & CR DG5. These were both applications for an order for sale under TLATA 1996 where the rights of the creditor prevailed and a sale was ordered.

outright order and no order at all.[96] The discretion to postpone or suspend is available whether the order is made against property of which the debtor is the sole legal and beneficial owner or is a joint beneficial owner.[97]

Procedure for application

Steps prior to making an application

Overview

- There should first be pre-action correspondence with the judgment debtor and any other prior incumbrancers.
- The judgment creditor will need to establish the nature of the judgment debtor's title or interest in the charged property. This is because the claim to be made differs depending on whether the interest is legal or beneficial only. It is also useful to identify anyone else, for example a spouse or partner with home rights, as they will also need to be made a party to the claim.
- The claim should be made by Part 8 claim form, with supporting details of claim and witness evidence.

---

96 In *Close Invoice Finance Ltd v Pile* [2008] EWHC 1580 (Ch), [2009] 1 FLR 873, possession pursuant to an order for sale was postponed for a year, in view of the possible disruption to the debtor's family, the fact that the debtor's financial situation might improve and because the value of the property would be sufficient to discharge the debt on sale, even following a year's postponement. In *Pritchard Englefield (A Firm) v Steinberg* [2004] EWHC 1908 (Ch), [2004] All ER (D) 580 (Jul), the judge made an order for sale with vacant possession but provided that possession was to be delivered up within 2 months to give the judgment debtor's mother (who had lived at the property for 40 years and was found to have a life interest in the property) time to find a buyer who would purchase subject to her beneficial interest: see [63]. In *C Putnam & Sons v Taylor* [2009] EWHC 317 (Ch), [2009] BPIR 769, the court postponed the date by which possession was ordered to be given in order to provide an opportunity to the debtor to effect a private sale and find an alternative property: see [38]. In *Fred Perry (Holdings) Ltd v Genis* [2015] 2 P & CR DG5, possession was postponed for one year so as to enable to defendants to relocate and make arrangements for the education of their children who were attending specialist Jewish schools. Postponement may also be granted where the debtor has applied to set aside the judgment on which the debt is based. Thus, in *Royal Oak Property Co Ltd v Iktilat* [2008] EWHC 1703 (Ch), the court ordered sale, but stayed the order until final judgment of the debtor's pending application to set aside the judgment on which the debt was based: the stay was made conditional upon the judgment debtor's undertaking to pursue the application with due diligence: see [64].

97 *Close Invoice Finance Ltd v Pile* [2008] EWHC 1580 (Ch), [2009] 1 FLR 873 was a case involving a sole legal and beneficial owner, whereas *C Putnam & Sons v Taylor* [2009] EWHC 317 (Ch), [2009] BPIR 769 was a TLATA 1996 case.

- The witness evidence should include evidence from estate agents as to the value of the property and redemption figures provided by prior incumbrancers to show that the proceeds of sale will likely be enough to repay at least some of the judgment debt once prior incumbrances have been redeemed.

6.45 No specific pre-action protocol applies to an application for an order for sale brought by a judgment creditor to enforce a charging order. However, it is advisable for a creditor who is contemplating an enforcement claim to engage in constructive pre-action correspondence both with the debtor (who may have proposals for raising funds to discharge the debt) and with any prior incumbrancers (to establish what their attitude would be to an enforcement claim).[98]

6.46 Before a judgment creditor commences enforcement proceedings there are several steps which he should first take.

6.47 First, if he has not done so already, the judgment creditor should establish the nature of the debtor's title.[99] The form and substance of the application to be made varies according to whether the debtor is a sole legal and beneficial owner or a sole or joint beneficial owner. Accordingly, the creditor must establish the nature of the debtor's title before applying for an order for sale, to ensure that he makes the application in the correct form. In any event, the court will not grant an order for sale until and unless the nature of the debtor's title has been established. A creditor who commences an enforcement claim without having gathered sufficient evidence on this point will be directed by the court to do so.

6.48 Secondly, the judgment creditor should investigate whether there are any prior incumbrancers. If there are, he should ascertain their identity, the nature of their security and the amounts secured. A judgment creditor is required to make reasonable enquiries regarding those matters, prior to commencing his claim, by Practice Direction 73 of the Civil Procedure Rules.[100] The judgment creditor should try to ascertain the attitude of prior incumbrancers to the prospective enforcement claim. If a prior incumbrancer is about to make an application for an order for sale, the judgment creditor should normally abandon his own prospective enforcement application and await satisfaction of the sum secured by his charging order from the proceeds of the sale conducted by the other creditor.

6.49 Thirdly, the judgment creditor should investigate who, in addition to other chargees, may need to be informed of the claim or made a party. In particular,

---

98 See further para 6.48.

99 As to investigation of the debtor's title, see para 6.28 *et seq*.

100 See CPR PD 73, para 4.3(4).

he should ascertain whether the debtor's spouse or civil partner has home rights in the property, protected by a Class F land charge under section 2(7) of the Land Charges Act 1972 (if the title to the land is unregistered) or a notice under section 31(10) of the Family Law Act 1996 (for registered land).[101] This can be done by making a search at HM Land Registry in the case of registered land or by carrying out an official search at the Land Charges Department using Form K15[102] in the case of unregistered land. If those enquiries disclose that some person has the benefit of home rights in the property, that person must be notified of the claim.[103] A debtor's spouse, and any other adult who occupies the property, either with the debtor or as a tenant, will need to be added as a defendant to the claim in order for possession to be granted against them. The creditor should therefore investigate who is in possession, if necessary, by engaging an enquiry agent.[104]

6.50 Fourthly, the judgment creditor should give consideration to the possibility of appointing one or more estate agents to conduct an external-view[105] valuation of the property ahead of making his application. There is no express requirement to do so, but the creditor must provide an estimate of the price which would be obtained on the sale of the property[106] and the court is likely to direct a valuation if one has not already been obtained. The court will wish to know the ratio of the debt to the value of the property when exercising its discretion as to whether to make an order for sale.[107] Furthermore, any order for sale ultimately made by the court will likely set a threshold price below which the property may not be sold.[108]

6.51 Fifthly, the judgment creditor will need to give consideration as to whether there are any other legal bars to successfully obtaining an order for sale. A potential example of this is where the debtor in question (or a co-owner with the

---

101 See CPR PD 73, para 4.3(7).

102 LCA 1972, s 10 and Land Charges Rules 1974 (SI 1974/1286) (as amended by the Land Charges Amendment Rules 2012 (SI 2012/2884)), r 16.

103 See CPR PD 73, para 4.3(7)(b)(ii). It may be necessary to seek an order that that person's home rights are terminated: see *Fred Perry (Holdings) Ltd v Genis* [2015] 1 P & CR DG5.

104 See CPR PD 73, para 4.3(6).

105 In most cases the judgment debtor is unlikely to allow an internal inspection. If that were to become necessary following the issue of the claim, the court could grant an appropriate injunction to allow access.

106 See CPR PD 73, para 4.3(5).

107 As to the relevance of the debt-to-value ratio in the exercise of the court's discretion, see para 6.38.

108 The sample orders at CPR PD 73, Appendix A make provision for such a minimum price threshold at para 2.

debtor) is sanctioned, for example, if they are a 'designated person' under the Russia (Sanctions) (EU Exit) Regulations 2019.[109]

6.52 A detailed consideration of the law of sanctions falls outside the scope of this work. By way of worked example, however, if the judgment debtor were a 'designated person' for the purposes of the 2019 Regulations, the creditor would seem to be caught by regulation 11, which provides that: 'A person ("P") must not deal with funds or economic resources owned, held or controlled by a designated person if P knows, or has reasonable cause to expect, that P is dealing with such funds or economic resources'. Under regulation 60, land is an 'economic resource' and a sale of land would be 'dealing with' an economic resource and, as such, in breach of these asset-freezing provisions.

6.53 Regulation 64, however, provides that the above provisions 'do not apply to anything done under the authority of a licence issued by the Treasury under this paragraph'.

6.54 The Treasury, through the Office of Financial Sanctions Implementation (OFSI), only has power to issue licences where it is 'appropriate' to do so for certain prescribed purposes, which are set out in Part I of Schedule 5.[110] In the context of enforcement of charging orders, two of the prescribed purposes would appear to be of note:

(a) *Paragraph 6*: to enable, by the use of the designated person's frozen funds or economic resources, the implementation or satisfaction of a judicial decision provided that, amongst other things, the funds or economic resources so used are the subject of the relevant decision, and it was made before the date when the person became a designated person.
(b) *Paragraph 8*: to enable, by the use of the designated person's frozen funds or economic resources, the satisfaction of an obligation of that person (whether arising from a contract, other agreement or otherwise) provided that the obligation arose before the date on which the person became a designated person and no payments are made to another designated person, whether directly or indirectly.

6.55 In a case where the creditor obtains an order for sale *before* the debtor becomes a designated person, the creditor, it seems, would need to apply to OFSI for a licence to enforce the order in reliance on paragraph 6: the order for sale would be a 'judicial decision', the property in question would have been the

[109] SI 2019/855.

[110] Russia (Sanctions) (EU Exit) Regulations 2019, reg 64(2)(a).

subject of that decision and the decision would have been made before the debtor or relevant co-owner became a designated person.

6.56 Similarly, where the relevant judgment debt/charging order arises *after* a person becomes a designated person[111] but in pursuance of an obligation of that person arising *before* his designation, it ought to be possible to apply to OFSI for a licence before seeking an order for sale in reliance on paragraph 8.

6.57 There is considerably more uncertainty where the cause of action giving rise to the judgment debt only arises *after* the person becomes a designated person. This is because it is presently unclear from the wording of paragraph 8 whether it catches all contractual obligations entered into prior to designation (whether or not the specific contractual obligation has fallen due for performance before designation) or whether it simply embraces those obligations which have actually fallen due for performance by the date of designation. In such a case, specialist advice is likely to be necessary.

6.58 Of course, the analysis may differ depending on the specific sanctions regime which applies. The key point for practitioners to be aware of, however, is the potential need for a licence permitting the enforcement of an order for sale. It should be noted in this regard that it is OFSI's policy not to grant licences retrospectively.[112]

Creditor's decision as to whether or not to apply for an order for sale

6.59 The outcome of the investigations discussed at paras 6.45–6.48 should assist a judgment creditor in deciding whether or not to apply for an order for sale. He will retain the security of his charging order whether or not he makes an enforcement claim.

6.60 Two factors that will be particularly relevant to the judgment creditor's decision whether or not to seek an order for sale are:

(a) whether the debtor is the sole legal and beneficial owner or is merely a beneficial co-owner. This will indicate the extent of the debtor's equity in the property and the creditor's prospects of recovering the sum secured by his charging order upon a sale; and

---

111 The recent decision in *PJSC National Bank Trust v Mints* [2023] EWHC 118 (Comm) suggests that this is possible.

112 Guidance on how to apply for a licence can be found on OFSI's website, see www.gov.uk/guidance/licences-that-allow-activity-prohibited-by-financial-sanctions.

(b) whether there are prior incumbrancers and whether any of them proposes to seek a sale. This may influence the judgment creditor's decision of whether or not to seek a sale.[113]

6.61 A decision by the judgment creditor to seek a sale should not be taken lightly because:

(a) the court has a discretion whether or not to order a sale; it is not certain that the judgment creditor's claim will succeed;
(b) an application for an order for sale may not result in the swift satisfaction of the judgment debt. Unless the debtor pays the debt immediately, the creditor will face at least one court hearing and, if he is unable to produce all the necessary evidence at that hearing,[114] or if any dispute arises (e.g. as to the level of the debt[115]), there may be one or more subsequent hearings; and
(c) even when an order is made, the sale may be postponed or suspended. Even if it is not, any sale will involve the usual delays between finding a buyer, exchanging contracts and completion.

6.62 If an order for sale is made, the judgment creditor or his solicitors are likely to be given conduct of the sale and so will have to instruct an estate agent or auctioneer to carry it out. Although the creditor's costs of sale will ultimately be recoverable from the sale proceeds, he will nevertheless be personally liable for the professional fees of those whom he instructs. Furthermore, in a case where the debtor is the sole legal and beneficial owner, and in some cases, where he is a joint beneficial owner,[116] the creditor will be the party who contracts to sell and convey the land. He will therefore be personally liable to the purchaser on the contract and on the covenants for title given in the conveyance.

6.63 All of the above factors should be considered carefully by a creditor in deciding whether or not to apply for an order for sale.

Procedure for an application for an order for sale

6.64 The procedure on a claim to enforce a charging order by way of order for sale is set out in rule 73.10C and paragraph 4 of Practice Direction 73 of the Civil Procedure Rules. The procedural steps set out in these provisions should be followed whether the debtor is sole legal and beneficial owner or co-beneficial owner of the property sought to be sold. However, the precise form of the

---

113 See para 6.48.

114 As to the evidence which is to be produced, see paras 6.77–6.79.

115 As to other possible disputes which may arise, see paras 6.81–6.86.

116 See para 6.91 *et seq*.

application will be different in each case.[117] Where the debtor is a co-beneficial owner, additional evidence beyond that identified in paragraph 4.3 of Practice Direction 73 will be needed.[118] An outline of the procedure applicable to a claim for an order for sale is set out below.

6.65 The claim should be made to the court which made the charging order, unless that court does not have jurisdiction to make an order for sale.[119]

6.66 Consideration must be given as to who should be joined as a defendant to the claim and who should be notified of the claim. The position is as follows:

(a) In all cases, the following must be parties:

  (i) the debtor; and
  (ii) all other adult occupiers of the property (whether tenants or otherwise) against whom possession will be sought as a precursor to sale.

(b) Where the debtor is a co-beneficial owner, the trustee legal owners, along with other beneficial owners, may be added as defendants. Depending upon the circumstances, such parties may simply be notified of the claim.[120]
(c) Other interested persons, such as secured creditors, should also be notified of the proceedings, but need not be added as defendants. Such parties may apply to be joined as parties, if they so wish.
(d) Where, in relation to the land subject to the charging order, a Class F land charge or a notice under section 31(10) of the Family Law Act 1996[121] has been registered, the judgment creditor must serve notice of the claim on the person on whose behalf it has been registered.[122] He need not join that person as a defendant.

In all cases where persons are notified of the claim but are not joined as defendants, copies of the issued claim form and supporting evidence should be

---

117 See paras 6.70–6.71.

118 See para 6.78.

119 CPR r 73.10C(3). As to the jurisdiction of different courts, see paras 6.16–6.27. If the charging order was made in a county court different to that for the district in which the property is situated, the claim may be transferred to the latter court if, for example, the property is the debtor's home and the debtor defends the application for sale, having not previously defended the application for a charging order to be made.

120 In the usual case of a couple's co-owned home, the debtor and his or her spouse or partner should both be made defendants. In other cases, beneficiaries whose interests are small, or who do not occupy the property, need not necessarily be joined as defendants, but should in any event be notified of the claim.

121 Or any of its statutory predecessors.

122 See CPR PD 73, para 4.3(7)(b)(ii).

sent to these persons, together with an explanatory letter giving notice of the hearing date fixed on issue. The claimant should complete and file a certificate of service in Form N215 to prove service of these documents.

6.67 A claim to enforce a charging order by way of order for sale is brought under Part 8 of the Civil Procedure Rules.[123] The requirements of Part 8 must be followed by both the claimant and the defendant.

6.68 The claim form must be in prescribed Form N208 and must comply with the requirements of rule 8.2 of the Civil Procedure Rules. Accordingly, it must state:

(a) that Part 8 applies to the claim;
(b) the remedy which the claimant is seeking and the legal basis for the claim to that remedy;
(c) if the claim is being made under an enactment, what that enactment is;
(d) if the claimant is claiming in a representative capacity, what that capacity is; and
(e) if the defendant is sued in a representative capacity, what that capacity is.

6.69 In all cases, the claim form should identify the enactment under which it is made[124] and identify the charging order on which the claimant relies. A copy of the charging order itself must be filed with the claim form.[125] Two precedent claim forms, for a claim where the debtor is sole legal and beneficial owner and for a claim where the debtor is a beneficial co-owner, are in Appendix Precedent B12 and Precedent B13, respectively. Reference should be made to these precedents for an illustration of the matters to be covered in each case, although an outline commentary is given at paras 6.70–6.71.

6.70 Where the debtor is the sole legal and beneficial owner of the property, the claim form should, among other things:

(a) state that the claim is made under the Charging Orders Act 1979;
(b) identify the charging order on which the claimant relies;
(c) set out, briefly, the circumstances in which the charging order was made and the sums which it secures;
(d) identify the property which is subject to the charge;
(e) explain the sums outstanding under the charge at the date of issue of the claim; and

---

123 CPR r 73.10C(4).

124 See paras 6.70–6.71 for further discussion.

125 CPR r 73.10C(5).

(f) identify the remedies sought as being an order for sale, an order for possession to enable the sale to proceed (together with a vesting order under section 90(1) of the Law of Property Act 1925), an order that the conduct of the sale be given to the claimant or to the claimant's solicitors.[126]

6.71 Where the debtor is a beneficial co-owner, the claim form should, among other things:

(a) state that the claim is made under sections 14 and 15 of the Trusts of Land and Appointment of Trustees Act 1996;
(b) identify the charging order on which the claimant relies;
(c) set out, briefly, the circumstances in which the charging order was made and the sums which it secures;
(d) identify the property which is subject to the charge;
(e) explain the sums outstanding under the charge at the date of issue of the claim;
(f) state that the charging order is over the debtor's interest in the property, which property is held on trust; and
(g) identify the remedies sought as being an order for sale, an order for possession to enable the sale to proceed (together with orders under sections 47 and/or 50 of the Trustee Act 1925, as necessary),[127] and an order that the conduct of the sale be given to the claimant or to the claimant's solicitors.

6.72 Under rule 8.9(c) of the Civil Procedure Rules, all Part 8 claims are automatically allocated to the multi-track. Normally a hearing date will be given when the claim form is issued. If the claim is in the High Court, the hearing will be before a Chancery Master in the Royal Courts of Justice or a District Judge in a Chancery District Registry. If the claim is in the county court, it will be before a District Judge.

6.73 As the claim is made under Part 8 of the Civil Procedure Rules, the claimant must file and serve the written evidence on which he intends to rely, together with the claim form. If he does not, the claimant may not rely on his written evidence at the hearing of his claim without the permission of the court.[128] If the defendant wishes to defend the claim (the grounds on which he may seek

---

[126] For a detailed discussion of why these orders are legally and practically necessary, and for further information regarding additional orders which can be claimed in certain cases (such as an order permitting the judgment creditor to take steps to terminate any tenancies of the property to enable a sale with vacant possession), see para 6.91 *et seq*.

[127] For a further discussion of this jurisdiction, and whether or not such an order should be sought, see paras 6.100–6.102.

[128] CPR r 8.6(1). As to what a claimant's written evidence must contain, see paras 6.77–6.79.

to do so are set out below[129]), he must file and serve an acknowledgement of service within 14 days after service of the claim form, together with any written evidence on which he wishes to rely.[130] If he does not file an acknowledgement of service, he may attend the hearing but may not take part without the court's permission; if he does not file his written evidence, it may not be relied on at the hearing without the court's permission.[131]

6.74 The hearing that is listed upon the issue of the claim form will usually be a short first hearing. The claimant will present his case by dealing with the matters set out in his evidence in support. The claimant may provide a draft order, either filed and served with his claim form or ahead of the hearing, or simply brought to the hearing on the day.[132] Where the claim is opposed, the defendant will then make his submissions. In most cases,[133] his best hope of resisting an outright order for sale will be to make an offer of payment, which should, if possible, be supported by convincing evidence as to how and when he will obtain the means to make that payment. That may result in a postponed or suspended order. He may also raise matters relevant to the court's discretion, such as his own welfare and that of other occupiers of the property. He may also raise other matters to challenge the basis of the claim or to secure a stay or an adjournment.[134] Persons who were notified of the claim, but have not been joined as defendants, may apply at the hearing to be joined as parties so that they can put forward a defence.

6.75 If the claim is straightforward, and the claimant has presented all the required evidence, the court may exercise its discretion to make an order for sale at the first hearing. However, if:

(a) the claim is more complex or is substantively defended;
(b) necessary evidence has not been presented by the claimant; or
(c) the evidence is in dispute, as for example, if the debtor disputes the amount of the outstanding debt;

the court will use this first hearing to give directions for the future conduct of the case.

---

129 See paras 6.81–6.86 for the grounds on which he may do so.

130 CPR rr 8.3 and 8.5(3).

131 CPR rr 8.4 and 8.6(1).

132 As to the form of the order, see para 6.87 *et seq*. Sample orders (which can be tailored to meet the circumstances of the particular case) are at CPR PD 73, Appendix A.

133 Although see para 6.83 for the possibility of temporarily preventing enforcement by obtaining a breathing space or mental health crisis moratorium under the Debt Respite Scheme (Breathing Space and Mental Health Crisis Moratorium) Regulations 2020 (SI 2020/1311).

134 For full discussion, see paras 6.81–6.86.

6.76 For an example of the type of directions which might be expected to be given, see Appendix Precedent B17. This is based on a case where a third party appears at the first hearing and claims the entire beneficial interest in the property, albeit the legal title is registered in the debtor's name at HM Land Registry. As with any case management order, however, the precise directions given will depend on the issues in the case.[135]

Evidence in support

6.77 As already noted, a claimant's written evidence in support of his claim for an order for sale must be filed and served with the claim form.[136] Paragraph 4.3 of Practice Direction 73 of the Civil Procedure Rules provides that the claimant's written evidence must:

(a) identify the charging order and the property sought to be sold;[137]
(b) state the amount in respect of which the charge was imposed and the amount due at the date of issue of the claim;
(c) verify, so far as known,[138] the debtor's title to the property charged;
(d) state, so far as the claimant is able to identify:

    (i) the names and addresses of any other creditors who have a prior charge or other security over the property; and
    (ii) the amount owed to each such creditor;

(e) give an estimate of the price which would be obtained on sale of the property;[139]
(f) if the claim relates to land, give details of every person who to the best of the claimant's knowledge is in possession of the property; and
(g) if the claim relates to residential property:

---

135 Further example directions would include: an order that an account be taken of the debt, if it is in dispute or if it includes interest and the claimant does not have a calculated interest figure available at the hearing; an order that the claimant obtain a valuation of the property, if he has not already done so; or an order that evidence be gathered as to the debtor's title or the position as to prior incumbrancers, if satisfactory evidence has not already been obtained.

136 See para 6.73.

137 CPR r 73.10C(5) requires that a copy of the charging order be filed together with the claim form.

138 Despite the words 'so far as known' in CPR PD 73, para 4.3(3), the court will in fact require detailed evidence as to the nature of the debtor's title at the stage of making an order for sale. See further para 6.28 *et seq*.

139 Ideally, this should be supported by a valuation (or valuations) from an estate agent (or agents). Note, however, that this need not be a formal expert valuation. The purpose of this requirement is for the court to set a lower price limit below which the property should not be sold. The court does not require a precise valuation for this purpose.

(i) state whether either of the following has been registered:

(1) a land charge of Class F; or
(2) a notice under section 31(10) of the Family Law Act 1996 or under any provision of an Act which preceded that section; and

(ii) if so, state:

(1) on whose behalf the land charge or notice has been registered; and
(2) that the claimant will serve notice of the claim on that person.

6.78 The prescription of required evidence given by paragraph 4.3 of Practice Direction 73 of the Civil Procedure Rules applies only to applications for an order for sale where the debtor is sole legal and beneficial owner of the property. However, where the debtor is co-beneficial owner and the claim is brought under section 14 of the Trusts of Land and Appointment of Trustees Act 1996, this evidence will be required and should be given in any event. Additionally, the claimant should provide evidence as to the identity of the trustee legal owner(s) of the property, the identity of the other beneficiaries and the extent of the debtor's beneficial interest.

6.79 Two precedent witness statements, for a claim where the debtor is sole legal and beneficial owner and for a claim where the debtor is a joint beneficial owner, are in Appendix Precedent B14 and Precedent B15, respectively. These cover only the most straightforward case but are nevertheless an illustration of how a practitioner should go about complying with the requirements of Practice Direction 73. A well-drafted witness statement should, of course, contain all matters relevant to the application for sale, including, for example, any history of payment or non-payment, whether there are any tenancies which require termination before sale,[140] etc.

Checklist for an applicant for an order for sale

6.80 There follows a table outlining in summary the steps which an applicant should take in preparing for and making an application for an order for sale (Table 6.1). It should be read in conjunction with the more detailed commentary set out above.

---

[140] For a fuller discussion of this topic, see para 6.95 *et seq*.

Table 6.1: Order for sale checklist for an applicant

Step	*Form*	*Rule*
Before making an application		
Establish conclusively the nature of the debtor's title		
(1) Determine whether or not the property is registered by a search of the Public Index Map at HM Land Registry	SIM	CPR PD 73, para 4.3(3)
(2) If property is registered, obtain an office copy entry of the registered title or if the property is unregistered and the creditor has not previously had sight of the title deeds, then either:	OC1	
(a) make an official search of the Land Charges register and if a class C(i) land charge is registered, obtain an official copy of the application for the charge and enquire of the chargee as to the names on the title deeds; or	K15 K19	
(b) apply for an order for the debtor to attend court and give evidence on oath as to his title: obtain an injunction for him to lodge title deeds in court with an affidavit as to their completeness	N316	CPR r 71.2
(3) If the charge is against the debtor's beneficial interest, obtain evidence of the nature and extent of the beneficial interest: i.e. trust deed or judgment/order giving effect to resulting or constructive trust		
Establish whether there are any prior incumbrancers If the property is registered, check the charges register on the official copy of the registered title or if the property is unregistered, carry out a search at the Land Charges Department	OC1 K15	CPR PD 73, para 4.4
Establish whether the debtor's spouse has protected matrimonial home rights If the land is registered, carry out a matrimonial home rights search at HM Land Registry or if the land is unregistered, carry out a search at the Land Charges Department	HR3 (registered land) K15 (unregistered land)	CPR PD 73, para 4.3(7)
Consider obtaining one or more external-view valuations of the property		CPR PD 73, para 4.3(5)

Step	*Form*	*Rule*
The application		
Ensure the claim is commenced in the correct court The claim should be commenced in the court which made the charging order, unless that court does not have jurisdiction		CPR r 73.10C(3)
Claims commenced in the High Court should generally be started in Chancery Chambers at the RCJ or in a Chancery District Registry[141]		CPR PD 73, para 4.2
The county court's jurisdiction is generally limited to cases where the sum outstanding under the charge does not exceed the county court limit of £350,000:[142] the upper limit of the county court's jurisdiction is unlimited where the debt arises under a regulated consumer credit agreement,[143] but there can be no sale where the debt is less than £1,000[144]		CPR PD 73, para 4.1A
Commence the claim under CPR Part 8 Ensure that the claim form complies with the requirements of CPR Part 8 and, in cases where the debtor is joint beneficial owner, that it specifies that the claim is made under TLATA 1996, ss 14–15 Ensure that all necessary parties are added as defendants; some persons need not be added as defendants but must be notified of the claim	Claim form N208	CPR r 73.10C(4) CPR r 8.2
Attach a copy of the charging order to the claim form		CPR r 73.10(5)
File written evidence together with the claim form Ensure that the written evidence covers all the matters prescribed by CPR PD 73 and, in the case of property of which the debtor is joint beneficial owner, that additional evidence is given as to the identity of the trustee legal owners, the identity of the other beneficiaries and the extent of the beneficiaries' respective interests		CPR r 8.5 PD 73, para 4.3

141 But see para 6.17. It appears in some circumstances that enforcement claims may be made in other divisions of the High Court.

142 But see para 6.20 *et seq* for the potential position where the debtor is the sole legal and beneficial owner of the property.

143 But see para 6.26.

144 See para 6.5.

Step	*Form*	*Rule*
Serve copies of the claim form and its attachments on interested parties Copies should be served on those with matrimonial home rights and other secured creditors, if these persons have not been added as defendants Evidence of service should be produced in the form of a certificate of service	N215	CPR PD 73, para 4.3(7)

Opposing an application for an order for sale

6.81 An enforcement application is brought by a creditor who wishes to recover the sums secured by his charging order by sale of the debtor's property. Most of the grounds on which a defendant may resist such an application, whether by seeking an outright dismissal of the application or the postponement or suspension of the order for sale, flow from that.

6.82 If the debtor has no grounds upon which he can challenge the basis of the claim,[145] his best hope of resisting an application for an order for sale is to satisfy, or to show that he can satisfy, the judgment debt and the interest and costs secured with it, along with the claimant's costs of the enforcement process to date, within a reasonable time. If he is in a position to pay these sums immediately, he should do so, and the claim will be discontinued by the claimant or dismissed by the court. The debtor will, however, be liable for the claimant's costs to the date of payment. If the debtor is not in a position to pay immediately, he should propose to pay by a specified future date or in specified instalments. As matters have now reached the stage of an enforcement claim, it is likely either that the debtor did not oppose the making of a final charging order or that he has breached the terms (e.g. as to payment by instalments) on which enforcement of the final charging order was made conditional. Both the claimant's and the court's view of any payment proposals at this stage are therefore likely to be coloured by the debtor's past conduct in these respects. The debtor should therefore be prepared to explain his past conduct, as well as to provide full, detailed and convincing evidence of his means and his financial commitments (generally and to other creditors). Any reasons for non-payment to date (e.g. unemployment, commitments to other creditors) and any prospects of payment in the future (e.g. new employment, agreeing payment plans with other creditors) should be put in evidence.

6.83 Alternatively, if appropriate, the debtor may wish to consider applying for a breathing space or mental health crisis moratorium under the Debt Respite Scheme (Breathing Space Moratorium and Mental Health Crisis Moratorium) (England and

---

145 As to those grounds, see paras 6.84–6.85.

Wales) Regulations 2020.[146] Once in force, a moratorium will have the effect of preventing the judgment creditor from taking any action to enforce the charging order whilst the moratorium is in force. Importantly for creditors, any enforcement action taken in violation of the moratorium will be null and void.[147]

6.84 A defendant may also resist a claim by inviting the court to exercise its discretion not to make an order for sale. He may, for example:

(a) seek to rely on the property being his and his family's only home; and/or
(b) submit that the ratio of the debt to the value of the property would make an order for sale too extreme and draconian a step; or
(c) attempt to show that an order for sale would not in fact result in recovery by the claimant of the sums owed to him, on the basis that there is insufficient equity in the property, or that making an order for sale would otherwise be futile or of no benefit to the creditor.[148]

6.85 A defendant may be able to resist a claim for an order for sale by attacking the basis on which it is made. For example, he may:

(a) dispute the debtor's interest in the property or the extent of that interest;
(b) show that the sum secured by the charging order has in fact been paid;
(c) challenge the level of the alleged debt; or
(d) show that an application has been made to set aside the judgment on which the charging order is based.

If *prima facie* evidence is shown to support such assertions, the first hearing of the claim is likely to be adjourned, with directions given for further investigations to be made.

6.86 As already noted, a defendant seeking to resist a claim for an order for sale should file and serve an acknowledgement of service, together with any written evidence on which he wishes to rely, within 14 days of service of the claim form upon him.[149]

---

146 SI 2020/1311 (Debt Respite Scheme Regs 2020). For further discussion, see Chapter 2, paras 2.58–2.60 and Chapter 8, paras 8.122–8.123.

147 Debt Respite Scheme Regs 2020, reg 7(12). For a recent cautionary tale where a sale which was completed during the course of a moratorium and was subsequently declared null and void, see *Lees v Kaye* [2022] EWHC 1151 (QB). Note that HHJ Dight held that, whilst reg 7(13)(a) means that a moratorium would not affect the existence of a charging order, it would prevent its enforcement, so long as the moratorium lasts: see [62].

148 *Amari Lifestyle v Warnes* [2017] EWHC 1891 (Ch). For full discussion of the factors relevant to the exercise of the court's discretion, see paras 6.37–6.43.

149 See further para 6.73.

Form of an order for sale

6.87 Appendix A to Practice Direction 73 of the Civil Procedure Rules sets out two sample forms of order for sale, copies of which may be found in Appendix A3 of this work. The first is applicable to cases where the judgment debtor is the sole legal and beneficial owner of the property. The second applies to cases where the judgment debtor is the beneficial co-owner of the property. These sample forms of order are for guidance only. They are not prescribed forms and may be adapted or varied by the court to meet the requirements of individual cases.[150]

6.88 In practice, it will often be necessary to modify the sample forms in accordance with the discussion provided immediately below. Two modified versions of the standard forms may be found in Appendix Precedent B18 and Precedent B19, respectively. The following paragraphs provide commentary on those matters for which orders for sale are likely to make provision.

6.89 Whether the debtor is the sole legal and beneficial owner of the property or a co-beneficial owner, the order may make provision for the following matters:

(a) It is common for a conditional rather than an outright order for sale to be made, which postpones or suspends the sale upon terms that the debtor pay the judgment debt, interest and costs either in full by a fixed date or alternatively by fixed instalments. Paragraph 1 of the sample orders at Appendix A to Practice Direction 73 of the Civil Procedure Rules contemplates the making of such a conditional order. The order should also make it clear that if the judgment debtor has not discharged the judgment debt (and any relevant interest and costs) prior to the judgment creditor entering into a contract to sell the property, the sale can proceed to completion even if the judgment debtor subsequently tenders the sums owed.[151]

(b) If the order is conditional, then it may direct the creditor to apply to cancel registration of the charge and any restriction in his favour on the registered title to the property (if the property is registered land) or registration of his charge on the Land Charges register (if the property is unregistered land), in the event that the secured sum is paid by the debtor. If this is not done, the charging order may remain registered against the property following satisfaction. If the judgment debt arises out of a county court judgment, the order may also direct the creditor to apply to the court which made the judgment for the judgment to be marked as satisfied in the judgment list in the event that the secured sum is paid.

---

[150] CPR PD 73, para 4.5.

[151] See further paras 6.117–6.118.

(c) There is no requirement for the sale to be by public auction or private treaty and it is generally for the applicant to choose which method he believes will be most effective. However, the order will commonly provide that the sale may take place at a price not less than a figure specified by the court (which figure may be varied by further court order).[152]

(d) The order should usually provide for the claimant or the claimant's solicitors to have conduct of the sale.[153]

(e) The order should specify precisely what property is to be included in the sale.

(f) The order will usually provide for the debtor and any others who are in possession of the property[154] to deliver vacant possession to the creditor. If the order for sale is suspended, the order for possession will be suspended on the same terms.[155]

6.90 The further terms of the order will depend upon whether the debtor is the sole legal and beneficial owner of the property or the joint beneficial owner of the property. This is discussed in further detail below.

Debtor sole legal and beneficial owner of the property

6.91 Where the debtor is the sole legal and beneficial owner of the property, the order will first have to make appropriate provision to ensure that there can be a valid conveyance of the legal estate. This is achieved by obtaining an order under section 90(1) of the Law of Property Act 1925.

6.92 Section 90(1) of the Law of Property Act 1925 provides as follows:

> Where an order for sale is made by the court in reference to an equitable mortgage on land (not secured by a legal term of years absolute or by a charge by way of legal mortgage) the court may, in favour of a purchaser, make a vesting order conveying the land or may appoint a person to convey the land or create and vest in the mortgagee a legal term of years absolute to enable him to carry out the sale, as the case may require, in like manner as if the mortgage had been created by deed by way of legal mortgage pursuant to this Act, but without prejudice to any incumbrance having priority to the equitable mortgage unless the incumbrancer consents to the sale.

---

152 See para 2 of the sample orders at CPR PD 73, Appendix A.

153 See para 3 of the sample orders at CPR PD 73, Appendix A.

154 Including, if relevant, a person whose home rights are protected by a class F land charge or a notice under Family Law Act 1996, s 31(10): see *Fred Perry (Holdings) Ltd v Genis* [2015] 1 P & CR DG5.

155 See para 5 of the sample orders at CPR PD 73, Appendix A.

6.93 In the context of applications to enforce charging orders, the most common strategy is to seek an order vesting a legal term of years in the creditor to enable him to carry out the sale.[156] Where the land charged is freehold land, the practice is to seek an order that a term be vested in the creditor for 3,000 years from the date of the court's order.[157] Where the claim relates to leasehold land, the term to be vested will depend on the length of the interest charged but it has been described as a 'safe formula' to seek the vesting of a term which is one day shorter than the debtor's own term.[158]

6.94 A vesting order has some important practical – and legally necessary – effects. Primarily, the vesting of a term of years will enable the creditor to carry out a sale 'in like manner as if the mortgage had been created by deed by way of legal mortgage pursuant to this Act'. This means that the creditor will, by the operation of statutory magic, benefit from the power of sale conferred on mortgagees by section 101(1) of the Law of Property Act 1925, which he otherwise would not have had as a mere equitable chargee. It will also confer upon the judgment creditor the power to sell the entirety of the debtor's legal and beneficial interest in the property, subject only to prior incumbrances, rather than the mere beneficial interest.[159]

6.95 Secondly, where the relevant property is tenanted and the judgment creditor's interest has priority over that tenancy,[160] the effect of a legal term of years being vested in the creditor will be to create a concurrent lease. Accordingly, the judgment creditor will stand in the position of the reversioner to the occupational tenancy, thus giving him the power to take steps to terminate that tenancy and to achieve vacant possession (if that is desirable to achieve the best price upon sale).[161]

6.96 Accordingly, where it is known that a property is leased and the judgment creditor has priority over that lease, it is likely to be beneficial to ask the court to order, or at least record, that the judgment creditor is at liberty to take steps to

---

156 Although LPA 1925, s 90 expressly provides for the alternatives of the court making a vesting order directly in favour of a purchaser or to appoint some other person to convey the land, these are less commonly encountered, not least because a purchaser is unlikely to have been found before the court exercises its discretion to grant an order for sale and the judgment creditor will usually wish to have full conduct or the sale himself.

157 See para 4 of the relevant sample order at CPR PD 73, Appendix A.

158 See Walker and Buckley, p 276, and para 4 of the relevant sample order at PD 73, Appendix A.

159 See, in this regard, LPA 1925, ss 88 and 89.

160 For a detailed discussion of this important question, see Chapter 4.

161 See Falcon Chambers and Sir Paul Morgan, *Fisher & Lightwood's Law of Mortgage* (LexisNexis, 15th edn, 2019), para 29.17.

terminate the occupational tenancy in light of the vesting order which the court has made under section 90(1).

6.97 Thirdly, following the enactment of the Economic Crime (Transparency and Enforcement) Act 2022, the creditor will now have to give consideration to whether the debtor is an 'overseas entity'.[162] Where this is the case, HM Land Registry will enter a restriction against the title prohibiting the registration of any disposition including a transfer of the title, a grant of a lease for 7 years or more, or the grant of a legal charge unless:

(a) the entity is a registered overseas entity or is exempt at the time of the disposition;
(b) the disposition is made in pursuance of a statutory obligation, court order, or occurs by operation of law;
(c) the disposition is made in pursuance of a contract made before the restriction is entered in the register;
(d) the disposition is made in exercise of a registered mortgagee's power of sale or leasing, or by a receiver appointed by the mortgagee;
(e) the Secretary of State gives consent;
(f) the disposition is made by a specified insolvency practitioner in circumstances set out in regulations.[163]

6.98 Where an order for sale is sought against a debtor which is an overseas entity, registration of the disposition is likely to be possible, despite the presence of the above restriction, by reference to exception (b) above. In such a case, however, it would seem advisable for the creditor to seek an express order from the court giving permission for the sale and its registration in accordance with the above exception.

6.99 Lastly, the order should make provision as to the application of the proceeds of sale, in accordance with the respective entitlements of the interested parties.[164] Alternatively, if there is a dispute between subsequent incumbrancers as to which of them has priority next after the judgment creditor, the order may make provision for the proceeds of sale or part of them to be paid into court, pending resolution of the dispute. It is preferable to make such provision in the order for sale itself, to save the creditor the costs and trouble of a further application to the court following the sale.

---

162 See Economic Crime (Transparency and Enforcement) Act 2022, s 2(1).

163 See LRA 2002, Sch 4A, para 3.

164 See paras 6 and 7 of the first sample order at CPR PD 73, Appendix A. As to the application of the proceeds of sale, see further paras 6.121–6.131.

Debtor joint beneficial owner

6.100 Where the debtor is the co-beneficial owner of the property (or the beneficial owner of the property under a bare trust), then in addition to the matters outlined at para 6.89, the order may also make provision for the following matters.

6.101 First, if it is anticipated that there may be any difficulty in requiring the trustee(s) to convey the legal estate in the property,[165] the order should include a provision that appoints some other person (the claimant or the claimant's solicitors) to convey the property pursuant to section 50 of the Trustee Act 1925.[166] Alternatively, the order may provide for the legal estate to be vested in the claimant or, if a purchaser has already been found, in that purchaser, pursuant to section 47 of the Trustee Act 1925.[167]

6.102 Where the property is tenanted, it is thought that an order under section 47 of the Trustee Act 1925 is likely to be preferable. The vesting of the legal estate in the judgment creditor will enable him to take steps to terminate any tenancies over which the judgment creditor has priority in order to obtain vacant possession. If such an order is not sought, the trustees will retain the legal title and thus the reversion to the tenancies.

6.103 The order should also make provision as to the application of the proceeds of sale.[168]

Costs of the application for an order for sale

6.104 A creditor who successfully obtains an order for sale should seek an order that the debtor pay his costs of the application. Such costs are payable out of the proceeds of sale of the property charged.[169] The award of costs is discretionary, but the normal rule applies on applications for an order for sale, namely that costs will follow the event unless the creditor has acted unreasonably. Costs will be assessed on the standard basis, either by summary or detailed assessment. If summary assessment is sought, a schedule of costs should be filed and served.

---

165 In the common case of a co-owned marital home, the trustees will be the debtor and the debtor's spouse. The debtor may be obstructive.

166 See para 4 of the second sample order at CPR PD 73, Appendix A.

167 See further paras 6.119–6.120.

168 See paras 6 and 7 of the second sample order at CPR PD 73, Appendix A. As to the application of the proceeds of sale, see further paras 6.121–6.131.

169 See *Holder v Supperstone* [2000] 1 All ER 473 at 479–80. This entitlement arises from the nature of the creditor's security. If the creditor's costs are not recouped at the time of sale or the charging order is discharged before payment, there will be no entitlement to costs in the absence of a specific contractual agreement between the parties: see *Brierley v Otuo & Others* [2023] EWHC 919 (Ch).

If costs are summarily assessed, then a costs order will be included in the order for sale.[170]

6.105 Where the debtor is a beneficial co-owner, it is usual for the creditor's costs to be recovered from the debtor alone. However, the court retains a discretion as to who should be liable in respect of costs, and other beneficiaries (such as the debtor's spouse or cohabitant) may be made liable for a share of the creditor's costs if their conduct merits such an order, as for example if the co-beneficiary has delayed the proceedings by obstructing service. The court should also determine who is to bear the costs of the sale itself.

6.106 After the order has been made, the creditor may recover his costs of the sale itself out of the proceeds of sale.[171] His solicitor's conveyancing costs are allowable on the same basis as if the bill were being assessed for non-contentious business under the Solicitors Act 1974.

6.107 Where costs have been incurred in recovering vacant possession from any occupational tenants[172] but the judgment creditor has not been able to recover those costs from that party,[173] it is thought that any costs which have not been recovered may be added to the costs of sale. This is under the general principle that a chargee is entitled to reimbursed for the costs of enforcing his security, which often includes obtaining vacant possession from third parties.

The mechanics of sale

Sale by the judgment creditor

Conduct of the sale

6.108 It will normally be appropriate for the order for sale to provide that the judgment creditor will have conduct of the sale. The reasons for this are obvious: the judgment debtor will usually have resisted or failed to agree to a sale, which is why the judgment creditor has had to make an application for an order for sale; and furthermore, the proceeds of sale may not be sufficient to discharge the judgment debt. If, however, the secured debt is small in relation to the value of the property, it may sometimes be appropriate to entrust the sale to the judgment debtor, on the basis that he will have a greater interest in the proceeds of sale, and

---

170 See para 1 of the sample orders at CPR PD 73, Appendix A.

171 See para 6 of the sample orders at CPR PD 73, Appendix A.

172 See paras 6.96 and 6.102 for a further discussion of how the judgment creditor can seek to lawfully do this.

173 For example, because of any applicable fixed costs regime or because the tenants have not paid them.

more incentive to obtain the highest price reasonably obtainable, but the court would need to be confident that the judgment debtor would proceed promptly to sell.[174]

6.109 In his conduct of the sale, the judgment creditor can act primarily in his own interests, with the aim of obtaining payment of his secured debt. However, he owes a duty to any subsequent incumbrancers and to the judgment debtor to act in good faith, and to take reasonable care to obtain the best sale price reasonably obtainable at the date of sale.[175]

6.110 The judgment creditor must also comply with any particular requirements or restrictions specified in the order for sale (for instance, if a minimum sale price has been specified).[176]

6.111 The order should have specified precisely what property was to be included in the sale, and whether the sale was to be subject to any prior incumbrances.[177]

6.112 The order should also have specified that the judgment creditor may sell the property by any means considered appropriate by the court (such as auction or private treaty), and may instruct any appropriate estate agent or auctioneer and conveyancing solicitors (either specified in the order, or to be selected at the judgment creditor's discretion).[178] A prudent judgment creditor will take appropriate advice concerning the manner in which the sale is conducted, and should ensure that the sale is suitably advertised.[179]

6.113 The judgment creditor will be primarily responsible for the fees of any agents or others whom he instructs on the sale, although, once any prior incumbrancers have been paid, he will be entitled to recoup those fees from the net proceeds of sale.[180]

6.114 If the order for sale ordered the debtor (or others) to give vacant possession of the property,[181] the judgment creditor should ordinarily secure possession

---

174 *Re Jordan* (1884) 13 QBD 228; *Cheltenham & Gloucester plc v Krausz* [1997] 1 WLR 1558.

175 *Palk v Mortgage Services Funding plc* [1993] Ch 330; *Yorkshire Bank v Hall* [1999] 1 WLR 1713; *Silven Properties v Royal Bank of Scotland plc* [2003] EWCA Civ 1409, [2004] 1 WLR 997.

176 See para 6.89(c).

177 See para 6.89. He is under the duties of a mortgagee when selling.

178 See para 6.89.

179 See e.g. *Michael v Miller* [2004] EWCA Civ 282, [2004] 2 EGLR 151.

180 See paras 6.104–6.107.

181 See para 6.89(f).

before the sale proceeds, on the basis that that will enable a higher price to be achieved.

6.115 The judgment creditor need not improve the property before sale, even if an owner-occupier might have done so.[182]

6.116 Because the sale has been ordered by the court, the judgment creditor or those connected with him can buy the charged property if the court gives permission. However, the court will wish to be sure in such circumstances that the price is the best price reasonably obtainable.[183]

If the judgment debtor pays the debt prior to completion

6.117 If the judgment debtor pays in full the sums secured by the charging order – judgment debt, interest and costs – before the judgment creditor has entered into a contract for the sale of the property, the judgment creditor will have no interest in proceeding with the sale, and the judgment debtor would be entitled to apply to the court to stop it.[184]

6.118 However, once the judgment creditor has entered into a contract for the sale of the property, pursuant to the order, then (unless there is something improper about the transaction) the court will not stop the sale even if, at that late stage, the judgment debtor tenders in full the sums secured by the charging order. The judgment creditor will be entitled to proceed with the sale, and indeed, if he does not do so, he is likely to put himself in breach of his contract with the purchaser (unless the sale contract provides otherwise).[185] Nevertheless, to minimise the risk of any dispute with the judgment debtor in such a situation, the judgment creditor should ensure that the order for sale specifies that if the judgment debtor has not discharged the debt (and any relevant interest and costs) prior to the judgment creditor entering into a contract for the sale of the property,

---

182 *Silven Properties v Royal Bank of Scotland plc* [2003] EWCA Civ 1409, [2004] 1 WLR 997. Further consideration of a chargee's duties upon sale falls outside the scope of this book. Further discussion can be found in Falcon Chambers and Sir Paul Morgan, *Fisher and Lightwood's Law of Mortgage* (LexisNexis, 15th edn, 2019) (*Fisher and Lightwood's Law of Mortgage*).

183 *Palk v Mortgage Services Funding plc* [1993] Ch 330; *Polonski v Lloyds Bank Mortgages Ltd* (1997) 31 HLR 721.

184 Although in such circumstances a subsequent, but unpaid, incumbrancer might wish himself to pursue an application for an order for sale.

185 *Lord Waring v London and Manchester Assurance Co Ltd* [1935] Ch 310; *Property and Bloodstock Ltd v Emerton* [1968] Ch 94; *Duke v Robson* [1973] 1 WLR 267; *National and Provincial Building Society v Ahmed* [1995] 2 EGLR 127.

the sale can proceed to completion even if the judgment debtor subsequently tenders the sums owed.[186]

Sale by trustees

6.119 If the charging order was over the judgment debtor's beneficial interest in land held on trust, and the court has ordered a sale by the trustees, the trustees must ensure that they comply with any directions in the order, and otherwise comply fully with their duties as trustees of the property and of the proceeds of sale.

6.120 Since the legal estate in the property will be vested in the trustees, they are in a position to convey it to any purchaser. Alternatively, if they are unwilling to do so or are unduly dilatory (for instance, if the judgment debtor is also a trustee, and obstructs the sale or its completion), the court can either appoint a nominee to convey it on their behalf,[187] or vest the property in the purchaser or in someone who can convey it to the purchaser.[188] In such cases, the purchaser is entitled to rely on the relevant order, and need not enquire into whether the court had jurisdiction or grounds to make it.[189]

Proceeds of sale

Sale by the judgment creditor

6.121 As already explained, a well-drawn order for sale should specify how the proceeds of sale should be applied.[190]

6.122 If the judgment creditor sells the charged land or interest in land pursuant to an order for sale, he becomes a trustee of the proceeds of sale as soon as he receives them. Subject to any specific directions which the court has made, he

---

[186] In *Barrett v Charles*, 1 July 1983, unreported, CA, the order for sale had expressly stated that the order for sale would cease to have effect if the debt and costs were discharged, but without specifying the latest date on which the debtor could pay the debt. The judgment debtor paid the secured sums after the judgment creditor had entered into a contract for the sale of the land, but before completion. That resulted in litigation between the judgment debtor, the judgment creditor and the purchaser as to whether the sale could proceed. After 4 months of litigation it was held that the judgment debtor was not entitled to restrain the sale from completing, but the dispute could have been avoided if the terms of the order had put the matter beyond doubt. The judgment is now available on Westlaw at [1983] 7 WLUK 92.

[187] Under TA 1925, s 50.

[188] Under TA 1925, s 47.

[189] TA 1925, s 66.

[190] See para 6.87 *et seq*.

must distribute the proceeds of sale in the order of priority that is set out in section 105 of the Law of Property Act 1925. This is explained in Chapter 4.[191]

6.123 If there is any doubt or dispute as to who is entitled to any part of the proceeds of sale, the judgment creditor can pay the relevant monies into court,[192] or can seek appropriate directions from the court as to their distribution.

6.124 If, by mistake, the judgment creditor pays over to a subsequent incumbrancer or the judgment debtor more than he should have done, he can claim repayment.[193]

Sale by a prior incumbrancer

6.125 If the charged property is sold by a prior incumbrancer, a judgment creditor with the benefit of a charging order will be entitled to be paid any relevant residue of the proceeds of sale in accordance with the same order of priorities explained in Chapter 4.[194]

Sale by trustees

6.126 If the charging order was over the judgment debtor's beneficial interest in land held under a trust, and the court ordered a sale by the trustees,[195] the trustees will hold the proceeds of sale on trust for those interested in them. They will be liable to distribute those proceeds to such persons in accordance with their respective entitlements and priorities.

6.127 Once again, a well-drafted order for sale will have specified how the proceeds of sale should be applied.[196]

6.128 Subject to any specific directions which the court has made, the trustees should first apply the proceeds of sale towards paying off all incumbrances affecting the *legal* estate, according to their order of priority. That will apply to all such incumbrances, even those which arose after the charging order was made,

---

191 See Chapter 4, paras 4.63–4.67.

192 Under TA 1925, s 63.

193 *Weld-Blundell v Synott* [1940] 2 KB 107.

194 Chapter 4, paras 4.63–4.67.

195 Or their nominees.

196 See para 6.87 *et seq*.

since the grant of those charges will ordinarily have overreached the judgment debtor's beneficial interest and the charging order over it.[197]

6.129 The residue of the proceeds of sale should then be distributed between the owners of the respective beneficial interests and those with incumbrances over them, including the judgment creditor with the benefit of the charging order, in accordance with their respective entitlements and priorities. Any beneficial owners with unencumbered shares will be entitled to be paid in accordance with their respective beneficial entitlements. The judgment creditor will be entitled to be paid the sums secured by the charging order from the judgment debtor's beneficial share, and the judgment debtor will then be entitled to any residue of that share, unless there are any subsequent incumbrancers.[198]

6.130 The order for sale should have made provision as to who was to bear the costs of the application for the order for sale and the costs of the sale itself.[199]

6.131 If there is any doubt or dispute as to who is entitled to any part of the proceeds of sale, the trustees can pay the relevant monies into court[200] or seek appropriate directions from the court as to their distribution.

Enforcement against proceeds of sale

6.132 Nevertheless, there may be still cases in which a sale occurs and trustees fail to account for the proceeds of sale in the proper manner. This section considers the extent to which a judgment creditor can take steps to enforce his claim against the proceeds of sale if such a situation arises.

6.133 First, if the judgment creditor is put on notice that a trustee may take, or is taking, steps to unlawfully dissipate the proceeds of sale without accounting to him, it may be possible to avoid any need for enforcement against the proceeds of sale. An injunction can be sought prohibiting the trustee from further dealing with the proceeds of sale except in accordance with the court's previous order.[201]

---

197 Provided that the mortgage money was advanced to at least two trustees or a trust corporation: LPA 1925, ss 2 and 27.

198 For the analogous position where a prior incumbrancer is the trustee of the proceeds of sale, see *Banner v Berridge* (1881) 18 ChD 254, esp at 269; *Charles v Jones* (1887) 35 ChD 544 at 549; *Adams v Bank of New South Wales* [1984] 1 NSWLR 285.

199 See paras 6.104–6.107.

200 TA 1925, s 63.

201 See, e.g. *Central Europe Business Development Ltd v Property Transfer Coordination Ltd* [2016] EWHC 2480 (Ch) at [7]. See also Tucker, Le Poidevin and Brightwell, *Lewin on Trusts* (Sweet & Maxwell, 20th edn, 2020), para 40-010.

6.134 If, however, a sale occurs and the proceeds are dissipated, the judgment creditor will have to give consideration to his other enforcement options.

6.135 The central point, already considered above,[202] is that the trustee will hold the proceeds of sale on trust for those interested in them. Any dissipation of those monies without the judgment creditor's consent will therefore amount to a breach of trust.

6.136 A detailed consideration of the remedies available for breach of trust falls outside the scope of this work. Reference should be made to other more detailed practitioner's texts on the topic.[203] In very brief outline, however, if the trustee has wholly dissipated the proceeds of sale, the judgment creditor will have a personal claim against him, seeking an account with a view to restoration of the trust fund or compensation for the creditor's loss. Alternatively, if the judgment creditor can show that the proceeds of sale have been used to acquire a substitute asset, such as another property, he could seek to rely on the principles of equitable tracing to make a proprietary claim over that asset and then take further steps to realise its value.

6.137 Depending on the circumstances, a creditor may also wish to consider whether it is possible to bring a claim against the defaulting trustee's conveyancing solicitor. In that regard, it is important to note that the conveyancing solicitor will usually have been acting merely as the trustee's agent. He will not be made a constructive trustee merely because he receives the proceeds of sale from the purchaser;[204] nor if, acting honestly and on the instructions of the trustee, he deals with the proceeds of sale in a manner which is inconsistent with the terms of the trust (even if he suspects that the proceeds may be applied inconsistently with the terms of the trust).[205] In this regard, it is not dishonest to transfer the proceeds of sale to the trustee in circumstances where the solicitor merely suspects that the proceeds may be applied inconsistently with the terms of the trust.[206] If, however, the solicitor knows that a trustee intends to commit a fraud and proceeds to transfer the proceeds of sale to him, then he may be liable under the doctrine of

---

202 See para 6.121 *et seq*.

203 See, e.g. Tucker, Le Poidevin and Brightwell, *Lewin on Trusts* (Sweet & Maxwell, 20th edn, 2020); McGhee and Elliott, *Snell's Equity* (Sweet & Maxwell, 34th edn, 2020).

204 See Tucker, Le Poidevin and Brightwell, *Lewin on Trusts* (Sweet & Maxwell, 20th edn, 2020), para 42-114.

205 See Tucker, Le Poidevin and Brightwell, *Lewin on Trusts* (Sweet & Maxwell, 20th edn, 2020), para 42-117.

206 *Adams v Bank of New South Wales* [1984] 1 NSWLR 285, esp at 290.

dishonest assistance[207] or, to the extent that the proceeds of sale cover his fees, knowing receipt.[208]

APPOINTMENT OF A RECEIVER

6.138 An alternative remedy that is available to a judgment creditor, although it is one that is rarely exercised, is to apply to the court for the appointment of a receiver over the debtor's land or interest in land.

Court's jurisdiction to appoint a receiver

6.139 The appointment of a receiver by the court was originally a purely equitable remedy, and hence discretionary, but it was normally available to an equitable mortgagee or chargee.[209] Since 1873, the court has had a statutory jurisdiction to appoint a receiver in all cases where it appears to the court to be just and convenient to do so;[210] and since 1956, the court has had the power to appoint a receiver by way of equitable execution over legal as well as equitable estates or interests in land.[211] Thus a receiver can now be appointed either for the specific purpose of enforcing the charging order, or more generally (whether or not a charging order has already been made in respect of the same judgment) by way of equitable execution.[212]

6.140 A receiver can generally be appointed over any property, real or personal, which can be taken in execution.[213] The receiver's powers will be determined by the terms of the order under which he is appointed.

---

[207] For a further discussion, see Tucker, Le Poidevin and Brightwell, *Lewin on Trusts* (Sweet & Maxwell, 20th edn, 2020), Chapter 43.

[208] See Tucker, Le Poidevin and Brightwell, *Lewin on Trusts* (Sweet & Maxwell, 20th edn, 2020), para 42-059.

[209] *Berney v Sewell* (1821) 1 Jac & W 647; *Re Pope* (1886) 17 QBD 743.

[210] Originally under Judicature Act 1873, s 25(8).

[211] Originally under AJA 1956, s 36, which was enacted following the reforms proposed by the Evershed Committee (*Supreme Court Practice and Procedure Report*).

[212] In the High Court, under Senior Courts Act 1981, s 37; and in the county courts, under CCA 1984, ss 38 and 107. See further CPR Part 69; and also paras 6.13–6.15.

[213] *Hope v Croydon and Norwood Tramways Co* (1887) 34 Ch D 730.

When it may be advantageous to seek the appointment of a receiver

6.141 Normally, there will be a practical advantage to the judgment creditor in appointing a receiver, rather than applying for an order for sale, in just two situations.

6.142 First, where land which belongs to the debtor is let and produces a rent, the judgment creditor can apply for the appointment of a receiver to collect the rents and pay them to the judgment creditor, rather than allowing the debtor to collect them and apply them to his own purposes.[214] Any tenant will be liable to pay his rents (including any arrears) to the receiver, rather than the debtor, once the receiver has given him notice to do so.[215] The order appointing the receiver can give him the power to re-let the property, but otherwise the receiver should seek directions from the court before doing so.[216]

6.143 Secondly, where the judgment creditor has obtained a charging order against the debtor's beneficial interest in land under a trust, the judgment creditor's interest is vulnerable. A conveyance or mortgage by the legal owners and trustees of the property will ordinarily overreach both that beneficial interest and the charging order over it.[217] In such circumstances (for instance, where a property is jointly owned by husband and wife, and where the judgment creditor has obtained a charging order over the husband's beneficial interest), unscrupulous trustees and co-owners may disappear with the proceeds of sale, without paying the judgment creditor his share.[218] Accordingly, if the judgment creditor becomes aware that the legal owners and trustees of the property have contracted to sell it, and considers there is a risk that they will not pay the judgment creditor his share of the proceeds of sale, the judgment creditor can apply to the court for the appointment of a receiver to intercept the judgment debtor's share of the proceeds of sale, and pay over to the judgment creditor his share of those proceeds. The judgment creditor must ensure that the order appointing the receiver gives him power to issue instructions to the legal owners

---

214 If the debtor has only a partial beneficial interest in the land, the receiver can be appointed to receive the debtor's share of the rents.

215 *Codrington v Johnstone* (1838) 1 Beav 520; *Re Ind Coope* [1911] 2 Ch 223; and see further *Fisher and Lightwood's Law of Mortgage*, para 28.28.

216 *Re Cripps* [1946] Ch 265; and see further *Fisher and Lightwood's Law of Mortgage*, para 28.28.

217 For an example, however, of a claim where overreaching failed, see *Banwaitt v Dewji* [2015] EWHC 3441 (Ch).

218 For this problem, and another way in which it may be overcome, see Chapter 4, paras 4.37–4.44 and Chapter 3, paras 3.16–3.18.

and trustees, and any solicitors acting for them, in the name of (and to the exclusion of) the judgment debtor.

6.144 In the past, a judgment creditor who had obtained a charging order against the debtor's beneficial interest in land under a trust sometimes applied for the appointment of a receiver to seek the execution of the trust by an order for sale (or to sell the beneficial interest). It is now clearly established that a judgment creditor can himself apply for the execution of the trust.[219]

Procedure for seeking the appointment of a receiver

6.145 An application for the appointment of a receiver must be made in accordance with Parts 69 and 23 of the Civil Procedure Rules.

6.146 Although a judgment creditor with a charging order will generally be entitled to the appointment of a receiver over the charged property, the court has a wide discretion as to whether or not to make the appointment, having regard to all the relevant circumstances. If there is a prior incumbrancer, any appointment of a receiver on the application of the judgment creditor will be subject to the rights of that prior incumbrancer. It will not usually be possible if the prior incumbrancer has already appointed a receiver or taken possession of the property.[220]

6.147 If the court is willing to appoint a receiver, it will normally be willing to appoint the applicant's nominee, provided that he is suitably qualified and there are no proper objections to his appointment (such as a conflict of interest). A court-appointed receiver is an officer of the court, and must act in good faith and fairly in the interests of both the judgment creditor and the judgment debtor.[221]

6.148 To be binding on third parties, an appointment of a receiver should be protected by an appropriate form of registration.[222]

---

219 *Midland Bank v Pike* [1988] 2 All ER 434. See paras 6.10–6.11.

220 *Berney v Sewell* (1821) 1 Jac & W 647; and see further *Fisher and Lightwood's Law of Mortgage*, para 28.19.

221 *Re Newdigate Colliery* [1912] 1 Ch 468; and see further *Fisher and Lightwood's Law of Mortgage*, para 28.26.

222 Registration would be under the register of writs and orders affecting land where title is unregistered (see LCA 1972, s 6(1)(b)) and as a restriction where title is registered (see LRA 2002, s 87(2)(b)).

6.149 For further details of the law of receivership, reference should be made to the specialist works on the subject.[223]

LIMITATION

6.150 An application for a charging order is a form of execution. It is not a fresh action on a judgment. In consequence, the judgment creditor is entitled to apply for a charging order even if more than 6 years have elapsed since the money judgment became enforceable.[224] However, undue delay on the part of the judgment creditor may be relevant to the exercise of the court's discretion as to whether or not to grant the charging order.[225] The judgment creditor will not, however, ordinarily be able to secure any interest which accrued on the debt post-judgment but more than 6 years before the application for the charging order was made (since such interest will ordinarily have become irrecoverable).[226]

6.151 There is no limitation period for the enforcement of a charging order (by an order for possession and sale, or by the appointment of a receiver).[227] Upon enforcement of the charging order, the judgment creditor is entitled to receive from the proceeds of sale all interest which was secured by the charging order (including any interest which has accrued since the charging order was made), and not merely the interest which accrued in the 6 years prior to enforcement.[228]

---

[223] See e.g. *Fisher and Lightwood's Law of Mortgage*, Chapter 28; and on receivership generally, see S Tozer and C Crampin, *Mortgage Receivership: Law and Practice* (Wildy, Simmonds & Hill Publishing, 2018); P Walton, T Robinson and S Mann, *Kerr & Hunter on Receivers and Administrators* (Sweet & Maxwell, 21st edn, 2020); G Lightman, G Moss, H Anderson, I Fletcher and R Snowden, *Lightman & Moss: The Law of Administrators and Receivers of Companies* (Sweet & Maxwell, 6th edn, 2017).

[224] This is because Limitation Act 1980, s 24, does not apply to such an application: *Lowsley v Forbes* [1999] 1 AC 329.

[225] See Chapter 2, para 2.26 *et seq*.

[226] Limitation Act 1980, s 24(2); *Lowsley v Forbes* [1999] 1 AC 329. Interest which accrued more than 6 years before the application was made may be recoverable if the judgment creditor has been under a relevant disability: Limitation Act 1980, s 28; or there was a relevant acknowledgement or part-payment: see Limitation Act 1980, s 29.

[227] *Yorkshire Bank v Mulhall* [2008] EWCA Civ 1156 (holding that neither Limitation Act 1980, s 20 nor s 24 applies).

[228] *Ezekiel v Orakpo* [1997] 1 WLR 340; *Yorkshire Bank v Mulhall* [2008] EWCA Civ 1156.

Chapter 7

Other Types of Charging Order

7.1 In addition to charging orders obtainable pursuant to the Charging Orders Act 1979, with which the rest of this book has been concerned, there are a number of other statutory provisions which provide for the creation of charging orders and statutory charges in specific circumstances. This chapter considers these other types of charging order, and the means by which they can be obtained.

COUNCIL TAX (ADMINISTRATION AND ENFORCEMENT) REGULATIONS 1992

Circumstances in which a charging order may be imposed

7.2 The first relevant provisions are the Council Tax (Administration and Enforcement) Regulations 1992.[1] Where a person who is liable to pay council tax has failed to make the required payments, it is open to the local authority charging that tax to apply to the magistrates' court for a 'liability order' specifying the amount that the debtor is liable to pay.[2] If the court is satisfied that the sum has become payable and has not been paid, the liability order is made in respect of the aggregate of the sum payable for council tax and the costs reasonably incurred by the applicant authority in obtaining that order.[3]

7.3 Subsequently, if payment is not made, it is open to the local authority to apply for a charging order in respect of the outstanding debt, provided that:

---

1 SI 1992/613 (CT (A&E) Regs 1992).

2 CT (A&E) Regs 1992, reg 34.

3 CT (A&E) Regs 1992, reg 34(6) and (7).

(a) a magistrates' court has made one or more liability orders;
(b) the amount in respect of which the liability order was made[4] or, where there is more than one liability order, the aggregate of those amounts, is an amount the debtor is liable to pay under the billing provisions;[5] and
(c) at the time the application is made, at least £1,000 of that amount remains outstanding.[6]

Procedure

7.4 Part 73 of the Civil Procedure Rules makes specific reference to charging orders obtainable pursuant to the Council Tax (Administration and Enforcement) Regulations 1992,[7] and the procedure for obtaining them, once the conditions set out above are fulfilled, is substantially the same as it is on an application for a charging order under the Charging Orders Act 1979, with only minor variation.

7.5 The principal features of an application for a charging order under the Council Tax (Administration and Enforcement) Regulations 1992 are as follows:

(a) The only property over which such an order can be sought is the debtor's[8] interest in the dwelling in relation to which the debtor has incurred the council tax liability which the authority seeks to enforce.[9]
(b) The application must be issued in the county court for the district in which that dwelling is situated.[10]
(c) In deciding whether or not to make a charging order, the court is required to consider all the circumstances of the case, in the usual manner, but also specifically:

    (i) the personal circumstances of the debtor; and
    (ii) whether any other person would be likely to be unduly prejudiced by the making of the order.[11]

---

4 That is, the amount specified in either reg 34(7)(a) or reg 36A(5)(a).

5 That is, the provisions of CT (A&E) Regs 1992, Part V.

6 CT (A&E) Regs 1992, reg 50(1).

7 See CPR r 73.2(b).

8 Or 'debtors', since a liability order may be made in respect of more than one person: see CT (A&E) Regs 1992, reg 35(1).

9 CT (A&E) Regs 1992, reg 50(2) and (3).

10 CT (A&E) Regs 1992, reg 50(2) and (3); CPR r 73.3(1)(b).

11 CT (A&E) Regs 1992, reg 51(1).

7.6 The order, if it is made, will secure:

(a) the outstanding sums owed under the liability order or orders; and
(b) a sum equal to the applicant authority's costs reasonably incurred in obtaining it.[12]

It is also required to specify the relevant dwelling and the debtor's interest in it.[13] The court has a discretion to decide whether to make the order absolute or subject to conditions as to the time when the charge is to become enforceable or as to other matters.[14]

7.7 Once made, the charging order has the same effect and is enforceable in the same manner as an equitable charge created by the debtor by writing under his hand,[15] and can be protected by registration in the usual way.[16]

7.8 An application to vary or discharge a charging order made under the Council Tax (Administration and Enforcement) Regulations 1992 may be made not only by the debtor or any person with an interest in the dwelling to which it relates, but also by the authority which applied for it.[17]

SOLICITORS ACT 1974, SECTION 73

7.9 Solicitors[18] enjoy two common law liens. These are:[19]

(a) A general lien entitling a solicitor to retain all papers or other chattels belonging to his client of which he has possession in his capacity as the client's solicitor, until all his costs and charges in that capacity have been paid.

---

12 CT (A&E) Regs 1992, reg 50(2) and (3).

13 CT (A&E) Regs 1992, reg 51(2)(a).

14 CT (A&E) Regs 1992, reg 51(2)(b).

15 CT (A&E) Regs 1992, reg 51(3).

16 CT (A&E) Regs 1992, reg 51(5) and (6). For the registration of charging orders, see Chapter 4.

17 CT (A&E) Regs 1992, reg 51(4), CPR r 73.10B.

18 Barristers have no similar lien, despite that distinction being 'illogical, unprincipled and potentially unfair' according to Robin Dicker QC, sitting as a Deputy High Court Judge, in *Glasgow v ELS Law Ltd* [2017] EWHC 3004 (Ch), [2018] 1 WLR 1564 at [55].

19 See *Halsbury's Laws of England* (LexisNexis, 5th edn, 2008), Vol 65, para 720.

(b) A right to ask the court to direct that all property other than real property[20] which is recovered or preserved by the solicitor's efforts on behalf of his client stand as security for his costs of that recovery or preservation,[21] which lien extends only to those specific costs.[22]

It was thought[23] until recently that this second lien was engaged only when litigation was commenced. However, in *Bott & Co Solicitors Ltd v Ryanair DAC*,[24] the Supreme Court considerably widened the scope of the lien, as explained by Lord Burrows JSC:[25]

> the appropriate test for a solicitor's equitable lien is whether a solicitor provides services (within the scope of the retainer with its client) in relation to the making of a client's claim (with or without legal proceedings) which significantly contribute to the successful recovery of a fund by the client.

7.10 Section 73 of the Solicitors Act 1974, which has had several statutory predecessors (with minor variations in the wording of the provision between them),[26] extended the second form of common law lien. It provides that:

---

20 *Shaw v Neale* (1858) 6 HLC 581 at 601–602, where Baron Chelmsford LC explained: 'There can be no lien upon any property unless it is in the possession of the party who claims the lien. But if an estate is recovered by a solicitor, or if through a solicitor it is conveyed to the client, the solicitor is not in possession of the estate, but his client is in possession of it. All that the solicitor has are the deeds and documents. He has a lien upon them. He may render them available for the purpose of establishing his claim. But it is quite clear that he cannot say that he has any such lien upon the estate as, within the principle of the doctrine which I have suggested, can entitle him to maintain it as a charge upon the property.'

21 *Lord v Colvin* (1862) 2 Drew & Sm 82 at 92–93, where Kindersley V-C explained that: 'The law, in respect of his employment as solicitor, gives him a lien upon whatever he may recover for his client but the fact of his being a solicitor for a party in a suit does [93] not, per se, give him any lien on any particular fund in Court. He has no interest in or lien upon the fund; and although, in all probability, in an administration suit the costs will be ordered to be paid out of the fund, yet, unless and until such an order has been made, he has no charge or lien upon it.'

22 See e.g. *Smith v Betty* [1903] 2 KB 317 at 322 ('The lien of a solicitor on a fund recovered is confined to the costs of the action in which it is recovered', per Stirling LJ).

23 Based on the decision of the Court of Appeal in *Meguerditchian v Lightbound* [1917] 2 KB 298.

24 *Bott & Co Solicitors Ltd v Ryanair DAC* [2022] UKSC 8, [2022] 2 WLR 634.

25 *Bott & Co Solicitors Ltd v Ryanair DAC* [2022] UKSC 8, [2022] 2 WLR 634 at [88].

26 See Solicitors Act 1860, s 28; Solicitors Act 1932, s 69; Solicitors Act 1957, s 72.

any court in which a solicitor has been employed to prosecute or defend any suit, matter or proceedings may at any time –

(a) declare the solicitor entitled to a charge on any property recovered or preserved through his instrumentality for his assessed costs in relation to that suit, matter or proceeding.[27]

Property within the jurisdiction

7.11 The jurisdiction to make a charging order pursuant to section 73 of the Solicitors Act 1974 applies to every form of property, including real property.[28] The extent of the property 'recovered or preserved' by the efforts of the solicitor is 'in the nature of salvage',[29] and consequently, the charge attaches to any such preserved property, and not only to the interest of the solicitor's client in it.[30] The court may also make the charge over property belonging to third parties to the relevant proceedings, even where they have been under a disability, provided that they have benefited from the preservation or recovery of it.[31] The court is not bound to do so, however, because the remedy is discretionary.[32]

7.12 Whether property has been 'recovered or preserved' is a question of fact,[33] and it is not important at what stage it is recovered or preserved, even where part of that process pre-dates the retention of the solicitor, provided that his efforts are material to its preservation or recovery.[34]

7.13 Furthermore, property may be recovered or preserved not only in a successful action, but also where a party has been unsuccessful. Thus, property has been found to have been recovered or preserved both where an action to prove

---

27 Solicitors Act 1974 (SA 1974), s 73(1)(a). The lien may, in certain circumstances, be waived by the solicitor, whether by taking other security or for other reasons: see *Candey Ltd v Crumpler* [2020] EWCA Civ 26, [2020] Bus LR 1452; *Clifford Harris & Co v Solland International Ltd* [2005] EWHC 141 (Ch); *Currie & Co v Law Society* [1977] QB 990.

28 *Foxon v Gascoigne* (1874) LR 9 Ch App 654 at 660, where Mellish LJ explained, 'No doubt [the section] applies to property of all kinds: personal property and real property, corporeal and incorporeal property, property in possession and property in remainder or reversion'.

29 *Greer v Young* (1883) 24 Ch D 545 at 552, per Brett MR, who explained that, 'I do not adopt the idea of salvage as an accurate analogy in all respects, but I think the fundamental theory is, that what is recovered by the action of the solicitor is to be treated as if he had earned salvage, and that he is to be paid for his services on the theory that salvage services have been rendered'.

30 *Scholey v Peck* [1893] 1 Ch 709.

31 *Greer v Young* (1883) 24 Ch D 545; *Wright v Sanderson* [1901] 1 Ch 317.

32 *Wimbourne v Fine* [1952] Ch 869; and see SA 1974, s 73(1), which provides that, 'the court ... may ... declare the solicitor entitled to a charge'.

33 *Rowland v Williams* [1885] WN 194.

34 *Wimbourne v Fine* [1952] Ch 869.

a will was successfully brought,[35] and also where such a claim failed, but where the unsuccessful party recovered property from the estate under an intestacy.[36] Where a claim to the defendant's property is dismissed, that property may have been preserved for the defendant so as to fall within section 73 of the Solicitors Act 1974,[37] and where a claim is successfully resisted in part, the difference between the amount claimed and that established may be charged.[38] Similarly, the balance between a successful claim and a successful counterclaim may be made subject to the statutory order.[39]

7.14 On the other hand, where proceedings were brought, a receiver successfully appointed, and the proceedings then abandoned, the claimant's solicitors were not allowed to impose a charge on the defendant's property relating to their costs of appointing the receiver.[40] The court will also not ordinarily exercise its discretion in relation to property which statute or rules provide is intended to benefit the client or to be inalienable, notably periodic maintenance payments.[41]

Costs in relation to which a charging order may be made

7.15 Only costs incurred in the relevant litigation or arbitration may be protected by a section 73 charging order.[42] Costs that are otherwise incurred, even in related proceedings, may not be so protected.[43] However, the costs of proving the solicitor's retainer and of applying for the charging order may be protected by a statutory charging order.[44]

Practice

7.16 An application for a charging order pursuant to section 73 of the Solicitors Act 1974 is made to a Master, costs judge or District Judge in the court in which the property to be charged has been preserved or recovered, by a claim pursuant to Part 8 of the Civil Procedure Rules. The claim should make clear on its face

---

35 *Ex p Tweed* [1899] 2 QB 167.

36 *Hyde v White* [1933] P 105.

37 *Bulley v Bulley* (1874) LR 9 Ch App 739.

38 *The Birnam Wood* [1907] P 1.

39 *Westacott v Bevan* [1891] 1 QB 774.

40 *Wingfield v Wingfield* [1919] 1 Ch 462.

41 *Watkins v Watkins* [1896] P 222; but *cf Harrison v Harrison* (1888) 13 PD 180.

42 SA 1974, s 73(1); Arbitration Act 1996, s 75; *Bozon v Bolland* (1839) 4 My & Cr 354 at 357–8; *Mackenzie v Mackintosh* (1891) 64 LT 706; *Smith v Betty* [1903] 2 KB 317 at 322; *Re Clayton* [1940] Ch 539 at 545–7.

43 *Wilson v Round* (1863) 4 Giff 416; *MacFarlane v Lister* (1887) 37 Ch D 88.

44 *Re Hill* (1886) 33 Ch D 266; *Re Meter Cabs* [1911] 2 Ch 557.

that its purpose is to assist the solicitor and not his client.[45] The claim may be brought by an executor[46] or assignee[47] of the solicitor entitled to the charge. A solicitor who has ceased to act may also apply, although any charge he obtains will be subject to an equivalent charge over the same property to which any replacement solicitor is entitled.[48]

7.17 The making of the charging order is in the discretion of the court,[49] and the claim may be brought at any time when the requirements of section 73 of the Solicitors Act 1974 are made out.[50] The court cannot, however, make the order where the claim to the costs on which it is founded is barred by limitation.[51] Mere delay does not prevent the exercise of the discretion, although the acquisition of rights over the property to be charged by third parties may prevent it.[52]

7.18 It is expressly stated in section 73 of the Solicitors Act 1974 that all conveyances and acts done to defeat, or operating to defeat, the statutory charge are void as against the solicitor, except for conveyances made in favour of a bona fide purchaser for value without notice.[53] 'Notice' in this context means notice of the solicitor's entitlement to apply for a charging order, not the existence of such an order.[54] In most of the reported cases, the party with notice was directly aware of the underlying litigation in which the costs giving rise to the charge were

---

45 *Harrison v Cornwall Minerals Ry* (1883) 53 LJ Ch 596.

46 *Baile v Baile* (1872) LR 13 Eq 497.

47 *Briscoe v Briscoe* [1892] 3 Ch 543.

48 *Rhodes v Sugden* (1886) 34 Ch D 155; *Knight v Gardner* [1892] 2 Ch 368; *Hyde v White* [1933] P 105.

49 SA 1974, s 73(1). See e.g. *Re Born, Curnock v Born* [1900] 2 Ch 433 at 435, where Farwell J explained that, 'It is clear on the authorities that the applicants have no absolute right to a charging order under [what is now s 73], but that the Court has a discretion in the matter, which it must exercise according to the circumstances of the particular case'; and *Re Cockrell's Estate* [1912] 1 Ch 23 at 27, where Cozens-Hardy MR said that, 'it is perfectly plain that the Court has a discretion and is not bound to make a charging order'. The court must take into account the rights of the client in exercising its discretion: *Re Fuld (No 4)* [1968] P 727, where, at 737, Scarman J explained that, 'the duty of the court is to intervene only if it be necessary for the solicitor's protection, and then only to the extent necessary to safeguard his lien. The intervention, if the court thinks it right to intervene, must not prejudice the rights of the client'. Generally, the authorities show that the court is very willing to assist the solicitor where a client appears to be attempting to take the benefit of his efforts without payment.

50 SA 1974, s 73(1); *Harris v Yarm* [1960] Ch 256.

51 SA 1974, s 73(2).

52 *Re Born* [1900] 2 Ch 433.

53 SA 1974, s 73(1). The making of a third party debt order (formerly known as a garnishee order) is such an act: see e.g. *Dallow v Garrold* (1884) 14 QBD 543; as is an assignment of the relevant property: *Cole v Eley* [1894] 2 QB 350.

54 *Dallow v Garrold* (1884) 14 QBD 543; *Cole v Eley* [1894] 2 QB 350.

incurred.[55] However, in principle there would be nothing to stop a solicitor advertising more widely, for example in *The Gazette*, in the hope of proving later that a wider group of persons had notice of the right. The order gives priority over all other creditors and claims, including mortgages, to the solicitor,[56] save that where what is preserved is trust property the trustee's right to an indemnity for his expenses has priority.[57] A conveyance of the relevant property before the making of the order does not affect the right of the solicitor to the charge.[58] Where there is a change of solicitors during the proceedings, the latter solicitor's charge takes priority over that of the former.[59]

7.19 The court may make such orders as it thinks fit for the assessment of the solicitor's costs and for raising the money to pay them or for paying them out of the property recovered or preserved.[60]

7.20 Where a solicitor takes security which is inconsistent with the lien which he hopes to protect by the imposition of the charge, he will be taken to have waived his entitlement to seek an order under section 73 of the Solicitors Act 1974, whether or not he has demonstrated a positive intention to waive, unless he has expressly or impliedly reserved his right.[61]

INSOLVENCY ACT 1986, SECTION 313

7.21 Pursuant to section 313 of the Insolvency Act 1986,[62] where any property consisting of an interest in a dwelling house which is occupied by a bankrupt or his spouse or civil partner, or by his former spouse or civil partner, is comprised in the bankrupt's estate and the trustee is, for any reason, unable to realise that property, the trustee may apply to the court for an order imposing a charge on the

---

55 See e.g. *Faithfull v Ewen* (1878) 7 Ch D 495.

56 See e.g. *Re Suffield and Watts* (1888) 20 QBD 693 at 696, where Lord Esher MR explained that, 'so long as a fund upon which such a charging order has been made has not been paid away to any one, the order is effectual against every one except a bona fide purchaser for value without notice'.

57 *Re Turner* [1907] 2 Ch 126.

58 *Baile v Baile* (1872) LR 13 Eq 497.

59 *Knight v Gardner* [1892] 2 Ch 368.

60 SA 1974, s 73(1)(b).

61 Although if that security proves invalid, the right is treated as never having been waived: see *Clifford Harris & Co v Solland International Ltd* [2005] EWHC 141 (Ch). See *Candey Ltd v Crumpler and Farmer* [2019] EWHC 282 (Ch), [2019] Bus LR 1901 at [117], per Andrew Hochhauser QC, sitting as a Deputy Judge of the Chancery Division.

62 As amended by the Enterprise Act 2002 and the Civil Partnership Act 2004.

property for the benefit of the bankrupt's estate.[63] Such an order can only be made, however, where the value of the interest to be charged is greater than a prescribed minimum.[64]

7.22 If made, the charge itself becomes part of the bankrupt's estate and is enforceable, up to the 'charged value' from time to time, for the payment of any amount which is payable otherwise than to the bankrupt out of the estate and of interest at the prescribed rate.[65] The 'charged value' for these purposes is the amount specified in the charging order as the value of the bankrupt's interest in the property at the date of the order, and interest on that amount from the same date at the prescribed rate.[66] The prescribed rate of interest is that set out in section 17 of the Judgments Act 1838 on the date on which the charge is imposed, and that rate must be stated in the order imposing the charge.[67]

Practice

7.23 Subsections (1), (2), (4), (5) and (6) of section 3 of the Charging Orders Act 1979 have effect in relation to charging orders made under section 313 of the Insolvency Act 1986 as in relation to charging orders made under the Charging Orders Act 1979,[68] except that the charged value may not be varied under section 3(5) of that Act.[69]

7.24 The terms of a charging order made under the section are to be agreed between the trustee in bankruptcy and the bankrupt or, if they cannot be so agreed, settled by the court.[70]

7.25 The respondents to an application for a charging order under section 313 of the Insolvency Act 1986 must include any spouse or civil partner, or former spouse or civil partner, of the bankrupt who has or claims to have an interest in

---

63 IA 1986, s 313(1). For discussion of the origins and effect of such a charging order, see *Doodes v Gotham & Perry* [2005] EWHC 2576 (Ch), [2006] 1 WLR 729 at [3] (reversed on appeal: *Gotham v Doodes* [2006] EWCA Civ 1080, [2007] 1 WLR 86).

64 IA 1986, s 313A(2). The current prescribed minimum value is £1,000: see Insolvency Proceedings (Monetary Limits) Order 1986 (SI 1986/1996), art 3 and Sch, Pt II. In determining the value of the bankrupt's interest the court is required to disregard certain matters, being a sum equal to the value of any loans secured by mortgage or other charge against the property, any other third party interest, and the reasonable costs of sale: see IA 1986, s 313(2B); 1986 Order, art 5; IA 1986, ss 384(1) and 412; Insolvency Rules 1986 (SI 1986/1925), r 6.237D(10).

65 IA 1986, s 313(2).

66 IA 1986, s 313(2A).

67 Insolvency (England and Wales) Rules 2016 (SI 2016/1024), r 10.171(5).

68 IA 1986, s 313(4).

69 IA 1986, s 313(5).

70 Insolvency (England and Wales) Rules 2016, r 10.171(4).

the property, anyone else having an interest in that property, and such other persons as the court may direct.[71]

7.26 The trustee is obliged to make a report to the court, containing the following particulars:

(a) the extent of the bankrupt's interest which is the subject of the application;
(b) the amount which, at the date of the application, remains owing to unsecured creditors of the bankrupt; and
(c) an estimate of the costs of realising the interest.[72]

7.27 If the court makes an order, its terms must:[73]

(a) describe the property to be charged;
(b) state whether the title to the property is registered and, if it is, specify the title number;
(c) set out the extent of the bankrupt's interest in the property which has vested in the trustee;
(d) indicate, by reference to any, or the total, amount which is payable otherwise than to the bankrupt out of the estate and of interest on that amount, how the amount of the charge is to be ascertained;
(e) set out the conditions (if any) imposed by the court under section 3(1) of the Charging Orders Act 1979; and
(f) identify the date any property charged under section 313 of the Insolvency Act 1986 shall cease to be comprised in the bankrupt's estate and shall, subject to the charge (and any prior charge), vest in the bankrupt.

7.28 The date on which the property is to be vested in the bankrupt is ordinarily the date on which the charge is registered in accordance with section 3(2) of the Charging Orders Act 1979.[74]

7.29 A suggested precedent designed to ensure that all of these matters are included is in Appendix Precedent B16.

---

[71] Insolvency (England and Wales) Rules 2016, r 10.171(2)

[72] Insolvency (England and Wales) Rules 2016, r 10.171(3).

[73] Insolvency (England and Wales) Rules 2016, r 10.171(6)

[74] Insolvency (England and Wales) Rules 2016, r 10.171(7).

7.30 Once an order has been made, the trustee is required to register the resulting charge, as soon as is reasonably practical thereafter.[75]

Effect

7.31 The order, once made, has the same effect and is enforceable in the same manner as an equitable charge created by the bankrupt under his own hand.[76]

7.32 An order under section 313 of the Insolvency Act 1986 is unusual because there is no preceding enforceable debt between the applicant trustee and respondent bankrupt, since it is made 'for the payment of any amount which is payable otherwise than to the bankrupt out of the estate'.[77] Consequently, time does not start to run for the purposes of section 20 of the Limitation Act 1980 upon the making of the order, but only upon the making of an order for sale of the property under section 335A of the Insolvency Act 1986.[78]

7.33 The matters to which the court is to have regard where an application for an order for sale is made pursuant to section 14 of the Trusts of Land and Appointment of Trustees Act 1996 are set out in section 335A of the Insolvency Act 1986.

7.34 Broadly, the intention and ultimate effect of allowing the trustee in bankruptcy to obtain a charging order is to enable the bankrupt to deal with his home without excessive constraint. It protects any subsequent increase in the value of his home from his bankruptcy creditors. However, it also allows the trustee in bankruptcy:

(a) to protect the interests of the bankrupt's creditors; and
(b) at the same time to summon the final meeting of creditors required by section 331 of the Insolvency Act 1986.

---

75 Insolvency (England and Wales) Rules 2016, r 10.171(8). An order made over a beneficial interest under a trust of land cannot be registered as a land charge under LCA 1972, s 6: see *Perry v Phoenix Assurance plc* [1988] 1 WLR 940.

76 COA 1979, s 3(4), applied, together with s 3(1), (2), (5) and (6), by IA 1986, s 313(4).

77 IA 1986, s 313(2).

78 *Gotham v Doodes* [2006] EWCA Civ 1080, [2007] 1 WLR 86.

AGRICULTURAL HOLDINGS ACT 1986, SECTIONS 85, 86 AND 87

7.35 Lettings of agricultural holdings made prior to 1 September 1995 are regulated by the Agricultural Holdings Act 1986.[79] Under the Act, the tenant becomes entitled to compensation payments from the landlord in a variety of circumstances and, in particular, on the termination of the tenancy.[80] The Act makes provision for the Secretary of State[81] – not a court – to make a charging order to secure the payments due to the tenant, and also to enable a landlord who has had to make compensation payments to charge them on the land by way of a charging order.

Tenant's charge

7.36 Section 85(2) of the Agricultural Holdings Act 1986 provides that, where a sum becomes due to a tenant of an agricultural holding in respect of compensation from the landlord, and the landlord fails to discharge his liability within one month of the payment becoming due, the tenant is entitled to obtain from the Minister an order charging the holding with payment of the amount due. The sums due include the costs of obtaining the charge.[82] By section 85(3), where the landlord is entitled to receive the rents and profits of the holding otherwise than for his own benefit,[83] the tenant is not entitled to sue him personally in respect of any sum agreed or awarded under the Act to be paid to him by the landlord,[84] but he is entitled, if such sum has not been paid to him within one month after it becomes due, to obtain from the Minister an order charging the holding with payment of such a sum, and with the costs of obtaining it.[85]

7.37 These rights are in addition to the tenant's right to enforce payment of a sum agreed or awarded under the Agricultural Holdings Act 1986 as a county court judgment, if the county court so orders.[86]

---

79 Thereafter, such tenancies create farm business tenancies under the Agricultural Tenancies Act 1995.

80 See Agricultural Holdings Act 1986 (AHA 1986), Part V.

81 Referred to in the relevant sections as 'the Minister': see AHA 1986, s 96(1).

82 AHA 1986, s 87(1).

83 As, for instance, a trustee.

84 AHA 1986, s 85(3)(a). *Cf* AHA 1986, s 85(1).

85 AHA 1986, ss 85(3)(b) and 87(1).

86 AHA 1986, s 85(1).

Landlord's charge

7.38 By section 86 of the Agricultural Holdings Act 1986, where the landlord of a holding to which the Act applies has paid to the tenant of the holding in respect of compensation for:

(a) improvements;[87]
(b) tenant-right matters;[88]
(c) disturbance; or
(d) defraying the costs of executing an improvement[89] required of him by notice;[90]

he is entitled to obtain from the Minister an order charging the holding or any part of it with repayment of the amount of the compensation or the costs, together with the costs of obtaining the order.[91] Where the relevant sum falls to be determined by arbitration, the landlord may require the arbitrator to certify the amount of compensation and the term for which the charge may properly be made, having regard to the time at which the matter compensated is to be deemed to be exhausted.[92]

7.39 Similarly, where the landlord is entitled to receive the rents and profits of the holding otherwise than for his own benefit,[93] he is entitled, either before or after paying to the tenant of the holding any sum agreed or awarded under the Act to be paid to the tenant by him, to obtain an order charging the holding with repayment of that amount.[94]

7.40 A charge pursuant to section 86 of the Agricultural Holdings Act 1986 may not be obtained by trustees holding land for ecclesiastical or charitable purposes except with the written approval of the Charities Commission.[95]

7.41 These provisions are probably of more assistance to landlords with only a limited interest in the holding, such as a tenant for life, than to ordinary landlords,

---

87 Under AHA 1986, s 64(1) or (4).

88 Under AHA 1986, Sch 8, Part II.

89 Within AHA 1986, Sch 7, Part II.

90 Under AHA 1986, s 67(5).

91 AHA 1986, ss 86(1) and 87(1).

92 AHA 1986, s 86(2).

93 As, for instance, a trustee.

94 AHA 1986, s 86(3).

95 AHA 1986, s 86(4).

although it is conceivable that a landlord might prefer to transfer the burden of a debt onto the holding in any event.

Practice

7.42 Section 87 of the Agricultural Holdings Act 1986 contains provisions about the imposition of charges under sections 85 and 86. In particular, it provides that any such charging orders:

(a) are to be made in favour of the person obtaining them and of his executors, administrators and assigns;[96]
(b) shall make provision for the payment of interest and for the payment of the sum charged by instalments, and shall contain such directions for giving effect to it, as the Secretary of State thinks fit.[97]

7.43 A charge under section 86 of the Agricultural Holdings Act 1986 is a charge on the landlord's interest in the holding or part of it charged, and on all interests in it subsequent to the landlord's holding, but where the landlord's holding is leasehold, it shall not extend beyond the interest of the landlord, his executors, administrators and assigns.[98] Furthermore, in the case of a charge under section 86, where the landlord is not the absolute owner of the holding for his own benefit, no instalment or interest is to be made payable after the time when the improvement to which the compensation relates will, in the opinion of the Minister, be exhausted.[99]

7.44 There may be a provision in a will, deed or other instrument, under which an estate or interest in the landlord's agricultural holding may be determinable or liable to forfeiture if he charges the land or allows it to be charged. Such a provision will not operate if a tenant obtains a charge under section 85(2) of the Agricultural Holdings Act 1986, or if the landlord obtains a charge under section 86.[100]

7.45 A company incorporated by Parliament with power to advance money for the improvement of land may take an assignment of any charge created under

---

96 AHA 1986, s 87(2). The express inclusion of executors, administrators and assigns avoids the arguments considered in *Re the Agricultural Holdings (England) Act 1883, Gough v Gough* [1891] 2 QB 665, where executors of a tenant for life, who were required to pay compensation to a tenant whose interest had terminated before the landlord's death, were entitled to a charge under the Agricultural Holdings (England) Act 1883.

97 AHA 1986, s 87(2).

98 AHA 1986, s 87(3).

99 AHA 1986, s 87(4).

100 AHA 1986, s 87(5).

these provisions upon such terms as may be agreed between it and the person entitled to the charge, and thereafter may itself assign it.[101]

7.46 Charges which are created pursuant to these provisions[102] rank in priority to any other charge, however created and whenever arising, although as between themselves, they rank in order of their creation.[103] They are registrable as Class A land charges under the Land Charges Act 1972 in respect of unregistered land,[104] and can be protected by notice on the Charges Register of a registered title.

LANDLORD AND TENANT ACT 1927

7.47 Very similar provisions to those considered above under the Agricultural Holdings Act 1986 apply where a landlord of business premises has paid his tenant a sum in respect of compensation for improvements or has expended the cost of executing works following a notice given in accordance with the Landlord and Tenant Act 1927.[105]

7.48 The charge is to be obtained from the Minister of Agriculture, Fisheries and Food[106] and is registrable as a Class A land charge where title to the land charged is unregistered[107] or by a notice where the property to be charged is registered. There is no special provision relating to the priority of such a charge, so it will not rank in priority to a pre-existing mortgage.

7.49 The order is made in favour of the landlord and persons deriving title under him, and it charges the holding or part of it with repayment of the amount paid or expended, as appropriate, with such interest and by such instalments, and with such directions for giving effect to the charge, as the Minister thinks fit.[108]

---

101 AHA 1986, s 87(7). The best-known example of such a company is the Agricultural Mortgage Corporation plc. For land improvement companies and their history, see *Halsbury's Laws of England* (LexisNexis, 5th edn, 2008), Vol 1, paras 608–610.

102 Or under AHA 1948, s 74 (now repealed).

103 AHA 1986, s 87(6).

104 LCA 1972, s 2(2) and Sch 2. Failure so to register it will render it void against a purchaser for value of the land charged: LCA 1972, ss 4(2) and 17(1).

105 Landlord and Tenant Act 1927 (LTA 1927), s 12 and Sch 1.

106 The Ministry of Agriculture, Fisheries and Food was dissolved in March 2002: see the Ministry of Agriculture, Fisheries and Food (Dissolution) Order 2002 (SI 2002/794). Its functions passed to the Department for Environment, Food and Rural Affairs. Presumably, the order would therefore be made by the Secretary of State, as in the case of agricultural holdings, or possibly by the Minister of State for Agriculture, Fisheries and Food.

107 LTA 1927, Sch 1, para (7).

108 LTA 1927, Sch 1, para (1).

7.50 Where the landlord who obtains the charge is not an absolute owner of the holding for his own benefit, no instalment or interest shall be made payable after the time when the improvement in respect whereof compensation is paid will, in the opinion of the Minister, have become exhausted.[109]

7.51 Where the estate or interest of a landlord is determinable or liable to forfeiture by reason of his creating or suffering any charge thereon, that estate or interest shall not be determined or forfeited by reason of his obtaining such a charge, anything in any deed, will or other instrument to the contrary thereof notwithstanding.[110]

7.52 The sum charged is a charge on the holding, or the part of the holding that is charged. The charge is for the landlord's interest in the holding and for interests in the reversion immediately expectant on the termination of the lease. However, where the landlord's interest is an interest in a leasehold, the charge shall not extend beyond that leasehold interest.[111]

7.53 Any company incorporated by Parliament which has power to advance money for the improvement of land is entitled take an assignment of such a charge, on terms agreed between the company and the chargee, and the company may itself assign the charge.[112]

7.54 Where such a charge is made for compensation due under an award, the person entitled to the charge can require the tribunal making the award to certify the amount to be charged and the term for which the charge may properly be made, having regard to the time at which each improvement in respect of which compensation is awarded is to be deemed to be exhausted.[113]

PARTNERSHIP ACT 1890, SECTION 23

7.55 Section 23(1) of the Partnership Act 1890 provides that a judgment creditor of a partner may not issue a writ of execution against property belonging to the partnership in respect of that partner's individual debt.[114] This provision

---

109 LTA 1927, Sch 1, para (2).

110 LTA 1927, Sch 1, para (3).

111 LTA 1927, Sch 1, para (4).

112 LTA 1927, Sch 1, para (5).

113 LTA 1927, Sch 1, para (6).

114 It provides that, 'A writ of execution shall not issue against any partnership property except on a judgment against the firm'.

thereby abrogated a previously cumbersome procedure under which the business of solvent partners could be severely disrupted by the seizure of shared assets.[115]

7.56 Instead, the section provides that a judgment creditor of a partner in a partnership may obtain an order charging that partner's interest in the partnership property and profits.[116]

7.57 If such an order is made, its effect is the same as if the partner owing the debt had executed a document charging his interest in the partnership property with the debt.[117] Consequently, one result of the imposition of such a charge is that the other partners may choose to dissolve the partnership.[118] They are also given power to redeem the charge themselves, or to purchase the charged property, if a sale is directed.[119]

Practice

7.58 Practice Direction 73 of the Civil Procedure Rules sets out a specific procedure for applications under section 23 of the Partnership Act 1890.[120]

7.59 The powers granted by section 23 of the Partnership Act 1890 are to be exercised by:

(a) a Master;
(b) the Admiralty Registrar; or
(c) a District Judge;[121]

and an application under the section is to be made in accordance with Part 23 of the Civil Procedure Rules,[122] in either the High Court or the county court.[123]

7.60 All application notices filed by a judgment creditor in relation to section 23 of the Partnership Act 1890, and all orders made pursuant to them,

---

115 See *Brown, Janson & Co v A Hutchinson & Co* [1895] 1 QB 737 at 738–9, where Lindley LJ graphically described the former practice. Partnership Act 1890 (PA 1890), s 23 is unusual because, as Lindley LJ pointed out at 738, the Act 'made very little alteration in the legal procedure except by s 23'.

116 PA 1890, s 23(2).

117 *Brown, Janson & Co v A Hutchinson & Co (No 2)* [1895] 2 QB 126.

118 PA 1890, s 33(2); *Brown, Janson & Co v A Hutchinson & Co* [1895] 1 QB 737 at 740.

119 PA 1890, s 23(3).

120 CPR r 73.22; CPR PD 73, para 6.

121 CPR PD 73, para 6.3.

122 CPR Part 23 contains the general rules about applications for court orders.

123 CPR PD 73, para 2; PA 1890, 23(2).

must be served on the judgment debtor and on any of his partners who are within the jurisdiction.[124] All application notices filed by a partner of a judgment debtor in relation to section 23, and all orders relating to them, must be served on the judgment creditor and the judgment debtor, as well as on all the other partners of the judgment debtor who are not joined in the application and are within the jurisdiction.[125] Where, however, an application notice has been served on one or more, but not all, of the partners of a partnership, it is deemed to have been served on all of them.[126]

7.61 If, notwithstanding section 23(1) of the Partnership Act 1890:

(a) execution is levied against a partner;
(b) it is claimed that the property which has been seized is partnership property;
(c) the execution creditor either disputes that there is a partnership, or that the relevant property is property of a partnership;

the dispute is the proper subject of interpleader proceedings.[127]

ROAD TRAFFIC ACT 1991

7.62 Part 75 of the Civil Procedure Rules deals with enforcement proceedings relating to parking offences, which are within the jurisdiction of the county court. The local authority to which parking charges are due is entitled to make a request, for which there are various specified procedural requirements,[128] to the court, whereupon a court officer will make an order that the amount claimed is recoverable as if it were payable under an order of the county court.[129] By rule 75.6 of the Civil Procedure Rules, the provisions of Part 73 are applied for the purpose of enforcement of specified debts[130] arising out of the Road Traffic Act 1991. In consequence, a charging order can be obtained pursuant to that Part in order to enforce an order made under rule 75.3.[131]

---

[124] CPR PD 73, para 6.4.

[125] CPR PD 73, para 6.5.

[126] CPR PD 73, para 6.6.

[127] See *Peake v Carter* [1916] 1 KB 652.

[128] For which see CPR r 75.3 and CPR PD 75.

[129] CPR r 75.3(3).

[130] As defined in Enforcement of Road Traffic Debts Order 1993 (SI 1993/2073), art 2.

[131] Subject to the provisions set out in the remainder of CPR Part 75.

CHILD SUPPORT ACT 1991, SECTIONS 33 AND 36

7.63 By section 33 of the Child Support Act 1991, the Secretary of State may apply to the magistrates' court for the making of a liability order against a person if that person has failed to pay an amount of child support maintenance which he is obliged to pay, and it appears to the Secretary of State that it would be inappropriate or ineffective to make a deduction from earnings order.[132] Where such a liability order has been made, the amount in respect of which it was made, to the extent that it remains unpaid, is recoverable as though it were payable under a county court judgment,[133] by means of a third party debt order or charging order,[134] if the court so orders.[135] It follows that the provisions of Part 73 of the Civil Procedure Rules apply to a charging order sought under the Act. Although only the Secretary of State can apply for the liability order, there is no restriction in the Act as to who may apply for the consequential orders.

MENTAL CAPACITY ACT 2005, SECTION 18

7.64 The Mental Capacity Act 2005 gives to the court, or to a deputy appointed by it under the Act,[136] a general power to impose charges on the property of a person who lacks capacity[137] within the meaning of the Act.[138]

7.65 The Act also makes provision, where the court has ordered or directed the expenditure of money either for the carrying out of permanent improvements on any property belonging to a person who lacks capacity, or otherwise for the permanent benefit of any of his property, for the court to order that the whole or part of the money so expended is to be charged against the property, with or without the payment of interest at a specified rate.[139]

7.66 A charge made under this latter provision may be made in favour of such person as may be just and, in particular, where the money is paid out of the general estate of the person who lacks capacity, may be made in favour of a person as

---

132 Child Support Act 1991 (CSA 1991), s 33(2).

133 CSA 1991, s 33(5).

134 CSA 1991, s 36(1).

135 The words 'if the court so orders' will be repealed by Child Maintenance and Other Payments Act 2008, ss 28, 58 and Sch 8, which are not yet in force.

136 See Mental Capacity Act 2005 (MCA 2005), s 16.

137 MCA 2005, s 18(1)(b).

138 See MCA 2005, s 2.

139 MCA 2005, Sch 2, para 9(1) and (2).

trustee for that person.[140] But the charge so made is restricted, in that it cannot confer any right of sale or foreclosure during the lifetime of the person who lacks capacity.[141]

HOUSING ACT 2004, SECTIONS 49 AND 50, SCHEDULE 3

7.67 Under the Housing Act 2004, a local housing authority is entitled to make such reasonable charge as it considers appropriate in order to recover certain administrative and other expenses incurred by it in:[142]

(a) serving an improvement notice;[143]
(b) making a prohibition order;[144]
(c) serving a hazard awareness notice;[145]
(d) taking emergency remedial action;[146]
(e) making an emergency prohibition order;[147] or
(f) making a demolition order.[148]

7.68 Only specified expenses give rise to the right to make such a charge.[149] The charge is recoverable for the person on whom the relevant notice or order was served.[150] A demand for payment must be served on that person,[151] and if it is not satisfied within 21 days of service, subject to appeal,[152] it automatically becomes a charge on the property of that person, until the sum demanded is recovered.[153]

7.69 The charge is registrable as a local land charge,[154] and it confers on the local authority all the same powers and remedies under the Law of Property Act

---

[140] MCA 2005, Sch 2, para 9(4).

[141] MCA 2005, Sch 2, para 9(5).

[142] Housing Act 2004 (HA 2004), s 49(1).

[143] Under HA 2004, s 11 or s 12.

[144] Under HA 2004, s 20 or s 21.

[145] Under HA 2004, s 28 or s 29.

[146] Under HA 2004, s 40.

[147] Under HA 2004, s 43.

[148] Under HA 1985, s 265.

[149] HA 2004, s 49(2), (3) and (4).

[150] See HA 2004, s 50.

[151] HA 2004, s 50(5).

[152] HA 2004, s 50(6), (7) and (8).

[153] HA 2004, s 50(9).

[154] HA 2004, s 50(10).

1925 and otherwise as if it were a mortgagee by deed having powers of sale and lease, of accepting surrenders of leases and of appointing a receiver.[155]

7.70 Where an improvement notice is not complied with, or where reasonable progress is not being made towards compliance with it, the local authority is entitled to carry out the required works itself.[156] If it does so, the local authority is then entitled to recover its reasonable expenses of so doing from the person on whom the notice was served.[157] A demand must then be served,[158] and rights of appeal apply.[159] However, subject to compliance with those pre-conditions, the demand becomes operative after 21 days. Once it is, the local authority can claim receipt of the rents and profits of the property,[160] but until the sum demanded is recovered,[161] it automatically becomes a charge on the property.[162]

7.71 Once again, the charge is registrable as a local land charge, and it confers on the local authority all the same powers and remedies under the Law of Property Act 1925 and otherwise as if it were a mortgagee by deed having powers of sale and lease, of accepting surrenders of leases and of appointing a receiver.[163]

7.72 These charges take priority over all other mortgages and rent charges on the relevant property.[164]

HIGHWAYS ACT 1980

7.73 Under the Highways Act 1980, where a local authority has carried out works to make up a private street it is entitled to impose a charge for so doing on the owners of the properties fronting the street.[165]

---

155 HA 2004, s 50(11), subject to a delay of one month before a receiver can be appointed: see s 50(12).

156 HA 2004, Sch 3, para 3.

157 HA 2004, Sch 3, paras 7 and 8.

158 HA 2004, Sch 3, para 9.

159 HA 2004, Sch 3, paras 9 and 11.

160 HA 2004, Sch 3, para 12.

161 Together with interest: see HA 2004, Sch 3, para 10.

162 HA 2004, Sch 3, para 13.

163 HA 2004, Sch 3, para 13, subject to a delay of one month before a receiver can be appointed.

164 *Paddington Borough Council v Finucane* [1928] Ch 567 (followed in *Westminster City Council v Haymarket Publishing Ltd* [1981] 1 WLR 677); *Bristol Corporation v Virgin* [1928] 2 KB 622; see also *Hackney LBC v Crown Estate Commissioners* (1996) 72 P & CR 233.

165 See, for instance, HA 1980, ss 212 and 305.

7.74 Once the sum owed has been determined, it is automatically a charge on the relevant premises, registrable as a local land charge. Although a failure to register such a charge does not render it unenforceable, it does in some circumstances entitle a purchaser to compensation.[166]

7.75 The charge brings with it all of the powers and remedies under the Law of Property Act 1925 as would be available to the local authority if it were a mortgagee having powers of sale, leasing and appointing a receiver.[167] As chargee, the authority is given a power of sale in priority to earlier mortgages or rent charges.[168] Since this is an exception to the usual rules of priority and the impact can be severe, it is important for conveyancers to ensure that searches for such charges are carried out, and that purchasers are made aware of the effect of any such charge.

LEGAL AID, SENTENCING AND PUNISHMENT OF OFFENDERS ACT 2012

7.76 The first edition of this work discussed[169] the historical provisions relating to the recovery of legal aid. Those provisions have now been repealed by the Legal Aid, Sentencing and Punishment of Offenders Act 2012[170] and replaced by a new regime set out in the 2012 Act itself.

7.77 The Legal Services Commission having been abolished,[171] it is now the Lord Chancellor who is responsible for the provision of public funding in litigation, which he is to do through a civil servant designated as the 'Director of Legal Aid Casework' and acting independently of him.[172]

7.78 Provision for an automatic statutory charge is now contained in section 25 of the Legal Aid, Sentencing and Punishment of Offenders Act 2012, with

---

[166] Local Land Charges Act 1975, s 10.

[167] HA 1980, s 212(3); *Payne v Cardiff RDC* [1932] 1 KB 241, a case under the similarly worded Private Street Works Act 1892, s 13.

[168] *Paddington Borough Council v Finucane* [1928] Ch 567; *Bristol Corporation v Virgin* [1928] 2 KB 622; see also *Hackney LBC v Crown Estate Commissioners* (1996) 72 P & CR 233.

[169] At paras 7.76–7.78.

[170] Legal Aid, Sentencing and Punishment of Offenders Act 2012 (LASPO), s 39(1) and Sch 5, para 51.

[171] By LASPO, s 38(1).

[172] LASPO, ss 1 and 4.

detailed provisions relating to its function and enforcement appearing in the Civil Legal Aid (Statutory Charge) Regulations 2013.[173]

7.79 Section 25(1) of the Legal Aid, Sentencing and Punishment of Offenders Act 2012 confirms that the charge constitutes a first charge on any property recovered or preserved by a funded individual in proceedings, or in any compromise or settlement of a dispute, in connection with which the funded services were provided, and that it applies to property preserved or recovered for persons other than the funded party. It is suggested that authorities decided under the historical regime will apply in the same way to the new regime. If this is correct, then property is recovered where a claimant claims property in proceedings, and he established a right to some form of ownership of it, and where a defendant's ownership of property is disputed in proceedings, and that right is vindicated and preserved.[174] A reduction in the amount of a debt secured on a property, even by way of compromise, is preservation of that property.[175] Similarly, property which is released from an encumbrance as a result of the relevant proceedings has been preserved.[176] A money judgment is relevant property for the purposes of the section.[177] Notably, though, the new regime extends the charge also to costs payable to the funded individual in connection with the relevant proceedings.

7.80 Provision for calculation of the amounts secured by the statutory charge is set out in regulations 4–6 of the Civil Legal Aid (Statutory Charge) Regulations 2013. In the ordinary case, the charge is in favour of the Lord Chancellor, though in certain circumstances it may operate in favour of the person who has provided the legal services for which funding has been given.[178] The Lord Chancellor is given power to waive the charge in specified circumstances.[179]

7.81 Where there is a statutory charge in favour of the Lord Chancellor, Part 3 of the Civil Legal Aid (Statutory Charge) Regulations 2013 makes provision for its enforcement, postponement of its enforcement, and the payment of interest at the (current) rate of 8% per annum. The imposition of a charge under s 25 of the Legal Aid, Sentencing and Punishment of Offenders Act 2012 will not breach the human rights of the chargor, even if the result is that the chargor retains none of

---

173 SI 2013/503.

174 *Hanlon v Law Society* [1981] AC 124.

175 *McPherson v Legal Services Commission* [2008] EWHC 2865 (Ch).

176 *Morgan v Legal Aid Board* [2000] EWHC 462 (Ch), [2000] 1 WLR 1657.

177 *Legal Services Commission v Banks* [2008] EWHC 1035 (QB).

178 Civil Legal Aid (Statutory Charge) Regulations 2013, reg 7.

179 Civil Legal Aid (Statutory Charge) Regulations 2013, regs 8 and 9.

the damages that he was awarded.[180] However, in an appropriate case, the Legal Aid Agency may co-operate with legal representatives to structure litigation in such a way as to avoid the statutory charge applying, although this will need to be addressed at the inception of any claim.[181]

180 *R (Tirkey) v Director of Legal Aid Casework & Another* [2017] EWHC 3403 (Admin), [2018] 1 WLR 2112.

181 See *Northamptonshire CC v Lord Chancellor* [2018] EWHC 1628 (Fam), [2019] 1 FLR 169 for an example and the Legal Aid Agency's position statement.

Chapter 8

Insolvency

INTRODUCTION

8.1 As alluded to above,[1] several statutory provisions restrict, or bar altogether, steps in execution of judgments in cases of insolvency. This can be particularly relevant for practitioners dealing with charging orders in circumstances where the judgment debtor is insolvent or is at risk of insolvency.

8.2 In particular, if a charging order is obtained in breach of a mandatory moratorium on execution (i.e. without any requisite leave of the court), it is irregular and invalid. Although not a nullity as such, because it has been made without the court having power to do so it will be liable to be set aside.[2] Unless leave is granted retrospectively, the court must set aside the charging order as of right.[3]

8.3 This chapter offers a concise summary of the main individual and corporate insolvency procedures[4] and the extent to which they impact on the ability of a judgment creditor to apply for or (as the case may be) retain the benefit of a charging order.

---

1 See, for instance, Chapter 3, para 3.119 and see paras 2.33–2.44 for the relevance of insolvency to the exercise of a court's discretion in making a charging order final.

2 *Clarke v Coutts & Co (A Firm)* [2002] EWCA Civ 943, [2002] BPIR 916.

3 *Clarke v Coutts & Co (A Firm)* [2002] EWCA Civ 943, [2002] BPIR 916. It was said that the charging order was liable to be set aside *ex debito justitiae* on the debtor's application, the court having no discretion to leave it in place.

4 For more detailed consideration of the various insolvency procedures, readers are advised to make reference to specialist insolvency texts.

DEFINITION OF INSOLVENCY

8.4 The key piece of legislation is the Insolvency Act 1986, together with the Insolvency (England and Wales) Rules 2016.[5] Although the 1986 Act does not explicitly define the term 'insolvency', it encompasses the notion of being unable to pay one's debts.

OVERVIEW OF INDIVIDUAL INSOLVENCY PROCEDURES

8.5 In England and Wales, the main formal individual insolvency procedures are bankruptcy and individual voluntary arrangements (IVAs). IVAs comprise the majority of individual insolvencies.

Bankruptcy

8.6 The key provisions relating to bankruptcy can be found in Part 9 of the Insolvency Act 1986 and Parts 10 and 11 of the Insolvency (England and Wales) Rules 2016.

8.7 Each and every bankruptcy is under the general control of the court (section 363(1) of the Insolvency Act 1986). This means that the court has full power to decide all questions of priorities and all other questions – whether of law or fact – arising in any bankruptcy.

8.8 One of the distinguishing features of bankruptcy is that it may be instigated by third parties, as well as the putative bankrupt himself.

8.9 Where the procedure is instigated by third parties, the process begins with the presentation of a bankruptcy petition. Assuming the court has jurisdiction,[6] the court may make a bankruptcy order in relation to an individual on a petition by any of the following persons identified in section 264 of the Insolvency Act 1986:

(a) the creditor(s) of that individual;
(b) the supervisor of, or any person (other than the individual), who is, for the time being, bound by a voluntary arrangement (an IVA) proposed by the individual and approved under Part VIII of the Insolvency Act 1986; or

---

5 SI 2016/1024.

6 As to which, see IA 1986, s 265.

(c) where a criminal bankruptcy order has been made against the individual, by the Official Petitioner or by any person specified in the order in pursuance of section 39(3)(b) of the Powers of Criminal Courts Act 1973.

8.10 A creditor's petition must be in respect of one or more debts owed by the debtor, and the petitioning creditor must be a person to whom the debt or (as the case may be) at least one of the debts is owed.[7]

8.11 Further, by virtue of section 267(2) of the Insolvency Act 1986, petitioning creditors must satisfy the court that, at the time the petition is presented:

(a) the amount of the debt, or the aggregate amount of the debts, is equal to or exceeds the bankruptcy level (currently £5,000[8]);
(b) the debt, or each of the debts, is for an unsecured liquidated sum payable to the petitioning creditor (or one or more of the petitioning creditors) either immediately or at some certain, future time;
(c) the debt, or each of the debts, is a debt which the debtor appears either to be unable to pay or to have no reasonable prospect of being able to pay; and
(d) there is no outstanding application to set aside a statutory demand served (under section 268 of the Insolvency Act 1986) in respect of the debt or any of the debts.

8.12 Since 6 April 2016, debtors have no longer been able to petition the court for their own bankruptcy order. Instead, by virtue of changes introduced by the Enterprise and Regulatory Reform Act 2013, debtors must now make a bankruptcy application online to an 'adjudicator' via an online portal called Online Debt Solutions.[9] A debtor may make such an application only on the ground that he is unable to pay his debts.[10]

8.13 An adjudicator is an official appointed pursuant to section 398A of the Insolvency Act 1986. Section 263I confers a statutory jurisdiction on adjudicators to make bankruptcy orders without any involvement on the part of the court.[11] If the application provides all the prescribed information and is considered appropriate, then the adjudicator will make a bankruptcy order.

8.14 Although this process is administrative, rather than judicial, in nature, the bankruptcy order made by the adjudicator has the same statutory force as one

---

7 IA 1986, s 267(1).

8 IA 1986, s 267(4).

9 See https://apply-for-bankruptcy.service.gov.uk/.

10 IA 1986, s 263H(2).

11 Although the court has jurisdiction to hear appeals of an adjudicator's refusal to make a bankruptcy order: see IA 1986, s 263N.

made by the court after the presentation of a petition. Further, once the order has been made, the court retains the same general control of the bankruptcy under section 363(1) of the Insolvency Act 1986.

8.15 A bankruptcy commences on the day on which the bankruptcy order is made.

8.16 On the making of a bankruptcy order, the first trustee in bankruptcy is appointed.[12] The first trustee will be the official receiver, unless the court appoints another person under section 291A(2) of the Insolvency Act 1986. This subsection provides that, if, when the order is made, an IVA has been approved in relation to the bankrupt, then the bankrupt's IVA supervisor may be appointed as the first trustee.

8.17 A number of consequences follow from the making of a bankruptcy order. This is the case whether it is made by the court or an adjudicator. Chief amongst these is that, by virtue of section 306 of the Insolvency Act 1986, the bankrupt's estate automatically vests in the trustee in bankruptcy,[13] although the trustee is granted a power to disclaim 'onerous' property.[14]

8.18 The purpose of this vesting is to enable the trustee in bankruptcy to perform his statutory function – namely, to collect in, realise, and distribute the bankrupt's estate amongst the bankrupt's creditors.[15]

8.19 In performing this statutory function, the trustee is entitled to use his own discretion.

8.20 The bankrupt's estate must be distributed in accordance with the rules of priority laid down by section 328 of the Insolvency Act 1986.

8.21 The bankruptcy will continue until the individual is discharged or, alternatively, the bankruptcy order is annulled.[16] The bankrupt will be automatically discharged on the first anniversary of the bankruptcy order. However, the trustee in bankruptcy may apply to court to suspend the discharge for a specified period or until some specified condition is fulfilled. The court's power to make such an order suspending discharge is a relatively limited one.

---

12 IA 1986, s 291A(1).

13 Note that the IA 1986 makes special provision in relation to the bankrupt's interest in the family home: see IA 1986, s 283A.

14 See IA 1986, s 315.

15 IA 1986, s 305(2).

16 See IA 1986, ss 278–282.

Individual voluntary arrangements

8.22 The legislation governing IVAs can largely be found in Part VIII of the Insolvency Act 1986 and Part 8 of the Insolvency (England and Wales) Rules 2016.

8.23 An IVA is essentially contractual in nature, albeit that this contract is formed within a statutory framework. The principal consequence of this is that an IVA can be tailored to the needs of the individual debtor. This means that – generally speaking – an IVA is a more flexible procedure than bankruptcy, which may account for its relative prevalence.

8.24 Generally, an IVA begins with a debtor engaging an insolvency practitioner (IP) to act as his adviser.

8.25 Thereafter, the IP will usually work directly with the debtor to prepare a proposal for the debtor's creditors. This proposal may take two different forms, either a composition in satisfaction of the debtor's debts or a scheme of arrangement of his affairs.

8.26 Before the proposal is made, it is possible to apply to the court for what is known as an interim order.[17] The interim order has the effect that, whilst it is in force:

(a) no bankruptcy petition relating to the debtor may be presented or proceeded with;
(b) no landlord or other person to whom rent is payable may exercise any right of forfeiture by peaceable re-entry in relation to premises let to the debtor in respect of a failure by the debtor to comply with any term or condition of his tenancy of such premises, except with the leave of the court; and
(c) no other proceedings, and no execution or other legal process, may be commenced or continued and no distress may be levied against the debtor or his property except with the leave of the court.[18]

8.27 Once the proposal has been drawn up, the IP will call a meeting of the debtor's creditors (known as a creditors' meeting). At this meeting, the creditors will vote on the proposal.

---

17 As to which, see IA 1986, ss 252 and 253.

18 IA 1986, s 252(2).

8.28 Briefly, an IVA may be approved by creditors holding 75% of the debt by value.[19]

8.29 At a high level of abstraction, an IVA typically requires a debtor to make some funds available to his IVA supervisor. The debtor may make these funds available out of his assets, his income or a combination of both. In addition, third parties – such as the debtor's spouse or family members – may choose to contribute funds. The IVA supervisor will then divide those funds between the creditors in accordance with the proposal.

8.30 Unlike bankruptcy, where the bankrupt's estate vests in the trustee immediately upon the making of a bankruptcy order, a debtor who is subject to an IVA retains control of his assets.

8.31 Whereas, in a bankruptcy, the bankrupt is automatically discharged at the end of one year, it is necessary to look to the terms of the IVA itself in order to determine when it can be said to have been successfully completed (or, if not, when it terminates).

8.32 Generally speaking, IVAs tend to last somewhere in the region of 3–6 years.

THE DEBT RESPITE SCHEME

8.33 The Debt Respite Scheme (Breathing Space Moratorium and Mental Health Crisis Moratorium) (England and Wales) Regulations 2020[20] came into force on 4 May 2021.

8.34 Essentially, the Debt Respite (Breathing Space Moratorium and Mental Health Crisis Moratorium) (England and Wales) Regulations 2020 allow a debtor to enter a 'breathing space', during which a creditor is prevented from taking action in relation to a 'moratorium debt'. For example, the creditor is precluded from taking any enforcement in respect of the moratorium debt without the permission of the court.[21] Any action taken contrary to reg 7 is 'null and void'.[22]

8.35 A breathing space can only be started by either a 'debt advice provider' or a local authority (where the local authority provides debt advice to its residents).

19 Insolvency (England and Wales) Rules 2016, r 15.34(6).

20 SI 2020/1311 (Debt Respite Scheme Regs 2020).

21 Debt Respite Scheme Regs 2020, reg 7.

22 Debt Respite Scheme Regs 2020, reg 7(12). A good example of this is *Lees v Kaye* [2022] EWHC 1151 (QB).

Once the breathing space has commenced, debt advice providers are responsible for its administration.

8.36 Although a debt advice provider is required to consider any application for a breathing space moratorium which is made to it by a debtor,[23] the debt advice provider can only start a breathing space moratorium if it is satisfied that the debtor is eligible. An eligible debtor is a person who:[24]

(a) is an individual;
(b) owes a qualifying debt to a creditor;
(c) is domiciled or ordinarily resident in England or Wales;
(d) is not subject to a debt relief order;
(e) is not subject to an interim order or an IVA;
(f) is not an undischarged bankrupt;
(g) is not subject to another breathing space moratorium and, if he has previously been subject to a breathing space moratorium, that moratorium ended more than 12 months before the date of the application; and
(h) is not subject to a mental health crisis moratorium.

8.37 In addition, the debt advice provider must be satisfied that the debtor meets both of the following conditions:

(a) the debtor cannot, or is unlikely to be unable to, repay all or some of his debt; and
(b) a breathing space moratorium is appropriate for the debtor.[25]

8.38 In considering whether a breathing space moratorium is appropriate, the debt advice provider must consider the matters specified in reg 24(5)(a) of the Debt Respite (Breathing Space Moratorium and Mental Health Crisis Moratorium) (England and Wales) Regulations 2020 and may have regard to any other factor which they consider relevant, including (but not limited to) the matters enumerated in reg 24(5)(b).

8.39 Unless it is cancelled, the breathing space moratorium will last for 60 days[26] and cannot be extended further. The debt advice provider must conduct a review between days 25 and 35 of the moratorium in order to determine whether it should continue or be cancelled.[27]

---

23 Debt Respite Scheme Regs 2020, reg 24(1).

24 Debt Respite Scheme Regs 2020, reg 24(3).

25 Debt Respite Scheme Regs 2020, reg 24(4).

26 Debt Respite Scheme Regs 2020, reg 26(2).

27 Debt Respite Scheme Regs 2020, reg 27.

OVERVIEW OF CORPORATE INSOLVENCY PROCEDURES

8.40 Section 123 of the Insolvency Act 1986 provides that a company is unable to pay its debts where, *inter alia*:

(a) the company has failed to comply with a statutory demand;
(b) the company has failed to satisfy enforcement of a judgment debt;
(c) the court is satisfied that the company is unable to pay its debts as they fall due (the 'cash flow' test);
(d) the court is satisfied that the liabilities of the company exceed its assets (the 'balance sheet' test).

8.41 It is possible to divide insolvency procedures into two distinct categories.

8.42 The first class comprises those procedures which are designed to rescue the company as a going concern.

8.43 The second class comprises those procedures which are instead concerned with the cessation of business, the realisation of assets, and the distribution of the proceeds thereby obtained to the company's creditors.

Rescue procedures

Administration

8.44 The main 'rescue procedure' is administration. The statutory provisions governing this procedure are located in Schedule B1 to the Insolvency Act 1986.

8.45 Essentially, there are two routes into administration. These are often described as the 'court route' and the 'out-of-court route'.

8.46 The court route begins with the making of a formal administration application to court. Such an application can only be made by the company itself, its directors, one or more creditors of the company, the designated officer for a magistrates' court in the exercise of a power conferred by section 87A of the Magistrates' Courts Act 1980 (i.e. a fine imposed on the company) or a combination of the aforementioned persons.[28]

---

[28] IA 1986, Sch B1, para 12(1).

8.47 The company will enter administration if and when the court makes what is known as an 'administration order'.

8.48 Paragraph 11 of Schedule B1 to the Insolvency Act 1986 provides that the court may make an administration order in relation to a company only if satisfied:

(a) that the company is or is likely to become unable to pay its debts; and
(b) that the administration order is reasonably likely to achieve the purpose of the administration.

8.49 If the court elects to make an administration order, then a person known as an administrator will be appointed. The appointment of the administrator will take effect either at the time stated in the order or, if no time is stated in the order, when that order is made.[29]

8.50 The out-of-court route avoids the need for any application to court. Instead, the company, its directors or the holder of a qualifying floating charge over the company's assets may appoint an administrator.[30]

8.51 Where the out-of-court route is utilised, the appointment of the administrator will take effect when certain documents are filed at court[31] – namely, the notice of appointment and such other documents as may be prescribed.[32]

8.52 The notice of appointment must be accompanied by a statutory declaration by or on behalf of the person making the appointment,[33] as well as a statement by the administrator:

(a) that he consents to the appointment;
(b) that in his opinion the purpose of administration is reasonably likely to be achieved; and
(c) giving such other information and opinions as may be prescribed.[34]

8.53 The choice between these two routes – the court route and the out-of-court route – is not entirely unfettered.

---

29 IA 1986, Sch B1, para 13(2).

30 IA 1986, Sch B1, paras 14 and 22.

31 IA 1986, Sch B1, paras 19 and 31.

32 IA 1986, Sch B1, paras 18 and 29.

33 IA 1986, Sch B1, paras 18(2) and 29(2).

34 IA 1986, Sch B1, paras 18(3) and 29(3).

8.54 For example, the out-of-court route is not available where an administrative receiver is already in office.[35] By contrast, where a receiver has been appointed by a secured creditor of the company, the company can nevertheless go into administration via either route. The administrator can require the receiver to vacate his office.[36] However, if the administrator makes such a request, the administrator must ensure that he is not acting irrationally in doing so.[37]

8.55 Further, the out-of-court route is not available to the company or its directors if the company is already the subject of an outstanding winding-up petition,[38] unless the winding-up petition was only presented after the company or its directors (as the case may be) filed a notice of intention to appoint administrators.[39] The existence of an outstanding petition does not preclude the holder of a qualifying floating charge from using the out-of-court route, however.[40] Likewise, an outstanding winding-up petition does not impinge on the availability of the court route.

8.56 Part AI moratoriums are discussed in more detail below.[41] However, for present purposes, it suffices to note that, where a company goes into administration, any subsisting Part AI moratorium automatically comes to an end.[42]

8.57 Regardless of the route by which a company enters administration, an administrator is appointed. An administrator is a qualified IP and an officer of the

---

35 IA 1986, Sch B1, paras 17(b) and 25(c). Where an administrative receiver is already in place, the court may nevertheless make an administration order, but the court's ability to do so is circumscribed, such that the court is only able to make an administration order if certain prescribed conditions are met (as to which, see para 39).

36 IA 1986, Sch B1, para 41(2).

37 *Promontoria (Chestnut) Ltd v Craig & Another* [2017] EWHC 2405 (Ch).

38 IA 1986, Sch B1, para 25(a).

39 IA 1986, Sch B1, paras 25A(1) and 44(5).

40 If the holder of a qualifying floating charge opts to go down the 'out-of-court' route, then the outstanding winding-up petition will be automatically suspended on the appointment of an administrator: IA 1986, Sch B1, para 40(1)(b). The petition will be of no legal effect during the ensuing period of suspension: *Re J Smiths Haulage* [2007] BCC 135. However, when the administration comes to an end, the petition will be automatically revived.

41 See paras 8.80–8.85.

42 Likewise, even before a company goes into administration, where a notice of intention to appoint administrators is filed at court, or an application to appoint administrators is made to court, the temporary moratorium which thereby comes into effect (pursuant to IA 1986, Sch B1, para 44) automatically terminates any subsisting Part AI moratorium.

court. The latter will be the case even if the administrator was not appointed by the court.[43]

8.58 Once appointed, the administrator assumes responsibility for the running of the company. In exercising his functions, the administrator acts as the agent of the company.[44]

8.59 By virtue of paragraph 3(1) of Schedule B1 to the Insolvency Act 1986, the administrator must perform his functions with one of the following objectives in mind, namely:

(a) rescuing the company as a going concern; or
(b) achieving a better result for the company's creditors as a whole than would be likely if the company were wound up (without first being in administration); or
(c) realising property in order to make a distribution to one or more secured or preferential creditors.

8.60 However, it is important to note that the administrator does not have complete freedom in deciding which of these objectives ought to be pursued.

8.61 In effect, the first of these objectives – namely, rescuing the company as a going concern – is the primary or paramount objective. Accordingly, paragraph 3(3) of Schedule B1 to the Insolvency Act 1986 mandates that the administrator must perform his functions with this objective unless he thinks either that it is not reasonably practicable to achieve this objective or that the objective in sub-paragraph (1)(b) would achieve a better result for the company's creditors as a whole.

8.62 There are particular restrictions on the administrator's objective to pursue the final objective – namely, realising property in order to make a distribution to one or more secured or preferential creditors. Paragraph 3(4) of Schedule B1 to the Insolvency Act 1986 stipulates that an administrator may only perform his functions with the objective specified in sub-paragraph (1)(c) if he thinks that it is not reasonably practicable to achieve either of the other objectives *and* he does not unnecessarily harm the interests of the creditors of the company as a whole.

---

43 IA 1986, Sch B1, para 5.

44 IA 1986, Sch B1, para 69.

8.63 Subject to paragraph 3(4) of Schedule B1 to the Insolvency Act 1986, the administrator is obliged to perform his functions in the interests of the company's creditors as a whole.[45]

8.64 For the avoidance of doubt, neither the administrator nor the party appointing him (if the out-of-court route is employed) is required to specify in advance which of these statutory objectives the administration is intended to achieve.[46]

8.65 Turning, then, to the nature of an administration itself. An administration essentially involves the imposition of a statutory moratorium.

8.66 The moratorium comes into force as soon as the administrator is appointed. Thereafter, during its currency, the company's creditors are precluded from taking enforcement action against the company without the prior consent of either the administrator or the court.[47]

8.67 The statutory moratorium does not deprive the company's creditors of their substantive rights. Rather, for the duration of the statutory moratorium, the exercise of the rights is suspended.[48]

8.68 The company is thereby afforded some 'breathing space'. The administrator is given some room to manoeuvre, so that the company's affairs can be reorganised or its assets can be realised.

8.69 Having been appointed, the administrator must make a statement setting out proposals for achieving the purpose of the administration.[49]

8.70 The administrator's proposals may include a proposal for a voluntary arrangement under Part I of the Insolvency Act 1986 or a proposal for a compromise or arrangement to be sanctioned under Part 26 or Part 26A of the Companies Act 2006.[50]

8.71 As soon as is reasonably practicable after the company enters administration (and, in any event, within 8 weeks of the company entering

---

45 IA 1986, Sch B1, para 3(2).

46 *Hammonds (A Firm) v Pro-Fit USA Ltd* [2007] EWHC 1998 (Ch).

47 Although it seems that it is possible for this consent to be obtained retrospectively: *Bank of Ireland (UK) plc v Colliers International UK plc* [2012] EWHC 2942 (Ch).

48 *Barclays Mercantile Business Finance Ltd & Another v Sibec Developments Ltd* [1992] 1 WLR 1253.

49 IA 1986, Sch B1, para 49(1).

50 IA 1986, Sch B1, para 49(3).

administration), the administrator must send a copy of the statement of his proposals to the registrar of companies, to every creditor of the company (other than an opted-out creditor) of whose claim and address he is aware, and to every member of the company of whose address he is aware.[51]

8.72 In most cases, having sent out the statement, the administrator is then required to seek a decision from the company's creditors as to whether they approve the proposals set out therein.[52] The initial decision date for that decision must be within 10 weeks of the day on which the company entered administration,[53] although it is possible to vary this period in accordance with paragraph 107 of Schedule B1to the Insolvency Act 1986 .

8.73 As alluded to above, the administrator is not required to seek a decision in all cases. Specifically, the administrator is excused from this obligation if the statement of proposals states that, in the opinion of the administrator:[54]

(a) the company has sufficient property to enable each creditor of the company to be paid in full;
(b) the company has insufficient property to enable a distribution to be made to unsecured creditors other than by virtue of section 176A(2)(a) of the Insolvency Act 1986; or
(c) neither of the objectives specified in paragraph 3(1)(a) and (b) of Schedule B1 to the Insolvency Act 1986 can be achieved.

8.74 Notwithstanding the above, the administrator must nevertheless seek a decision from the company's creditors if requested to do so by creditors of the company whose debts amount to at least 10% of the total debts of the company and that request is made in the prescribed manner and in the prescribed period.[55]

8.75 If the creditors approve the administrator's proposals, then they may do either without modification or with such modifications as the administrator consents to.[56]

---

51 IA 1986, Sch B1, para 49(4) and (5).
52 IA 1986, Sch B1, para 51(1).
53 IA 1986, Sch B1, para 51(2).
54 IA 1986, Sch B1, para 52(1).
55 IA 1986, Sch B1, para 52(2).
56 IA 1986, Sch B1, para 53(1).

8.76 As soon as practicable, the administrator must report any decision taken by the company's creditors to the court, the registrar of companies, and such other persons as may be prescribed.[57]

8.77 Where the administrator reports to the court that the company's creditors have failed to approve the administrator's proposals (or revised proposals), the court may:

(a) provide that the appointment of the administrator shall cease to have effect from a specified time;
(b) adjourn the hearing conditionally or unconditionally;
(c) make an interim order;
(d) make an order on a petition for winding up suspended by virtue of paragraph 40(1)(b) of Schedule B1 to the Insolvency Act 1986;
(e) make any other order (including an order making consequential provision) that the court thinks appropriate.[58]

8.78 During the currency of the administration, the company's creditors may establish a creditors' committee.[59] The creditors' committee may require the administrator:

(a) to attend on the committee at any reasonable time (of which the administrator must be given at least 7 days' notice); and
(b) to provide the committee with information about the exercise of his functions.[60]

8.79 An administration comes to an end automatically after one year, unless its term is extended. It is only possible to extend the term of the administration prospectively.

Part AI moratorium

8.80 The Part AI moratorium is – unsurprisingly – so named because it is found in Part A1 of the Insolvency Act 1986.

8.81 This procedure was introduced relatively recently by the Corporate Insolvency and Governance Act 2020.

---

[57] IA 1986, Sch B1, para 53(2).

[58] IA 1986, Sch B1, para 55.

[59] IA 1986, Sch B1, para 57(1).

[60] IA 1986, Sch B1, para 57(3).

8.82 In essence, the Part A1 moratorium allows the directors of a company to put in place a moratorium on creditor action against the company. In that sense, it is similar to an administration.

8.83 However, there are a number of key differences between the Part A1 moratorium and administration. One of the principal differences is that the Part A1 moratorium is much shorter in duration. It lasts, initially, for only 20 business days, although the statute makes provision for it to be extended further.

8.84 It is also different from an administration in that, while the Part A1 moratorium is in force, the directors retain control of the company.

8.85 During this time, the directors' actions are overseen by a qualified IP known as a monitor.

Other rescue procedures

8.86 Other rescue procedures include company voluntary arrangements,[61] Part 26A restructuring plans, and schemes of arrangement.

Procedures designed to realise the company's assets

Winding up or liquidation

8.87 Liquidation falls into the second class of corporate insolvency procedures discussed above.[62]

8.88 Unlike those procedures canvassed in the preceding paragraphs, the aim of liquidation is not to rescue the company as a going concern. Instead, liquidation has as its objective the realisation of the company's assets in order to satisfy the company's debts.

8.89 Like many of the other insolvency procedures discussed in this chapter, liquidation involves the appointment of an IP, who is known as a liquidator.

8.90 The role of the liquidator is to collect in and sell the company's assets before distributing the proceeds thereby obtained to the company's creditors in order (so far as possible) to satisfy the company's debts. Once this process is complete, the company is dissolved.

---

61 CVAs.

62 See paras 8.41–8.43.

8.91 It is not uncommon for liquidation to be used in conjunction with other insolvency procedures. In particular, where an administration has not been effective to rescue the company as a going concern, the company may exit administration via liquidation.

8.92 There are two types of liquidation: compulsory and voluntary.

8.93 A compulsory liquidation is one which takes place pursuant to a court order (known as a winding-up order). A voluntary liquidation is one which takes place pursuant to a resolution of the company itself.

8.94 Turning to the former, the process of compulsory liquidation begins with the presentation of a winding-up petition at court. Typically, one would expect the petitioner to be one of the company's creditors. However, in addition to the company's creditor or creditors,[63] a petition may be presented by the company itself, the company's directors, a contributory or contributories, or by the designated officer for a magistrates' court in the exercise of the power conferred by section 87A of the Magistrates' Court Act 1980 (enforcement of fines imposed on companies).[64] The petition may be presented by any or all of these persons, together or separately.

8.95 In certain prescribed circumstances, a petition may also be presented by, *inter alia*, the Secretary of State, the Financial Conduct Authority, and the Regulator of Community Interest Companies.[65]

8.96 As to jurisdiction, the High Court has jurisdiction to wind up any company registered in England and Wales.[66] The county court has concurrent jurisdiction in relation to such a company where the amount of its share capital paid up or credited as paid up does not exceed £120,000.[67]

8.97 The court will only make a winding-up order if satisfied that one of the grounds for winding up is made out. These grounds are enumerated in section 122(1) of the Insolvency Act 1986. For present purposes, the most important grounds are that the company is unable to pay its debts (section 122(1)(f)) and the court is of

---

63 Including any contingent or prospective creditor(s).

64 IA 1986, s 124(1). There are restrictions on the entitlement of a contributory to present a winding-up petition: see IA 1986, s 124(2) and (3).

65 IA 1986, s 124(4), (4AA) and (4A).

66 IA 1986, s 117(1).

67 IA 1986, s 117(2). Subsection (5) provides, *inter alia*, that every court in England and Wales with winding-up jurisdiction has, for the purposes of that jurisdiction, all the powers of the High Court.

the opinion that it is just and equitable that the company should be wound up (section 122(1)(g)).[68]

8.98 If the court opts to make a winding-up order, then the liquidation is deemed to commence from the date when the petition was presented. In other words, unlike bankruptcy, the order is backdated, such that the liquidation takes effect retrospectively.

8.99 It is possible to put a company into provisional liquidation before a final winding-up order is granted.

8.100 With regard to voluntary liquidations, there are two distinct forms – namely, members' voluntary liquidation (MVL) and creditors' voluntary liquidation (CVL). Whether a voluntary liquidation is an MVL or a CVL depends, in essence, on whether or not the directors are willing and able to give a statutory declaration of solvency under section 89 of the Insolvency Act 1986.

8.101 A statutory declaration of solvency under section 89 of the Insolvency Act 1986 is a declaration made at a directors' meeting to the effect that the directors (or, if the company has more than two directors, the majority of them) have made a full enquiry into the company's affairs and, having done so, they have formed the opinion that the company will be able to pay its debts in full (together with interest at the 'official rate'[69]) within such period, not exceeding 12 months from the commencement of the winding up, as may be specified in the declaration.[70]

8.102 The declaration must be made before the passing of the resolution for winding up, but not earlier than 5 weeks before the date of the resolution.[71]

8.103 The directors are not under any obligation to make a statutory declaration of solvency. The consequences of making such a declaration without reasonable grounds for the opinion stated therein are serious. Specifically, a director who makes a statutory declaration without reasonable grounds is liable to imprisonment or a fine or both.[72] Section 89(5) of the Insolvency Act 1986 provides that, if the company is wound up in pursuance of a resolution passed within 5 weeks after the making of the declaration, and its debts (together with

---

68 IA 1986, s 122(1)(a) also provides that a company may be wound up by the court if the company has, by special resolution, resolved that the company be so wound up. Voluntary liquidation is discussed in more detail below, see para 8.100.

69 As defined in IA 1986, s 251.

70 IA 1986, s 89(1).

71 IA 1986, s 89(2). Having been made, the statutory declaration must then be delivered to the Registrar of Companies within 15 days of the resolution having been passed: IA 1986, s 89(3).

72 IA 1986, s 89(4).

interest at the official rate) are not paid or provided for in full within the period specified, then it is to be presumed – unless the contrary is shown – that the director did not have reasonable grounds for his opinion.

8.104 Section 90 of the Insolvency Act 1986 provides that, where such a declaration has been made, the winding up is an MVL and that, where such a declaration has not been made, the winding up is a CVL.

8.105 It is for this reason that an MVL is sometimes known as a 'solvent liquidation'. It follows that, in a CVL, it is generally more likely that the assets available will prove insufficient to repay the creditors in full. The corollary of this is that the creditors are more liable to be affected by the conduct of the winding-up in a CVL. In recognition of this fact, where the winding up is a CVL, the liquidator must produce progress reports and send these to, *inter alia*, the creditors.[73]

8.106 A voluntary winding up – whether an MVL or a CVL – is deemed to commence at the time when the members of the company pass a resolution for its voluntary winding up.[74]

8.107 In every liquidation – whether compulsory or voluntary – a liquidator is appointed to deal with the company's affairs. The liquidator is endowed with broad powers. These powers permit the liquidator to collect in the company's assets, realise them, and distribute the proceeds to the company's creditors.[75] On appointment, the liquidator will also assume the directors' powers.

INSOLVENCY RESTRICTIONS

8.108 The chapter now examines the numerous ways in which the insolvency legislation impacts on the ability of a judgment creditor to apply for or (as the case may be) retain the benefit of a charging order.

8.109 If the debtor's insolvency is actual or imminent, any judgment creditor who contemplates seeking a charging order should consider the potential ramifications of the relevant statutory provisions before proceeding. If the judgment creditor overlooks or ignores the restrictions and misguidedly seeks

---

73 IA 1986, s 104A(1).

74 IA 1986, s 86. Before a company passes such a resolution, it is required to give written notice of the resolution to the holder of any qualifying floating charge: IA 1986, s 84(2A). The purpose of this requirement is to give the holder of that qualifying charge a window of opportunity in which to appoint an administrator.

75 IA 1986, s 143.

(and perhaps even obtains) a charging order in such circumstances, he will ultimately achieve nothing from the exercise, apart from wasting costs.

8.110 The following is a summary of the most significant aspects of the insolvency legislation which may bear on charging orders, some of which are mentioned above.[76] For a full treatment of the topic, reference should be made to a specialist insolvency text.

Fetters in the case of corporate insolvency

Administration

8.111 Reference is made above to the statutory moratorium which comes into existence when a company enters administration.[77]

8.112 The effect of this moratorium is that, where a company is in administration, no execution may be instituted or continued against the company or property of the company except:

(a) with the consent of the administrator; or
(b) with the permission of the court.[78]

The same applies where, although the company is not yet in administration, a notice of intention to appoint administrators has been filed or an application to appoint administrators has been made.[79]

8.113 The process of obtaining a final charging order (after an interim charging order has been obtained) constitutes the continuation of an already-commenced execution,[80] and so both interim and final charging orders are caught by this restriction.

Part A1 moratorium

8.114 Similarly, where a company has the benefit of a moratorium under Part A1 of the Insolvency Act 1986,[81] no execution may be instituted, carried out or

---

76 See Chapter 2, para 2.33 *et seq*.

77 See paras 8.65–8.68.

78 IA 1986, Sch B1, para 43(6).

79 IA 1986, Sch B1, para 44.

80 *Clarke v Coutts & Co (A Firm)* [2002] EWCA Civ 943, [2002] BPIR 916.

81 Introduced by the Corporate Insolvency and Governance Act 2020.

continued against the company or its property without the permission of the court.[82] As already explained, this includes interim and final charging orders.

Winding-up

8.115 After the presentation of a winding-up petition, and before a winding-up order has been made, the company and any creditor may apply to stay or restrain any proceedings against the company (such as an application for a charging order).[83]

8.116 Further, the commencement of the winding-up process (the presentation of the petition) is itself generally a sufficient ground for an interim charging order not to be made final. In such a case the asset in question should be subject to the statutory insolvency scheme and one creditor ought not to be preferred over others.[84]

8.117 Also and significantly, where a creditor has issued execution against the land of a company, and the company is subsequently wound up, the creditor is not entitled to retain the benefit of the execution against the liquidator unless he has completed the execution before the commencement of the winding-up.[85] For these purposes, execution is completed by the making of a charging order under the Charging Orders Act 1979.[86] In this context, when the statute refers to 'the making of a charging order', it means the making of a *final* charging order, not merely the interim charging order.[87]

8.118 Consequently, where the debtor is wound up, the judgment creditor can rely on, and (normally) retain the benefit of, a charging order *only if* that order was made final before the commencement of the winding-up (i.e. prior to the presentation of the petition or the passing of a voluntary winding-up resolution[88]). If matters have not reached the relevant stage (i.e. a final charging order has not been obtained) when the winding-up commences, the creditor will be deprived of the benefit of the security provided by a subsequent charging order in the event that the company is wound up.

---

82 IA 1986, s A21(1)(e). This does not apply to proceedings relating to an employment relationship.

83 IA 1986, s 126(1).

84 *Roberts Petroleum Ltd v Bernard Kenny Ltd (In Liquidation)* [1983] 2 AC 192, HL.

85 IA 1986, s 183(1).

86 IA 1986, s 183(3)(a).

87 *Nationwide Building Society v Wright* [2009] EWCA Civ 811, [2010] Ch 318 at [19]. See also *Clarke v Coutts & Co (A Firm)* [2002] EWCA Civ 943, [2002] BPIR 916.

88 IA 1986, s 129.

8.119 Therefore, there is little merit in an interim charging order being made final after the commencement of the winding-up, although it is possible for a judgment creditor to seek an interim order and to ask the court to adjourn the hearing for further consideration until after the hearing of the winding-up petition.[89] If a winding-up order is made, the interim order will be discharged, whereas it could be made final if the petition were dismissed.

8.120 It should be noted that the statute does not say that a creditor who has completed execution before the commencement of the winding-up will in all circumstances be entitled to retain the benefit of that execution, although it is clear that a creditor in that position will not be denied its security by reason of the winding-up alone.[90]

8.121 Lastly, when a winding-up order is made, no action or proceeding may be commenced or proceeded with against the company or its property in respect of any debt of the company, except by leave of the court, and subject to such terms as the court may impose.[91]

Fetters in the case of an individual insolvency

Breathing space moratorium or mental health crisis moratorium

8.122 Where the judgment debtor has the benefit of either a breathing space moratorium or a mental health crisis moratorium under the Debt Respite Scheme (Breathing Space Moratorium and Mental Health Crisis Moratorium) (England and Wales) Regulations 2020, creditors are prevented from taking any enforcement action[92] in respect of a moratorium debt[93] without the court's permission.[94]

8.123 Therefore, if the judgment debt is a moratorium debt, the judgment debtor cannot apply for a charging order during the moratorium. If the application has already been made, then the creditor must notify the court of the moratorium[95] and the court must take all necessary steps to ensure that the proceedings are not progressed during the moratorium period.[96] Presumably, therefore, the court will not make an interim charging order or (if an interim order has already been made)

---

89 *Nationwide Building Society v Wright* [2009] EWCA Civ 811, [2010] Ch 318 at [26].

90 *Nationwide Building Society v Wright* [2009] EWCA Civ 811, [2010] Ch 318 at [18].

91 IA 1986, s 130(2).

92 Debt Respite Scheme Regs 2020, reg 7(6)(c).

93 Defined by Debt Respite Scheme Regs 2020, reg 6.

94 Debt Respite Scheme Regs 2020, reg 7(2).

95 Debt Respite Scheme Regs 2020, reg 10(1).

96 Debt Respite Scheme Regs 2020, reg 10(5).

a final charging order until after the moratorium period. Any existing charging order will continue unaffected by the moratorium, but cannot be enforced by sale during the moratorium period.[97]

Individual voluntary arrangement

8.124 Where an application for an interim order in connection with a proposed IVA has been made, the court may stay any execution against the property of the debtor.[98]

8.125 Once an interim order[99] has actually been made in connection with an IVA, no execution may be commenced or continued against the debtor or his property except with the leave of the court.[100] The court could, however, leave an existing interim charging order in place, pending the decision of the creditors to approve (or reject) the proposed IVA.

Bankruptcy

8.126 At any time when proceedings on a bankruptcy application or petition are ongoing, or an individual has been made bankrupt, the court may stay any execution against the property of the debtor or, as the case may be, bankrupt. This would include an application for a charging order.[101]

8.127 After a bankruptcy order is made, no person[102] who is a creditor of the bankrupt in respect of a debt provable in the bankruptcy shall have any remedy against the property of the bankrupt in respect of that debt or, before the discharge of the bankrupt, commence any action or other legal proceedings against the bankrupt except with leave of the court and on such terms as the court may impose.[103]

---

97 Debt Respite Scheme Regs 2020, reg 7(13)(a); *Lees v Kaye* [2022] EWHC 1151 (QB).

98 IA 1986, s 254.

99 This is a reference to an interim order under IA 1986, s 253, not to an interim *charging* order under the COA 1979.

100 IA 1986, s 252(2).

101 IA 1986, s 285(1).

102 Except a secured creditor enforcing its security: IA 1986, s 285(4).

103 IA 1986, s 285(3).

8.128 The making of a bankruptcy order is generally a sufficient ground for an interim charging order not to be made final, because the asset in question should be subject to the statutory insolvency scheme.[104]

8.129 Further, like the position with companies, where the creditor of any person who is made bankrupt has, before the commencement of the bankruptcy, issued execution against the land of that person, that creditor is not entitled, as against the official receiver or trustee of the bankrupt's estate, to retain the benefit of the execution, or any sums paid to avoid it, unless the execution was completed, or the sums were paid, before the commencement of the bankruptcy.[105] Again, for these purposes, execution is completed by the making of a charging order under the Charging Orders Act 1979.[106] And in this context the reference to 'the making of a charging order' means the making of a *final* charging order, not merely the interim charging order.[107]

8.130 Consequently, where the debtor is declared bankrupt, the judgment creditor can rely on, and (normally) retain the benefit of, a charging order only if that order was made final before the commencement of the bankruptcy, that is prior to the bankruptcy order.[108]

8.131 It will be apparent that, because of the differences in the timing of the commencement of the relevant insolvency process, the position in bankruptcy in respect of charging orders differs from the position in corporate insolvency.[109]

---

104 *Roberts Petroleum Ltd v Bernard Kenny Ltd (In Liquidation)* [1983] 2 AC 192, HL.

105 IA 1986, s 346(1). The court has a discretion to disapply this provision in favour of the judgment creditor: IA 1986, s 346(6). However, this should only be exercised in exceptional cases: *Tagore Investments SA v The Official Receiver* [2008] EWHC 3495 (Ch), [2009] BPIR 392.

106 IA 1986, s 346(5)(a).

107 *Nationwide Building Society v Wright* [2009] EWCA Civ 811, [2010] Ch 318 at [19]. See also *Clarke v Coutts & Co (A Firm)* [2002] EWCA Civ 943, [2002] BPIR 916.

108 IA 1986, s 278: bankruptcy commences on the day on which the order is made.

109 *Nationwide Building Society v Wright* [2009] EWCA Civ 811, [2010] Ch 318 at [17].

Appendices

APPENDIX A1: CHARGING ORDERS ACT 1979

CHARGING ORDERS

1 Charging orders.

(1) Where, under a judgment or order of the High Court [or the family court] or [the county court], a person (the "debtor") is required to pay a sum of money to another person (the "creditor") then, for the purpose of enforcing that judgment or order, the appropriate court may make an order in accordance with the provisions of this Act imposing on any such property of the debtor as may be specified in the order a charge for securing the payment of any money due or to become due under the judgment or order.

(2) The appropriate court is –

(a) in a case where the property to be charged is a fund in court, the court in which that fund is lodged;

(b) in a case where paragraph (a) above does not apply and the order to be enforced is a maintenance order of the High Court, the High Court [or an order for costs made in family proceedings in the High Court], the High Court or [the family] court;

[(ba) in a case where paragraph (a) does not apply and the order to be enforced is an order of the family court, the family court;]

(c) in a case where [none of paragraphs (a), (b) and (ba)] above applies and the judgment or order to be enforced is a judgment or order of the High Court for a sum exceeding [the county court limit], the High Court [or [the county court]]; and

(d) in any other case, [the county court].

In this section ["county court limit" means the county court limit for the time being specified in an Order in Council under [section 145 of the County Courts Act 1984]] as the county court limit for the purposes of this section and] "maintenance order" has the same meaning as in section 2(a) of the Attachment of Earnings Act 1971.

(3) An order under subsection (1) above is referred to in this Act as a "charging order".

(4) Where a person applies to the High Court for a charging order to enforce more than one judgment or order, that court shall be the appropriate court in relation to the application if it would be the appropriate court, apart from this subsection, on an application relating to one or more of the judgments or orders concerned.

(5) In deciding whether to make a charging order the court shall consider all the circumstances of the case and, in particular, any evidence before it as to –

(a) the personal circumstances of the debtor, and
(b) whether any other creditor of the debtor would be likely to be unduly prejudiced by the making of the order.

(6) Subsections (7) and (8) apply where, under a judgment or order of the High Court [or the family court] or [the county court], a debtor is required to pay a sum of money by instalments.
(7) The fact that there has been no default in payment of the instalments does not prevent a charging order from being made in respect of that sum.
(8) But if there has been no default, the court must take that into account when considering the circumstances of the case under subsection (5).
[(9) In this section "family proceedings" means proceedings in the Family Division of the High Court which are business assigned, by or under section 61 of (and Schedule 1 to) the Senior Courts Act 1981, to that Division of the High Court and no other.]

Amendments

Section 1(1): words 'or the family court' in square brackets inserted by Crime and Courts Act 2013, s 61(3), Sch 10, para 38(2); SI 2014/954 art 2(d) (with art 3); words 'the county court' in square brackets substituted by Crime and Courts Act 2013, s 61(3), Sch 9, para 52; SI 2014/954 art 2(c) (with art 3).
Section 1(2)(b): words 'or an order for costs made in family proceedings in the High Court' in square brackets inserted by SI 2014/605, arts 1, 15; Words 'the family' in square brackets substituted by Crime and Courts Act 2013, s 61(3), Sch 10, para 38(3); SI 2014/954, art 2(d) (with art 3).
Section 1(2)(ba): inserted by Crime and Courts Act 2013, s 61(3), Sch 10, para 38(4); SI 2014/954, art 2(d) (with art 3).
Section 1(2)(c): Words 'none of paragraphs (a), (b) and (ba)' in square brackets substituted by Crime and Courts Act 2013, s 61(3), Sch 10, para 38(5); SI 2014/954, art 2(d) (with art 3); words 'the county court limit' in square brackets substituted by Administration of Justice Act 1982 s 37, Sch 3, paras 2, 3(b)(iv); word 'or' in square brackets inserted by Administration of Justice Act 1982, s 34(3).
Section 1(2)(c), (d): words 'the county court' in square brackets substituted by Crime and Courts Act 2013, s 61(3), Sch 9, para 52; SI 2014/954, art 2(c) (with art 3).
Section 1(2): words '"county court limit" means the county court limit for the time being specified in an Order in Council under section 145 of the County Courts Act 1984 as the county court limit for the purposes of this section and' in square brackets inserted by Administration of Justice Act 1982, s 37, Sch 3, para 6, with words 'section 145 of the County Courts Act 1984' substituted by County Courts Act 1984, s 148(1), Sch 2, para 71.
Sections 1(6)–(8): added by Tribunals, Courts and Enforcement Act 2007, sections 93(2), (6), 148; SI 2012/1312, art 3.
Section 1(6): words 'or the family court' in square brackets inserted by Crime and Courts Act 2013, s 61(3), Sch 10, para 38(2); SI 2014/954, art 2(d) (with art 3); words 'the county court' in square brackets substituted by Crime and Courts Act 2013, s 61(3), Sch 9, para 52; SI 2014/954, art 2(c) (with art 3).
Section 1(9): added by SI 2014/605, arts 1, 16.

2 Property which may be charged.

(1) Subject to subsection (3) below, a charge may be imposed by a charging order only on –

(a) any interest held by the debtor beneficially –

(i) in any asset of a kind mentioned in subsection (2) below, or
(ii) under any trust; or

(b) any interest held by a person as trustee of a trust ("the trust"), if the interest is in such an asset or is an interest under another trust and –

(i) the judgment or order in respect of which a charge is to be imposed was made against that person as trustee of the trust, or
(ii) the whole beneficial interest under the trust is held by the debtor unencumbered and for his own benefit, or
(iii) in a case where there are two or more debtors all of whom are liable to the creditor for the same debt, they together hold the whole beneficial interest under the trust unencumbered and for their own benefit.

(2) The assets referred to in subsection (1) above are –

(a) land,
(b) securities of any of the following kinds –

(i) government stock,
(ii) stock of any body (other than a building society) incorporated within England and Wales,
(iii) stock of any body incorporated outside England and Wales or of any state or territory outside the United Kingdom, being stock registered in a register kept at any place within England and Wales,
(iv) units of any unit trust in respect of which a register of the unit holders is kept at any place within England and Wales, or

(c) funds in court.

(3) In any case where a charge is imposed by a charging order on any interest in an asset of a kind mentioned in paragraph (b) or (c) of subsection (2) above, the court making the order may provide for the charge to extend to any interest or dividend payable in respect of the asset.

3 Provisions supplementing sections 1 and 2.

(1) A charging order may be made either absolutely or subject to conditions as to notifying the debtor or as to the time when the charge is to become enforceable, or as to other matters.

(2) The Land Charges Act 1972 and the [Land Registration Act 2002] shall apply in relation to charging orders as they apply in relation to other orders or writs issued or made for the purpose of enforcing judgments.

(3) (repealed)

(4) Subject to the provisions of this Act, a charge imposed by a charging order shall have the like effect and shall be enforceable in the same courts and in the same manner as an equitable charge created by the debtor by writing under his hand.

(4A) Subsections (4C) to (4E) apply where –

- (a) a debtor is required to pay a sum of money in instalments under a judgment or order of the High Court [or the family court] or [the county court] (an "instalments order"), and
- (b) a charge has been imposed by a charging order in respect of that sum.

(4B) In subsections (4C) to (4E) references to the enforcement of a charge are to the making of an order for the enforcement of the charge.

(4C) The charge may not be enforced unless there has been default in payment of an instalment under the instalments order.

(4D) Rules of court may –

- (a) provide that, if there has been default in payment of an instalment, the charge may be enforced only in prescribed cases, and
- (b) limit the amounts for which, and the times at which, the charge may be enforced.

(4E) Except so far as otherwise provided by rules of court under subsection (4D) –

- (a) the charge may be enforced, if there has been default in payment of an instalment, for the whole of the sum of money secured by the charge and the costs then remaining unpaid, or for such part as the court may order, but
- (b) the charge may not be enforced unless, at the time of enforcement, the whole or part of an instalment which has become due under the instalments order remains unpaid.

(5) The court by which a charging order was made may at any time, on the application of the debtor or of any person interested in any property to which the order relates, make an order discharging or varying the charging order.

(6) Where a charging order has been protected by an entry registered under the Land Charges Act 1972 or the [Land Registration Act 2002], an order under subsection (5) above discharging the charging order may direct that the entry be cancelled.

(7) The Lord Chancellor may by order made by statutory instrument amend section 2(2) of this Act by adding to, or removing from, the kinds of asset for the time being referred to there, any asset of a kind which in his opinion ought to be so added or removed.

(8) Any order under subsection (7) above shall be subject to annulment in pursuance of a resolution of either House of Parliament.

AMENDMENTS

Section 3(2), (6): words 'Land Registration Act 2002' in square brackets substituted by Land Registration Act 2002, ss 133, 136(2), Sch 11, para 15 (with s 129), SI 2003/1725, art 2(1).

Section 3(3) repealed by Land Registration Act 2002, ss 135, 136(2), Sch 13 (with s 129, Sch 12 para 1); Sch 11, para 15 (with s 129); SI 2003/1725, art 2(1).

Section 3(4A)–(4E) added by Tribunals, Courts and Enforcement Act 2007, ss 93(3), (6), 148; SI 2012/1312, art 3.

Section 3(4A)(a): words 'or the family court' in square brackets inserted by Crime and Courts Act 2013, s 61(3), Sch 10, para 38(2), SI 2014/954, art 2(d) (with art 3); words 'the county court' in square brackets substituted by Crime and Courts Act 2013, s 61(3), Sch 9, para 52, SI 2014/954, art 2(c) (with art 3).

3A Power to set financial thresholds.

(1) The Lord Chancellor may by regulations provide that a charge may not be imposed by a charging order for securing the payment of money of an amount below that determined in accordance with the regulations.

(2) The Lord Chancellor may by regulations provide that a charge imposed by a charging order may not be enforced by way of order for sale to recover money of an amount below that determined in accordance with the regulations.

(3) Regulations under this section may –

(a) make different provision for different cases;
(b) include such transitional provision as the Lord Chancellor thinks fit.

(4) The power to make regulations under this section is exercisable by statutory instrument.

(5) The Lord Chancellor may not make the first regulations under subsection (1) or (2) unless (in each case) a draft of the statutory instrument containing the regulations has been laid before, and approved by a resolution of, each House of Parliament.

(6) A statutory instrument containing any subsequent regulations under those subsections is subject to annulment in pursuance of a resolution of either House of Parliament.

AMENDMENTS

Section 3A added by Tribunals, Courts and Enforcement Act 2007, ss 94, 148(5).

4 (repealed)

AMENDMENTS

Section 4 repealed by Insolvency Act 1985, s 235, Sch 10, Pt III.

STOP ORDERS AND NOTICES

5 Stop orders and notices.

(1) In this section –

"stop order" means an order of the court prohibiting the taking, in respect of any of the securities specified in the order, of any of the steps mentioned in subsection (5) below;

"stop notice" means a notice requiring any person or body on whom it is duly served to refrain from taking, in respect of any of the securities specified in the notice, any of those steps without first notifying the person by whom, or on whose behalf, the notice was served; and

"prescribed securities" means securities (including funds in court) of a kind prescribed by rules of court made under this section.

(2) The power to make rules of court under section 1 of, and Schedule 1 to, the Civil Procedure Act 1997 shall include power by any such rules to make provision –

(a) for the High Court to make a stop order on the application of any person claiming to be entitled to an interest in prescribed securities; and
(b) for the service of a stop notice by any person claiming to be entitled to an interest in prescribed securities.

(3) (repealed)
(4) Rules of court made by virtue of subsection (2) [or (3)] above shall prescribe the person or body on whom a copy of any stop order or a stop notice is to be served.
(5) The steps mentioned in subsection (1) above are –

(a) the registration of any transfer of the securities;
(b) in the case of funds in court, the transfer, sale, delivery out, payment or other dealing with the funds, or of the income thereon;

(c) the making of any payment by way of dividend, interest or otherwise in respect of the securities; and
(d) in the case of units of a unit trust, any acquisition of or other dealing with the units by any person or body exercising functions under the trust.

(6) Any rules of court made by virtue of this section may include such incidental, supplemental and consequential provisions as the authority making them consider necessary or expedient, and may make different provision in relation to different cases or classes of case.

Amendments
Section 5(2): substituted by SI 2002/439, art 5(a).
Section 5(3): repealed by SI 2002/439, art 5(b).
Section 5(4): words 'or (3)' in square brackets omitted by virtue of SI 2002/439, art 5(c).

SUPPLEMENTAL

6 Interpretation.

(1) In this Act –

"building society" has the same meaning as in the Building Societies Act [1986];
"charging order" means an order made under section 1(1) of this Act;
"debtor" and "creditor" have the meanings given by section 1(1) of this Act;
"dividend" includes any distribution in respect of any unit of a unit trust;
"government stock" means any stock issued by Her Majesty's government in the United Kingdom or any funds of, or annuity granted by, that government;
"stock" includes shares, debentures and any securities of the body concerned, whether or not constituting a charge on the assets of that body;
"unit trust" means any trust established for the purpose, or having the effect, of providing, for persons having funds available for investment, facilities for the participation by them, as beneficiaries under the trust, in any profits or income arising from the acquisition, holding, management or disposal of any property whatsoever.

(2) For the purposes of [sections 1 and 3] of this Act references to a judgment or order of the High Court [or the family court] or [the county court] shall be taken to include references to a judgment, order, decree or award (however called) of any court or arbitrator (including any foreign court or arbitrator) which is or has become enforceable (whether wholly or to a

limited extent) as if it were a judgment or order of the High Court [or the family court][the county court].

(3) References in section 2 of this Act to any securities include references to any such securities standing in the name of the Accountant General.

AMENDMENTS

Section 6(1): word '1986' in square brackets substituted by Building Societies Act 1986, ss 54(3)(a), (5), 120, Sch 18, Pt I, para 14.

Section 6(2): words 'sections 1 and 3' in square brackets substituted by Tribunals, Courts and Enforcement Act 2007, ss 93(4), (6), 148; SI 2012/1312, art 3.

Section 6(2): Words 'or the family court' in square brackets inserted by Crime and Courts Act 2013, Sch 10 para 38(2); SI 2014/954, art 2(d) (with art 3); Words 'the county court' in square brackets substituted by Crime and Courts Act 2013, Sch 9, para 52, SI 2014/956, art 2(c) (with art 3).

7 Consequential amendments, repeals and transitional provisions.

(1) (repealed)

(2) (repealed)

(3) Any order made or notice given under any enactment repealed by this Act or under any rules of court revoked by rules of court made under this Act (the "new rules") shall, if still in force when the provisions of this Act or, as the case may be, the new rules come into force, continue to have effect as if made under this Act or, as the case may be, under the new rules.

(4) (repealed)

AMENDMENTS

Section 7(1) repealed by County Courts Act 1984, s 148(3), Sch 4.

Section 7(2) repealed by virtue of Senior Courts Act 1981, s 153(2), Sch 7 and by County Courts Act 1984, s 148(3), Sch 4.

Section 7(4) repealed by Land Registration Act 2002, ss 135, 136(2), Sch 13 (with s 129, Sch 12, para 1).

8 Short title, commencement and extent.

(1) This Act may be cited as the Charging Orders Act 1979.

(2) This Act comes into force on such day as the Lord Chancellor may appoint by order made by statutory instrument.

(3) This Act does not extend to Scotland or Northern Ireland.

APPENDIX A2: CIVIL PROCEDURE RULES, PART 73, SECTION I

PART 73 – CHARGING ORDERS, STOP ORDERS AND STOP NOTICES

Scope of this Part and interpretation

73.1

(1) This Part contains rules which provide for a judgment creditor to enforce a judgment by obtaining –

  (a) a charging order (Section I);
  (b) a stop order (Section II); or
  (c) a stop notice (Section III),

  over or against the judgment debtor's interest in an asset.

(2) In this Part –

  (a) "the 1979 Act" means the Charging Orders Act 1979;
  (b) "the 1992 Regulations" means the Council Tax (Administration & Enforcement) Regulations 1992;
  (c) "judgment debtor's home court" means –

    (i) if the application for a charging order is proceeding in the County Court –

      (aa) in the case of an application under the 1992 Regulations, the County Court hearing centre for the district in which the relevant dwelling (as defined in regulation 50(3)(b) of those Regulations) is situated; or
      (bb) in other cases, the County Court hearing centre for the district in which the judgment debtor resides or carries on business; or

    (ii) if the application for a charging order is proceeding in the High Court, the district registry for the district in which the judgment debtor resides or carries on business or, where there is no such district registry, the Royal Courts of Justice;

  (ca) "final charging order" means an order confirming that a charge imposed by an interim charging order continues;
  (d) "funds in court" includes securities held in court; and

(e) "interim charging order" means an interim charging order made in accordance with rule 73.4(5), 73.4(6) or 73.6(3);

(ea) "legal adviser" means a court officer assigned to the county court who is –

(i) a barrister;
(ii) a solicitor; or
(iii) a Fellow of the Chartered Institute of Legal Executives,

who may exercise the jurisdiction of the county court with regard to matters set out in this Part to the extent specified in this Part, with the consent of the Designated Civil Judge for Greater Manchester, or their nominee;

(f) "securities" means securities of any of the kinds specified in section 2(2)(b) of the 1979 Act.

AMENDMENTS
Rule 73.1(2)(ca) inserted by SI 2020/82, r 9(2)(a).
Rule 73.1(2)(ea) inserted by SI 2020/82, r 9(2)(b).

SECTION I – CHARGING ORDERS

Scope of this Section

73.2
This Section applies to an application by a judgment creditor for a charging order under –

(a) section 1 of the 1979 Act; or
(b) regulation 50 of the 1992 Regulations.

Application for charging order

73.3
(1) An application for a charging order may be made without notice.
(2) Where an application for a charging order is to be made to the County Court, it must be made to the [Civil National Business Centre], unless the application is for a charging order over an interest in a fund in court.
(3) An application to the County Court for a charging order over an interest in a fund in court must be made to the County Court hearing centre where the order or judgment was made.

(Section 1 of the 1979 Act sets out when applications are to be made to the County Court and when they are to be made to the Family Court or the High Court.)

(4) Subject to paragraphs (2) and (3), a judgment creditor may apply for a single charging order in respect of more than one judgment or order against the same judgment debtor.

(5) The application notice must –

(a) be in the form and contain the information required by Practice Direction 73; and

(b) be verified by a statement of truth.

Amendments

Rule 73.3(2) words in square brackets substituted by SI 2023/788, r 31(b).

Interim charging order – [Civil National Business Centre]

73.4

(1) This rule applies where an application for a charging order is made to the [Civil National Business Centre].

(2) The application for a charging order will initially be dealt with without a hearing.

(3) Where –

(a) the application is only for a charging order on the judgment debtor's interest in land; and

(b) none of the exceptions listed in paragraph (4) apply,

the application may initially be dealt with by a court officer.

(4) The exceptions referred to are –

(a) an application under section 2(1)(b)(i) of the 1979 Act;

(b) an application for a charging order on the interest of a partner in the partnership property under section 23 of the Partnership Act 1890;

(c) where an instalment order has been made before 1 October 2012;

(d) where the court officer otherwise considers that the application should be dealt with by a judge.

(5) The court officer may make an interim charging order imposing a charge over the judgment debtor's interest in the asset to which the application relates.

(6) The judge may make an interim charging order –

(a) imposing a charge over the judgment debtor's interest in the asset to which the application relates; and

(b) if the judge considers it appropriate at that stage, transferring the application to the judgment debtor's home court for the fixing of a hearing to consider whether to make a final charging order as provided by rule 73.10A(3)(a).

(7) Where a matter has been transferred under paragraph (6), the court must serve notice of the hearing on the judgment creditor and all persons served with the interim charging order under rule 73.7.

AMENDMENTS

Rule 73.4 heading words in square brackets substituted by SI 2023/788, r 31(c).
Rule 73.4(1) words in square brackets substituted by SI 2023/788, r 31(c).

Review of a decision made by a court officer

73.5

(1) A party may request that a decision by a court officer be reconsidered by a District Judge.
(2) A request for reconsideration must be filed within 14 days after the party is served with notice of the decision.
(3) Reconsideration will take place without a hearing.

Interim charging order – venues other than the [Civil National Business Centre]

73.6

(1) This rule applies where an application for a charging order is made other than to the [Civil National Business Centre].
(2) An application for a charging order will initially be dealt with by a judge without a hearing.
(3) The judge may make an interim charging order –

  (a) imposing a charge over the judgment debtor's interest in the asset to which the application relates; and
  (b) fixing a hearing to consider whether to make a final charging order as provided by rule 73.10A(3)(a).

AMENDMENTS

Rule 73.6 heading words in square brackets substituted by SI 2023/788, r 31(d).
Rule 73.6(1) words in square brackets substituted by SI 2023/788, r 31(d).

Service of interim order

73.7

(1) Where the interim charging order has been made at the [Civil National Business Centre] and has not been transferred out of that Centre under rule 73.4(6) for a hearing, copies of the interim charging order, the application notice and any documents filed in support of it must be served by the judgment creditor on the persons listed in paragraph (7) within 21 days of the date of the interim charging order.
(2) Where paragraph (1) applies, the judgment creditor must file a certificate of service in relation to each person served together with a statement of the

amount due under the judgement or order including any costs and interest, within 28 days of the date of the interim charging order.

(3) Any application for an extension of time for service or filing specified in paragraph (1) or (2) –

(a) must be made to the [Civil National Business Centre]; and
(b) will be dealt with without a hearing.

[(Rule 73.10(6B) sets out the powers of a legal adviser to make an order where a judgment creditor has not, on time, filed certificates of service and a statement of the amount due or applied for an extension.)]

(4) (revoked)

(5) Where the interim charging order has been made at a court other than the [Civil National Business Centre], or where the matter has been transferred out of that Centre under rule 73.4(6) for a hearing, copies of the interim charging order, the application notice and any documents filed in support of it must, not less than 21 days before the hearing, be served by the judgment creditor on the persons listed in paragraph (7).

(6) Where paragraph (5) applies, the judgment creditor must either –

(a) file a certificate of service in relation to each person served not less than 2 days before the hearing; or
(b) produce a certificate of service at the hearing.

(7) The persons to be served in accordance with paragraph (1) or (5) are –

(a) the judgment debtor;
(b) if the order relates to an interest in land, any co-owner;
(c) the judgment debtor's spouse or civil partner (if known);
(d) such other creditors as are identified in the application notice or as the court directs;
(e) if the order relates to an interest under a trust, on such of the trustees as the court directs;
(f) if the interest charged is in securities other than securities held in court, then –

(i) in the case of stock for which the Bank of England keeps the register, the Bank of England;
(ii) in the case of government stock to which subparagraph (f)(i) does not apply, the keeper of the register;
(iii) in the case of stock of any body incorporated within England and Wales, that body;

(iv) in the case of stock of any body incorporated outside England and Wales or of any state or territory outside the United Kingdom, which is registered in a register kept in England and Wales, the keeper of that register;

(v) in the case of units of any unit trust in respect of which a register of the unit holders is kept in England and Wales, the keeper of that register; and

(g) if the interest charged is in funds in court, the Accountant General at the Court Funds Office.

(8) Where paragraph (1) or (5) requires service of the application notice, interim charging order and any documents filed in support of the application on a person who is outside the jurisdiction, the permission of the court is not required for service

AMENDMENTS

Rule 73.7(1) words in square brackets substituted by SI 2023/788, r 31(e).
Rule 73.7(3)(a) words in square brackets substituted by SI 2023/788, r 31(e).
Words in square brackets after para (3) inserted by SI 2020/747, r 13(1)(a).
Rule 73.7(4) revoked by SI 2020/747, r 13(1)(b).
Rule 73.7(5) words in square brackets substituted by SI 2023/788, r 31(e).
Para inserted by SI 2022/783 as para (8) of r 73.3 moved to become para (8) of r 73.7, by SI 2023/105, r 36.

Effect of interim order in relation to securities

73.8

(1) If a judgment debtor disposes of their interest in any securities while they are subject to an interim charging order which has been served on them, that disposition will not, so long as that order remains in force, be valid as against the judgment creditor.

(2) A person served under rule 73.7(7)(f) with an interim charging order relating to securities must not, unless the court gives permission –

(a) permit any transfer of any of the securities; or
(b) pay any dividend, interest or redemption payment relating to them.

(3) If a person acts in breach of paragraph (2), that person will be liable to pay to the judgment creditor –

(a) the value of the securities transferred or the amount of the payment made (as the case may be); or
(b) if less, the amount necessary to satisfy the debt in relation to which the interim charging order was made.

Effect of interim order in relation to funds in court

73.9

If a judgment debtor disposes of their interest in funds in court while they are subject to an interim charging order which has been served on them and on the Accountant General in accordance with rule 73.7(7), that disposition will not, so long as that order remains in force, be valid as against the judgment creditor.

Further consideration of the application where interim charging order was made at the [Civil National Business Centre] and has not been transferred under rule 73.4(6) for a hearing

73.10

(1) This rule applies where the interim charging order was made at the [Civil National Business Centre] and the matter has not been transferred under rule 73.4(6) for a hearing.

(2) If any person objects to the court making a final charging order, that person must –

(a) file; and
(b) serve on the judgment creditor,

written evidence stating the grounds of objection, not later than 28 days after service on that person of the application notice and interim order.

(3) If any person files evidence stating grounds of objection to the making of a final charging order, the court must, in accordance with paragraph (4), transfer the application for hearing to the judgment debtor's home court.

(4) Following receipt by the court of one or more objections, the matter must be transferred under paragraph (3) –

(a) once all persons served under rule 73.7 with a copy of the interim charging order have filed and served an objection; or
(b) upon expiry of the period allowed under paragraph (2) for the filing and service of any objection by the last person served under rule 73.7 with a copy of the interim charging order,

whichever is the earlier.

(5) Where a matter has been transferred under paragraph (3), the court must serve notice of the hearing on the judgment creditor and all persons served under rule 73.7 with the interim charging order.

(6) Unless the application has been transferred under paragraph (3) for a hearing, the application will be considered by a judge [or a legal adviser] [after] expiry of the period allowed under paragraph (2) for the filing and

service of any objection by the last person served under rule 73.7 with a copy of the interim charging order.

(6A) When considering the application under paragraph (6), a legal adviser may only –

(a) make a final charging order, if it provides that the charge imposed by the interim charging order is to continue without modification (except for the amount secured);
(b) discharge the interim charging order and dismiss the application, if the applicant has requested it; [...]
(c) refer the matter to a judge[; or]
(d) if paragraph (6B) applies, make an unless order, or refer the matter to a judge, in accordance with that paragraph.

(6B) This paragraph applies where the judgment creditor has not complied with rule 73.7(1) or (2) and has not applied for an extension of time within the period specified by those provisions or either of them as appropriate, or has been granted an extension of time but has not met the extended time limit. In those circumstances, a legal adviser must –

(a) order that unless, by a date specified in the order, the judgment creditor files a certificate of service in relation to each person served (together with a statement of the amount due under the judgment or order including any costs and interest), the application for a charging order is to be dismissed and the interim charging order discharged; or
(b) refer the matter to a judge to consider whether to dismiss the application and discharge the interim charging order.

(6C) A copy of any order made under paragraph (6B) is to be served by the court on all the parties.

(6D) Decisions of a legal adviser are to be made without a hearing.

(7) When considering the application (either at a hearing following a transfer under paragraph (3) or under paragraph (6)), the [judge] may –

(a) make a final charging order confirming that the charge imposed by the interim charging order continues, with or without modification;
(b) discharge the interim charging order and dismiss the application;
(c) decide any issues in dispute between the parties, or between any of the parties and any other person who objects to the [judge] making a final charging order;
(d) direct a trial of any such issues, and if necessary give directions; or
(e) make such other order as the court considers appropriate.

(8) If the court makes a final charging order which charges securities, the order must include a stop notice unless the court otherwise orders.

(Section III of this Part contains provisions about stop notices.)

(9) Any order made must be served by the court on all the persons on whom the interim charging order was required to be served.

AMENDMENTS
Rule 73.10 heading words in square brackets substituted by SI 2023/788, r 31(f).
Rule 73.10(1) words in square brackets substituted by SI 2023/788, r 31(f).
Rule 73.10(6) words in square brackets inserted by SI 2020/82, r 9(3)(a).
Rule 73.10(6) word in second set of square brackets substituted by SI 2020/747, r 13(2)(a).
Rule 73.10(6A), (6B) inserted by SI 2020/82, r 9(3)(b).
Rule 73.10(6A)(b) word revoked by SI 2020/747, r 13(2)(b)(i).
Rule 73.10(6A)(c) word substituted for punctuation by SI 2020/747, r 13(2)(b)(ii).
Rule 73.10(6A)(d) substituted by SI 2020/747, r 13(2)(b)(ii).
Rule 73.10(6B)–(6D) substituted for rule 73.10(6B) by SI 2020/747, r 13(2)(c).
Rule 73.10(7) words in square brackets substituted by SI 2020/82, r 9(3)(c).

Reconsideration of a decision made by a legal adviser
73.10ZA
(1) Any interested person may request any decision of a legal adviser to be reconsidered by a District Judge.
(2) A request must be filed within 14 days after the interested person is served with a notice of the decision, or becomes aware of the decision.
(3) The request may include a summary of the issue and an explanation of why the reconsideration is sought.
(4) Reconsideration may take place without a hearing.
(5) When reconsidering the decision of the legal adviser, the District Judge may exercise any of the powers listed in rule 73.10(7).

AMENDMENTS
Rule 73.10ZA added by SI 2020/82, r 9(4).

Further consideration of the application where interim charging order was made other than at the [Civil National Business Centre], or has been transferred out of that Centre under rule 73.4(6)

73.10A
(1) This rule applies where an interim charging order was made other than at the [Civil National Business Centre] or has been transferred out of that Centre under rule 73.4(6).

(2) If any person objects to the court making a final charging order, that person must –

(a) file; and
(b) serve on the judgment creditor,

written evidence stating the grounds of objection, not less than 7 days before the hearing.

(3) At the hearing the court may –

(a) make a final charging order confirming that the charge imposed by the interim charging order continues, with or without modification;
(b) discharge the interim charging order and dismiss the application;
(c) decide any issues in dispute between the parties, or between any of the parties and any other person who objects to the court making a final charging order;
(d) direct a trial of any such issues, and if necessary give directions; or
(e) make such other order as the court considers appropriate.

(4) If the court makes a final charging order which charges securities other than securities held in court, the order must include a stop notice unless the court otherwise orders.

(Section III of this Part contains provisions about stop notices.)

(5) Any order made at the hearing must be served by the court on all the persons on whom the interim charging order was required to be served.

AMENDMENTS
Rule 73.10A heading words in square brackets substituted by SI 2023/788, r 31(g).
Rule 73.10A(1) words in square brackets substituted by SI 2023/788, r 31(g).

Discharge or variation of order
73.10B
(1) Where the final charging order was made without a hearing under [rule 73.10(6A) or 73.10(7)] any application to discharge or vary a charging order must be made to the [Civil National Business Centre].
(2) Upon the filing of an application to discharge or vary a charging order at the [Civil National Business Centre], the application must be transferred for a hearing to the judgment debtor's home court.
(3) Where the final charging order was made at a hearing, any application to discharge or vary a charging order must be made to the court which made the charging order.

(4) The court may direct that –

(a) any interested person be joined as a party to such an application; or
(b) the application be served on any such person.

(5) An order discharging or varying a charging order must be served on all the persons on whom the charging order was required to be served.

AMENDMENTS
Rule 73.10B(1) words in square brackets inserted by SI 2020/82, r 9(5).
Rule 73.10B(1) words in second set of square brackets substituted by SI 2023/788, r 31(h).
Rule 73.10B(2) words substituted by SI 2023/788, r 31(h).

Enforcement of charging order by sale
73.10C
(1) Subject to the provisions of any enactment, the court may, upon a claim by a person who has obtained a charging order over an interest in property, order the sale of the property to enforce the charging order.
(2) Where the charging order was made at the [Civil National Business Centre] a claim for an order for sale under this rule must be made to the judgment debtor's home court.
(3) Subject to paragraph (2) a claim for an order for sale under this rule should be made to the court which made the charging order, unless that court does not have jurisdiction to make an order for sale.
(4) The claimant must use the Part 8 procedure.
(5) A copy of the charging order must be filed with the claim form.

AMENDMENTS
Rule 73.10C(2) words in square brackets substituted by SI 2023/788, r 31(i).

AMENDMENTS
Updated: Wednesday, 12 April 2023

APPENDIX A3: CIVIL PROCEDURE RULES, PRACTICE DIRECTION 73, SECTION I AND APPENDIX A

PRACTICE DIRECTION 73 – CHARGING ORDERS, STOP ORDERS AND STOP NOTICES

This Practice Direction supplements Part 73

SECTION I – CHARGING ORDERS

Application notice – rule 73.3

1.1 An application for a charging order must be made by filing an application notice in Practice Form N379 if the application relates to land, or N380 if the application relates to securities.

1.2 The application notice must contain the following information –

(1) the name and address of the judgment debtor;
(2) details of the judgment or order sought to be enforced;
(3) the amount of money remaining due under the judgment or order;
(4) if the judgment debt is payable by instalments –

    (a) whether the order was made on or after 1 October 2012; and
    (b) the amount of any instalments which have fallen due and remain unpaid;

(5) if the judgment creditor knows of the existence of any other creditors of the judgment debtor, their names and (if known) their addresses;
(6) identification of the asset or assets which it is intended to charge including, where applicable, the title number under which any land upon which it is sought to impose a charge is registered;
(7) details of the judgment debtor's interest in the asset; and
(8) the names and addresses of the persons on whom an interim charging order must be served under rule 73.7.

1.3 A judgment creditor may apply in a single application notice for charging orders over more than one asset, but if the court makes interim charging orders over more than one asset, it will draw up a separate order relating to each asset.

1.4 Where, under rule 73.3(2), an application to the County Court is to be made to the Civil National Business Centre, the address is:

Civil National Business Centre,
St Katharine's House,
21–27 St Katharine's Street,
Northampton, NN1 2LH,
DX 702885 Northampton 7

High Court and County Court jurisdiction

2. The jurisdiction of the High Court, Family Court and the County Court to make charging orders is set out in section 1(2) of the 1979 Act.

Transfer following receipt of objections to an application for a charging order

3. Where the application is made to the Civil National Business Centre the court must, (and in any other case the court may) on receipt of written evidence from any person who wishes to oppose an application for a charging order, transfer the application to the judgment debtor's home court.

Discharge or variation of order – rule 73.10B

3A. Section 3(5) of the 1979 Act and regulation 51(4) of the 1992 Regulations provide that the court may at any time, on the application of the judgment debtor, or of any person interested in any property to which the order relates, or (where the 1992 Regulations apply) of the authority, make an order discharging or varying the charging order.

Enforcement of charging orders by sale – rule 73.10C

4.1 The County Court has jurisdiction to determine a claim under rule 73.10C for the enforcement of a charging order if the amount owing under the charge does not exceed the County Court limit.

4.1A A claim under rule 73.10C is a proceeding for the enforcement of a charge, and section 23(c) of the County Courts Act 1984 provides the extent of the County Court's jurisdiction to hear and determine such proceedings.

4.2 A claim in the High Court for an order for sale of land to enforce a charging order must be started in Chancery Chambers at the Royal Courts of Justice, or a Chancery district registry.

(There are Chancery district registries at Birmingham, Bristol, Caernarfon, Cardiff, Leeds, Liverpool, Manchester, Mold, Newcastle upon Tyne and Preston.)

4.3 The written evidence in support of a claim under rule 73.10C must –

(1) identify the charging order and the property sought to be sold;
(2) state the amount in respect of which the charge was imposed and the amount due at the date of issue of the claim;
(3) verify, so far as known, the debtor's title to the property charged;
(4) state, so far as the claimant is able to identify –

    (a) the names and addresses of any other creditors who have a prior charge or other security over the property; and
    (b) the amount owed to each such creditor; and

(5) give an estimate of the price which would be obtained on sale of the property.
(6) if the claim relates to land, give details of every person who to the best of the claimant's knowledge is in possession of the property; and
(7) if the claim relates to residential property –

 (a) state whether –

  (i) a land charge of Class F; or
  (ii) a notice under section 31(10) of the Family Law Act 1996, or under any provision of an Act which preceded that section,

 has been registered; and
 (b) if so, state –

  (i) on whose behalf the land charge or notice has been registered; and
  (ii) that the claimant will serve notice of the claim on that person.

4.4 The claimant must take all reasonable steps to obtain the information required by paragraph 4.3(4) before issuing the claim.
4.5 Sample forms of orders for sale are set out in Appendix A to this practice direction for guidance. These are not prescribed forms of order and they may be adapted or varied by the court to meet the requirements of individual cases.

Charging orders made against partnership property
4A.1 A charging order or interim charging order may be made against any property, within the jurisdiction, belonging to a judgment debtor that is a partnership.
4A.2 For the purposes of rule 73.7(7)(a) (service of the interim order), the specified documents must be served on –

(1) a member of the partnership within the jurisdiction;
(2) a person authorised by a partner; or
(3) some other person having the control or management of the partnership business.

4A.3 Where an order requires a partnership to appear before the court, it will be sufficient for a partner to appear before the court.

Appendix A

Order for sale following a charging order

(property solely owned by judgment debtor)

In the

Claim No.

Appn. No.

Claimant

Defendant

On the ____________ 20 __, ________________ sitting at ___________

heard ________________________________

The claimant is entitled to an equitable charge upon the defendant's interest in the property ______

____

____

____

____

[registered at H.M. Land Registry under Title No. ____________________]

("the property") ________________________________

under a charging order made on the ______________________

in the __________________ in Claim No. ___________________

and the court orders that

1. The remainder of this order will not take effect if the defendant by 4.00 p.m. on the __________ 20 ___ pays to the claimant the judgment debt of £______ secured by the charge and his costs to date of this application assessed at £______, making together £______ [together ______ with interest at the rate of £______ per day from the date of this order until payment is received by the claimant].

2. The property shall be sold without further reference to the court at a price not less than £______, unless that figure is changed by a further order of the court.

3. The [claimant] [claimant's solicitor] will have conduct of the sale.

4. To enable the claimant to carry out the sale, there be created and vested in the claimant pursuant to section 90 of the Law of Property Act 1925 a legal term in the property of [3000 years] [one day less than the remaining period of the term created by the lease under which the defendant holds the property].

5. The defendant must deliver possession of the property to the claimant [on or before the _____ 20 ___] [within [______] days of this order being served on him].

6. The claimant shall first apply the proceeds of sale of the property –

   (i) to pay the costs and expenses of effecting the sale; and

   (ii) to discharge any charges or other securities over the property which have priority over the charging order.

7. Out of the remaining proceeds of sale the claimant shall –

   (i) retain the amount due to him as stated in paragraph 1; and

   (ii) pay the balance (if any) [to the Defendant] [to ________________________________] [into court].

8. Either party may apply to the court to vary any of the terms of this order, or for further directions about the sale or the application of the proceeds of sale, or otherwise

Order for sale
Following a charging order (property owned by judgment debtor and another person)

In the
Claim No.

Claimant

Defendants

On the 20 , sitting at

heard

The claimant is entitled to an equitable charge upon the first defendant's interest in the property

[registered at H.M. Land Registry under Title No.]
("the property")
under a charging order made on the
in the in Claim No.

and the court orders that

1. The remainder of this order will not take effect if the first defendant by 4.00 p.m. on the 20 pays to the claimant the judgment debt of £ secured by the charge and his costs to date of this application assessed at £ , making together £ [together with interest at the rate of £ per day from the date of this order until payment is received by the claimant].

2. The property shall be sold without further reference to the court at a price not less than £ , unless that figure is changed by a further order of the court.

3. The [claimant] [claimant's solicitor] will have conduct of the sale.

4. The court pursuant to section 50 of the Trustee Act 1925 appoints the [claimant] [claimant's solicitor] to convey the property.

5. The defendants must deliver possession of the property to the claimant [on or before the 20] [within [ ] days of this order being served on him].

6. The claimant shall first apply the proceeds of sale of the property –

(i) to pay the costs and expenses of effecting the sale; and

(ii) to discharge any charges or other securities over the property which have priority over the charging order.

7. The claimant shall then divide the remaining proceeds of sale into two equal shares and fi

(i) pay one equal share to the second defendant; and

(ii) out of the other equal share, retain the amount due to him as stated in paragraph 1, and pay the balance (if any) [to the rst defendant] [to] [into court].

8. Any party may apply to the court to vary any of the terms of this order, or for further directions about the sale or the application of the proceeds of sale, or otherwise.

AMENDMENTS
Updated: Thursday, 10 August 2023

CORRECTION NOTE

The errors on page 2 of the form 'Order for sale following a charging Order (property owned by judgment debtor and another person)' are in the original form as set out in the CPR.

The editors consider that the text might be read as meaning the following:

7. The claimant shall then divide the remaining proceeds of sale into two equal shares and then:

(ii) out of the other equal share, retain the amount due to him as stated in paragraph 1, and pay the balance (if any) [to the first defendant] [to] [into court].

APPENDIX A4: FAMILY PROCEDURE RULES, PART 40 CHARGING ORDER, STOP ORDER, STOP NOTICE

CHAPTER 1

GENERAL

Application of this Part

40.1. This Part contains rules which provide for a creditor to enforce a judgment or order by obtaining –

(a) a charging order (Chapter 2);
(b) a stop order (Chapter 3); or
(c) a stop notice (Chapter 4),

over or against the debtor's interest in an asset.

Interpretation of this Part

40.2. In this Part –

"the 1979 Act" means the Charging Orders Act 1979;
"creditor" means the person to whom payment of a sum of money is due under a judgment or order or a person who is entitled to enforce such a judgment or order;
"debtor" means the person against whom a judgment or other order for payment of a sum of money was given, made or ordered, as the case may be;
"interim charging order" means an interim charging order made in accordance with rule 40.5; and
"securities" means securities of any of the kinds specified in section 2(2)(b) of the 1979 Act.

CHAPTER 2

CHARGING ORDERS

Scope of this Chapter

40.3. This Chapter applies to an application by a creditor for a charging order under section 1 of the 1979 Act.

Application for a charging order

40.4.–

(1) An application for a charging order may be made without notice.

(2) An application must be made to the family court or to the High Court, as appropriate and as specified in section 1 of the 1979 Act.

([His Majesty's] Courts and Tribunals Service publishes information to identify the appropriate location of the family court or High Court to which an application for a charging order should be sent.)

(3) A creditor may apply for a single charging order in respect of more than one judgment or order against the same debtor.

(4) The application must –

  (a) be in the form and contain the information required by Practice Direction 40A; and
  (b) be verified by a statement of truth.

AMENDMENTS

Words in square brackets in rule 40.4(2) substituted by SI 2023/61, rr 1(3), 19.

Interim charging order

40.5.–

(1) An application for a charging order will initially be dealt with by the court without a hearing.

(2) The court may make an interim charging order –

  (a) imposing a charge over the debtor's interest in the asset to which the application relates; and
  (b) fixing a hearing to consider whether to make a final charging order as provided by rule 40.8.

Service of an interim charging order

40.6.–

(1) Copies of the interim charging order, the application and any documents filed in support of it must, not less than 21 days before the hearing, be served by the creditor on the persons listed in paragraph (3).

(2) The creditor must either –

  (a) file a certificate of service in relation to each person served not less than 2 days before the hearing; or
  (b) produce a certificate of service at the hearing.

(3) The persons to be served in accordance with paragraph (1) are –

(a) the debtor;
(b) if the order relates to an interest in land, any co-owner;
(c) the debtor's spouse or civil partner (if known);
(d) such other creditors as are identified in the application or as the court directs;
(e) if the order relates to an interest under a trust, on such of the trustees as the court directs; and
(f) if the interest charged is securities, then –

  (i) in the case of stock for which the Bank of England keeps the register, the Bank of England;
  (ii) in the case of government stock to which sub-paragraph (f)(i) does not apply, the keeper of the register;
  (iii) in the case of stock of any body incorporated within England and Wales, that body;
  (iv) in the case of stock of any body incorporated outside England and Wales or of any state or territory outside the United Kingdom, which is registered in a register kept in England and Wales, the keeper of that register; and
  (v) in the case of units of any unit trust in respect of which a register of the unit holders is kept in England and Wales, the keeper of that register.

Effect of interim charging order in relation to securities
[40.7 omitted]
40.8.–
(1) If any person objects to the court making a final charging order, that person must –

  (a) file; and
  (b) serve on the creditor,

  written evidence stating the grounds of objection, not less than 7 days before the hearing.
(2) At the hearing, the court may –

  (a) make a final charging order confirming that the charge imposed by the interim charging order continues, with or without modification;
  (b) discharge the interim charging order and dismiss the application;
  (c) decide any issues in dispute between the parties, or between any of the parties and any other person who objects to the court making a final charging order;
  (d) direct a trial of any such issues, and if necessary give directions; or
  (e) make such other order as the court considers appropriate.

(3) If the court makes a final charging order which charges securities, the order must include a stop notice unless the court otherwise orders.

(Chapter 4 of this Part contains provision about stop notices.)

(4) Any order made at the hearing must be served by the creditor on all the persons on whom the interim charging order was served.

Discharge or variation of order

40.9.–

(1) Where an application is made to discharge or vary a charging order, the court may direct that –

 (a) any interested person be joined as a party to such an application; or
 (b) the application be served on any such person.

(2) An order discharging or varying a charging order must be served, by the person who applied for that order, on all the persons on whom the charging order was required to be served.

APPENDIX A5: FAMILY PROCEDURE RULES, PRACTICE DIRECTION 40A – CHARGING ORDERS, STOP ORDERS AND STOP NOTICES

THIS PRACTICE DIRECTION SUPPLEMENTS PART 40

SECTION I – CHARGING ORDERS

Applicant and application notice – rules 40.2 and 40.4

1.1 A creditor may apply for a charging order. The term "creditor" is defined in rule 40.2 to mean "the person to whom payment of a sum of money is due under a judgment or order, or a person who is entitled to enforce such a judgment or order". A person who is entitled to enforce such a judgment or order would include a court officer who is able to take enforcement proceedings by virtue of rule 32.33.

1.2 An application for a charging order must be made by filing an application in Practice Form N379 if the application relates to land, or N380 if the application relates to securities.

1.3 The application notice must contain the following information –

(1) the name and address of the debtor;
(2) details of the judgment or order sought to be enforced;
(3) the amount of money remaining due under the judgment or order;
(4) if the judgment debt is payable by instalments, the amount of any instalments which have fallen due and remain unpaid;
(5) if the judgment creditor knows of the existence of any other creditors of the judgment debtor, their names and (if known) their addresses;
(6) identification of the asset or assets which it is intended to charge including, where applicable, the title number under which any land upon which it is sought to impose a charge is registered;
(7) details of the debtor's interest in the asset; and
(8) the names and addresses of the persons on whom an interim charging order must be served under rule 40.6.

1.4 A creditor may apply in a single application notice for charging orders over more than one asset, but if the court makes interim charging orders over more than one asset, it will draw up a separate order relating to each asset.

High Court and family court jurisdiction

2.1 The jurisdiction of the High Court and the family court to make charging orders is set out in section 1(2) of the 1979 Act.

Change of location

3.1 The court may, on an application by a debtor who wishes to oppose an application for a charging order, direct that the matter be dealt with in a court building serving the address where the debtor resides or carries on business, or in another location (see rule 29.18 FPR).

Enforcement of charging orders by sale

4.1 The High Court or, subject to the county court limit, the county court can enforce a charging order by an order for sale. Provision in respect of applications for an order for sale is made in rule 73.10C CPR.

Charging Orders made against partnership property

5.1 A charging order or interim charging order may be made against any property, within the jurisdiction, belonging to –

(1) a debtor that is a partnership, or
(2) a debtor who is in a partnership.

5.2 Where paragraph 5.1(1) applies, then for the purposes of rule 40.6 (service of the interim order), the specified documents must be served on –

(1) a member of the partnership within the jurisdiction;
(2) a person authorised by a partner; or
(3) some other person having the control or management of the partnership business.

5.3 Where an order requires a partnership to appear before the court, it will be sufficient for a partner to appear before the court.

PRECEDENT B1: COMPLETED SPECIMEN FORM N379: APPLICATION FOR CHARGING ORDER ON LAND

N379

Application for charging order on land

CPR Part 73

You can use this form to apply for an order imposing a charge on the interest of the judgment debtor in the land mentioned below to secure payment of the amount owing you under the judgment or order you have been given.

Name of court		**Claim no.**
CIVIL NATIONAL BUSINESS CENTRE		BBB0001
Fee account no. (if applicable)	**Help with Fees – Ref. no.** (if applicable)	
	H W F - -	
Claimant's name (including ref.) VEGGIES R US LIMITED		
Defendant's name (including ref.) MR JOHN TAYLOR		

1. Judgment creditor (the person making this application)

What is your full name?

VEGGIES R US LIMITED

Details of the judgment or order

What is the name of court where the judgment or order was made?

COUNTY COURT AT CASTLETOWN

On what date was the order or judgment given?

0 1 0 7 2 0 2 3

What is/are the claim number(s)? (if applicable)

AAA0001

If have more claim numbers please list them on a separate sheet.

2. Judgment debtor (the person who owes you money)

What is the full name of the judgment debtor?

MR JOHN TAYLOR

If known, what is their date of birth?

0 1 0 1 1 9 7 0

What is their address?

5 LONG STREET
SMITHFORD

Postcode C E 1 2 6 P Z

3. Judgment debt or enforcement of liability order (Complete only part A or B)

A. – Judgment debt

What does the judgment or order require the judgment debtor to pay?

£ 11,091.34 (including any costs and interest)

What amount is still owing?

£ 11,324.71 (which includes further interest payable on the judgment debt)

Tick the relevant box(es)

- ■ The judgment or order did not provide for payment by instalments
- ■ The judgment or order was made **after** 1 October 2012
- ☐ The judgment or order was made **before** 1 October 2012 **and**

  £ ______ of the instalments due under the judgment or order has fallen due and remains unpaid.

OR

~~**B. – Enforcement of a liability order**~~

~~A Magistrates' Court has made one or more liability order(s) for non-payment of council tax.~~

~~What does the liability order require the judgment debtor to pay?~~

~~£~~

~~The amount outstanding is **at least £1,000** and **evidence of the debt is attached** to this application.~~

~~What amount is still owing?~~

~~£~~ ~~(which includes further interest payable on the judgment debt)~~

4. The land

What is the address of the land upon which it is sought to impose a charge?

5 LONG STREET
SMITHFORD

Postcode | C | E | 1 | 2 | 6 | P | Z |

The evidence of the judgment debtor's interest in the land is:

☑ The title to the land **is registered** at HM Land Registry under Title Number CEX98765 and an Office copy of the Land Register entry(ies) for the title(s) is/are attached.

OR

☐ The land is **not registered** and alternative evidence of the judgment debtor's interest in the land is attached

5. Judgment debtor's interest in the land

☐ the judgment debtor is the sole owner

☑ the judgment debtor is a joint owner

☐ the judgment debtor is a beneficiary under a trust

☐ the judgment debtor, as a partner has an interest in partnership property

☐ the judgment or order was made against the judgment debtor as trustee under a trust

☑ debtor's interest in the land as shown by the office copy Land Register entries attached

OR

☐ the judgment creditor believes this to be so because:

6. Other creditors (please tick only one box)

☐ The judgment creditor does not know of any other creditors of the judgment debtor

OR

☑ The judgment creditor knows of the following other creditors of the judgment debtor (full name and address including postcode of each creditor, and if known, nature of debt and amount):

Full name	Address including postcode	Nature of debt	Amount
LENDING BANK PLC	MONEYBAGS AVENUE, RICHTOWN, RT1 32J	FIRST LEGAL CHARGE REGISTERED AGAINST THE PROPERTY	UNKNOWN
NOQUESTIONSASKED LIMITED	TOP RATES, CRISISVILLE, CV5 92E	UNSECURED	APPROXIMATELY £5000

7. Other persons to be served

☐ No other person has an interest in the property
(including any co-owners, trustees and persons with rights of occupation)

☑ The following persons have or may have an interest in the property
(please provide full names and full addresses and postcodes, and if known, nature of interest)

Full name	Address including postcode	Nature of interest
DR F TAYLOR	5 LONG STREET, SMITHFORD, CE12 6PZ	THE DEFENDANT'S WIFE AND THE JOINT REGISTERED OWNER OF THE PROPERTY.

8. Further information

The judgment creditor asks the court to take account of the following
(please provide any additional evidence to support your application):

A COPY OF THE ORDER OF THE COUNTY COURT SITTING AT CASTLETOWN DATED 1 JULY 2023 IS ATTACHED. TO DATE, THE DEFENDANT HAS NOT MADE ANY PAYMENTS TOWARDS THE SUMS DUE UNDER THAT ORDER.

THE DEFENDANT HAS NOT ENGAGED WITH THE CLAIMANT'S ATTEMPTS TO AGREE A PAYMENT PLAN. THE CLAIMANT HAS SENT LETTERS TO THE DEFENDANT (BY FIRST CLASS POST AND EMAIL) ON 31 JULY 2023, 31 AUGUST 2023, AND 31 SEPTEMBER 2023 BUT RECEIVED NO RESPONSE.

THE CLAIMANT COMPANY IS A FAMILY BUSINESS THAT IMPORTS AND SUPPLIES FRUIT AND VEGETABLES. THE BUSINESS HAS BEEN ADVERSELY AFFECTED BY BOTH BREXIT AND THE COVID-19 PANDEMIC.

THE CLAIMANT IS NOT AWARE OF ANY INSOLVENCY PROCEEDINGS AGAINST THE DEFENDANT.

9. Sources of information – Only complete this section where the judgment creditor is a firm or a company or other corporation

The information in this application is given after making proper enquiry of all persons within the judgment creditor's organisation who might have knowledge of the facts.

Name of person completing this form

STEPHEN COLLECTOR

Their position or office held

DIRECTOR

Name of the firm or company or other corporation

VEGGIES R US LIMITED

Statement of Truth

I understand that proceedings for contempt of court may be brought against anyone who makes, or causes to be made, a false statement in a document verified by a statement of truth without an honest belief in its truth.

☑ **I believe** that the facts stated in this application form are true.

☐ **The Judgment Creditor** believes that the facts stated in this section and any continuation sheets are true. **I am authorised** by the judgment creditor to sign this statement.

Signature

☑ Judgment creditor

☐ Litigation friend (where judgment creditor is a child or a patient)

☐ Judgment creditor's legal representative (as defined by CPR 2.3(1))

Date

Day	Month	Year
05	10	2023

Full name

STEPHEN COLLECTOR

Name of judgment creditor's legal representative's firm

If signing on behalf of firm or company give position or office held

DIRECTOR

Judgment creditor's or judgment creditor's legal representative's address to which documents should be sent.

Building and street

44 NEEDIT BACKSTREET

Second line of address

Town or city

PAYUP

County (optional)

Postcode

AT9 8BG

If applicable

Phone number

Fax phone number

DX number

Your Ref.

Email

Notice to judgment creditor

Further information on making an application for a charging order can be found in **EX325 Third Party Debt Orders and Charging Orders – How do I apply for an order? How do I respond to an order?** Available from http://hmctsformfinder.justice.gov.uk

Please complete your form in full and make sure that the required documents are attached. Your application will be returned to you if it is incomplete. This will delay issue of your application.

Please tick to confirm that you have done the following

☑ The names of the parties and the claim number are entered on the form

☐ You have entered the fee account number

or

☑ You have enclosed the fee of £ 119 Make your cheque payable to **HMCTS**

or

☐ You have completed and attached the 'Applying for help with fees' form (EX160)

☐ You have attached the documents or evidence required by Section 3B

☑ The documents or evidence required by Section 4 are attached.

☑ You have attached one additional copy of the application and supporting documents to be returned for service.

Where to send your completed form

For a County Court application	Civil National Business Centre St Katharine's House 21-27 St Katharine's Street Northampton NN1 2LH	~~County Court Money Claims Centre~~ ~~PO Box 527~~ ~~Salford~~ ~~Greater Manchester~~ ~~M5 0BY~~
OR		
For a county court application, that **includes an interest in a fund in court**, send your application to the County Court hearing centre where the order was made.		The addresses of County Court Hearing Centres can be found at **courttribunalfinder.service.gov.uk**
OR		
For High Court or District Registry applications		The addresses of High Court and District Registry can be found at **courttribunalfinder.service.gov.uk**

Find out how HM Courts and Tribunals Service uses personal information you give them when you fill in a form: https://www.gov.uk/government/organisations/hm-courts-and-tribunals-service/about/personal-in-formation-charter

PRECEDENT B2: COMPLETED SPECIMEN FORM FE6: APPLICATION FOR CHARGING ORDER ON LAND

FE6 – FAMILY COURT

Application for charging order on land

FPR Part 40

You can use this form to apply for an order imposing a charge on the interest of the judgment debtor in the land mentioned below to secure payment of the amount owing you under the judgment or order you have been given.

Name of court	Claim No.
FAMILY COURT SITTING AT CASTLETOWN	ZZZ0001
Fee Account no.	FEE56789
Help with Fees - Ref no. (if applicable)	H W F - -
Name of Creditor	MS CHARLOTTE PHILLIPS
Name of Debtor	MR DAVID BARCLAY

1. Creditor (the person entitled to receive payments)

What is the creditor's full name?

MS CHARLOTTE PHILLIPS

Details of the judgment or order

What is the name of court where the judgment or order was made?

FAMILY COURT SITTING AT CASTLETOWN

On what date was the order or judgment given?

1 2 0 7 2 0 2 2

What is the case number? (if applicable)

YYY0001

2. Debtor (the person who owes the money)

What is the full name of the debtor?

MR DAVID BARCLAY

If known, what is their date of birth?

1 4 0 3 1 9 7 7

What is their address?

22 SHORT STREET
SMITHFORD

Postcode C E 1 3 9 T J

What is their email address?

dbarclay@gmail.com

What is their phone number?

07809876543

3. Judgment debt

Judgment debt

What does the judgment or order require the judgment debtor to pay?

Lump sum

£ 60,000 (including any costs and interest)

Regular Payment

£ ☐ weekly ☐ monthly

What amount is currently owed?

£ 49,142.47 (which includes further interest payable on the judgment debt)

Tick the relevant box(es)

☑ The judgment or order did not provide for payment by instalments

☑ The judgment or order was made **after** 1 October 2012

☐ The judgment or order was made **before** 1 October 2012 **and**

£ ______ of the instalments due under the judgment or order has fallen due and remains unpaid.

4. The land

What is the address of the land upon which it is sought to impose a charge?

22 SHORT STREET
SMITHFORD

Postcode C E 1 3 9 T J

The evidence of the debtor's interest in the land is:

☑ The title to the land **is registered** at HM Land Registry under Title Number CEY43210 and an Office copy of the Land Register entry(ies) for the title(s) is/are attached.

OR

☐ The land is **not registered** and alternative evidence of the debtor's interest in the land is attached

5. Debtor's interest in the land

- [x] the debtor is the sole owner
- [ ] the debtor is a joint owner
- [ ] the debtor is a beneficiary under a trust
- [ ] the debtor, as a partner has an interest in partnership property
- [ ] the order was made against the debtor as trustee under a trust

- [x] debtor's interest in the land as shown by the office copy Land Register entries attached

OR

- [ ] the creditor believes this to be so because:

6. Other creditors (please tick only one box)

- [ ] The applicant creditor does not know of any other creditors of the debtor

OR

- [x] The applicant creditor knows of the following other creditors of the debtor (full name and address including postcode of each creditor, and if known, nature of debt and amount):

Full name	Address including postcode	Nature of debt	Amount
LENDING BANK PLC	MONEYBAGS AVENUE, RICHTOWN, RT1 32J	FIRST LEGAL CHARGE REGISTERED AGAINST THE PROPERTY	APPROXIMATELY £100,000

7. Other persons to be served

☐ No other person has an interest in the property
(including any co-owners, trustees and persons with rights of occupation)

☑ The following persons have or may have an interest in the property
(please provide full names and full addresses and postcodes, and if known, nature of interest)

Full name	Address including postcode	Nature of interest
MRS MARIA BARCLAY	22 SHORT STREET, SMITHFORD, CE13 9TJ	THE DEFENDANT'S WIFE

8. Further information

The creditor asks the court to take account of the following
(please provide any additional evidence to support your application):

A COPY OF THE ORDER OF THE FAMILY COURT SITTING AT CASTLETOWN DATED 12 JULY 2022 IS ATTACHED. THE DEFENDANT MADE A SINGLE PAYMENT OF £15,000 TO THE CLAIMANT IN AUGUST 2022.

SINCE THEN, NO FURTHER PAYMENTS HAVE BEEN MADE AND THE DEFENDANT HAS NOT RESPONDED TO ANY CORRESPONDENCE FROM THE CLAIMANT.

THE CLAIMANT IS A SINGLE MOTHER OF TWO. SHE IS IN PART-TIME EMPLOYMENT AS A CARER AND STRUGGLES TO MAKE ENDS MEET ON A MONTHLY BASIS. THE MONEY OWED BY THE DEFENDANT IS NEEDED URGENTLY.

THE CLAIMANT IS NOT AWARE OF ANY INSOLVENCY PROCEEDINGS AGAINST THE DEFENDANT.

9. Statement of Truth THE CREDITOR UNDERSTANDS THAT PROCEEDINGS FOR CONTEMPT OF COURT MAY BE BROUGHT AGAINST ANYONE WHO MAKES OR CAUSES TO BE MADE, A FALSE STATEMENT IN A DOCUMENT VERIFIED BY A STATEMENT OF TRUTH WITHOUT AN HONEST BELIEF IN ITS TRUTH.

*~~I believe (~~the creditor believes) that the facts stated in this application form are true.

*I am duly authorised by the creditor to sign this statement.

Signed   Date 0 5 0 9 2 0 2 3

~~*(Creditor) (Litigation friend (where creditor is a child or a patient))~~
(Creditor's legal representative)

**delete as appropriate*

Full name

MS LAURA DANIELS

Name of creditor's legal representative's firm

DANIELS & ROGERS LLP

Position or office held (if signing on behalf of a firm or company)

PARTNER

Creditor's or creditor's legal representative's address to which documents should be sent.

DANIELS & ROGERS LLP
LITIGATION HOUSE
122-142 ADVICE AVENUE
LONDON

Postcode E C 8 R 1 2 J

If applicable	
Telephone no.	
Fax no.	
DX no.	
Your ref.	

E-mail	ldaniels@danielsrogers.com

Notice to creditor

Further information on making an application for a charging order can be found in **EX325 Third Party Debt Orders and Charging Orders – How do I apply for an order? How do I respond to an order?** Available from http://hmctsformfinder.justice.gov.uk

Please complete your form in full and make sure that the required documents are attached. Your application will be returned to you if it is incomplete. This will delay issue of your application.

Please tick to confirm that you have done the following

☑ The names of the parties and the claim number are entered on the form

☑ You have entered the fee account number

or

☐ You have enclosed the fee of £ ______ Make your cheque payable to **HMCTS**

or

☐ You have completed and attached the 'Applying for help with fees' form (EX160)

☑ The documents or evidence required by Section 4 are attached.

☑ You have attached one additional copy of the application and supporting documents to be returned for service.

Where to send your completed form

Payments made directly between the parties

If your maintenance order was made in England or Wales, the debtor lives in England or Wales and payments are instead made directly between the parties, you should apply to your nearest designated Family Court. A full list of Family Courts is available on our website courttribunalfinder.service.gov.uk

You will need to select the issue category **'Children: child contact issues and disputes over maintenance payments'** to find your nearest designated Family Court.

Payments made through the court

If your maintenance order was made in England or Wales, the debtor lives in England or Wales and payments are made through the court, you should apply to a Maintenance Enforcement Business Centre based on where the debtor now lives.

The Maintenance Enforcement Business Centre - Wales

Port Talbot Justice Centre, Harbourside Road, Port Talbot, South Wales SA13 1SB

Phone: 01639 642267
Email: Wales_MEBC@hmcts.gsi.gov.uk

The Maintenance Enforcement Business Centre - England (excluding London)

Triton House, St Andrews Street North, Bury St Edmunds, Suffolk IP33 1TR

Phone: 0300 123 3034
Email: MEBC.BSE@hmcts.gsi.gov.uk

The Maintenance Enforcement Business Centre - London

Central Family Court, First Avenue House, 42-49 High Holborn, London WC1V 6NP

Phone: 020 7421 8657
Email: MEBC.London@hmcts.gsi.gov.uk

PRECEDENT B3: COMPLETED SPECIMEN FORM N86: INTERIM CHARGING ORDER – COURT ORDER

N86

Interim charging order

CPR Part 73

Name of court	Claim No.
CIVIL NATIONAL BUSINESS CENTRE	BBB0001
Name of Claimant	
VEGGIES R US LIMITED	
Name of Defendant(s)	
MR JOHN TAYLOR	

On 19 October 2023, [a Court Officer] ~~[Judge] [Master]~~ considered the application of the [claimant] ~~[defendant]~~ ('the judgment creditor(s)'), from which it appears:

SEAL

(a)a judgment or order given on 1 JULY 2023, by the ~~[CCMCC]~~ [County Court sitting at CASTLETOWN] ~~[District Registry of the High Court sitting at ....]~~ ~~[High Court other]~~ in claim number [AAA0001] ordered the [defendant] ~~[claimant]~~ ('the judgment debtor(s)') to pay money to the judgment creditor;

(b)the amount now owing under the judgment or order is £11,324.71 (including any interest and costs); and

(c)the judgment debtor~~(s)~~ [is]~~[are]~~ the owner~~(s)~~ of or [has]~~[have]~~ a beneficial interest in the asset described in the schedule below;

and the court orders that

1. The interest of the judgment debtor(s) MR JOHN TAYLOR in the asset described in the schedule below stand charged with payment of £11,324.71 together with any further interest becoming due and the costs of the application.

[2a. Unless the judgment debtor or any other person files and serves their objection to the continuation of the charge in writing, within 28 days of the date of service of the order, the application will be considered by a District Judge OR LEGAL ADVISER no later than 49 days from the date of the order. The District Judge OR LEGAL ADVISER will consider, without a hearing, whether the charge created by this order should be made final (with or without modification) or should be discharged.]

or

~~[2b. The application has been transferred to .... Any communication in respect of the application and Interim Charging Order must be made to that Court.~~

~~[3. The application will be heard at [a.m.] [p.m.] on .... 20....~~
~~at [..] when a judge will decide whether the charge created by this order should continue (with or without modification) or should be discharged.~~

~~The judgment debtor or any other person must file and serve any objection to the making of a final charging order in writing stating the grounds of the objection not less than 7 days before the hearing]~~

4. The judgment creditor must serve all relevant persons with the application notice, interim charging order and all documents filed in support in accordance with CPR 73.7.

Notice to parties served with this interim charging order
Where the interim charging order has been made by a court officer, any party may request that the decision be reconsidered by a District Judge. A request for reconsideration must be filed at the ~~County Court Money Claims Centre~~ Civil National Business Centre within 14 days after a party is served with this order. Reconsideration of the decision will take place without a hearing.

The Schedule

[The address of the land charged is 5 LONG STREET, SMITHFORD, CE12 6PZ.]

[the title to which is registered at H. M. Land Registry under Title No. CEX98765]

~~[particulars of securities, funds etc. charged ....].~~

PRECEDENT B4: WITNESS STATEMENT TO OPPOSE MAKING OF FINAL CHARGING ORDER

Defendant
John Taylor
First statement
Exhibit: JT1
11 November 2023

IN THE CIVIL NATIONAL BUSINESS CENTRE Claim No: BBB0001

BETWEEN:

VEGGIES R US LIMITED

Claimant

– and –

MR JOHN TAYLOR

Defendant

WITNESS STATEMENT OF MR JOHN TAYLOR

I, JOHN TAYLOR, of 5 LONG ROAD, SMITHFORD, CE12 6PZ do say as follows:

Introduction

1. I am the Defendant in these proceedings.

2. I make this witness statement to explain why I oppose the interim charging order which was made by the Civil National Business Centre on 19 October 2023 being made final.

3. I have prepared this witness statement myself. The facts and matters in this witness statements are, except where I indicate otherwise, within my own knowledge.

4. I attach to this statement an exhibit marked 'JT1' containing true copies of various documents to which I refer in this statement. Where I make reference to a page number, it is to the corresponding page of the exhibit.

5. My current occupation is explained at paragraph 10 of this witness statement.

Background

6. My wife and I are the joint owners of the property (5 Long Road) against which the charging order has been imposed.

7. In 2016 I started my own business as a greengrocer, trading from town centre premises in Smithford which I rented at the time. The Claimant supplied me with fruit and vegetables in connection with my business.

8. All went well for a couple of years but in early 2018 a superstore opened just a couple of miles outside Smithford. This had a significant adverse effect on my trade and I really struggled to make ends meet; it was a constant challenge juggling the need to pay my staff (I had two part-time employees), my landlord, HMRC, my various suppliers, the business rates and the utilities.

9. Matters became increasingly difficult but, by one means or another, I just about kept my head above water until January 2020 when I was unable to pay the rent then due and my landlord repossessed the unit. I could not discharge the arrears and my efforts to reach an agreement for further time to pay the rent failed. Unable to trade, my business came to an end quite literally overnight. I lost my livelihood and my staff lost their jobs. Inevitably this meant that I had no chance of paying my creditors, including the Claimant.

10. Since then, I have been looking for new business opportunities but that has been difficult due to the Covid-19 pandemic. In January 2023, I started an online business sourcing rare and antiquarian books for collectors. This draws on my extensive knowledge and experience in this field which has been acquired over some 25 years, although I have not previously deployed this with a view to profit. Having no alternative accommodation, I run the operation from 5 Long Road. I have created a website and had stationery and business cards designed and printed. All of these identify 5 Long Road as my business address. My start-up costs have been about £2,500. At this stage the venture is in its infancy and as yet it is too early to say how it will fare, although I am optimistic. Copies of my stationery, business cards and screenshots of my website are at **pages 1 to 10**.

My financial position

11. As I said above, my wife and I own 5 Long Road together. We bought it in the spring of 2015 for £200,000. However, property prices in the area have declined since then. This is primarily because the town is situated on a flood plain and there have been a number of significant floods in the past few years. Recently, the neighbouring property (which is virtually identical to our property) was marketed for £150,000 and sold for £125,000. Copies of the newspaper advertisement and a printout from the estate agent's website confirming this are at **pages 11 and 12**.

12. Our property is mortgaged to Lending Bank plc. Currently we owe the bank £135,000. I attach at **page 13** our latest mortgage statement. Therefore, I do not believe that there is any equity in our house at this time.

13. We are currently managing to pay the monthly instalments due under the mortgage. We rely heavily on my wife's income to do so. She is a general practitioner at the local surgery.

14. Apart from the mortgage, my wife has no significant debts. We have no credit cards. We have a small agreed overdraft (£1,000) on our bank current account but otherwise have no joint borrowings.

15. However, I myself owe various creditors. In addition to the amount I owe to the Claimant (which I do not dispute), I owe my former landlord £3,500 in respect of rent arrears. He took me to court and obtained a judgment for this sum from the County Court at Castletown. A copy of the court order is at **page 14**.

16. Also, I owe £1,250 to FatCats Limited. That is a debt which I incurred in connection with my former business. Further, another such debt, of £4,000, is outstanding to Noquestionsasked Limited. This was a loan which was originally £6,000 but over time I have succeeded in repaying some of it, thanks largely to some gifts from my daughter-in-law. Correspondence in relation to these matters is at **pages 15 to 20**.

The way forward

17. I have visited my local advice centre for help. I went through with them all the figures relating to our income and outgoings. They helped me to produce a considered and detailed budget and a repayment schedule in respect of my various debts. A copy of this is at **pages 21 to 23**.

18. I should explain that, although not legally liable for the various debts (except the mortgage and the bank overdraft), my wife is fully supportive of my attempts to 'do the right thing' and pay off my liabilities over time. We pool our income and resources and will continue to do so. The paperwork reflects this.

19. I was advised that, treating all my creditors fairly, I can reasonably afford to repay the Claimant the sum of £200 per month. My payment proposals in respect of the various debts are outlined on the spreadsheet at **page 24**.

20. I have contacted the other creditors. They have indicated, albeit with some understandable reluctance, that they are prepared to give me time to repay what I owe and to accept repayment in instalments. Letters showing this are at **pages 25 and 26**. My former landlord has agreed to this but only on the telephone so I do not have a letter from him.

21. I am doing my best to clear the slate. But it will take time. And I only have a realistic chance of avoiding bankruptcy if the Claimant takes a similar view to the other creditors. I have telephoned and left messages with the Claimant (offering the £200 per month) but my calls have not been returned.

Our home

22. 5 Long Road is our family home. My wife and I live there as does our son who is an undergraduate studying medicine at Paythefees University. He lives at home with us in order to save money. Obviously, the costs associated with a medicine degree are not small. He could ill afford being forced to live elsewhere. This would only increase his already sizeable borrowings or perhaps even lead to him having to quit the course altogether.

My proposal/position

23. In the circumstances I ask the court not to make the charging order final or, if it does make it final, to impose conditions on its enforcement in order to give me a fair and realistic opportunity to clear the debt over time and to retain our home.

24. As stated above, I am willing and able to repay the debt I owe to the Claimant at the rate of £200 per month. This can be reviewed every few months as my new business develops and hopefully turns into profit.

25. If the charging order were imposed, it would not benefit the Claimant because of the negative equity in our home. There is thus really no point in making the order final.

26. Also, I know of no reason why the Claimant should be preferred (by means of a charging order) over and above my other creditors, all of whom are realistic and willing to accept the deferred repayment terms I have offered on advice.

27. If I am given the chance to sort out my financial affairs in the way I have proposed, I believe that this represents the best possible outcome for all concerned. Indeed, if the Claimant is allowed to insist on full and immediate repayment, this will mean that my arrangements with those others to whom I owe money will not be met. There simply is not enough money to go around.

28. If our home were to be sold, three people would have nowhere to live. In addition, all the money I have invested in my new business (the stationery, etc.) would have been wasted. Further, the consequences for our son's education and future career could be devastating.

Conclusion

29. I ask the court not to make the charging order final but instead to discharge the interim charging order, and to order that I can repay the judgment debt which I owe to the Claimant at the rate of £200 per month.

STATEMENT OF TRUTH

I believe that the facts stated in this witness statement are true. I understand that proceedings for contempt of court may be brought against anyone who makes, or causes to be made, a false statement in a document verified by a statement of truth without an honest belief in its truth.

Signed ....

Dated ....

Defendant
John Taylor
First statement
Exhibit: JT1
11 November 2023

IN THE CIVIL NATIONAL BUSINESS CENTRE

CLAIM No: BBB 0001

BETWEEN:

TRADE FUNDS LIMITED

Claimant

– and –

MR JOHN TAYLOR

Defendant

WITNESS STATEMENT OF MR JOHN TAYLOR

PRECEDENT B5: ORDER FOR DISCHARGE OF CHARGING ORDER WHERE NO FINAL ORDER MADE

IN THE COUNTY COURT AT CASTLETOWN CLAIM NO: BBB0001

DISTRICT JUDGE EVERYDAY

15 January 2024

BETWEEN:

VEGGIES R US LIMITED

Claimant

– and –

MR JOHN TAYLOR

Defendant

ORDER (DISCHARGING INTERIM CHARGING ORDER)

FURTHER TO the interim charging order made on 19 October 2023

UPON the Defendant having filed and served a witness statement dated 11 November 2023 objecting to the making of a final charging order

AND UPON the proceedings having been transferred from the County Court Business Centre to the County Court at Castletown by order dated 20 November 2023

AND UPON hearing the Claimant and the Defendant and reading the evidence filed with the Court

IT IS ORDERED THAT:

1. The interim charging order made on 19 October 2023 is hereby discharged.

2. The Chief Land Registrar cancel and remove any entry made on the register of title CEX98765 (being the registered title for 5 LONG ROAD, SMITHFORD CE12 6PZ) made in support of or connection with the interim charging order.

3. The Claimant send a copy of this Order to HM Land Registry (Luckless District Registry) forthwith.

4. There be no order as to Costs.

PRECEDENT B6: COMPLETED SPECIMEN FORM N87: FINAL CHARGING ORDER – COURT ORDER

N87

Final charging order

CPR Part 73

Name of court	Claim No.
COUNTY COURT AT CASTLETOWN	BBB0001
Name of Claimant	
VEGGIES R US LIMITED	
Name of Defendant(s)	
MR JOHN TAYLOR	

On 15 JANUARY 2024, ~~[Master]~~ [Judge] EVERYDAY sitting at COUNTY COURT AT CASTLETOWN heard THE CLAIMANT AND THE DEFENDANT

SEAL

and the court orders that

1. The charge created by the order made on the 19 OCTOBER 2023 shall continue [as modified by this order], NAMELY THAT THE CHARGE SHALL NOT BE ENFORCED IF AND FOR SO LONG AS THE DEFENDANT DO PROMPTLY AND PUNCTUALLY PAY TO THE CLAIMANT THE SUM OF £200 PCM TOWARDS THE JUDGMENT DEBT REFERRED TO IN PARAGRAPH 2 BELOW, THE FIRST SUCH PAYMENT TO BE MADE ON 1 FEBRUARY 2024 AND THEREAFTER ON THE 1ST OF EACH SUCCEEDING MONTH UNTIL THE JUDGMENT DEBT IS CLEARED.

2. The interest of the [defendant~~(s)~~] ~~[claimant]~~ in the asset described in the schedule below stand charged with payment of the sum of £11,570.24 the amount now owing under a judgment or order given on 1 JULY 2023 [by the COUNTY COURT AT CASTLETOWN in claim no. AAA0001] together with any further interest becoming due and £229 the costs of the application.

3. Those costs are to be added to the judgment debt.

[4. The Chief Land Registrar enter the following restriction on the register of title CEX98765 (being the registered title for the asset described in the schedule below): "No disposition of the registered estate, other than a disposition by the proprietor of any registered charge registered before the entry of this restriction, is to be registered without a certificate signed by the applicant for registration or their conveyancer that, at least 14 days prior to the disposition, written notice of the disposition was given to Veggies R Us Limited at 44 Needit Backstreet, Payup, AT9 8BG being the person with the benefit of a final charging order on the beneficial interest of Mr John Taylor made by the County Court at Castletown on 15 January 2024 (Court reference BBB0001)"]

The Schedule
[The address of the land or property charged is 5 LONG STREET, SMITHFORD, CE12 6PZ
[the title to which is registered at H. M. Land Registry under Title No. CEX98765]]

~~[(particulars of securities, funds etc. charged) ....].~~

~~**[STOP NOTICE**~~
~~**To [the Bank of England] [...]**~~
~~Take notice that, in relation to the securities specified in the schedule to this order, you may not, without notice to .... at ....~~
~~register any transfer, or make any redemption payment, or, in the case of a unit trust, deal with the units, or, where dividends or interest are included in the order, pay any dividend or interest.]~~

PRECEDENT B6A: SUGGESTED WORDING FOR AN APPLICATION FOR A NON-STANDARD RESTRICTION

The Claimant also applies for an order pursuant to section 46(1) of the Land Registration Act 2002, requiring the Chief Land Registrar to enter the following restriction on the register of title number CEX98765:

> No disposition of the registered estate, other than a disposition by the proprietor of any registered charge registered before the entry of this restriction, is to be registered without a certificate signed by the applicant for registration or their conveyancer that, at least 14 days prior to the disposition, written notice of the disposition was given to Veggies R Us Limited at 44 Needit Backstreet, Payup AT9 8BG being the person with the benefit of a final charging order on the beneficial interest of Mr John Taylor made by the County Court at Castletown on *[date]* (Court reference *[ref]*)

The Claimant submits that it is necessary or desirable for this restriction to be entered for the purpose of protecting the Claimant's position, because there is otherwise a risk that the Claimant would not be informed of a disposition of the registered estate until after that disposition had occurred, by which time the proceeds of sale may have been dissipated and put out of the Claimant's reach.

PRECEDENT B7: STANDARD ORDER 4.13

In the Family Court
sitting at [*Court name*]

No: [*Case number*]

[The Matrimonial Causes Act 1973]
[The Civil Partnership Act 2004]
[Schedule 1 to the Children Act 1989]
[The Inheritance (Provision for Family and Dependants) Act 1975]
[The Matrimonial and Family Proceedings Act 1984 and Schedule 7 to the Civil Partnership Act 2004]
(DELETE AS APPROPRIATE)

The [Marriage] / [Relationship] / [Family] of [*applicant name*] and [*respondent name*]
(ADAPT AS NECESSARY)

After hearing [*name the advocate(s) who appeared*]
After consideration of the documents lodged by the parties
(IN THE CASE OF AN ORDER MADE WITHOUT NOTICE) After reading the statements and hearing the witnesses specified in para [*para number*] of the Recitals below

INTERIM CHARGING ORDER MADE BY [*NAME OF JUDGE*] ON [*DATE*] SITTING IN [OPEN COURT] / [PRIVATE]
(DELETE AS APPROPRIATE)

The parties

1. The applicant is [*applicant name*]
   The respondent is [*respondent name*]
   Further respondent[s]: [*further respondents names*]
   (SPECIFY IF ANY PARTY ACTS BY A LITIGATION FRIEND)

Recitals

2.
   a. This order was made without a hearing in accordance with Family Procedure Rules, rule 40.4(1).
   b. The Judge read the application notice in Form N379 verified by a statement of truth as required by Family Procedure Rules, Practice Direction 40A.

3. On [*date and time*], [*name of judge*] considered the application of the applicant, from which it appears that:

   a. on [*date*], [*name of judge*] made an order under case number [*case number*] requiring the respondent to pay money to the applicant;
   b. the amount now owing under that order is £[*amount*] including interest and costs as follows:

Sums remaining due for payment under the order	£[*amount*]
Interest to the date of the order	£[*amount*]
Costs to the date of the order	£[*amount*]

   c. the respondent is the owner of, or has a beneficial interest in, the asset described in the schedule below.

IT IS ORDERED THAT:

4. The interest of the respondent in the asset described in the schedule below shall stand charge with payment of £[*amount*], together with any further interest becoming due, and the costs of the application.

5. The application shall be listed for a further hearing before a [District] / [Circuit] / [High Court] Judge at the Family Court sitting at [*name of court*] on [*date*] at [*time*] when the judge will decide whether the charge created by this order should continue (with or without modification) or should be discharged.

SCHEDULE

[The property at [property full address and the Land Registry title number].]

[The holding of [description] shares in [company] and all dividends of other interest that accrues on these shares.]

Dated [*date*]

PRECEDENT B8: STANDARD ORDER 4.14

In the Family Court
sitting at [*Court name*]

No: [*Case number*]

[The Matrimonial Causes Act 1973] /
[The Civil Partnership Act 2004] /
[Schedule 1 to the Children Act 1989] /
[The Inheritance (Provision for Family and Dependants) Act 1975] /
[The Matrimonial and Family Proceedings Act 1984 and Schedule 7 to the Civil Partnership Act 2004]
(DELETE AS APPROPRIATE)

The [Marriage] / [Relationship] / [Family] of [*applicant name*] and [*respondent name*]

After hearing [*name the advocate(s) who appeared*]
After consideration of the documents lodged by the parties
(IN THE CASE OF AN ORDER MADE WITHOUT NOTICE) After reading the statements and hearing the witnesses specified in para [*para number*] of the Recitals below

FINAL CHARGING ORDER MADE BY [*NAME OF JUDGE*] ON [*DATE*] SITTING IN [OPEN COURT] / [PRIVATE]
(DELETE AS APPROPRIATE)

The parties

1. The applicant is [*applicant name*]
   The respondent is [*respondent name*]
   Further respondent(s): [*further respondents names*]
   (SPECIFY IF ANY PARTY ACTS BY A LITIGATION FRIEND)

Recitals

2. (IN THE CASE OF AN ORDER MADE WITHOUT NOTICE)

   a. This order was made at a hearing without notice to the respondent. The reason why the order was made without notice to the respondent was [*insert*].
   b. The Judge read the following [affidavits] / [witness statements] / [*insert*] and heard oral testimony from [*name*].

3. (IN THE CASE OF AN ORDER MADE FOLLOWING THE GIVING OF SHORT INFORMAL NOTICE) This order was made at a hearing without full notice having been given to the respondent. The reason why the order was made without full notice having been given to the respondent was [*insert*].

Findings of the court

4. On [*date and time*], [*name of judge*] considered the application of the applicant for the interim charging order to be made final.

5. On [*date*], [*name of judge*] made an order under case number [*case number*] requiring the respondent to pay money to the applicant.

6. The amount now owing under that order is £[*amount*] including interest and costs as follows:

Sums remaining due for payment under the order	£[amount]
Interest to the date of the order	£[amount]
Costs to the date of the order	£[amount]

7. The respondent is the owner of, or has a beneficial interest in, the asset described in the schedule below.

8. [The parties have been reminded of their duties to identify relevant other parties and have not indicated any such party who should be served with notice prior to this charge being made final. (OR AS APPROPRIATE)]

9. There is no interim order made under section 252 of the Insolvency Act 1986 and no restraint order under the Proceeds of Crime Act 2002.

10. There is no other justification for the refusal of the charge

IT IS ORDERED THAT:

11. The charge created by the interim charging order of this court made on [*date*] shall continue (as modified by this order).

12. The interest of the respondent in the asset described in the schedule below shall stand charged with payment of the sum £[*amount*] including interest to [*date*], together with any further interest becoming due at the rate of £[*amount*] from [*date*], and the costs of this application [summarily assessed at £[*amount*]] / [to be subject to detailed assessment in accordance with the Civil Procedure Rules 1998 Part 47 if not agreed] by [*date and time*]].

SCHEDULE

[The property at [*property full address and the Land Registry title number*].]

[The holding of [*description*] shares in [*company*] and all dividends of other interest that accrues on these shares.]

Dated [*date*]

PRECEDENT B9: FORM N244, APPLICATION NOTICE

N244

Application notice

For help in completing this form please read the notes for guidance form N244Notes.

Find out how HM Courts and Tribunals Service uses personal information you give them when you fill in a form: https://www.gov.uk/government/organisations/hm-courts-and-tribunals-service/about/personal-information-charter

Name of court COUNTY COURT AT CASTLETOWN	**Claim no.** CCC0001
Fee account no. (if applicable)	**Help with Fees – Ref. no.** (if applicable) H W F - -
Warrant no. (if applicable)	
Claimant's name (including ref.) TRADE FUNDS LIMITED	
Defendant's name (including ref.) MR JOHN TAYLOR	
Date	17 MAY 2023

1. What is your name or, if you are a legal representative, the name of your firm?

   THE BEST SOLICITOR

2. Are you a ☐ Claimant ☐ Defendant ☐ Legal Representative

   ☐ Other (please specify)

   If you are a legal representative whom do you represent? DR FRANCES TAYLOR

3. What order are you asking the court to make and why?

   AN ORDER DISCHARGING THE CHARGING ORDER DATED 26 APRIL 2023, AND ANCILLARY ORDERS IN ACCORDANCE WITH THE ATTACHED DRAFT, BECAUSE THE DEFENDANT HAS NO BENEFICIAL INTEREST IN THE CHARGED PROPERTY, ALTERNATIVELY THE APPLICANT HAS SOUGHT A PROPERTY ADJUSTMENT ORDER IN RELATION TO ANY INTEREST WHICH HE HAS.

4. Have you attached a draft of the order you are applying for? ☑ Yes ☐ No

5. How do you want to have this application dealt with? ☑ at a hearing ☐ without a hearing ☐ at a remote hearing

6. How long do you think the hearing will last? [ ] Hours [20] Minutes

   Is this time estimate agreed by all parties? ☐ Yes ☐ No

7. Give details of any fixed trial date or period: NOT APPLICABLE

8. What level of Judge does your hearing need? DISTRICT JUDGE

9. Who should be served with this application? CLAIMANT AND DEFENDANT

9a. Please give the service address, (other than details of the claimant or defendant) of any party named in question 9.

10. What information will you be relying on, in support of your application?

- [x] the attached witness statement
- [ ] the statement of case
- [ ] the evidence set out in the box below

If necessary, please continue on a separate sheet.

11. Do you believe you, or a witness who will give evidence on your behalf, are vulnerable in any way which the court needs to consider?

☐ Yes. Please explain in what way you or the witness are vulnerable and what steps, support or adjustments you wish the court and the judge to consider.

☑ No

Statement of Truth

I understand that proceedings for contempt of court may be brought against a person who makes, or causes to be made, a false statement in a document verified by a statement of truth without an honest belief in its truth.

☐ **I believe** that the facts stated in section 10 (and any continuation sheets) are true.

☑ **The applicant believes** that the facts stated in section 10 (and any continuation sheets) are true. **I am authorised** by the applicant to sign this statement.

Signature

☐ Applicant

☐ Litigation friend (where applicant is a child or a Protected Party)

☑ Applicant's legal representative (as defined by CPR 2.3(1))

Date

Day	Month	Year
17	May	2023

Full name

Best Solicitor

Name of applicant's legal representative's firm

The Best Solicitor

If signing on behalf of firm or company give position or office held

Partner

Applicant's address to which documents should be sent.

Building and street

High Street

Second line of address

Town or city

Castletown

County (optional)

Postcode

C E 4 1 A A

If applicable

Phone number

0123456789

Fax phone number

123 456789

DX number

3 CASTLETOWN

Your Ref.

TD/AS/10000001

Email

admin@bestsolicitor.com

Application Notice (Form N244) – Notes for Guidance

> Court Staff cannot give legal advice. If you need information or advice on a legal problem you can contact Community Legal Service Direct on 0845 345 4 345 or www.clsdirect.org.uk, or a Citizens Advice Bureau. Details of your local offices and contact numbers are available via their website www.citizensadvice.org.uk

Paying the court fee
A court fee is payable depending on the type of application you are making. For example:

- To apply for judgment to be set aside
- To apply to vary a judgment or suspend enforcement
- To apply for a summons or order for a witness to attend
- To apply by consent, or without service of the application notice, for a judgment or order.

No fee is payable for an application by consent for an adjournment of a hearing if it is received by the court at least 14 days before the date of the hearing.

What if I cannot afford the fee?
If you show that a payment of a court fee would involve undue hardship to you, you may be eligible for a fee concession.

For further information, or to apply for a fee concession, ask court staff for a copy of the combined booklet and form EX160A - Court fees - Do I have to pay them? This is also available from any county court office, or a copy of the leaflet can be downloaded from our website www.hmcourts-service.gov.uk

Completing the form

Question 3
Set out what order you are applying for and why; e.g. to adjourn the hearing because..., to set aside a judgment against me because... etc.

Question 5
Most applications will require a hearing and you will be expected to attend. The court will allocate a hearing date and time for the application. Please indicate in a covering letter any dates that you are unavailable within the next six weeks.
The court will only deal with the application 'without a hearing' in the following circumstances.

- Where all the parties agree to the terms of the order being asked for;
- Where all the parties agree that the court should deal with the application without a hearing, or
- Where the court does not consider that a hearing would be appropriate.

Telephone hearings are only available in applications where at least one of parties involved in the case is legally represented. Not all applications will be suitable for a telephone hearing and the court may refuse your request.

Question 6
If you do not know how long the hearing will take do not guess but leave these boxes blank.

Question 7
If your case has already been allocated a hearing date or trial period please insert details of those dates in the box.

Question 8
If your case is being heard in the High Court or a District Registry please indicate whether it is to be dealt with by a Master, District Judge or Judge.

Question 9
Please indicate in the box provided who you want the court to sent a copy of the application to.

Question 10
In this section please set out the information you want the court to take account of in support of the application you are making.
If you wish to rely on:

- **a witness statement,** tick the first box and attach the statement to the application notice. A witness statement form is available on request from the court office.
- **a statement of case,** tick the second box if you intend to rely on your particluars of claim or defence in support of your application.
- **written evidence** on this form, tick the third box and enter details in the space provided. You must also complete the statement of truth. Proceedings for contempt of court may be brought against a person who signs a statement of truth without an honest belief in its truth.

Question 11
The application must be signed and include your current address and contact details. If you agree that the court and the other parties may communicate with you by Document Exchange, telephone, facsimile or email, complete the details

Before returning your form to the court

Have you:

- signed the form on page 2,
- enclosed the correct fee or an application for fee remission,
- made sufficient copies of your application and supporting documentation. You will need to submit one copy for each party to be served and one copy for the court.

N244 Notes Application Notice (Form N244) – Notes for Guidance (05.08)

PRECEDENT B10: WITNESS STATEMENT IN SUPPORT OF APPLICATION TO DISCHARGE FINAL CHARGING ORDER

Third Party
Dr F Taylor
First statement
Exhibits: FT1–FT2
1 June 2013

IN THE COUNTY COURT SITTING AT CASTLETOWN CLAIM NO: CCC 0001

BETWEEN:

TRADE FUNDS LIMITED

Claimant

– and –

MR JOHN TAYLOR

Defendant

WITNESS STATEMENT OF DR FRANCES TAYLOR

---

1. My name is Dr Frances Taylor, and I am (presently) married to the Defendant herein, Mr John Taylor. My address is 5 Long Street, Smithsford CE12 6PZ.

2. I make this witness statement in support of my application to be joined to these proceedings and for the discharge of the charging order which was made by this Court on 17 May 2023.

Background

3. I married John Taylor ('John') on 31 August 2006. At the time, he was a professional boxer, and he enjoyed a very good standard of living. However, soon after we married, he was injured in a fight and he had to give up boxing. It became apparent very quickly afterwards that he had not saved any money at all. Although we had been hoping to buy a large house in the centre of Castletown, we had to pull out of that, and instead I bought 5 Long Street with the proceeds of my former home, and the benefit of a mortgage which my salary as a GP justified. I put 5 Long Street into joint names because we were newly married and I wanted John to feel secure despite the end of his boxing career. In fact, all the money was put in by me.

4. That continued to be the pattern throughout our married life. I was becoming increasingly unhappy that I was having to keep bailing him out of financial scrapes (and paying for him to start up fresh business ventures) instead of

enjoying the money that I earned and using it to help my son by a previous marriage, Toby (who is training to become a doctor). When I learnt about the charging order (which I explain in more detail below), I snapped – and I threw John out of the house. He has not been back since, and I have issued a divorce petition. A copy of this is annexed marked 'FT1'.

My involvement in the proceedings

5. Although I knew that Trade Funds Limited, the Claimant, had obtained a judgment against John for his trade debts, I thought that John was negotiating to pay off those debts by instalments and I was not aware that it had applied for a charging order against 5 Long Street. I did not learn of this until I returned home from work on 5 April 2023, and John told me that he had been to court that day and what had happened. I was furious that he had not told me in advance and, as I have already mentioned, it resulted in me deciding to end our marriage.

6. I consulted my solicitor a few days later. He asked me whether I was sure that I had not had notice of the hearing, and he explained that normally the court would have sent me a copy of the interim charging order and notice of the hearing date. On a subsequent appointment, he showed me a copy of the interim charging order, and I confirmed again that I had not seen this before. If it was sent to me, I can only assume that John intercepted it so that I did not see it. I normally leave for work before the post has arrived in the morning, and only see the post that John leaves out for me after he has sorted it.

My position

7. Although 5 Long Street is in joint names, I do not accept that John is entitled to any interest in it. I initially purchased it for £200,000 in April 2007, with the benefit of a mortgage of £140,000 from Lending Bank plc which was given solely on the basis of my salary. As I have mentioned, the balance of £60,000 was also funded by me from the proceeds of sale of my previous property in the past. I accept that I did put the property into joint names when it was bought, and therefore that John was, then, entitled to 50% of the equity.

8. Since then, I have paid all the mortgage repayments, and the balance on the account is now £135,587.04. However, more importantly, I have also paid numerous debts on behalf of John. Until 2009 (when he set up a greengrocers in Smithsford, as the Claimant is aware), John did not work at all. It took him a considerable amount of time to adjust to not having the income that he had previously had as a boxer, and he ran up numerous credit card debts. By December 2008, he had run up debts of over £75,000 on various store and credit cards, mainly buying rare books. I was very concerned about the situation. Fortunately, I inherited some money from my aunt just before Christmas, and we agreed that I would pay off all his debts with that money rather than paying a lump sum off the mortgage on 5 Long Street. However, it was clearly understood between us that this was nonetheless to be treated as

an investment in 5 Long Street by me, in the sense that I was buying back his share of the equity.

9. Because of everything stated above, I do not accept that John has any interest in 5 Long Street, and I do not consider that his trade debts ought to be secured against it.

10. I have also applied for a property adjustment order in respect of John's interest (if any) in 5 Long Street by way of ancillary relief, although, for the reasons I have already referred to, I do not believe that he has any interest anyway.

11. My solicitor has written to the Claimant, Trade Funds Limited, to explain all of this, and seek their consent to the discharge of the charging order, but they have not replied to his letter. A copy of his letter is annexed marked 'FT2'.

STATEMENT OF TRUTH

I believe that the facts stated in this witness statement are true. I understand that proceedings for contempt of court may be brought against anyone who makes, or causes to be made, a false statement in a document verified by a statement of truth without an honest belief in its truth.

Signed ....
Dr Frances Taylor

Dated ....

CLAIM NO: CCC 0001

IN THE COUNTY COURT SITTING AT CASTLETOWN

BETWEEN:

TRADE FUNDS LIMITED
Claimant

– and –

MR JOHN TAYLOR
Defendant

WITNESS STATEMENT OF DR FRANCES TAYLOR

The Best Solicitor
High Street
Castletown CE4 1AA

REF: TD/AS/10000001

PRECEDENT B11: DRAFT ORDER FOR DISCHARGE OF CHARGING ORDER AFTER FINAL CHARGING ORDER MADE

IN THE CASTLETOWN COUNTY COURT CLAIM NO: CCC 0001

BETWEEN:

TRADE FUNDS LIMITED

Claimant

– and –

MR JOHN TAYLOR

Defendant

DRAFT ORDER

UPON HEARING [ ] FOR DR F TAYLOR AND [ ] FOR THE CLAIMANT

AND UPON DR F TAYLOR'S APPLICATION DATED 1 JUNE 2023

IT IS ORDERED THAT:

1. Dr Frances Taylor shall be joined as Second Defendant herein for the purposes of this application only.

2. The charging order dated 17 May 2023 is discharged.

3. The restriction at entry [ ] in the Proprietorship Register for title number CEX98765 shall be cancelled forthwith.

4. The Claimant shall pay Dr F Taylor's costs of this application, summarily assessed in the sum of £14,750.

PRECEDENT B12: COMPLETED SPECIMEN CLAIM FORM (CPR PART 8): APPLICATION TO ENFORCE CHARGING ORDER BY MEANS OF ORDER FOR SALE – I

Claim Form (CPR Part 8)

In the	COUNTY COURT AT CASTLETOWN
Claim no.	RCC0999
Fee Account no.	
Help with Fees - Ref no. (if applicable)	H W F - -

Claimant

BAD DEALS LIMITED
WANT IT BACK HOUSE
SILVER LINING
AT5 1BY

SEAL

Defendant(s)

MR R BROKE
13 SKINT STREET
LUCKLESS
VP8 0MG

Does your claim include any issues under the Human Rights Act 1998? ☐ Yes ☑ No

Details of claim (see also overleaf)

1. This claim is made under the Charging Orders Act 1979.

2. On 19 March 2022 in claim number RC00002 in this court the Claimant was granted a final charging order ("the Charging Order") over the Defendant's freehold interest in the property known as 13 Skint Street, Luckless, VP8 0MG ("the Property"), of which the Defendant is the sole legal and beneficial owner. The Charging Order order was granted to secure payment of £13,819.78, the amount then owing to the Claimant from the Defendant under a judgment given on 9 October 2021 by the Local County Court in claim number LCC00002, together with any further interest becoming due and £114, the cost of the application for the Charging Order.

3. No payment has been made from the Defendant to the Claimant and the balance due as at 4 January 2023 is £14,728.43 with interest accruing at a daily rate of £3.02.

(continued on next page)

Defendant's name and address

MR R BROKE
13 SKINT STREET
LUCKLESS
VP8 0MG

	£
Court fee	355.00
Legal representative's costs	TBA
Issue date	5 January 2023

For further details of the courts www.gov.uk/find-court-tribunal.
When corresponding with the Court, please address forms or letters to the Manager and always quote the claim number.

Claim no.	RCC0999

Details of claim (continued)

4. Accordingly, the Claimant seeks an order that:

4.1 The Property, which is subject to the Charging Order in favour of the Claimant, be sold without further reference to the court at a price not less than £250,000 unless that figure is changed by the court;
4.2 The Claimant's solicitor shall have conduct of the sale;
4.3 To enable the Claimant to conduct the sale there be created and vested in the Claimant pursuant to section 90 of the Law of Property Act 1925 a legal term in the Property of 3,000 years;
4.4 To enable the sale to proceed, the Defendant shall give the Claimant possession of the Property on or before the date 21 days after the order is made;
4.5 On sale of the Property, the Claimant will apply the proceeds of sale to pay the costs of sale, to the discharge of prior encumbrances and to discharge the sum then due to the Claimant with the balance, if any, to be paid to the Defendant, or into court as the court shall direct;
4.6 The Defendant shall pay the costs of this claim, such costs to be added to the Claimant's security.

CAN'T PAY WE'LL TAKE IT AWAY & CO
58 OUT OF LUCK LANE
BETTERTIMES
BT69 9JQ

Claimant's or claimant's legal representative's address to which documents should be sent if different from overleaf. If you are prepared to accept service by DX, fax or e-mail, please add details.

Statement of Truth

I understand that proceedings for contempt of court may be brought against anyone who makes, or causes to be made, a false statement in a document verified by a statement of truth without an honest belief in its truth.

☐ **I believe** that the facts stated in these particulars of claim are true.

☑ **The Claimant believes** that the facts stated in these particulars of claim are true. **I am authorised** by the claimant to sign this statement.

Signature

Glv. Me-More

☐ Claimant

☐ Litigation friend (where claimant is a child or a Protected Party)

☑ Claimant's legal representative (as defined by CPR 2.3(1))

Date

Day	Month	Year
4	1	2023

Full name

GIVERNY ME-MORE

Name of claimant's legal representative's firm

CAN'T PAY WE'LL TAKE IT AWAY & CO

If signing on behalf of firm or company give position or office held

PARTNER

Find out how HM Courts and Tribunals Service uses personal information you give them when you fill in a form: https://www.gov.uk/government/organisations/hm-courts-and-tribunals-service/about/personal-information-charter

PRECEDENT B13: COMPLETED SPECIMEN CLAIM FORM (CPR PART 8): APPLICATION TO ENFORCE CHARGING ORDER BY MEANS OF ORDER FOR SALE – II

Claim Form (CPR Part 8)

In the	COUNTY COURT AT CASTLETOWN
Claim no.	RC00666
Fee Account no.	
Help with Fees - Ref no. (if applicable)	H W F - -

Claimant

OUT OF POCKET LIMITED
NEED IT BACK HOUSE
SILVER LINING
AT9 8BG

SEAL

Defendant(s)

(1) MR V POOR AND (2) MRS V V POOR
HARD TIMES
TOUGH MEASURES
LUCKLESS
VP1 0MY

Does your claim include any issues under the Human Rights Act 1998? ☐ Yes ☑ No

Details of claim (see also overleaf)

1. This claim is made under sections 14 and 15 of the Trusts of Land and Appointment of Trustees Act 1996.

2. On 26 April 2022 in claim number RC00001 in this court the Claimant was granted a final charging order ("the Charging Order") over the First Defendant's beneficial interest in the property known as Hard Times, Tough Measures, Luckless, VP1 0MY ("the Property") to secure payment of the sum of £110,401.56, the amount then owing to the Claimant from the First Defendant under a judgment given on 13 October 2021 by the Local County Court in claim number LCC00001, together with any further interest becoming due and £114, the costs of the application for the Charging Order.

3. The First Defendant has failed to make payments to the Claimant stipulated by the Charging Order of £2,500pcm and has not in fact made any payments to the Claimant since the date the Charging Order was made. The balance due from the First Defendant as at 15 February 2023 is £115,926.34 with interest accruing at a daily rate of £2.49.

(continued on next page)

Defendant's name and address

(1) MR V POOR AND (2) MRS V V POOR
HARD TIMES
TOUGH MEASURES
LUCKLESS
VP1 0MY

	£
Court fee	355.00
Legal representative's costs	TBA
Issue date	16 February 2023

For further details of the courts www.gov.uk/find-court-tribunal.
When corresponding with the Court, please address forms or letters to the Manager and always quote the claim number.

Claim no.	RC00666

Details of claim (continued)

4. Accordingly, the Claimant seeks an order that:

4.1 The Property, which is subject to the Charging Order in favour of the Claimant, be sold without further reference to the court at a price not less than £670,000 unless that figure is changed by order of the court;
4.2 The Claimant's solicitor shall have conduct of the sale;
4.3 Pursuant to section 50 of the Trustee Act 1925, the Claimant's solicitor, Ruth Less of Less, More & Co be appointed to convey the Property;
4.4 To enable the sale to proceed, the Defendants shall give possession of the Property to the Claimant on or before the date 21 days after the order is made;
4.5 On sale of the Property, the Claimant will apply the proceeds of sale to the discharge of prior incumbrances over the legal estate, and shall then divide the remaining proceeds into two equal shares, paying one share to the Second Defendant and, after retaining the sum then due to the Claimant from the other share, paying the balance of that other share to the First Defendant;
4.6 The First Defendant shall pay the Claimant's costs of this claim, such costs to be added to the Claimant's security.

LESS, MORE & CO
GET IT BACK HOUSE
SILVER LINING
AT9 8DY

Claimant's or claimant's legal representative's address to which documents should be sent if different from overleaf. If you are prepared to accept service by DX, fax or e-mail, please add details.

Statement of Truth

I understand that proceedings for contempt of court may be brought against anyone who makes, or causes to be made, a false statement in a document verified by a statement of truth without an honest belief in its truth.

☐ **I believe** that the facts stated in these particulars of claim are true.

☑ **The Claimant believes** that the facts stated in these particulars of claim are true. **I am authorised** by the claimant to sign this statement.

Signature

R. Less

☐ Claimant

☐ Litigation friend (where claimant is a child or a Protected Party)

☑ Claimant's legal representative (as defined by CPR 2.3(1))

Date

Day	Month	Year
15	02	2023

Full name

RUTH LESS

Name of claimant's legal representative's firm

LESS, MORE & CO

If signing on behalf of firm or company give position or office held

SENIOR ASSOCIATE

Find out how HM Courts and Tribunals Service uses personal information you give them when you fill in a form: https://www.gov.uk/government/organisations/hm-courts-and-tribunals-service/about/personal-information-charter

PRECEDENT B14: WITNESS STATEMENT IN SUPPORT OF APPLICATION FOR SALE – I

On behalf of: Claimant
Name of witness: G. Memore
Statement Number: First
Exhibits: GM1–GM5
Date of Statement: 27 February 2023
Date of Translation: N/A

IN THE COUNTY COURT AT CASTLETOWN — CLAIM NO: RCC 0999

BETWEEN:

BAD DEALS LIMITED

Claimant

– and –

MR R BROKE

Defendant

WITNESS STATEMENT OF GIVERNY MEMORE

I, GIVERNY MEMORE, Solicitor, of 58 Out of Luck Lane, Bettertimes BT69 9JQ, WILL SAY AS FOLLOWS:

1. I am a partner in the firm of Can't Pay We'll Take it Away & Co, solicitors for the Claimant, and have care and conduct of this matter on behalf of the Claimant. I am duly authorised by the Claimant to make this witness statement on the Claimant's behalf.

2. The facts and matters herein stated are, except where it expressly appears otherwise, within my own knowledge. My knowledge is derived from a combination of my personal involvement in the subject matter of these proceedings and also from the documentation which I have seen and to which I refer in this statement.

3. I make this statement in support of the Claimant's application under the Charging Orders Act 1979 for an order for sale of the Defendant's property known as 13 Skint Street, Luckless VP8 0MG ('the property'). I can confirm, for the purposes of paragraph 18.1(5) of Practice Direction 32, that I have prepared this witness statement personally.

4. On 9 October 2021, in claim number LC00002 between the Claimant and the Defendant in Local County Court, the Claimant was granted judgment against the Defendant for the sum of £12,569.78 and costs summarily assessed at

£1,250.00. The claim was brought in respect of trade debts owed to the Claimant by the Defendant.

5. On 19 March 2022, in claim number RCC00002 in this court, the Claimant was granted a final charging order over the Defendant's freehold interest in the property to secure payment of the sums then owing under the judgment. A copy of the final charging order is attached to this witness statement as exhibit 'GM1'.

6. Since the final charging order was made, the Defendant has not made any payments to the Claimant at all. As at the date of this statement, the balance due from the Claimant is £14,728.43, with interest accruing at a daily rate of £3.02.

7. Accordingly, the Claimant seeks an order for the sale of the property.

8. The freehold title to the property is registered at HM Land Registry under title number HT5678. The Defendant is the sole registered proprietor of the freehold estate. An official copy of the registered freehold title to the property is attached to this witness statement as exhibit 'GM2'.

9. To the best of the Claimant's knowledge, the only other creditor with a prior charge or security over the property is Biggest Bank plc of Bigbucks Street, Richtown. As appears from the official copy of the registered title, Biggest Bank plc has a first legal charge over the property. I have made enquiries of Biggest Bank plc on behalf of the Claimant and have discovered that the balance due under the charge is £142,819.72. Biggest Bank plc is not opposed to an order for sale. A letter from Biggest Bank plc confirming these matters is attached to this witness statement at exhibit 'GM3'.

10. The Claimant has obtained two valuations of the property from local estate agents: the first, from Treat Mean Estate Agents, values the property at £270,000; the second, from Keep Keen Estate Agents, values the property at £260,000. Copies of these valuations are attached to this witness statement at exhibit 'GM4'. Accordingly, the Claimant seeks an order that the property be sold for a price not less than £250,000.

11. The property consists of residential property.

12. To the best of the Claimant's knowledge, the only persons in possession of the property are the Defendant and his wife.

13. I can confirm that no Class F land charge or notice under section 31(10) of the Family Law Act 1996 or any predecessor provision has been registered against the property. A copy of the matrimonial home rights search carried out at HM Land Registry is attached to this witness statement as exhibit 'GM5'.

STATEMENT OF TRUTH

I believe that the facts stated in this witness statement are true. I understand that proceedings for contempt of court may be brought against a person who makes, or causes to be made, a false statement in a document verified by a statement of truth without an honest belief in its truth.

Signed ....
Giverny Memore

Dated ....

CLAIM NO: RCC 0666

IN THE COUNTY COURT AT CASTLETOWN

BETWEEN:

BAD DEALS LIMITED
Claimant

– and –

Mr R BROKE
Defendant

WITNESS STATEMENT OF GIVERNY MEMORE

CAN'T PAY WE'LL TAKE IT AWAY & CO
58 OUT OF LUCK LANE
BETTERTIMES
BT69 9JQ

PRECEDENT B15: WITNESS STATEMENT IN SUPPORT OF APPLICATION FOR SALE – II

On behalf of: Claimant
Name of witness: R. Less
Statement Number: First
Exhibits: RL1–RL4
Date of Statement: 7 September 2023
Date of Translation: N/A

IN THE COUNTY COURT AT CASTLETOWN CLAIM NO: RCC 0666

BETWEEN:

OUT OF POCKET LIMITED

Claimant

– and –

MR V POOR

Defendant

WITNESS STATEMENT OF RUTH LESS

I, RUTH LESS, Solicitor, of Get It Back House, Silver Lining AT9 8DY, WILL SAY AS FOLLOWS:

1. I am a partner in the firm of Less, More & Co, solicitors for the Claimant, and have care and conduct of this matter on behalf of the Claimant. I am duly authorised by the Claimant to make this witness statement on the Claimant's behalf.

2. The facts and matters herein stated are, except where it expressly appears otherwise, within my own knowledge. My knowledge is derived from a combination of my personal involvement in the subject matter of these proceedings and also from the documentation which I have seen and to which I refer in this statement.

3. I make this statement in support of the Claimant's application under sections 14 and 15 of the Trusts of Land and Appointment of Trustees Act 1996 for an order for sale of the Defendants' property known as Hard Times, Tough Measures, Luckless VP1 0MY ('the property'). I can confirm, for the purposes of paragraph 18.1(5) of Practice Direction 32, that I have prepared this witness statement personally.

4. On 13 October 2021, in claim number LC00001 between the Claimant and the First Defendant in Local County Court, the Claimant was granted judgment

against the First Defendant for the sum of £100,421.56 and costs summarily assessed at £9,800.00. The claim was brought in respect of trade debts owed to the Claimant by the First Defendant.

5. On 26 April 2022, in claim number RCC00001 in this court, the Claimant was granted a final charging order over the First Defendant's beneficial interest in the property to secure payment of the sums then owing under the judgment. A copy of the final charging order is attached to this witness statement as exhibit 'RL1'.

6. When making the final charging order, the court ordered that the charge could not be enforced for so long as the First Defendant paid the Claimant £2,500 pcm towards the judgment debt on the 1st of each month, until such time as the judgment debt was discharged. The first payment was to be made on 1 May 2022.

7. Since the final charging order was made, the First Defendant has not made any payments to the Claimant at all. As at the date of this statement, the balance due from the First Defendant is £115,926.34, with interest accruing at a daily rate of £2.49.

8. Accordingly, the Claimant seeks an order for the sale of the property.

9. The freehold title to the property is registered at HM Land Registry under title number HT1234. The Defendants are joint registered proprietors of the freehold estate. An official copy of the registered freehold title to the property is attached to this witness statement as exhibit 'RL2'.

10. The Defendants have informed the Claimant that they hold the property on trust for themselves in equal beneficial shares, having purchased it together as the family home.

11. As the party in whose favour the final charging order was made, the Claimant is a person interested in the property, which is held on a trust of land, and so is entitled to make an application to court for the sale of the property under section 14 of the Trusts of Land and Appointment of Trustees Act 1996.

12. To the best of the Claimant's knowledge, the only other creditor with a prior charge or security over the property is Lending Bank plc of Moneybags Avenue, Richtown. As appears from the official copy of the registered title, Lending Bank plc has a first legal charge over the property. I have made enquiries of the Lending Bank plc on behalf of the Claimant and have discovered that the balance due under the charge is £105,061.82. Lending Bank plc is not opposed to an order for sale. A letter from Lending Bank plc confirming these matters is attached to this witness statement at exhibit 'RL3'.

13. The Claimant has obtained two valuations of the property from local estate agents: the first, from Sell Quickly Estate Agents, values the property at £700,000; the second, from Sell Cheaply Estate Agents, values the property at £680,000. Copies of these valuations are attached to this witness statement at exhibit 'RL4'. Given the vagaries of the market, the Claimant seeks an order that the property be sold for a price not less than £670,000.

14. The property consists of residential property.

15. To the best of the Claimant's knowledge, the only persons in possession of the property are the Defendants and their two children.

STATEMENT OF TRUTH

I believe that the facts stated in this witness statement are true. I understand that proceedings for contempt of court may be brought against a person who makes, or causes to be made, a false statement in a document verified by a statement of truth without an honest belief in its truth.

Signed ....
Ruth Less

Dated ....

CLAIM NO: RCC 0666

IN THE COUNTY COURT AT CASTLETOWN

BETWEEN:

OUT OF POCKET LIMITED
Claimant

– and –

MR V POOR
Defendant

WITNESS STATEMENT OF RUTH LESS

LESS, MORE AND CO, SOLICITORS
GET IT BACK HOUSE
SILVER LINING
AT9 8DY

PRECEDENT B16: STANDARD FORM OF CHARGING ORDER (BANKRUPTCY)

IN THE HIGH COURT OF JUSTICE CLAIM NO: BR-2021-000255

BUSINESS AND PROPERTY COURTS OF ENGLAND AND WALES
INSOLVENCY AND COMPANIES LIST (ChD)

Before: INSOLVENCY AND COMPANIES COURT JUDGE SMITH

Dated: 24 February 2023

BETWEEN:

MR REGINALD SMITH
(as trustee in bankruptcy of OLIVER SMITHSON)

Applicant

– and –

OLIVER SMITHSON
ABEBA SMITHSON

Respondent

ORDER

UPON HEARING Shazia Afridi counsel for the trustee in bankruptcy and John Betjeman counsel for the bankrupt

AND UPON the trustee in bankruptcy's application under section 313 of the Insolvency Act 1986

IT IS ORDERED THAT:

1. The interest of the trustee and his successors in title in the property specified in the schedule to this order shall stand charged for the benefit of the bankrupt's estate with:

   (a) £100,000 being the total sum which on present information remains owing to unsecured creditors of the bankrupt;
   (b) all other amounts which are payable otherwise than to the bankrupt out of the estate;
   (c) interest on the said sums and other amounts at the rate of 2% per annum from the date of this order.

2. Upon registration of a unilateral notice over the said title in the property by the Chief Land Registrar under the Land Registration Act 2002, the said title shall

cease to be comprised in the bankrupt's estate and shall vest in the bankrupt subject to the charge created by this order and any prior charges.

SCHEDULE

The leasehold interest in 3 the Haven, Portsmouth PO4 8UP registered under title LN567893.

SERVICE OF THIS ORDER

3. This order shall be served by the trustee in bankruptcy on the bankrupt.

4. The court has provided a sealed copy of this order to the serving party:

   Falcon Lawyers LLP
   Falcon Court
   London EC4Y 1AA

PRECEDENT B17: DRAFT DIRECTIONS

IN THE COUNTY COURT AT MOLD　　　　CLAIM NO: J01MO123

BETWEEN:

SKINT LIMITED

Claimant

– and –

(1) MR JOHN SMITH
(2) MR JOSEPH SMITH

Defendants

ORDER

ON 24 February 2023

BEFORE District Judge Ruthless sitting at the County Court at Mold, County Civic Centre, Mold CH7 1AE

UPON the Claimant having the benefit of a charge upon the First Defendant's interest in the property known as 77 Hard Luck Lane, Mold, Flintshire, CH7 8QQ, which is registered at HM Land Registry under title number CYM5672 ('the Property') pursuant to a final charging order made on 18 December 2018 in the County Court at Mold ('the Charging Order')

AND UPON the Court holding a Part 8 hearing remotely by Microsoft Teams

AND UPON the Second Defendant, being the First Defendant's brother, being represented at the hearing and claiming the entire beneficial interest in the Property

AND UPON hearing counsel for the Claimant, counsel for the First Defendant and counsel for the Second Defendant

IT IS ORDERED THAT:

1. There shall be a trial of a preliminary issue ('the Preliminary Issue'), namely the extent of the Second Defendant's beneficial interest (if any) in the Property.

2. The Defendants shall file and serve all witness evidence and documentation upon which they rely in relation to the Preliminary Issue by 4 pm on Friday, 17 March 2023.

3. The Claimant shall, if so advised, file and serve a witness statement in response by 4 pm on Friday, 10 April 2023.

4. The Court shall list a further directions hearing on the first open date after 17 April 2023, time estimate 90 minutes, to consider what further directions, if any, are necessary in advance of trial.

5. Costs in the case.

DATED 24 February 2023

PRECEDENT B18: ORDER: JOINT OWNERS TENANTED

IN THE COUNTY COURT AT PORTSMOUTH CLAIM NO: J01PO967

BETWEEN:

CORPORATE LARGESSE LIMITED

Claimant

– and –

(1) MRS BERNADETTE WILSON
(2) MR JAKE SPIVEY

Defendants

ORDER

ON 24 February 2023

BEFORE Deputy District Judge Jamieson sitting at the County Court at Portsmouth, Winston Churchill Avenue, Portsmouth PO1 2EB

UPON the Claimant having the benefit of an equitable charge on the First Defendant's beneficial interest in the property known as 89 Hope Avenue, Portsmouth PO7 7AZ, which is registered at HM Land Registry under title number HAM085946 ('the Property') under a charging order made on 20 September 2008 in the County Court at Portsmouth under claim number G01PO925 ('the Charging Order')

AND UPON the Claimant's Part 8 claim for an order for sale of the Property

AND UPON the Court noting that the Property is let out pursuant to a residential tenant

AND UPON hearing counsel for the Claimant and counsel for the Defendant

IT IS ORDERED THAT:

1. By 4 pm on 24 March 2023, the Defendants must provide to the Claimant's solicitors copies of the current tenancy of the Property, any relevant information as to rent payments and arrears, tenancy deposits and their protection, and the Defendants' compliance or non-compliance, as the case may be, with other statutory requirements for valid service of notices under section 8 and/or section 21 of the Housing Act 1988 or any other relevant statute.

2. The remainder of this order shall not take effect if the First Defendant by 4 pm on 24 April 2023 pays to the Claimant the judgment debt of £14,356.23 secured by the Charging Order and its costs to date of this application,

summarily assessed in the sum of £6,314.00 (including VAT), making together £20,670.23, together with interest, currently amounting to £45.67 and continuing at the rate of £0.56 per day until final payment.

3. The Property shall be sold without further reference to the Court at a price not less than £615,000 unless that figure is changed by a further order of the Court.

4. The Claimant's solicitors will have conduct of the sale.

5. To enable the Claimant to recover vacant possession of the Property and to sell the same, the legal title to the Property shall be vested in the Claimant pursuant to section 47 of the Trustee Act 1925. For the avoidance of doubt, any reasonable costs incurred by the Claimant in recovering vacant possession of the Property which are not recovered from the occupier of the Property may be added to the Claimant's security and paid out of the proceeds of sale.

6. The Claimant shall first apply the proceeds of sale of the Property:

   (a) to pay the costs and expenses of sale (including, for the avoidance of doubt, any costs referred to at paragraph 5 above);
   (b) to discharge any other charges or securities over the Property which have priority over the charging order.

7. The Claimant shall then divide the remaining proceeds of sale into two equal shares and:

   (a) pay one equal share to the Second Defendant; and
   (b) out of the other equal share, retain the amount due to him as stated in paragraph 2 of this Order, and pay the balance (if any) to the First Defendant.

8. For the avoidance of doubt, if the First Defendant has not paid to the Claimant the sums due under paragraph 2 of this Order by the date the Claimant exchanges contracts for the sale of the Property, the sale shall proceed even if the First Defendant subsequently tenders all sums due. If such sums are paid prior to that date, the Claimant shall apply to HM Land Registry to cancel the notice of the Charging Order registered against the Defendants' title and any relevant restriction(s) in the Claimant's favour.

9. Either party may apply to vary any of the terms of this order, or for further directions about the sale or the application of the proceeds of sale, or otherwise.

DATED 24 February 2023

PRECEDENT B19: ORDER: SOLE LEGAL OWNER OVERSEAS ENTITY TENANTED

IN THE COUNTY COURT AT PORTSMOUTH CLAIM NO: J01PO967

BETWEEN:

CORPORATE LARGESSE LIMITED

Claimant

– and –

BV ISLAND ENTERPRISES LIMITED
(A company incorporated under the laws of the British Virgin Islands)

Defendant

ORDER

ON 24 February 2023

BEFORE Deputy District Judge Jamieson sitting at the County Court at Portsmouth, Winston Churchill Avenue, Portsmouth PO1 2EB

UPON the Claimant having the benefit of an equitable charge on the Defendant's freehold property known as 79 Grand Villas, Highgrove Avenue, Portsmouth PO1 7EQ, which is registered at HM Land Registry under title number HAM10976 ('the Property') under a charging order made on 5 January 2017 in the County Court at Portsmouth under claim number F00PO145 ('the Charging Order')

AND UPON the Claimant's Part 8 claim for an order for sale of the Property

AND UPON the Court noting that the Property consists of five flats ('the Flats'), each of which are let out to residential tenants

AND UPON hearing counsel for the Claimant and counsel for the Defendant

IT IS ORDERED THAT:

1. By 4 pm on 24 March 2023, the Defendant must provide to the Claimant's solicitors copies of the current tenancies of the Flats, any relevant information as to rent payments and arrears, tenancy deposits and their protection, and the Defendant's compliance or non-compliance, as the case may be, with other statutory requirements for valid service of notices under section 8 and/or section 21 of the Housing Act 1988 or any other relevant statute.

2. The remainder of this order shall not take effect if the Defendant by 4 pm on 24 May 2023 pays to the Claimant the judgment debt of £52,103.47 secured

by the Charging Order and its costs to date of this application, summarily assessed in the sum of £8,500 (including VAT), making together £60,603.47, together with interest, currently amounting to £1,203.67 and continuing at the rate of £3.45 per day until final payment.

3. The Property shall be sold without further reference to the Court at a price not less than £375,000 unless that figure is changed by a further order of the Court.

4. For the avoidance of doubt, as the sale of the Property will occur in pursuance of this Order, HM Land Registry shall have power to register any disposition of the Property notwithstanding the overseas entity restriction registered against the title to the Property.

5. The Claimant's solicitors will have conduct of the sale.

6. To enable the Claimant to carry out the sale, there shall be created and vested in the Claimant pursuant to section 90 of the Law of Property Act 1925 a legal term in the Property for 3,000 years.

7. By virtue of paragraph 6 above, the Claimant shall be at liberty to take steps to determine the tenancies of the Flats and to recover possession thereof. For the avoidance of doubt, any reasonable costs incurred by the Claimant in recovering vacant possession of the Flats which are not recovered from the occupiers of the Flats may be added to the Claimant's security and paid out of the proceeds of sale.

8. The Claimant shall first apply the proceeds of sale of the Property:

   (a) to pay the costs and expenses of sale (including, for the avoidance of doubt, any costs referred to at paragraph 7 above);
   (b) to discharge any other charges or securities over the Property which have priority over the charging order.

9. Out of the remaining proceeds of sale, the Claimant shall:

   (a) retain the amount due to him at paragraph 2 of this Order;
   (b) pay the balance (if any) to the Defendant.

10. For the avoidance of doubt, if the Defendant has not paid to the Claimant the sums due under paragraph 2 of this Order by the date the Claimant exchanges contracts for the sale of the Property, the sale shall proceed even if the Defendant subsequently tenders all sums due. If such sums are paid prior to that date, the Claimant shall apply to HM Land Registry to cancel the notice of the Charging Order registered against the Defendant's title and any relevant restriction(s) in the Claimant's favour.

11. Either party may apply to vary any of the terms of this order, or for further directions about the sale or the application of the proceeds of sale, or otherwise.

DATED 24 February 2023

Index

References are to page numbers